Women's Literary Education, 1690–1850

Women's Literary Education, 1690–1850

Edited by
Jessica Lim and Louise Joy

EDINBURGH
University Press

Edinburgh University Press is one of the leading university presses in the UK. We publish academic books and journals in our selected subject areas across the humanities and social sciences, combining cutting-edge scholarship with high editorial and production values to produce academic works of lasting importance. For more information visit our website: edinburghuniversitypress.com

Edinburgh University Press Ltd
The Tun – Holyrood Road
12(2f) Jackson's Entry
Edinburgh EH8 8PJ

Typeset in Sabon and Futura
by Manila Typesetting Company, and
printed and bound in Great Britain

A CIP record for this book is available from the British Library

ISBN 978 1 4744 9734 3 (hardback)
ISBN 978 1 4744 9736 7 (webready PDF)
ISBN 978 1 4744 9737 4 (epub)

Contents

Notes on Contributors

Rebecca Anne Barr is Assistant Professor at the Faculty of English, University of Cambridge, and a Fellow of Jesus College. She has published widely on gender and sexualities, including articles in *The Eighteenth Century: Theory and Interpretation*, *Women's Writing*, *Studies in Eighteenth-Century Culture* and *Eighteenth-Century Fiction*. Recent edited collections include *Bellies, Bowels and Entrails in the Eighteenth Century* (Manchester University Press, 2018) and *Ireland and Masculinities in History* (Palgrave Macmillan, 2019).

Rachel Bryant Davies is a lecturer in Comparative Literature at Queen Mary University of London. She researches classical reception during the long nineteenth century (c.1750–1914) and her publications include *Troy, Carthage and the Victorians: The Drama of Ruins in the Nineteenth-Century Imagination* (Cambridge University Press, 2018). She has edited *Victorian Epic Burlesque* (Bloomsbury Academic, 2018) and co-edited *Pasts at Play: Childhood Encounters with History in British Culture, c.1750–1914* (Manchester University Press, 2020) and *Intersectional Encounters in the Nineteenth-Century Archive: New Essays on Discourse and Power* (Bloomsbury Academic, 2022).

Michèle Cohen is Emeritus Professor at Richmond American International University in London. Having researched education and gender for many years, she has recently been focusing on pedagogy and gender and on gender in children's literature. Her publications include *Fashioning Masculinity* (Routledge, 1996), 'A Habit of Healthy: Boys' Underachievement in Historical Perspective' in *Failing Boys?* (Open University Press, 1998) and 'The Pedagogy of Conversation in the Home' (*Oxford Review of Education*, 2015).

Her chapter 'Balls and Pincushions: Representations of Gender in Children's Literature in the Long Eighteenth Century' is forthcoming in the *Cambridge History of Children's Literature* (Cambridge University Press), and her latest book, *Educating Differently: Changing Pedagogies for Girls and Boys in the Eighteenth Century*, is forthcoming with Boydell.

Aileen Douglas teaches in the School of English, Trinity College Dublin. Her publications include *Work in Hand: Script, Print, and Writing, 1690–1840* (Oxford University Press, 2017); a co-edition of Elizabeth Sheridan's *The Triumph of Prudence over Passion* (Four Courts, Dublin, 2011) and many articles on eighteenth-century women's writing. She is currently co-editing *The Vicar of Wakefield* for the Cambridge University Press edition of *The Collected Works of Oliver Goldsmith*.

Katie Halsey is Professor of Eighteenth-Century Literature at the University of Stirling. Her research interests centre around Jane Austen and the History of Reading. Her current research project, the AHRC-funded 'Books and Borrowing, 1750–1830', focuses on book circulation in Scotland in the period. Publications include *Shakespeare and Authority* (Palgrave Macmillan, 2018; with Angus Vine), *Jane Austen and Her Readers, 1786–1945* (Anthem Press, 2012) and *The History of Reading: A Reader* (Routledge, 2011; with Shafquat Towheed and Rosalind Crone).

Felicity James is Associate Professor of Eighteenth- and Nineteenth-Century English Literature at the University of Leicester. She has published widely on the Lambs and their circle, and on women writers of religious Dissent, and is currently editing the children's writing of Charles and Mary Lamb for the new Oxford Collected Works. She would like to thank the Leverhulme Trust for their support of her work on the Lambs through a Research Fellowship.

Louise Joy is a Fellow, Director of Studies and College Associate Professor in English at Homerton College, University of Cambridge. She is the author of *Eighteenth-Century Literary Affections* (Palgrave, 2020) and *Literature's Children: The Critical Child and the Art of Idealisation* (Bloomsbury, 2019), and the co-editor of *The Aesthetics of Children's Poetry: A Study of Children's Verse in English (Routledge, 2018) and Poetry and Childhood (Trentham Press, 2010)*. Her articles have appeared in journals including *Studies in Romanticism*,

History of European Ideas, *European Romantic Review*, *Philosophy and Literature*, *Literature and Theology* and *Children's Literature Association Quarterly*. With Eugene Giddens and Zoe Jaques, she is co-editing volumes 1 and 2 of *The Cambridge History of Children's Literature* (Cambridge University Press).

Laura Kirkley is Senior Lecturer in Eighteenth-Century Literature at Newcastle University. She is a comparatist with particular expertise in women's writing and translation in the Revolutionary era. She has published widely on Wollstonecraft, including articles in the *Journal for Eighteenth-Century Studies* and *European Romantic Review*. Her monograph, *Mary Wollstonecraft: Cosmopolitan*, was published by Edinburgh University Press in 2022. She is currently working on scholarly editions of Wollstonecraft's three extant translations.

Jessica Lim teaches English at St Andrew's Cathedral School Sydney. She previously supervised English literature at the University of Cambridge where she was a Director of Studies in English at Lucy Cavendish College. Her research centres on women's writing and children's literature from the eighteenth and nineteenth centuries, with a focus on literary explorations of theological and pedagogical concerns. Her articles have appeared in *Journal for Eighteenth Century Studies*, *The Charles Lamb Bulletin*, *Notes and Queries* and *Oxford Research in English*.

Jack Orchard is Content Editor for the Electronic Enlightenment (EE) project, based at the Bodleian Libraries, University of Oxford. Since completing his PhD at Swansea University in 2019 he has worked as Editorial Associate for the Elizabeth Montagu's Correspondence Online project (EMCO), before joining EE in 2021. His research focuses on literary analysis of eighteenth-century women's correspondence, digital humanities and digital scholarly editing, and the resonances between historical reading practices and contemporary digital culture.

Jonathan Padley is a Fellow, Tutor, and the Lead Admissions Tutor at Churchill College, Cambridge, and Director of Studies in Education at Lucy Cavendish, Newnham, and St Edmund's Colleges. He is an Affiliated Lecturer at the Cambridge Faculty of Education and an Honorary Member of the English Faculty. Jonathan is a specialist in English children's literature from the eighteenth century to the present day. His work explores margins, particularly the marginalisation of authors, texts, and characters.

Lissa Paul, a Professor at Brock University in St. Catharines, Ontario, Canada, is the Director of the PhD Programme in Interdisciplinary Humanities. Her most recent monograph is *Eliza Fenwick: Early Modern Feminist* (Delaware, 2019). With Philip Nel and Nina Christensen, she is a co-editor of the recently published second edition of *Keywords for Children's Literature* (New York University Press, 2021). Currently, Lissa is working on a scholarly edition of Fenwick's letters (1797–1840). The volume will be the third in her Fenwick trilogy. The first was *The Children's Book Business: Lessons from the Long Eighteenth Century* (Routledge, 2011). Lissa's work on Eliza Fenwick is generously funded by the Social Sciences and Humanities Research Council of Canada.

Jennifer Robertson is a doctoral candidate at the University of Stirling and the University of Strathclyde. Her thesis, entitled 'Jane Austen and Authority', examines Austen's engagement with contemporary debates about the legitimacy of narrative authority. She has published on evangelicalism in *Mansfield Park* with *Persuasions On-Line*.

Jennifer Wallace is Harris Fellow and Director of Studies in English at Peterhouse, University of Cambridge. She works in the fields of classical reception, comparative tragedy, Romantic Hellenism and archaeological poetics. Recent publications include *The Oxford History of Classical Reception in English Literature, 1790–1880* (2015; rev. edn 2020); 'Picturing Antiquity: Photography, Performance and Julia Margaret Cameron' in Edmund Richardson (ed.), *Classics in Extremis: The Edges of Classical Reception* (Bloomsbury, 2019); and *Tragedy Since 9/11: Reading a World Out of Joint* (Bloomsbury, 2019).

Laura White is John E. Weaver Professor of English at the University of Nebraska-Lincoln. She is the author of three books on Jane Austen; her latest, *The Alice Books and the Contested Ground of the Natural World*, concerns Lewis Carroll's adult-level satires. She has also published widely in interdisciplinary nineteenth-century topics. Her most recent book project is tentatively titled *Politics, Belief, and Disenchantment in Nineteenth-Century Fairy Tales and Fairy Narratives*.

Introduction

Jessica Lim and Louise Joy

At some point in the last few years, discussions about female *identity*, which for so long preoccupied, and in some quarters strangulated, second- and third-wave feminist thought, have transmuted into discussions about *participation*. Where once we worried about who we are, now we worry about how we are. Such concern, seen, for example, in Judith Butler's *Notes toward a Performative Theory of Assembly* (2015), Sara Ahmed's *Living a Feminist Life* (2017) and Carol Gilligan and David Richards' *Darkness Now Visible* (2018), no longer restricts the object of study to 'woman', which, as Monique Wittig persuasively argued back in 1990, has meaning 'only in heterosexual systems of thought and heterosexual economic systems'.[1] Instead, for Sara Ahmed feminism is concerned with *movement*. She writes, 'individual struggle does matter; a collective movement depends upon it'.[2] Carol Gilligan and David Richards have framed this project more explicitly as a 'movement to free democracy from patriarchy'.[3] As they put it, 'the gender binary that splits intelligence (masculine) from emotion (feminine) and the self (masculine) from relationships (feminine), constrains our humanity'.[4]

The insight that the personal and the political are embroiled has been a mainstay of feminist thought at least since Virginia Woolf

---

[1] Monique Wittig, 'The Straight Mind', in *Feminism and Sexuality: A Reader*, ed. by Stevi Jackson and Sue Scott (Edinburgh: Edinburgh University Press, 1996), pp. 144–50 (p. 148).

[2] Sarah Ahmed, *Living a Feminist Life* (Durham, NC and London: Duke University Press, 2017), p. 6.

[3] Carol Gilligan and David A. J. Richards, *Darkness Now Visible: Patriarchy's Resurgence and Feminist Resistance* (Cambridge: Cambridge University Press, 2018), p. 6.

[4] Ibid.

forcefully made the point in *Three Guineas* (1938) that 'the public and the private worlds are inseparably connected' and that 'the tyrannies and servilities of the one are the tyrannies and servilities of the other'.[5] In its twenty-first-century iteration, this feminist commitment to the belief that the personal is political has coalesced into a view that we all gain when that which has previously been designated feminine is reclaimed as human. The particular interest in a consonance between feminism and democracy has especially caught the imagination of those on the radical left. Where once Judith Butler was preoccupied by the performativity of gender, now she writes about the performativity of collective resistance, or what she calls 'concerted bodily enactment, a plural form of performativity'.[6] Pessimistic about the gains that have been made – or could ever be made – through the spoken word alone, she postulates that collective action speaks louder, even in its silence:

> when bodies assemble on the street, in the square, or in other forms of public space (including virtual ones) they are exercising a plural and performative right to appear, one that asserts and instates the body in the midst of the political field, and which, in its expressive and signifying function, delivers a bodily demand for a more livable set of economic, social, and political conditions no longer afflicted by induced forms of precarity.[7]

Butler's notion of a 'plural form of performativity' provides us with a beguiling way of thinking about the assembly of female 'bodies' entailed in the explosion of a particular print phenomenon during the long eighteenth century: educational literature authored by women. In this period – roughly 1690 to 1850 – sizeable numbers of women took to print to intervene in public debates about who might provide and receive education; what education might consist of; how and where and when and why it might take place. Limited in the public platforms available to them to shape the direction of travel, women's chosen vehicle for the exploration of educational ideas was frequently the literary text. As Jennie Batchelor and Cora Kaplan have highlighted, there were 'myriad' ways in which women could enter the literary marketplace, not just as writers, but also as printers,

---

[5] Virginia Woolf, *Three Guineas*, 2nd edn (London: Hogarth Press, 1943), p. 270.
[6] Judith Butler, *Notes toward a Performative Theory of Assembly* (Cambridge, MA and London: Harvard University Press, 2015), p. 8.
[7] Butler, p. 11.

as publishers, as patrons and of course as readers.[8] In their shared interest in the project of educating oneself and others, and in the shared gender of their authorship, it is easy to assume that eighteenth-century female educationalists, by anticipating Butler's 'plural form of performativity', together constitute a 'collective movement' – perhaps one that can be characterised as *feminist*: one that calls for equality expressed through uniformity; justice achieved through collective resistance; change modelled on designed order. But do collected bodies necessarily occupy a political field? Is the character of political occupation necessarily one of assertion and instatement? Must an assembly entail bodies operating in concert? Is the feminine plural always performative – always legible as a feminist *movement*?

This volume, *Women's Literary Education, 1690–1850*, seeks to identify some of the common interests among educational writings authored by women in the long eighteenth century, which for the purposes of this book reaches back to the last decade of the seventeenth century and forward into the first half of the nineteenth century. In so doing, it draws out some of the ways in which long-eighteenth-century discourses of education shaped what it meant for women to write and the ways in which women writers shaped long-eighteenth-century discourses of education, spotlighting the influence of female authors on eighteenth-century debates about education as they are conducted in and through literary form. Literature and education share certain perceived aims in the eighteenth century: transmission of knowledge, strengthening of understanding, acculturation, in some cases even empowerment. They also share certain structural forms: lessons, conversations, letters, dramatisations, confessions, narratives, examples, imitations, sometimes fantasies. Indeed, in the long eighteenth century the authors of literary texts and the authors of educational treatises were often the very same people who saw their activity in both spheres as interrelated. Moreover, in the cases of both literature and education, the power dynamics at play between the various parties (teacher and pupil; author and reader) are susceptible to organisation along ideological lines. A historically sensitive understanding of the fraught relations between these various parties therefore requires us to be alert to the subtle shades of the period's vexed debates about authority and freedom, particularly as they relate to matters of gender, race, religion, age and class.

---

[8] Jennie Batchelor and Cora Kaplan, eds, 'Introduction', in *British Women's Writing in the Long Eighteenth Century: Authorship, Politics and History* (Basingstoke: Palgrave Macmillan, 2005), pp. 1–15 (p. 7).

By restoring female writers to the centre of the stage, this book seeks to correct – and to add its voice to existing scholarly efforts to correct – the ongoing critical tendency to marginalise the contribution of women to the history of educational thought.[9] Together, the essays in this volume reveal the complex, various, sometimes contradictory and in many cases profoundly significant ways in which female literary artists interrogated and advanced educational philosophy and practice during this period. Further, one of the beliefs underpinning this project is that a nuanced understanding of women's contributions to the period's various strands of educational thought will enable us better to understand the intricate ways in which authors and readers of the period envisaged that literary texts might fulfil, fail, or refuse to fulfil, educational functions.

* * *

In the eighteenth century, education was often deemed to be a female preserve: teaching was a legitimate occupation for women, and a culturally approved subject about which women could write. As a result, discourses of education were often central to discussions of what it meant to be a woman writer, and women writers made a significant contribution to the direction and evolution of ideas about education. The forms in which women posed questions about education were heterogeneous: novels, poems, plays, treatises, letters, memoirs, autobiographical writings and translations. They included both published works and unpublished material, the latter often existing in manuscript or idiosyncratic form, such as homemade teaching aids or toys and artefacts used to nurture and develop intellectual growth in the domestic sphere. Certain thematic motifs recur across this body of female-authored work. One such motif, which rears its head as an educational priority throughout the writings considered

---

[9] See, for example, William Boyd, *The History of Western Education* (London: Black, 1969); Steven M. Cahn, *Classic and Contemporary Readings in the Philosophy of Education* (New York: Oxford University Press, 1997). Revisionist accounts that have sought to acknowledge the contribution of women to educational thought include: Mary Hilton, *Women and the Shaping of the Nation's Young: Education and Public Doctrine in Britain 1750–1850* (Aldershot: Ashgate, 2007); Mitzi Myers, 'Impeccable Governesses, Rational Dames, and Moral Mothers: Mary Wollstonecraft and the Female Tradition in Georgian Children's Books', *Children's Literature*, 14 (1986), 31–59; Rebecca Davies, *Written Maternal Authority and Eighteenth-Century Education in Britain: Educating by the Book* (Farnham: Ashgate, 2014).

by this volume, is the pursuit and attainment of human happiness, both individual and collective:

> [W]e ought as much as we can to endeavour the Perfecting of our Beings, and that we be as happy as possibly we may. [. . .] altho we all pursue the same end, yet the means we take to obtain it are Indefinite: [. . .] We all agree that its fit to be as Happy as we can, and we need no Instructor to teach us this Knowledge, 'tis born with us, and is inseparable from our Being, but we very much need to be Inform'd what is the true Way to Happiness.[10]

So wrote Mary Astell in 1694 in Part II of *A Serious Proposal to the Ladies*, asserting that the purpose of education is to inform the 'true Way to Happiness'. The rational education that provides personal fulfilment, Astell suggests, is religious in kind. Radically, the education she envisages takes place in a women's-only space, one modelled on a nunnery, a place where women temporarily withdraw from social participation to devote themselves to logical and philosophical thought and religious worship, without the distractions of fashion and culture. Astell's textual account of her anthropological theology, which obliquely discards the doctrine of Original Sin by insisting that people can perfect themselves with effective guidance, provides us with a means of perceiving how literature presented unique educational possibilities for female authors during the period. Astell's philosophical stance rests on a belief that the written word, in the right hands, can itself unfold and deliver a virtuous education. And this is critical. For although *A Serious Proposal* suggests that true knowledge is best acquired in a community of religious retreat – and although Astell clearly hoped to actualise the material reality of such a retreat – a real-world educational establishment never eventuated from Astell's proposal. The retreat remains virtual – a literary idea. In Astell's seminal work, then, the text itself becomes the locus for imagination. The literary text does not merely provide an analogue for educational exchange; it constitutes the thing itself. It functions as the medium for the delivery of a first-hand, asynchronous educational process, one which anticipates and theoretically might correspond with, but cannot yet be translated into, what today we might term 'in-person learning'.

---

[10] Mary Astell, *A Serious Proposal to the Ladies: Part I and II*, edited by Patricia Springborg (Peterborough, ON: Broadview Press, 2002), p. 129.

As Karen Detlefsen points out, Astell's vision modifies Cartesian dualism, extrapolating from Descartes's concept of the non-gendered soul not just women's rights but moreover their religious duty to cultivate their souls alongside those of men – a cultivation which for Astell is enabled by community, not Cartesian isolated reflection.[11] In Astell's proposal, right knowledge is the way to true happiness; what makes her account distinctive, and distinctively feminine, is that right knowledge is relational. Indeed, female friendships become the ultimate and true reflection of the love of the God who underpins Astell's worldview. Such friendships perform 'the search of Knowledge, and acquisition of Virtuous Habits, a mutual Love to which was the Origin of 'em'.[12] A century after Astell wrote her influential work, the evangelical author and educator Hannah More took up this question of the right knowledge for women, similarly focusing on the formation of relationships as the primary object of learning. The opening pages of More's *Strictures on the Modern System of Female Education* (1799) announce that her concern, too, is human contentment, framed, in More's work, as 'Domestic happiness'. Like Astell, More condemns the 'singular injustice which is often exercised towards women, first to give them a most defective Education, and then to expect from them the most undeviating purity of conduct'.[13] The goal and method of female education in More's vision, then, is to form women who, with

> learning which would be thought extensive in the other sex, set an example of deep humility to their own; – women who, distinguished for wit and genius, are eminent for domestic qualities; – who, excelling in the fine arts, have carefully enriched their understandings; – who, enjoying great affluence, devote it to the glory of God; – who, possessing elevated rank, think their noblest style and title is that of a Christian.[14]

---

[11] Karen Detlefsen, 'Cartesianism and Its Feminist Promise and Limits: The Case of Mary Astell', in *Descartes and Cartesianism: Essays in Honour of Desmond Clarke*, ed. by Stephen Gaukroger and Catherine Wilson (Oxford: Oxford Scholarship Online, 2017), pp. 191–206.

[12] Astell, p. 123.

[13] Hannah More, *Strictures on the Modern System of Female Education, with a View of the Principles and Conduct Prevalent among Women of Rank and Fortune*, vol. I of II (London: Printed for T. Cadell Jun. and W. Davies, 1799), p. ix.

[14] More, pp. xii–xiii.

More's rhetorical procedure recalls the parallelisms of the King James Bible, anaphorically building to the ultimate vision and basis on which she centres her vision of female education: the production of Christian women. More's celebration of female learning, particularly of knowledge and skill that pertains to the arts, reveals the influence on her thought of her Bluestocking associations. Yet the aim of female education for More is not to promote female intellectualism for its own sake. Neither does More consider personal fulfilment an end in itself, in contrast with Maria Edgeworth's vision for *her* female pupils, articulated in *Letters for Literary Ladies* (1794): 'I am more intent upon their happiness than ambitious to enter into a metaphysical discussion of their rights.'[15] Nor is education for More a question of rights – giving women access to the skills and knowledge held by men is not a motive of its own. As the cadence of More's sentence accentuates, her concern lies beyond the fate of the individual: the acquisition of 'humility' through education enables that individual to fulfil their altruistic (Christian) responsibilities to others. The gains breach the bounds of one singular life, both in this world and the next.

The implicit tensions at work here between personal fulfilment, spiritual salvation and social good acquire renewed political freight in the wake of the French Revolution, when what women did or should read was intensely scrutinised along political lines. In conservative, anti-Jacobin formulations, 'pleasure' could arouse suspicion due to its associations with uncontrollable desire for satiation. 'Happiness', by contrast, became associated with domesticity, and hence played a function in furthering the nationalist cause. This patriotism can be witnessed, for example, in Laetitia Matilda Hawkins' *Letters on the Female Mind* (1793), which sacrifices personal gratification on the altar of communal advantage, insisting that

> Instead of founding the motives of our conduct on the laws of instructed
> nature, and looking to our hearts for the impulses of duty, we shall, if
> we are good wives, be so, because the well-being of a state is connected

---

[15] Maria Edgeworth, *Letters for Literary Ladies, to Which Is Added, an Essay on the Noble Science of Self-Justification* (London: Joseph Johnson, 1795), p. 45. Robin Runia has suggested that good and right in Edgeworth's pedagogical fiction are 'behaviours upon which intelligent women and men must determine to act according to their own potential for happiness'. Robin Runia, 'Edgeworth's *Letters for Literary Ladies*: Publication Peers and Analytical Antagonists', in *Women's Literary Networks and Romanticism: 'A Tribe of Authoresses'*, ed. by Andrew O. Winckles and Angela Rehbein (Liverpool: Liverpool University Press, 2017), pp. 226–44 (p. 240).

with our virtue; not because [of] the affection we feel towards the man
we are devoted to [. . .] we shall be careful mothers, if such cares are not
beneath our notice, because we hope to rear a progeny of patriots [. . .][16]

Hawkins' natural rights lexis recalls the pretext of her anti-Jacobin
piece as a riposte to Helen Maria Williams' *Letters from France*
(1790–6). The dialogic nature of her *Letters* testifies to the energetic
public literary exchanges that took place between female writers at
this volatile moment at the end of the eighteenth century, and the perceived urgency of the role played by female education in national, and
indeed international, affairs. Hawkins' response constitutes an em-
phatic denial of the revolutionary insistence on the political value of
individualism, seen expressed a year before in Mary Wollstonecraft's
courageous personal avowal: 'Independence I have long considered
the grand blessing of life, the basis of every virtue – and independence I will ever secure by contracting my wants.'[17] In this radical reimagining of the social contract, Wollstonecraft had repositioned the
female desire for self-fulfilment as a matter of civic importance. This
logic underpins her insistence that female education should facilitate
consideration of 'the moral and civil interest of mankind'.[18] While
Wollstonecraft and Hawkins share a conviction, then, that female
education is a political priority, Wollstonecraft's 'first object of laud-
able ambition is to obtain a character as a human being'[19] – women's
psychological freedom; their power over themselves. Hawkins' self-
abnegating construction of female identity, meanwhile, reinforces the
patriarchal assumption that women exist to serve, an assumption
that would prove intractable during the period considered by the
essays in this volume.

For all that the reach of Wollstonecraft's radical philosophy
on the *practice* of female education would remain limited in her
own lifetime, it can be heard echoed in the words of her daughter,
Mary Shelley, ventriloquised through the creature in *Frankenstein*

---

[16] Laetitia Matilda Hawkins, 'Letter II', in *Letters on the Female Mind, Its Powers
and Pursuits: Addressed to Miss H. M. Williams, with Particular Reference to
Her Letters from France* (London: Printed for Hookham and Carpenter, 1793),
p. 30.

[17] Mary Wollstonecraft, *A Vindication of the Rights of Woman, with Strictures on
Political and Moral Subjects* (London: Printed for J. Johnson, 1792), p. iv.

[18] Wollstonecraft, p. viii.

[19] Wollstonecraft, p. 7.

(1818): 'Make me happy, and I shall again be virtuous.'[20] Its transmission in textual form kept the hope alive despite the conservative backlash in the wake of revolutionary turmoil across Europe. It surfaces again in 1847, when Charlotte Brontë published *Jane Eyre: An Autobiography*, which triumphantly culminates with Jane's declaration of personal happiness, albeit that the fantasy encoded in Brontë's use of the romance form hints at the exceptionality, the real-world unavailability, of such a fate in a society in which women's education is decided and circumscribed by women's designation as caregivers.[21]

But, as the example of Mary Astell's *Serious Proposal* vividly shows, literary texts can reach places to which worldly experiences are denied access. One of the period's most provocative contributions to discussions about female education came in the form of Sarah Scott's *A Description of Millenium Hall* (1762), which, like Astell's work, provides a way of imagining women as extricated from their matrimonial and familial contexts. Scott's thriving all-female community, unlike Astell's temporary refuge, provides a permanent way of being female. Scott produces an assembly of women collected, to recall Judith Butler's vocabulary, in a discernible 'field' – the eponymous house and the physical fields in which it is situated. The women who congregate at Millenium Hall exist happily alongside one another without men and outside of the nuclear family. The characters' evident delight in this prospect and the pleasure and awe that it inspires in its male narrator have routinely led to the novel being read as a feminist utopia. Christine Rees identifies it as a 'women's utopia', and Mary Louise Pratt calls it a 'feminotopia', which is to say that it contains 'episodes that present idealized worlds of female autonomy, empowerment and pleasure'.[22] Johanna Devereaux,

---

[20] Mary Shelley, *Frankenstein*, ed. by Marilyn Butler (Oxford: Oxford University Press, 1998), p. 78.

[21] Charlotte Brontë, *Jane Eyre*, ed. by Margaret Smith and Juliette Atkinson (Oxford: Oxford University Press, 2019), p. 439. For a discussion of *Jane Eyre*'s treatment of education, see Mary Poovey, 'The Anathematized Race: The Governess and *Jane Eyre*', in *Feminism and Psychoanalysis*, ed. by Richard Feldstein and Judith Roof (Ithaca, NY: Cornell University Press, 1989), pp. 230–54; Marianne Thormählen, *The Brontës and Education* (Cambridge: Cambridge University Press, 1999).

[22] See Christine Rees, *Utopian Imagination and Eighteenth-Century Fiction* (London: Longman, 1996), p. 7; M. L. Pratt, *Imperial Eyes: Travel Writing and Transculturation* (London: Routledge, 1992), p. 167; and Felicity Nussbaum, *Torrid Zones: Maternity, Sexuality, and Empire in Eighteenth-Century English Narratives* (Baltimore: Johns Hopkins University Press, 1995), p. 152.

searching to characterise it more narrowly to acknowledge that the novel's female characters do not experience any real empowerment, proposes the Foucauldian term 'heterotopia' to connote a 'kin[d] of effectively enacted utopia' whose role 'is to create a space of illusion that exposes every real space, all the sites inside of which human life is partitioned, as still more illusory'.[23] What all of these views share in common is that they see the novel's whimsicality – they position literary fantasy – as political in spirit. For all that critics have disputed the particular political character of Scott's feminism, with some seeing her as a conservative and others insisting that she is a radical,[24] the view that Scott's novel presents a theory of female education, that it functions as an 'expression of the social manifesto of the "Bluestocking" movement',[25] is entrenched.

But the premise that this novel – or indeed, any literary treatment of education – refracts a system of thought independent from the text itself warrants careful consideration. As Toril Moi has recently proposed, theory might not always be a benign instrument, particularly in the domain of feminist thought, snagged as such thought can be on debates about the meanings of their own key terms. Our alacrity to generalise and to fix meaning through rigid categories and stubborn definitions can cause us to miss the obvious or distort our vision so that what we see fits the shape we expect to see. As Moi puts it,

> feminist identity theory – and any other theory-formation obsessed with 'exclusionary' concepts – is bound to be self-defeating. The very idea of 'exclusionary' concepts [. . .] presupposes the very 'exclusionariness' or 'boundedness' that feminist theorists are eager to undo. The effect is to render feminist theorists unable to pay attention to the particular case, and thus unable to provide the kind of concrete, feminist analysis that helps to make women's lives intelligible.[26]

---

[23] Johanna Devereaux, 'Paradise Within? Mary Astell, Sarah Scott and the Limits of Utopia', *Journal for Eighteenth-Century Studies*, 32.1 (2009), 53–67 (p. 58).

[24] Susan Staves, for example, has seen the novel as 'politically and socially conservative'. Susan Staves, *A Literary History of Women's Writing in Britain, 1660–1789* (Cambridge: Cambridge University Press, 2006), p. 355. Betty Rizzo, however, sees the conservative elements of Scott's novel as a foil to enable her to sneak in a more radical agenda. Betty Rizzo, 'Introduction', in Sarah Scott, *The History of Sir George Ellison* (Lexington: University of Kentucky, 1996), p. xxxi.

[25] Brean Hammond and Shaun Regan, *Making the Novel: Fiction and Society in Britain, 1660–1789* (Basingstoke: Palgrave Macmillan, 2006), p. 177.

[26] Toril Moi, *Revolution of the Ordinary: Literary Studies after Wittgenstein, Austin, and Cavell* (Chicago and London: University of Chicago Press, 2017), p. 88.

For Moi, the pursuit of the rule is the problem. Far more enabling, she proposes, is Wittgensteinian ordinary language, which, she claims, 'teaches us to think through examples'[27]– to look for family resemblances instead of essential, intrinsic properties. In fact, one of the characters in Scott's *Millenium Hall* had already made much the same point. 'Philosophers, who have formed their judgements more on reason than the knowledge of mankind', laments Lady Mary, have fundamentally and perpetually misunderstood what women want.[28] Moi's cautioning against theory functions as a salutary reminder of the dangers of Procrustean literary critical methods that distort a text, which, in its interest in the feminine and in the particular, even when this feminine particular is a feminine plural, may have a family resemblance with a feminist system of thought, but which, as a particular example, and furthermore as a novel, cannot be reduced to it. The feminine plural of the particular exemplary case of *Millenium Hall*, then, as is the case for the feminine plural voice articulated through this volume, must be a definite feminine plural. That is, it cannot remain *in*definite, forced to encompass other or all feminine plurals. In this, it may transpire that the very insistence on particularity and plurality – the repudiation of consistency, coherence, homogeneity – is a standout contribution that female authors like Sarah Scott brought to eighteenth-century educational debate: what eighteenth-century women's literary educators together provide is a way of thinking through the plural without reducing it to the abstract.

In *Millenium Hall*, Scott's refusal to reduce women's stories in this way is indicated through the noun Scott uses to designate the activity of her hall: 'description'. This evokes a sense of the documentary: the narrative eye stumbles on that which falls beneath the normative gaze and reports what it sees. However, crucially, in *Millenium Hall* description merely forms a surface. The texture of the novel is provided by a series of discrete stories that are told to the male narrator by a character within the novel, Mrs Maynard. The narrator then relays these stories to his addressee in an epistolary frame. This collection of stories, each of which delineates the abuses of one or more women at the hands of men, creates a sense of equivalence. The stories remain separate and individual; no attempt is made to connect them. Their accumulation therefore leads to accretion, not

---

[27] Moi, p. 90.
[28] Sarah Scott, *Millenium Hall* (New York: Penguin, 1986), p. 60.

distillation. In their equivalence, the female characters are never elevated to the status of protagonists: they do not act or determine; they
are bounced into decline, unable materially to resist the alterations in
their circumstances. But each character shares in common that, even
as their circumstances deteriorate, their internal resolution, what the
text repeatedly calls their 'virtue', does not. Of course, for readers
of eighteenth-century fiction, notably Samuel Richardson's *Pamela*
(1740) and *Clarissa* (1748), this narrative conceit is familiar. Sarah
Scott, though, documents the psychological predicament of her female characters not from the cloying perspective of first-person narrative, awkwardly contrived through the voice of the implied author.
Instead, she modestly layers a series of narrative filters. The effect
is to alienate the reader from the characters' interiority – the lived
experience of affect – and instead to narrate these women as completed, finished, spent products of their education and experience.
Where Richardson offers protracted analysis of subjectivity, Scott
turns the gaze outwards towards those aspects of female experience
that are not individual but shared – what in the novel is called 'humanity', and what in contemporary feminist vocabulary we might
frame as the central insight 'that self and other are interdependent'.[29]
If, following Carol Gilligan, we perceive that

> women's construction of the moral problem as a problem of care and
> responsibility in relationships rather than one of rights and rules ties the
> development of their moral thinking to their understanding of responsi-
> bility and relationships, just as the conception of morality as justice ties
> development to the logic of equality and reciprocity,[30]

then Scott's shift away from the subjective and towards the 'interdependent' or the collective reveals a feminine voice at work – a voice
that recalls Astell and anticipates More – a feminine voice which
necessarily presents itself in the plural, since it cannot (yet) entertain
the self-serving individualism that makes possible the articulation,
without fear of rebuke (as Wollstonecraft discovered to her cost), of
a distinction between self and other.

Identifying the texts considered in this volume as particular exemplary cases, and as both *feminine* and as *literary*, goes some way
to divert the Procrustean urge, since it enables us to pose questions

[29] Carol Gilligan, *In a Different Voice: Psychological Theory and Women's
Development* (Cambridge, MA: Harvard University Press, 2003), p. 74.
[30] Gilligan, p. 73.

about each in turn – what kind of a work is this? What is it like? – without automatic recourse to existing taxonomical categories. All too often, women's writing has suffered at the hands of critics who have posed the questions they ask of it with reference to typologies drawn from surveys of male-authored works. Homer Obed Brown's *Institutions of the English Novel: From Defoe to Scott* (1997), for instance, recapitulates the familiar Wattian position that Daniel Defoe, Henry Fielding, Laurence Sterne and Walter Scott inaugurated the dominant kinds of novels of the period. Like Michael McKeon's capacious account of the novel's generic instability in the period, Brown's account refers to virtually no novels authored by women. For all that Terry Eagleton, among others, has popularised a view that we witness a 'feminization of discourse' in eighteenth-century fiction, particularly after the publication of *Clarissa*,[31] the 'unspoken masculinist assumptions' of such versions of literary history are, as Paula R. Backscheider and John J. Richetti have argued, 'embarrassingly apparent'.[32] This has resulted in a tendency to position works which do not fit the contours established by conventional histories of the rise of the novel as 'lawbreakers', that is to say, 'generically hybrid texts [which] challenge the discourses of power'.[33] The problem resides in the fact that if genre is a law, as Jacques Derrida has put it, then it ought to be obvious to us what the genre is. 'As soon as genre announces itself,' Derrida avers, 'one must respect a norm, [. . .] one must not risk impurity, anomaly, or monstrosity'.[34] For centuries, many of the works authored by writers considered in this volume – Mary Wollstonecraft, Sarah Trimmer, Hannah More – in their anomalousness, have been dismissed as monstrous: irrelevant, laughable, despicable. But what happens when we place such texts not alongside male-authored works by Daniel Defoe and Walter Scott, but alongside one another? What creative and critical norms, what creative or critical anarchy, comes into view when we adopt this line of sight?

In its interest in the plural contribution of women to eighteenth-century educational thought, this volume builds on recent critical

[31] Terry Eagleton, *The Rape of Clarissa: Writing, Sexuality and Class Struggle in Samuel Richardson* (Oxford: Basil Blackwell, 1982), p. 13.
[32] Paula R. Backscheider and John J. Richetti, *Popular Fiction by Women, 1660–1730: An Anthology* (Oxford: Clarendon Press, 1996), p. ix.
[33] Nicole Tabor, *Gender, Genre, and the Myth of Human Singularity* (New York: Peter Lang, 2013), pp. 1–2.
[34] Jacques Derrida, 'Law of Genre', in *Acts of Literature*, ed. by Derek Attridge (New York: Routledge, 1992), p. 224.

work that has begun to deepen and broaden our understanding of the ways in which women used literary forms in conversation with one another to carve out distinctive public literary identities. Rebecca D'Monté and Nicole Pohl's collection, *Female Communities 1600–1800: Literary Visions and Cultural Realities* (2000), and Andrew O. Winckles and Angela Rehbein's *Women's Literary Networks and Romanticism: 'A Tribe of Authoresses'* (2017), for example, have highlighted the ways in which both horizontal and vertical women's literary networks shaped women's creativity during the period.[35] But, like the women gathered in *Millenium Hall*, the female authors considered in *Women's Literary Education* do not act in concert (to recall Butler's term); they do not think in unison. As in Scott's novel, each contributes a different story to the assemblage; no one story can stand in for another, since each is unique and irreducible. Scott's narrative form is a composite structure which attests to multiple simultaneous separate experiences, and this volume takes its cue from the exemplary case of *Millenium Hall*. Its assertion of the presence of women as a critical mass endorses Simone de Beauvoir's phenomenological insistence that we encounter the world as embodied, gendered beings, but it also seeks to hold on to the notion of the continuum brought into play through Adrienne Rich's notion of 'lesbian existence'.[36] Crucially, then, it seeks to listen to the differences at play, the discreteness of the stories told, which together document the definite feminine plurality of eighteenth-century women's literary education.

* * *

While female authors in the period in question sought to sound their own individual voices, they did so in a context in which generalisations *about* women, and general rules about the education that women deserved, abounded. When Aphra Behn wrote in her sensationalist amatory novella, *The History of the Nun* (1689), 'Women

---

[35] *Female Communities 1600–1800: Literary Visions and Cultural Realities*, ed. by Rebecca D'Monté and Nicole Pohl (Basingstoke: Palgrave Macmillan, 2000); *Women's Literary Networks and Romanticism: 'A Tribe of Authoresses'*, ed. by Andrew O. Winckles and Angela Rehbein (Liverpool: Liverpool University Press, 2017).

[36] Simone de Beauvoir, *The Second Sex* (London: Picador, 1988); Adrienne Rich, 'Compulsory Heterosexuality and Lesbian Existence', in *Feminism and Sexuality: A Reader*, ed. by Stevi Jackson and Sue Scott (Edinburgh: Edinburgh University Press, 1996), pp. 130–44.

are by Nature more Constant and Just, than Men [. . .] But Customs of Countries change even Nature her self [. . .] The Women are taught, by the Lives of Men, to live up to all their Vices, and are become almost as inconstant',[37] the exaggerated tone already has the feel of cliché and a veneer of potentially justificatory defensiveness. Though Behn's arch sentiments playfully angle for readerly dismay, compounding the narrative shocks on offer in a plot hinging on big-amy, her phrases speak to a deep-seated and persistent cultural at-tempt to define women by some fundamental quality of constancy. They betray a recurrent suspicion that existing forms of women's education, and therefore existing models for female behaviour, were morally and intellectually deficient.

As Charlotte Lennox's *The Female Quixote* (1752) memorably chronicles, one vulnerability to which women were believed to be es-pecially prone by virtue of their inadequate education was a propen-sity for misreading, a trope which was hardened into a quintessential attribute of femininity in the female Gothic, particularly in the hands of Ann Radcliffe. As Amelia Dale has suggested, perceptions of wom-en's heightened physiological and mental impressionability meant that women were seen as particularly susceptible to being 'imprinted' on by the literature they read, heightening cultural anxieties con-cerning the importance of what women read and guidance for how to read it.[38] The assumption that women were physically frail, and hence, by implication, intellectually feeble, was echoed by both male and female writers, even by those arguing for improved women's educations. James Fordyce's observation of women's lack of 'vigour' reverberates in Mary Wollstonecraft's resignation to women's gen-eral physical weakness.[39] As has been well documented, the cultural acceptance of women's physiological fragility held women hostage to theories concerning their susceptibility to moral, social, sexual or supernatural corruption. In certain American Puritan communities, for instance, the belief that Satan attacked the soul by assaulting the body rendered women objects of universal suspicion.[40]

---

[37] Aphra Behn, *The History of the Nun: or, The Fair Vow-Breaker* (London: Printed for A. Baskervile, 1689), p. 3.

[38] Amelia Dale, *The Printed Reader: Gender, Quixotism, and Textual Bodies in Eighteenth-Century Britain* (Lewisburg, PA: Bucknell University Press, 2019).

[39] James Fordyce, *Sermons to Young Women*, vol. II of II (London: Printed for A. Millar and T. Cadell, 1746), pp. 9–10; see also Wollstonecraft, p. 3.

[40] Elizabeth Reis, 'The Devil, the Body, and the Feminine Soul in Puritan New England', *The Journal of American History*, 82 (1995), 15–36 (p. 15).

Against this backdrop of ingrained belief in women's essential fallibility, even depravity, it is unsurprising that even many women were pessimistic about what could be achieved for women through education. Mary Martha Sherwood, a bestselling late Georgian children's author and then-strict evangelical Calvinist, doubted that much good could come of it, describing literary works as 'the best means which we can use' for religious education, but warning that they 'must of themselves fall far short of the proposed end'.[41] The overt didacticism of her literary approach has led to her disdain among critics, who have bemoaned her 'heavy-handed religious bullying', her 'dogmatic fervour' and her 'unwilling[ness] to temper her conviction of inherent human corruption'.[42] Even F. J. Harvey Darton finds it hard to reconcile Sherwood's 'magnificent story-tell[ing]' with the 'extreme Puritan[ism]' of her outlook.[43] As several essays in this volume show, ideological and artistic ends are frequently in competition in eighteenth-century women's educational literature. Sherwood's evangelical belief in the power of introspection to transform the human heart stands in tension with her conviction that reading and writing are corrupt communicative processes destined (without intervention by the Holy Spirit) to fail.[44]

Yet, as the essays in this volume demonstrate, the dominance of this narrative of female delinquency did not deter women, and in some quarters men, from agitating for improvements in female education, however pessimistic the prognosis might be for its actualisation. Cultural and religious expectations may well have dictated that women become wives and mothers, and, consequently, legally disenfranchised, since it was impossible for a woman to enter into contracts that would 'suppose her separate existence', given that, as Sir William Blackstone explains in *Commentaries on the Laws of England* (1765), 'the very being or legal existence of a woman is suspended during the marriage, [and] incorporated and consolidated

---

[41] Mary Martha Sherwood, *The Governess; or, Little Female Academy* (London: F. Houlston and Son, 1820), p. 134.

[42] Hilton, p. 171; also Patricia Demers, 'Sherwood, Mary Martha (1775–1851)', in *Oxford Dictionary of National Biography* (Oxford: Oxford University Press, 2004); online edn, May 2011 <http://www.oxforddnb.com/view/article/25397> [accessed 13 July 2017].

[43] F. J. Harvey Darton, *Children's Books in England: Five Centuries of Social Life*, 3rd edn, rev. by Brian Alderson (London: British Library, 1999), p. 173.

[44] For more on this paradox, see Neil Cocks, 'Scripture Its Own Interpreter: Mary Martha Sherwood, the Bible and Female Autobiography', *Nineteenth-Century Gender Studies*, 7 (2011), 1–33.

into that of the husband'.[45] Nevertheless, there is evidence that, against all the odds, by the end of the eighteenth century the visibility of female-authored works testifying to their writers' capacity for learning, and consequently their capacity to participate in the public sphere, had caused sufficient consternation to motivate a prescriptive moralist backlash designed to encourage women to remain in the domestic sphere.[46] This in itself speaks volumes about the perceived threat of women's literary education.

*   *   *

Undermined from the start, and marginalised since, the many educational works produced by women during the long eighteenth century have not previously been identified as a discernible literary tradition. By bringing into the same frame works designed for older and younger audiences, works designed to please and instruct, works which became mainstream and works which remained obscure, this collection of essays reveals some of the many ways in which women writers innovated educational practice as they practised literary innovations.

The essays in Part I, 'Moulding Forms', examine some of the ways in which female educationalists pioneered new literary forms and techniques. Jessica Lim's essay shows how Anna Letitia Barbauld, Sarah Trimmer and Ellenor Fenn developed the conversational primer, tapping into the pedagogic potential of familial dialogues to enact educational ends and to model distinctive roles of female educators in the domestic sphere. Through a discussion that situates two different volumes entitled *Poetry for Children* in the wider context of eighteenth-century children's poetry, Felicity James draws out the uneasiness of the relationships between poetry and children's education during the period, highlighting the efforts of poets such as Lucy Aikin and Charles and Mary Lamb to reconcile the educational and the playful. Turning our gaze away from the imaginative realm and instead inviting us to contemplate the literary qualities of

---

[45] William Blackstone, *Commentaries on the Laws of England: Book the First*, 2nd edn (Oxford: Clarendon Press, 1765), chapter 15, p. 442.

[46] Linda Colley, *Britons: Forging the Nation 1707–1837* (London: Random House, 1992), pp. 241–50; Elaine Chalus, '"That Epidemical Madness": Women and Electoral Politics in the Late Eighteenth Century', *Gender in Eighteenth-Century England*, ed. by Hannah Barker and Elaine Chalus (Abingdon: Routledge, 1997), pp. 151–78.

non-fictional educational texts, Michèle Cohen's essay demonstrates the contributions made by women to the development of geography as a science in the nineteenth century. It highlights the role played by female authors in developing forms for representing and understanding the physical world, and in so doing, consolidating a newly emerging discipline. The final essay in this section, by Aileen Douglas, explores how Maria Edgeworth experimented with the possibilities inherent in the novel form by writing sequels to her earlier works of prose fiction for children. These sequels for older child readers provide opportunities for children's stories to anticipate how the child's gendered subjectivity will play out in the world.

As the essays in Part II, 'Acknowledging the Past', remind us, the education that women typically received in the long eighteenth century impeded access to the forms of knowledge and cultural capital that schools and universities routinely made available to men. Such educational differences shaped the ways in which female authors could situate themselves within existing traditions and make sense of their own intellectual contribution. Jennifer Wallace discusses the work of two women, Laetitia Elizabeth Landon and Elizabeth Barrett Browning, who were exceptional in their prodigious classical learning. Wallace examines how these nineteenth-century female poets' classical imitations perform a critique of nineteenth-century modes of engagement with the classical past, revealing the peculiar ways in which the ancient past haunted female poets who were debarred from classical education through conventional means. Rachel Bryant Davies' essay considers how eighteenth-century educators sought to transmit classical antiquity to the next generation. Focusing on two high-profile Quaker authors, Priscilla Wakefield and Maria Hack, she assesses the interactive opportunities that works by these female authors created for children to inherit practical wisdom from the ancient world. Through a discussion of Catherine Talbot and Elizabeth Carter, the third essay in this section, by Jack Orchard, shows how essential shared reading practices were to the self-education and self-fashioning of female Bluestockings whose mutual veneration of the classics engendered close collaborative creative relationships and facilitated female sociability and friendships.

The variety of literary approaches and political perspectives showcased in the texts considered in Part III, 'Responding to the Present', is an important reminder that for all that shared gender might have constrained female authors in discernibly similar ways, it does not follow that they shared a common sense of the status quo. Rebecca Anne Barr's chapter alerts us to the danger that the preponderance of the belief that education is a serious business can cause us to over-look the educative power of mirth, particularly in writing by women. Through an examination of works by Sarah Fielding, Barr charts the troubling ways in which female laughter affords possibilities for so-cial critique – even as it may be embroiled in the patriarchal systems that it brings into question. The second essay in this section, jointly written by Katie Halsey and Jennifer Robertson, considers how nov-els by Jane West and Mary Brunton seek to protect the social fab-ric by making a case for a female education that emphasises rigour, regulation and self-control, promoting a patriotic agenda designed to safeguard Britain from the perceived emotional excesses of the French – and how Jane Austen's novels trouble the efficacy of this ed-ucation. In the novels discussed in Laura White's chapter, patriotism takes the form of overtly anti-Jacobin polemic. White traces the con-sonances between Hannah More and Laetitia Matilda Hawkins, who both turned to the novel form as their chosen vehicle to drive home moral lessons in the wake of Britain's victory over France in 1815.

The final section, 'Shaping the Future', shows female educators turning to literature and female authors turning to education to con-ceptualise imagined, altered ways of being and improved prospects for the next generation. Laura Kirkley charts how Mary Wollstonecraft's cosmopolitan philosophy informs her theory of education. Kirkley demonstrates the European influences on Wollstonecraft's insis-tence that the path to freedom lies in the exercise of reason, com-passion and imagination, both as a guide to right conduct and as a means of identifying and rejecting unjust authorities. Jonathan Padley's chapter emphasises the importance of imagination for Sarah Trimmer too, offering a revisionist reading of Trimmer's *Fabulous Histories* in which the child reader's empathy for animals, and hence their capacity for Christian benevolence, is dependent on their capac-ity to project themselves into the position of another. As with Mary Wollstonecraft and Sarah Trimmer, for Eliza Fenwick, the subject of the final essay of the volume, education was not merely a literary activity, it was a professional practice too. Lissa Paul's essay traces the development of Eliza Fenwick's educational philosophy as she evolved from a British author to a colonial educator in Barbados and North America, showing how the late Enlightenment principles of the literary education that had shaped her early writing found new form in her teaching across the Atlantic.

Women's Literary Education, 1690–1850 brings together critical voices from a range of different sub-disciplines within literary studies, including history, book history, eighteenth- and nineteenth-century studies, comparative literature, gender studies, the history of philosophy, the history of political thought, the history of education, theological studies and childhood studies, reflecting the ways in which this body of educational writing is drawn from and has shaped a number of disciplinary traditions, but also requires us to read across, and to transfer knowledge and skills beyond, traditional disciplinary boundaries. In establishing a conversation between scholars who have themselves been educated according to different disciplinary protocols, this volume attempts to recreate the plurality, multiplicity and asynchronicity of the conversations that took place in and through long-eighteenth-century women's educational writings.

Works Cited

Primary

Astell, Mary, *A Serious Proposal to the Ladies: Part I and II*, edited by Patricia Springborg (Peterborough, ON: Broadview Press, 2002)

Behn, Aphra, *The History of the Nun: or, The Fair Vow-Breaker* (London: Printed for A. Baskervile, 1689)

Blackstone, William, *Commentaries on the Laws of England: Book the First*, 2nd edn (Oxford: Clarendon Press, 1765)

Brontë, Charlotte, *Jane Eyre*, ed. by Margaret Smith and Juliette Atkinson (Oxford: Oxford University Press, 2019)

Edgeworth, Maria, *Letters for Literary Ladies, to Which is Added, an Essay on the Noble Science of Self-Justification* (London: Joseph Johnson, 1795)

Fordyce, James, *Sermons to Young Women*, vol. II of II (London: Printed for A. Millar and T. Cadell, 1746)

Hawkins, Laetitia Matilda, 'Letter II', *Letters on the Female Mind, Its Powers and Pursuits: Addressed to Miss H. M. Williams, with Particular Reference to Her Letters from France* (London: Printed for Hookham and Carpenter, 1793)

Lennox, Charlotte, *The Female Quixote: or, The Adventures of Arabella*, ed. by Margaret Dalziel (London: Oxford University Press, 1970)

More, Hannah, *Strictures on the Modern System of Female Education, with a View of the Principles and Conduct Prevalent among Women of Rank and Fortune*, vol. I of II (London: Printed for T. Cadell Jun. and W. Davies, 1799)

Richardson, Samuel, *Clarissa: or, The History of a Young Lady*, ed. by Angus Ross (Harmondsworth: Penguin, 1985)

——, *Pamela: or, Virtue Rewarded*, ed. by Peter Sabor (Harmondsworth: Penguin, 1980)

Scott, Sarah, *The History of Sir George Ellison* (London: A. Millar, 1766)
——, *Millenium Hall* (New York: Penguin, 1986)
Shelley, Mary, *Frankenstein*, ed. by Marilyn Butler (Oxford: Oxford University Press, 1998)
Sherwood, Mary Martha, *The Fairchild Family* (London: F. Houlston and Son, 1818)
Wollstonecraft, Mary, *The Works of Mary Wollstonecraft*, ed. by Janet Todd and Marilyn Butler, 7 vols (New York: New York University Press, 1989)
——, *A Vindication of the Rights of Woman, with Strictures on Political and Moral Subjects* (London: Printed for J. Johnson, 1792)
Woolf, Virginia, *Three Guineas*, 2nd edn (London: Hogarth Press, 1943)

Secondary

Ahmed, Sara, *Living a Feminist Life* (Durham, NC and London: Duke University Press, 2017)
Backscheider, Paula R. and John J. Richetti, *Popular Fiction by Women, 1660–1730: An Anthology* (Oxford: Clarendon Press, 1996)
Batchelor, Jennie and Cora Kaplan, eds, *British Women's Writing in the Long Eighteenth Century: Authorship, Politics and History* (Basingstoke: Palgrave Macmillan, 2005)
Beauvoir, Simone de, *The Second Sex* (London: Picador, 1988)
Boyd, William, *The History of Western Education* (London: Black, 1969)
Brown, Homer Obed, *Institutions of the English Novel: From Defoe to Scott* (Philadelphia: University of Philadelphia Press, 1997)
Butler, Judith, *Gender Trouble: Feminism and the Subversion of Identity* (New York: Routledge, 1990)
——, *Notes toward a Performative Theory of Assembly* (Cambridge, MA and London: Harvard University Press, 2015)
Cahn, Steven M., *Classic and Contemporary Readings in the Philosophy of Education* (New York: Oxford University Press, 1997)
Chalus, Elaine, '"That Epidemical Madness": Women and Electoral Politics in the Late Eighteenth Century', in *Gender in Eighteenth-Century England*, ed. by Hannah Barker and Elaine Chalus (Abingdon: Routledge, 1997), pp. 151–78
Cocks, Neil, 'Scripture Its Own Interpreter: Mary Martha Sherwood, the Bible and Female Autobiography', *Nineteenth-Century Gender Studies*, 7 (2011), 1–33
Colley, Linda, *Britons: Forging the Nation 1707–1837* (London: Random House, 1992)
Dale, Amelia, *The Printed Reader: Gender, Quixotism, and Textual Bodies in Eighteenth-Century Britain* (Lewisburg, PA: Bucknell University Press, 2019)

Darton, F. J. Harvey, *Children's Books in England: Five Centuries of Social Life*, 3rd edn, rev. by Brian Alderson (London: British Library, 1999)

Davies, Rebecca, *Written Maternal Authority and Eighteenth-Century Education in Britain: Educating by the Book* (Farnham: Ashgate, 2014)

Demers, Patricia, 'Sherwood, Mary Martha (1775–1851)', in *Oxford Dictionary of National Biography* (Oxford: Oxford University Press, 2004); online edn, May 2011 <http://www.oxforddnb.com/view/article/25397> [accessed 13 July 2017]

Derrida, Jacques, 'Law of Genre', in *Acts of Literature*, ed. by Derek Attridge (New York: Routledge, 1992)

Detlefsen, Karen, 'Cartesianism and Its Feminist Promise and Limits: The Case of Mary Astell', in *Descartes and Cartesianism: Essays in Honour of Desmond Clarke*, ed. by Stephen Gaukroger and Catherine Wilson (Oxford: Oxford Scholarship Online, 2017), pp. 191–206

Devereaux, Johanna, 'Paradise Within? Mary Astell, Sarah Scott and the Limits of Utopia', *Journal for Eighteenth-Century Studies*, 32.1 (2009), 53–67

D'Monté, Rebecca and Nicole Pohl, eds, *Female Communities 1600–1800: Literary Visions and Cultural Realities* (Basingstoke: Palgrave Macmillan, 2000)

Eagleton, Terry, *The Rape of Clarissa: Writing, Sexuality and Class Struggle in Samuel Richardson* (Oxford: Basil Blackwell, 1982)

Gilligan, Carol, *In a Different Voice: Psychological Theory and Women's Development* (Cambridge, MA: Harvard University Press, 2003)

Gilligan, Carol and David A. J. Richards, *Darkness Now Visible: Patriarchy's Resurgence and Feminist Resistance* (Cambridge: Cambridge University Press, 2018)

Hammond, Brean and Shaun Regan, *Making the Novel: Fiction and Society in Britain, 1660–1789* (Basingstoke: Palgrave Macmillan, 2006)

Hilton, Mary, *Women and the Shaping of the Nation's Young: Education and Public Doctrine in Britain 1750–1850* (Aldershot: Ashgate, 2007)

McKeon, Michael, *The Origins of the English Novel 1600–1740* (Baltimore and London: Johns Hopkins University Press, 1987)

Moi, Toril, *Revolution of the Ordinary: Literary Studies after Wittgenstein, Austin, and Cavell* (Chicago and London: University of Chicago Press, 2017)

Myers, Mitzi, 'Impeccable Governesses, Rational Dames, and Moral Mothers: Mary Wollstonecraft and the Female Tradition in Georgian Children's Books', *Children's Literature*, 14 (1986), 31–59

Poovey, Mary, 'The Anathematized Race: The Governess and *Jane Eyre*', in *Feminism and Psychoanalysis*, ed. by Richard Feldstein and Judith Roof (Ithaca, NY: Cornell University Press, 1989), pp. 230–54

Pratt, M. L., *Imperial Eyes: Travel Writing and Transculturation* (London: Routledge, 1992)

Rees, Christine, *Utopian Imagination and Eighteenth-Century Fiction* (London: Longman, 1996)

Reis, Elizabeth, 'The Devil, the Body, and the Feminine Soul in Puritan New England', *The Journal of American History*, 82 (1995), 15–36

Rich, Adrienne, 'Compulsory Heterosexuality and Lesbian Existence', in *Feminism and Sexuality: A Reader*, ed. by Stevi Jackson and Sue Scott (Edinburgh: Edinburgh University Press, 1996), pp. 130–44

Rizzo, Betty, 'Introduction', in Sarah Scott, *The History of Sir George Ellison* (Lexington: University of Kentucky, 1996)

Runia, Robin, 'Edgeworth's *Letters for Literary Ladies*: Publication Peers and Analytical Antagonists', in *Women's Literary Networks and Romanticism: 'A Tribe of Authoresses'*, ed. by Andrew O. Winckles and Angela Rehbein (Liverpool: Liverpool University Press, 2017), pp. 226–44

Staves, Susan, *A Literary History of Women's Writing in Britain, 1660–1789* (Cambridge: Cambridge University Press, 2006)

Tabor, Nicole, *Gender, Genre, and the Myth of Human Singularity* (New York: Peter Lang, 2013)

Thormählen, Marianne, *The Brontës and Education* (Cambridge: Cambridge University Press, 1999)

Winckles, Andrew O. and Angela Rehbein, eds, *Women's Literary Networks and Romanticism: 'A Tribe of Authoresses'* (Liverpool: Liverpool University Press, 2017)

Wittgenstein, Ludwig, *Philosophical Investigations*, 4th edn, trans. G. E. M. Anscombe, P. M. S. Hacker and Joachim Schulte, ed. by P. M. S. Hacker and Joachim Schulte (Oxford: Wiley-Blackwell, 2009)

Wittig, Monique, 'The Straight Mind', in *Feminism and Sexuality: A Reader*, ed. by Stevi Jackson and Sue Scott (Edinburgh: Edinburgh University Press, 1996), pp. 144–50

Part I

Moulding Forms

Chapter 1

Important Familial Conversations: Anna Letitia Barbauld, Sarah Trimmer and Ellenor Fenn*

Jessica Lim

When Anna Letitia Barbauld popularised the 'New Walk' with *Lessons for Children*, sparking the creation of the genre of the conversational primer, she united women with significantly different educational goals.[1] Charles Lamb misogynistically excoriated 'the cursed Barbauld crew' for writing books 'in the shape of knowledge', identifying Anna Letitia Barbauld and Sarah Trimmer as key criminals in this apparent travesty.[2] Unnamed in Lamb's tirade, but almost certainly present in this 'crew', was Lady Ellenor Fenn, whose works were sold under at least eight pseudonyms revolving around the names 'Lovechild' and 'Teachwell'.[3] Barbauld, Trimmer and Fenn all published rational educations for young children packaged as home-based conversations directed by an affectionate Mamma. Indeed, Trimmer and Fenn paid homage to *Lessons for Children* in their prefaces, acknowledging Barbauld as their literary progenitor in *An Easy Introduction to Nature* (1780) and *Cobwebs to Catch Flies* (1783), respectively. Yet these women's pedagogical goals and literary contributions differed vastly. Barbauld was a liberal Arian Presbyterian and a political radical who wrote political polemics, devotional

---

* With thanks to Gareth Atkins for sharing his knowledge of late eighteenth-century Anglicanism.

1   Frances Burney [1798], in *Diary and Letters of Madam D'Arblay*, ed. by Charlotte Barrett (London: Macmillan, 1904–5), vol. 5 of 6, p. 418. On the conversational primer see Jessica W. H. Lim, 'Barbauld's Lessons: The Conversational Primer in Late Eighteenth-Century British Children's Literature', *Journal for Eighteenth-Century Studies* (2019) 43, 101–20.

2   Charles Lamb, letter no. 136 to S. T. Coleridge, 23 October 1802, *The Letters of Charles and Mary Lamb*, vol. 2, ed. by Edwin W. Marrs, Jr. (New York: Cornell University Press, 1976), pp. 81–2.

3   David Stoker, 'Establishing Lady Fenn's Canon', *Papers of the Bibliographical Society of America* (2009), 43–72.

essays, poems and children's literature, and was active in manuscript and print cultures.[4] Unconventionally, Barbauld's *Lessons* omits references to God, reflecting her belief that strict doctrine and liturgies are not central to faith.[5] Trimmer's educational agenda, by contrast, is contextualised by her devotion to the Church of England and political conservatism.[6] An Arminian-leaning orthodox Anglican,[7] Trimmer used *An Easy Introduction* to lay the groundwork for her nationally aimed religious education programme. She explicitly framed later editions of *An Easy Introduction* as part of an induction into Anglican faith. Fenn's *Cobwebs to Catch Flies*, meanwhile, 'recruits mothers to take control of their children's early reading in the nursery'.[8] Like a strand of its eponymous web, *Cobwebs* functions as a part of Fenn's broader teaching schemes, which encompassed educational games and toys.[9] Glancing at the women's philosophical allegiances side by side, one feels like exclaiming alongside Barbauld, 'There is no bond of union among literary women.'[10]

Though there is truth in accusations that a simplistic grouping of 'sister authors for the young [. . .] collapses together [. . .] liberal

---

[4] For more on Barbauld's religious associations see Daniel E. White, '"With Mrs Barbauld it is different": Dissenting Heritage and the Devotional Taste', in *Women, Gender and Enlightenment*, ed. by Sarah Knott and Barbara Taylor (Basingstoke: Palgrave Macmillan, 2005), 474–92; Michelle Levy, 'Barbauld's Poetic Career in Script and Print', *Anna Letitia Barbauld: New Perspectives*, ed. by William McCarthy and Olivia Murphy (Lewisburg, PA: Bucknell University Press, 2014), pp. 37–58.

[5] William McCarthy, *Anna Letitia Barbauld: Voice of the Enlightenment* (Baltimore: Johns Hopkins University Press, 2008), p. 200.

[6] Robert M. Andrews is one of few to note this, in *Lay Activism and the High Church Movement: The Life and Thought of William Stevens 1732–1804* (Brill's Series in Church History, Leiden and Boston: Brill, 2015), pp. 64–6.

[7] Peter Nockles, 'Church Parties in the Pre-Tractarian Church of England 1750–1833: The "Orthodox" – Some Problems of Definition and Identity', in *The Church of England c.1689–c.1833: From Toleration to Tractarianism*, ed. by John Walsh, Colin Haydon and Stephen Taylor (Cambridge: Cambridge University Press, 1993), pp. 334–59.

[8] Lesley Jane Delaney, 'Key Developments in the Nursery Reading Market 1783–1900' (unpublished doctoral thesis, University College London, 2012), p. 51.

[9] Andrea Immel, '"Mistress of the Infantine Language": Lady Ellenor Fenn, Her *Set of Toys*, and the "Education of Each Moment"', *Children's Literature*, 25 (1997), 214–28; also Stoker, p. 6.

[10] Anna Letitia Barbauld, letter to Maria Edgeworth, 30 August 1804, *Memoir of Mrs Barbauld, Including Letters and Notices of Her Family and Friends*, ed. by Anna Letitia LeBreton (London: George Bell and Sons, 1874), p. 86.

compromises [. . . and] deep-seated conservatism',[11] Barbauld, Trimmer and Fenn can be considered together as popular authors of conversational primers. This chapter studies their shared use of genre as a way of participating in politicised debates in which women's voices were denied public institutionalised platforms, including discussions on intercultural engagement, the reasonableness of Anglican liturgy, and the possibilities of ethical commerce and benevolence.[12] Histories of these ideas tend to overlook female contributions, especially in the form of children's literature. However, in *Lessons*, *An Easy Introduction* and *Cobwebs*, Barbauld, Trimmer and Fenn turned the conversational primer into a medium providing women with textual authority and cultural influence, transforming the home into a site of cultural and even political authority. This power was rooted in the verisimilar voice of the affectionate and educated middle- or upper-middle-class mother, and the books became a platform from which women could address a wide number of (often politically charged) sociocultural debates. As the conversational primer invoked its verisimilar origins and implied its real-life applicability, the genre suggests that all implied middle- and upper-class British mothers reading the texts could use their authority as mothers to speak on similar cultural and political concerns. In this way, the conversational primer confirmed the family home as a site of induction into broader (often national) communities, creating a non-institutionalised platform for Barbauld, Trimmer and Fenn to influence broader social discussions.

In *Lessons*, Barbauld established the key generic expectations in conversational primers: the assumption that the author's lived experience as maternal pedagogue and the conversational verisimilitude of her writing guaranteed the book's effectiveness as an educational tool in real-life middle-class British homes. Using her preface to establish these expectations, Barbauld notes that she wrote *Lessons* 'for a particular child [. . . but] the public is welcome to the use

---

[11] Alan Richardson, *Literature, Education, and Romanticism: Reading as Social Practice, 1730–1832* (Cambridge: Cambridge University Press, 1994), p. 168; this objection is echoed by Mary Hilton, *Women and the Shaping of the Nation's Young: Education and Public Doctrine in Britain 1750–1850* (Abingdon and New York: Ashgate, 2007), p. 4.

[12] In my focus on women's use of genre as the method by which women engaged with intellectual and political subfields, I build on and refocus Hilton's premise (note 11).

of it'.[13] Barbauld places the intimate relationship of mother and child at the centre of public discourse and literary focus, addressing middle-class parents and their toddlers at home as the 'public' and presenting her book as a functional object for their 'use'.[14] Since Barbauld's Mamma is a '"representative" middle-class mother', her verisimilar conversations intimate their repeatability by readers at home.[15] When Mamma tells Charles to sit on her lap and point at words, the scene feels like a record of an actual encounter. Real-life adults would be encouraged to mimic similar postures with accompanying children, as the book's size (3.5 × 4 inches) almost necessitates that the illiterate child(ren) must be on or near the reader's lap.[16] Barbauld's unillustrated book appears to have been a further conscious attempt to encourage such reading practices. Although Barbauld published *Lessons* through Joseph Johnson, who contracted engravers, each Johnson-published edition of *Lessons for Children* remains unillustrated. This creates textual gaps that must be bridged by real-life interactions. At one point Mamma teaches Charles how to stroke a cat and says, 'You stroke her the wrong way. This is the right way.'[17] As there are no further instructions or engravings, the episode is a non sequitur unless an implied adult reader provides an explanation or demonstration. The conversational primer, in Barbauld's hands, becomes an inherently interactive and relational book requiring close physical proximity between the literate reader and the illiterate or semi-literate child.

Moreover, Barbauld's preface presents a pedagogical case for publishing ordinary day-to-day parent–child conversations, introducing the element of authorial justification that persists in Trimmer's and Fenn's conversational primer prefaces. In place of tutor-led educations that marginalise the family home, Barbauld prioritises

---

[13] Anna Letitia Barbauld, *Lessons for Children Part I: For Children from Two to Three Years Old* (London: Printed for J. Johnson, 1787), p. iii. Hereafter *Lessons*, I.

[14] At sixpence per volume with fewer words per page, due to Barbauld's insistence that children's books should have large fonts and generous spacing, the books would be expensive for lower-class labourers. Teresa Michals observes this in *Books for Children, Books for Adults: Age and the Novel from Defoe to James* (Cambridge: Cambridge University Press, 2014), p. 111.

[15] McCarthy, p. 197.

[16] These measurements are based on the Joseph Johnson editions of *Lessons for Children* held in the British Library and the Cambridge University Library, printed over a span of twenty years.

[17] Barbauld, *Lessons*, I, p. 7.

experiential learning within the home. Claiming 'A grave remark, or a connected story, however simple, is above [a young child's] capacity; and *nonsense* is always below it',[18] Barbauld suggests that verisimilar depictions of mother–child interactions at home form an essential and unacknowledged stage in child development. Although Charles receives Lockean-like lessons in empirical observation and natural science – watching caterpillars metamorphose into butterflies, observing natural seasonal changes and interpreting compass directions using the sun in the sky – *Lessons for Children* begins with Mamma reading to Charles in her lap and ends with Mamma putting Charles to bed. These affectionate mother–child interactions bookend each of the four parts of *Lessons for Children*, suggesting that maternal domesticity is the fundamental seat from which intelligent, affectionate human development is performed and sustained.[19]

In *An Easy Introduction to Nature* Sarah Trimmer makes further claims for the role of the maternal domestic space, transforming her conversational primer into an initiation into Anglicanism.[20] Like Barbauld, Trimmer uses her preface to justify her literary efforts by asserting her credentials as a real-life caretaker of young children, and she also appeals to her implied mother-readers (even expressing frustration over the difficulty and expenses of child-rearing in a passage that possibly comforted real-life mothers with a sense of solidarity).[21] Like *Lessons*, Trimmer's *An Easy Introduction* revolves around the replicable acts of a mother accompanying her children on rural walks near the house, promoting empirical observation and conversation as methods of imparting knowledge and affection.[22] By adopting this culturally acceptable stance as a maternal, domestic figure, Trimmer positioned herself as a leading figure in a freighted

---

[18] Ibid., I, p. iii.
[19] Barbauld expanded *Lessons for Children* between 1778 and 1779. The following editions were used: *Lessons*, I; Anna Letitia Barbauld, *Lessons for Children Aged Three Years Old: Part I* (London: Joseph Johnson, 1788); Anna Letitia Barbauld, *Lessons for Children of Three Years Old: Part II* (London: J. Johnson, 1788); *Lessons for Children Aged Three to Four Years Old* (London: Joseph Johnson, 1788).
[20] Sarah Trimmer, *An Easy Introduction to the Knowledge of Nature, and Reading the Holy Scriptures: Adapted to the Capacities of Children* (London: Printed for the Author and sold by Dodsley, Robson, Longman and Robinson, Johnson, Welles and Grosvenor, Shave, 1780).
[21] Trimmer, *Easy Introduction*, p. 87.
[22] Lim.

national theological conversation about the relationships between rationality and faith in the fragmenting late eighteenth-century Anglican Church.

Similarly, Lady Ellenor Fenn's hugely popular *Cobwebs to Catch Flies* reinforces its likely applicability in the home by noting its verisimilar origins.[23] Like Trimmer and Barbauld, Fenn emphasises her family-oriented experience in her prefatory material, and even acknowledges the stylistic similarities between *Cobwebs* and Barbauld's *Lessons*.[24] Like Barbauld, Fenn publicises the private specificity of the *Cobwebs* conversations, revealing that she wrote the lessons for a particular child, 'from me; – from me who love him', and that the second volume was designed 'to please a set of children dear to the writer [. . .] and it did please them'.[25] Like Barbauld, Fenn publicises the personal origins and real-life reception of her book to cement the perception of the domestic space as an area for public scrutiny and interpretive activity. In this porous space where the familial is publicised, Mamma transforms the domestic platform to be simultaneously private and social. As Fenn used pseudonyms (her name was revealed in her obituary in *Gentleman's Magazine*),[26] Fenn's authorial Mamma flattens herself into obscurity, implicitly enabling any mother who 'loves children' and desires to 'teach well' to assume Fenn's literary identity as the Mamma in the dialogues. Although Fenn claims that her book is for 'none but fond mothers', seemingly limiting the scope of her book to the realm of familial affection, her directive that mothers should oversee their children's education is laden with economic language: 'It is your business (Mothers! To you I speak!)'[27] Fenn asserts that educating children is a mother's 'business', demonstrating her interest in the philosophical basis for

[23] *Cobwebs* remained in print for over 120 years; see Stoker, pp. 43–5; Delaney, pp. 3, 51, 54.
[24] Mrs Lovechild [Lady Ellenor Fenn], *Cobwebs to Catch Flies: or, Dialogues in Short Sentences, Adapted for Children from the Age of Three to Eight Years. In two volumes* (London: John Marshall, 1783), 'Dedication', pp. vi–vii. For more on genre as the invocation of stylistic expectations see Stephen Neale, 'Questions of Genre', in *Approaches to Media: A Reader*, ed. by Oliver Boyd-Barrett and Chris Newbold (London: Arnold, 1995), pp. 460–72.
[25] Fenn, *Cobwebs*, I, pp. vi, xiv.
[26] 'Review of New Publications', July 1813, *The Gentleman's Magazine: and Historical Chronicle from July to December 1813*, volume 83, ed. by Sylvanus Urban (London: Nichols, Son, and Bentley, 1818), p. 58.
[27] Fenn, *Cobwebs*, I, pp. viii, ix.

economic and material transactions.[28] This intersection between familial affection, kindness and business lies at the heart of *Cobwebs*,
suggesting the capacity for the conversational primer to enable
women to enter debates about national philosophical-economic
values.

Despite the variations in the philosophical and political aims of
Barbauld, Trimmer and Fenn, *Lessons, An Easy Introduction* and
Cobwebs highlight the ways in which the conversational primer enabled women to influence public debates from outside official institutions: by domesticating public issues and asserting the authority of
the domestic Mamma to teach and talk on those topics.

Benevolence in Barbauld's *Lessons*

Few could have predicted Barbauld's move to publish books for
babies and their mothers. Having gained literary fame for *Poems*
in 1773, Barbauld attracted controversy for her *Devotional Pieces*
(1775), which many in the Established Anglican Church and in
Dissenting circles considered on the verge of religious enthusiasm.[29]
When Barbauld published *Lessons for Children Aged Two to Three
Years* in 1778, it was a cautious but pointed re-entrance into the con-
tentious print market.[30] *Lessons* immediately received critical adula-
tion and redefined the marketing age of a reading child. In the same
year that *Lessons* reached shelves, Thomas Beecroft sold *The Infant's
Miscellany* for 'the very first set of readers – children from the age
of four, to eight or nine years old'.[31] Barbauld's redefinition of the
reading child's age was not uncontroversial. Even the Edgeworths,
otherwise fans of *Lessons*, remarked that *Lessons* was probably better suited to four- and five-year-olds.[32] Yet Barbauld's expectation
persisted: volume 1 of Fenn's *Cobwebs to Catch Flies* is for children

---

[28] Fittingly, Fenn's primers were financially significant: their popularity secured John
Marshall's publishing prominence in the juvenile literary market; Delaney, p. 55.
[29] McCarthy, pp. 148–64.
[30] McCarthy, p. 191; Levy.
[31] *The Infant's Miscellany: or, Easy Lessons, Extracted from Different Authors. On
a New Plan. Intended to Facilitate the Attainment of the English Language to
the Youngest Readers, by Teaching Them Not Only to Read, but Likewise to
Understand Clearly What They Read* (London: Printed for the Author; sold by
T. Beecroft, 1778).
[32] Maria and Richard Lovell Edgeworth, *Practical Education* (1801), 2nd edn,
vol. 2 of 3 (New York: Woodstock Books, 1996), p. 81.

between three and five years, and Elizabeth Somerville titled her own conversational primer *Lessons for Children of Three Years Old* (1800).[33]

In *Lessons*, Charles is educated in a domestic setting coloured by maternal affection. Notably, his education is an immersion into the world, rather than a pre-emptive defensive 'filling' of his mind. In John Locke's *Some Thoughts Concerning Education*, the tutor (not the parent) must prepare the child to enter a potentially hazardous and temptingly dangerous world. Locke describes education as a 'fence' to the student's virtue, against the world's vice.[34] Similarly, Isaac Watts fears that a child may 'furnish' their mind with 'mindless sonnets' and presents his hymns as a preventative antidote.[35] There is no equivalent language of fencing in *Lessons*. While Part One ensconces Charles' education in the home – it opens with Mamma greeting Charles and ends with Charles going to bed – this conceptual space is not as an escape from the world, but as an induction into it. Mamma's lessons suggest that the home is the model for the world, in which mothers have the jurisdiction to speak and write about extensive matters, including the importance of tolerance and respect for others. By using analogies, Mamma teaches Charles to respect the customs and dwellings of other living beings. Charles is taught to recognise features in the natural world that are analogous to his existence: Mamma describes a snail's shell as its 'house' and a lamb's wool as its 'petticoat'.[36] This pattern of analogical, metaphorical thinking teaches Charles to consider the home as a paradigm for interpreting the world, as he recognises similarities between himself and others (like him, the snail has a house and the lamb must keep warm) and is taught to respect their differences – the snail's house is a shell, and the lamb has wool rather than clothing.

Lessons applies this recognition of similarity and difference in a lesson on intercultural interactions. In one of the most popular episodes of *Lessons for Children*, Charles and Mamma journey to France, unsettling Charles' Anglo-centric expectations. Barbauld

---

[33] Elizabeth Somerville, *Lessons for Children of Three Years Old* (London: Sampson Low, 1800).

[34] John Locke, *Some Thoughts Concerning Education and Of the Conduct of the Understanding* (1706 edn), ed. by Ruth W. Grant and Narthan Tarcov (Indianapolis and Cambridge: Hackett Publishing Company, 1996), §70, §94.

[35] Katherine Wakely-Mulroney, 'Isaac Watts and the Dimensions of Child Interiority', *Journal for Eighteenth-Century Studies*, 39 (2016), 103–19.

[36] Barbauld, *Lessons*, I, p. 20; *Lessons*, II, p. 51.

records Charles' confusion in the face of meeting people who do not speak English. 'But I do not understand French', Charles says, 'And why do you speak French?' He is chastised for assuming that Anglo-culture is a global norm: 'Here is a foolish little boy come from a great way over the sea, and does not know that every body speaks French in France.'[37] The additional adjective 'foolish' feels harsh when directed to a four-year-old, but it also identifies the folly of Charles' assumption that English is the normative global language. The episode emphasises the distinctiveness of languages to nations and cultures: 'every body speaks French in France'. This almost glaringly obvious aphorism challenges contemporaneous Anglo-centric attitudes regarding language attainment and cultural engagement. In a comparable conversation in Trimmer's *Easy Introduction*, Trimmer's Mamma warns her children that they must learn French 'or they will take us for vulgar ill-bred persons [. . . since] all genteel People in England learn that Language',[38] situating the acquisition of the French language as a signifier of English gentility rather than as a language worth learning because it is a living, much-used language. Conversely, Barbauld transforms Charles' return home as a chance to prepare for more profound future intercultural engagements. 'Teach the little boy French, before he goes a great way abroad again',[39] Mamma tells Papa, implying that Charles will travel again, and that his family can equip him with the tools to engage with other cultural groups on their terms.

Remarkably, Barbauld suggests that a genuine respect for others may equip children to interpret ambiguous ethical situations. In her 1808 extension, Mamma tells Charles a 'curious' story of a Duck and a Drake. Since it is a 'curious' story it is clear that the Duck and Drake are not heroes or cautionary figures, complicating the expected binary in moral tales. Encouraging readers to sympathise with the anthropomorphised ducks 'who were very fond of each other',[40] Mamma praises the Drake for being a 'good husband' who sat by the Duck as they waited for the eggs to hatch. The complication occurs when the ducklings are hatched 'and then they turned the poor Drake out of the duck-house', fearful he would trample his

---

[37] Barbauld, *Lessons*, IV, pp. 69–70.
[38] Trimmer, *Easy Introduction*, p. 109.
[39] Barbauld, *Lessons*, IV, pp. 71–2.
[40] Anna Letitia Barbauld, *Lessons for Children, in Four Parts* (London: printed for J. Johnson, 1808), Part III, p. 40.

ducklings.[41] While 'they' are unnamed, it is clear 'they' are the human farmers. The Drake, displaced from his home and separated from his children, adopts a brood of newly hatched chickens, and attempts to teach them to swim. The Hen resists, but 'nobody came to her assistance, though they saw from the house that something was the matter by her fluttering and screaming'.[42] Tragically, the Drake's paternal resolution to teach 'his little ones [. . .] to swim' results in the death of all five chickens. Yet Mamma makes it clear that neither the Drake nor the Hen is at fault. Mamma has positioned child readers to recognise the Drake as a loving husband and an affectionate father who sought to teach his 'little ones' important life skills, and she has cultivated sympathy for the anthropomorphised 'screaming' Hen. Instead, 'they' are the culprits: the humans who turn the Drake out of his home and refuse to help the Hen, though they can see 'her fluttering and screaming'. Mamma's story invites readers to consider the ethical responsibility that humans have towards all living beings and suggests that a hands-off approach leads to damaging decisions about when to intervene and when to not intervene. In one sense, the story introduces the problem of intentionality and the dilemma of benevolence.[43] Mamma allows her reader to make at least one clear, if implicit, ethical judgement: whether benevolence is or is not measured by intention or action, the human observers have failed to show benevolence by failing to respect the emotions and inclinations of their avian neighbours. To be inattentive to the cries of others is a tragedy, and the humans are culpable for treating the 'house' as a site separate from the struggles of individuals in the outside ('public') space. Rather, the home in Barbauld's *Lessons* is where Charles learns compassion and respect and is taught to criticise social practices that lead to the needless suffering of others.[44]

Within Barbauld's *Lessons*, Mamma is crucial in guiding her child's education. By colouring lessons with maternal affection, and teaching Charles that love for one's home should produce respect for others' homes and customs, *Lessons* enables Mamma (and by extension,

[41] Ibid.
[42] Ibid.
[43] For more on eighteenth-century ethical debates about intention and hospitality see Teresa Saxton, 'Benevolent Intentions: Hospitality, Ethics and the Eighteenth-Century Novel' (unpublished doctoral dissertation, University of Tennessee, 2012).
[44] For more on animals, ethics and Enlightenment narratives about social injustice, see McCarthy, pp. 202–3.

Barbauld) to provide a Dissenting-style vision of tolerance, asserting
the importance of interacting with others from a place of sympathy
and respect for others – both their similarities and their differences.

Tackling Anglican Partisanship in the Nursery

In 1780, when Trimmer published *An Easy Introduction*, the
Anglican Church was still reeling from the Feathers Tavern Petition
(1772), when a group of Latitudinarians petitioned Parliament to
abolish subscription to the Thirty-Nine Articles, a cornerstone of
Anglicanism. This petition had significant religious-political implications: Latitudinarianism, the liberal and rational school of
Anglicanism, became associated with political partisanship, and began disintegrating.[45] *An Easy Introduction* provided the Anglican
Church with an educational programme around which to rally. The
domestic space, seemingly removed from clerical debates and arguments about the intersections between citizenship rights and denom-
inational practice, became a site where Trimmer could assert her
orthodox Anglican ideologies with impunity.

Insisting upon the importance of learning to read 'nature' and 'the
Holy Scriptures', Trimmer's book emanates a missionary zeal that
was largely absent from Georgian Anglican clerical culture.[46] This
zeal is characterised by ecumenism: Trimmer was the first Anglican
to use the natural theology argument of the 'watchmaker' analogy
to prove God's existence. The 'watchmaker' analogy argues that a
logical and complex creation (a watch; the world) must be made by a
logical and complex creator (a watchmaker; God). Comparable logic
was invoked by the Roman Catholic René Descartes,[47] and Trimmer's

[45] John Walsh and Stephen Taylor, 'Introduction: The Church and Anglicanism in
the "Long" Eighteenth Century', *The Church of England c.1689–c.1833: From
Toleration to Tractarianism*, ed. by John Walsh, Colin Haydon and Stephen
Taylor (Cambridge: Cambridge University Press, 1993), pp. 1–66 (pp. 40–5).
On the complexity of the term 'Latitudinarian' see Walsh and Taylor, pp. 36–7;
Nockles, 'Church Parties 1750–1833'. On the disunity of the Anglican Church see
William J. Bulman, *Anglican Enlightenment: Orientalism, Religion and Politics
in England and Its Empire, 1648–1715* (Cambridge: Cambridge University Press,
2015).
[46] Walsh and Taylor, pp. 13–16.
[47] René Descartes, 'Treatise on Man', in *Descartes: The World and Other Writings*,
ed. by Stephen Gaukroger (Cambridge: Cambridge University Press, 1998),
pp. 97–169.

use of the analogy predates William Paley's *Natural Theology* by over twenty years. This reveals Trimmer's eirenicism: her invocation of the analogy shows an openness to general truths shared between Deist traditions. Moreover, this highlights Trimmer's significance in popularising the watchmaker analogy in Anglican educational circles prior to Paley.[48] Indeed, where Paley's work left readers questioning his potentially heterodox leanings, Anglican periodicals celebrated Trimmer's Anglican agenda. This indicates the capacity for the domestic aesthetic and content of the conversational primer to present ideas with a reduced risk of controversy.[49] In many ways, *An Easy Introduction* was (doctrinally) uncontroversial: focusing on rational observation and avoiding doctrinally weighted terms such as Original Sin, depravation and justification, it is decidedly not evangelical.[50] Neither is it 'High Church'.[51] Rather, *An Easy Introduction* follows an eirenic orthodox Anglican stance of acknowledging general truths across Christian denominations while promoting the Anglican framework as the ultimate paradigm for a 'good life'. The guide in this religious education is not a cleric but Mamma and, in the prefaces of *An Easy Introduction*, Trimmer herself.

In the preface to the first eight editions of *An Easy Introduction*, Trimmer positions herself as a moral guide in the form of a parent-teacher, dispensing domestic scientific knowledge as a handmaiden to Christianity.[52] She pays homage to Barbauld's *Lessons* as 'the best [book] adapted for the Purpose of teaching [children] to read [. . .] in a stile of familiar conversation', and asserts that she is building on

---

[48] William Paley is so associated with natural theology he is sometimes identified as its originator; Matthew D. Eddy and David Knight (eds), 'Introduction', in William Paley, *Natural Theology: or, Evidence of the Existence and Attributes of the Deity, Collected from the Appearances of Nature* (Oxford: Oxford University Press, 2006), pp. ix–xix.

[49] G. Cole, 'Doctrine, Dissent and the Decline of Paley's Reputation 1805–1825', *Enlightenment and Dissent*, 6 (1987), 19–30; Andrews, pp. 64–6.

[50] I have used Peter Nockles' definition of evangelicalism as a school of Protestantism that emphasises the centrality of Original Sin, depravity, justification and regeneration; Nockles, 'Church Parties 1750–1833'.

[51] Bulman, p. 7; Peter Nockles, *The Oxford Movement in Context: Anglican High Churchmanship, 1760–1857* (Cambridge: Cambridge University Press, 1994), pp. 27–9.

[52] For more on Trimmer's natural theology see Heather E. Weir, 'Reading Nature before Reading the Bible: Sarah Trimmer's Natural Theology', in *Breaking Boundaries: Female Biblical Interpreters Who Challenged the Status Quo*, ed. by Nancy Calvert-Koyzis and Heather Weir (New York: T & T Clark International), pp. 53–68.

Barbauld's 'ground work'.[53] This homage lies alongside Trimmer's acknowledgements to the Congregationalist Isaac Watts and the Roman Catholic François Fénelon, Archbishop of Cambray. The eirenic acknowledgement highlights the theological inclusiveness of Trimmer's religious programme. Yet Trimmer's religious programme does not draw indiscriminately from other denominations. In fact, *An Easy Introduction* shows Trimmer's distrust of evangelical programmes that placed the Bible, without guidance, into readers' hands.[54] Although the majority of *An Easy Introduction* is devoted to scientific lessons, thirty-one of the final pages are devoted to a discussion of the Holy Scriptures. In this section there is a significant exposition regarding Moses' calling as Trimmer 'prove[s]' the divine authority behind the first five books of the Bible.[55] In the ninth and tenth editions, Mamma replaces the narrative of Moses' life with a lesson on how to navigate the Bible by showing children how to identify the Old Testament, New Testament and the Apocrypha (including advice to consider the Apocrypha as 'pious good books' but not part of the Bible).[56] This later addition teaches children to navigate the Bible as a physical book compiled by humans, implicitly elevating Trimmer's *An Easy Introduction* to sit closer in authority to the human-compiled Scriptures. Nevertheless, both editions position child readers to see the Bible as a collection of books that should be approached with academic rigour and wonder. Crucially, Mamma provides this biblical guidance, not a cleric: the conversational primer enables her to adopt a more authoritative religious role than she would be accorded in Church contexts.

In the ninth and tenth editions of *An Easy Introduction* (1796 and 1799), Trimmer's preface emphasises that her conversational primer is the initial stage in her national religious education. Removing references to Barbauld and Fénelon in an apparently political

---

53   Trimmer, *Easy Introduction*, p. xii.
[53] Trimmer, *Easy Introduction*, p. xii.
[54] For more on orthodox Anglican distrust of evangelicalism see Nockles, *Oxford Movement*, pp. 107–8. This contrasts with claims that Trimmer was evangelical; cf. Barbara Brandon Schnorrenberg's entry on Sarah Trimmer for the *Oxford Dictionary of National Biography*, online edition <https://doi.org/10.1093/ref:odnb/27740> [accessed 18 June 2021].
[55] Trimmer, *Easy Introduction*, pp. 213–31.
[56] Sarah Trimmer, *An Easy Introduction to the Knowledge of Nature, and Reading the Holy Scriptures: Adapted to the Capacities of Children. By Mrs Trimmer. The ninth edition, with considerable additions and improvements* (London, 1796), digitized by *Eighteenth Century Collections Online*, Gale Document Number CB3326809317, p. 146.

move designed to assert her loyalty to the British conservatism, Trimmer reaffirms that *An Easy Introduction* is her primary literary-pedagogical contribution to Anglican education. Trimmer envisions that her revised work will be 'adopted in schools for the higher orders of children' and stresses that it is 'incumbent on all who engage in the important business of education, to fortify the yet uncorrupted minds of their young pupils' against radical sociopolitical ideas.[57] Adopting defensive language to describe education as 'fortification', Trimmer acknowledges the significant sociocultural role of schools, suggesting that she no longer believes that her work will be read primarily by mothers at home. Instead, she cedes implied real-life domestic authority to institutions while embedding home learning as an ideal paradigm within school institutions. Trimmer uses her preface to promote *An Abridgment of Scripture History* and laments that three of her books, *An Attempt to Familiarize the Catechism of the Church of England*, *An Explanation of the Office of Baptism, and the Order of Confirmation* and *A Companion to the Book of Common Prayer, with Questions for the Use of Teachers* 'are not so generally used in schools'. It is impossible to read the preface and miss Trimmer's Anglican educational agenda in promoting a catechised awareness of the Book of Common Prayer, the Church of England Catechism and Anglican sacramental liturgies.

In fact, *An Easy Introduction* normalises Christian rituals through its structure. Although Aileen Fyfe suggests that *An Easy Introduction* is designed primarily to overwhelm readers with a sense of awe,[58] as Heather Weir points out, there are six 'sets' of scientific lessons (plants; animals and birds; microscopes and insects; the globe and geography; basic economics; physics and astronomy), followed by a seventh 'set' of lessons: Trimmer's theological argument for God.[59] This pattern of learning follows a liturgical Christian pattern of employing the seventh phase (or day of the week) to reflect on God and recontextualise one's experience in the world. This seventh phase is Trimmer's ultimate educational goal. Mamma brings complex scientific lessons (including lessons on eclipses using a gold watch and the firelight)[60] into a framework to help children comprehend an orderly and benevolent God. She simultaneously brings both science

[57] Ibid., p. ix.
[58] Aileen Fyfe, 'Reading Children's Books in Late Eighteenth-Century Dissenting Families', *Historical Journal* 43 (2000), 453–73 (pp. 460–1).
[59] Weir, pp. 54–5.
[60] Trimmer, *Easy Introduction*, pp. 189–90.

and theology under her jurisdiction of domestic authority. Trimmer's conversational primer thus reveals a significant capacity for the genre to increase the authoritative potential for women to comment on matters of religion from the home, even as they were denied institutional religious platforms.

Potentially offsetting clerical discomfort, *An Easy Introduction* promotes the idea of being comfortable with one's space, presenting a politically conservative vision where social hierarchies correspond with the hierarchical structure of Anglicanism.[61] Mamma's class-inflected values conflate domestic-based scientific lessons with lessons in hierarchical sympathy. Mamma owns expensive educational toys like microscopes and glass hives, and she uses these tools to teach Charlotte and Henry lessons in science, sympathy and social hierarchies. When looking at the limbs of an ant under a microscope, Mamma tells Henry that he ought not to torture insects 'if [he] wish to be thought a boy'.[62] This emphasises that Henry's reputation and social standing as a young gentleman depend on his displays of benevolence. When Mamma teaches her children to observe how the colony of bees works together to build honeycomb, she explicitly informs her children that she invested in a glass hive so she wouldn't be 'obliged' to kill the bees when they had finished harvesting honey.[63] This affirms Mamma's benevolence and her power over the bees' lives: they are educational tools and commercial tools that *could* be killed after they have performed their useful functions. From the ninth edition onward, Mamma suggests that hierarchical superiority and benevolence coexist. Mamma tells Henry, 'You are an Englishman [. . .] if you travel all the world over, you will never find a better country', promoting a patriotic celebration of 'Englishness' (not Britishness), but she insists that Henry 'must not despise the people of other countries because they do not speak, act, and dress, as we do, for to them we appear as strange as they do to us'.[64] Rather than making positive statements about other cultural practices, Trimmer's Mamma speaks in the language of negation: Henry need not respect non-English people, he must merely 'not despise' them. Moreover, when discussing slavery, Trimmer's language is that of amelioration rather than abolition. Noting that sugar comes from

---

[61] Contrast this with democratically structured Dissenting faiths like Congregationalism and Unitarianism.

[62] Trimmer, *Easy Introduction*, p. 90.

[63] Ibid., p. 102.

[64] Trimmer, *Easy Introduction*, 9th edn, pp. 89–90.

the West Indies, she acknowledges that enslaved people 'undergo severe hardships', but she avoids the term slavery, describing instead individuals 'employed to work' in plantations.[65] By promoting an ameliorative stance on slavery, Trimmer again utilises the genre to contribute to an ongoing ethical, political debate, but as her stance is less radical than that of abolition, what is significant is less the capacity for the genre to house radical thoughts and more the possibility the conversational primer offers for women to comment on ongoing ethical and political debates.

Trimmer suggests that her conversational primer, based on rational observation and empirical learning, is an authoritative text on public debates on education and sympathy. She patterns her book on Christian rituals and even suggests that her book holds a similar level of textual authority to the Scriptures: though the Scriptures may be divinely inspired, her later editions emphasise the fact that the Bible is compiled by humans too. By claiming this religious and cultural authority in her much-reprinted conversational primers, Sarah Trimmer highlights the profound contributions of women to Anglican history, hidden in plain sight in the form of children's books.

Ethics of Exchange

Like Barbauld and Trimmer, Fenn establishes familial affection as the basis from which to shape young children's values and knowledge. *Cobwebs to Catch Flies* consists of two volumes: the first book of 'Easy' lessons for children aged three to five features words ranging from three to six letters, and the second set of 'Instructive' conversations features words of up to four syllables (for five- to eight-year-olds). The progression from 'Easy' to 'Instructive' lessons suggests an increasingly moral focus. In fact, *Cobwebs* was part of an immersive educational programme: Fenn listed *Cobwebs* as the book to buy after the completion of Fenn's *Spelling Book*.[66] Fenn's sequential educational programme is both a marketing ploy and an indicative suggestion that literacy should lead to lessons in moral values and ethical practices, to prepare children for societal participation. Indeed, *Cobwebs* suggests that upper-middle-class mothers should promote and sustain a polite and benevolent British class system.[67]

---

[65] Trimmer, *Easy Introduction*, p. 138; *Easy Introduction*, 9th edn, p. 100.
[66] Fenn, *Spelling Book*, p. xi; Delaney, p. 84.
[67] Delaney, pp. 95–7.

More specifically, *Cobwebs* is concerned with facilitating polite upper-middle-class commerce: conversations regularly take place in shops or anticipate shopping trips. The question of how to become a polite commercial society was, as Paul Langford's seminal study indicates, an active philosophical debate in eighteenth-century England.[68] This study places Fenn as an important figure in the development of that philosophical-economical thought.

In *Cobwebs*, Mamma is a gateway to the world of ethical consumption. In the conversation 'The Morning', the son asks Mamma, 'May I go to-day, and buy my top?' and Mamma answers, 'Yes, you may.'[69] The exchange provides a pattern for how a child may politely and successfully request an object from their parent. Moreover, the exchange implies that mothers can (or should) have control over the domestic purse. The boy, excited by the prospect of owning something new, begins to list objects. This is, on one level, a reading exercise: young children can read 'bat', 'cup' and 'mug'. The conversation also establishes a financial hierarchy. When the boy asks, 'And let us get a gun for *Sam*. [. . .] May I get a bag for *Bet*?' Mamma asks if the boy can pay for it. 'O no; but you can pay for all', the boy says.[70] Mamma does not berate her son for impudence: her silence suggests that the boy is, in fact, correct. He has understood that his mother buys her son's toys and his gifts, and he rightly defers to her. This suggests that establishing a parental hierarchy at home paves the way for wise consumption in the marketplace.

Fenn presents the ownership of material goods in *Cobwebs* as an opportunity for ethical development, as is seen in 'The Doll'. A girl exclaims to her Mamma, 'What a nice doll! I like this: pray may I have this?' and Mamma encourages her to consider the responsibility of ownership: 'You must then take care to keep her cool [. . .] You must then work for her [. . .] Will you not wish her in the shop?'[71] Through her imperatives and rhetorical questions, Mamma transforms the doll from an object to be possessed into an ethical demand for the girl to show responsibility for another. This stance is distinct from Barbauld's attitude towards dolls[72] – where Barbauld chastises

[68] Paul Langford, *A Polite and Commercial People: England 1727–1783* (Oxford: Clarendon Press, 1989).
[69] Fenn, *Cobwebs*, I, p. 32.
[70] Ibid., I, p. 33.
[71] Ibid., I, p. 62.
[72] Anna Letitia Barbauld, 'Live Dolls', in *Evenings at Home: or, the Juvenile Budget Opened. Consisting of a Variety of Miscellaneous Pieces for the Instruction and*

children for spending time and effort on toys rather than people, Fenn suggests that toys can teach children responsibility for others without distracting their sympathies.

The dialogue 'The Toy Shop' reaffirms that purchasing toys can enable children to exercise generosity. The opening engraving depicts a young boy almost overwhelmed by choice as he holds a toy musket and a rocking horse, and gazes towards several toys lined up on the toyshop-owner's desk. In the engraving, Mamma is the only figure whose body is not obscured by an object, a visual cue that corresponds with her conceptual command over the situation. Mamma knows the true focus: to educate her son, on whom her gaze is fixed. During the dialogue, the boy cannot decide which toy he wants, and Mamma shows both her affection and her financial stability in her willingness to indulge him with two toys, indicating that the episode is designed to teach financial responsibility within the context of financial comfort.[73] Upon seeing a rocking horse, the boy exclaims, 'I will be good to you, not whip you much [. . .] nor let the hair rub off [. . .] I will pat your neck [. . .] At night you must have a warm bed.' The boy's cumulative declarations 'I will' centre not upon his dominance over the rocking horse but on ways in which he will show affection. Upon hearing how the toy inspires kindness in her son, Mamma offers to buy the rocking horse, implicitly affirming the idea that shopping can improve an individual's capacity for kindness.[74] Ultimately, the boy chooses the rocking horse for himself, and a toy gun for a friend. This dialogue is designed to give child readers at home the excitement of imagining a visit to a toy shop while modelling how a successful shopping trip can provide opportunities to cultivate generosity. Mamma does not say that she cannot afford all the items the boy wants, only that she does not think purchasing multiple toys will help him. Lacking any financial restriction on his purchases, the boy models ethical consumption: he buys the toy that awakens his generous impulse, and in this generous spirit, he buys another item for a friend.

Fenn's celebration of the generous motive indicates that she is less concerned with the experience of the person on whom generosity

Amusement of Young Persons. Fourteenth edition. Carefully revised and corrected throughout by Arthur Aikin, Esq. FLS., &c. And with some additional pieces, by the authors. The whole newly arranged. In 4 volumes, ed. by Lucy Aikin (London: Baldwin, Cradock and Joy; Hunter; Longman, Rees and Co.; Booker; Harvey and Darton; Hamilton, Adams and Co.; and Simpkin and Marshall, 1826).
[73] Fenn, *Cobwebs*, I, pp. 75–6.
[74] Ibid., I, pp. 78–80.

is bestowed, and more concerned with the intentions of the giver.[75] Fenn repeatedly indicates that the benevolent actor's intentions must align with their actions. Modifying Adam Smith's concept of the 'impartial spectator' who can judge conduct to (ostensibly) ensure that benevolent intention aligns with benevolent practice, in 'The Happy Family' Fenn gives the 'impartial spectator' a physical form: Mrs Freelove.[76] The Freelove children are 'used to control', and in this context of familial obedience, Fenn illustrates how Mamma's implied omnipresence is sufficient to enable her children to cultivate the stance of the 'impartial spectator'. George reads a phrase to his brother, William: 'Do as you would be done by.' When William asks what this means, George feeds nearby sheep and explains he has performed the lesson. Later, William gives most of his bread to a hungry woman, saying, 'We should do as we would be done by', and his mother praises him.[77] The story is incomplete without Mamma's affirmation that William is a 'Good' boy, as this confirms that William has seen, understood and replicated the lesson in benevolence. Moreover, Fenn interpolates several perspectives in this story: William sees George feed the hungry sheep, and Mamma sees William feed the hungry woman; the reader sees all. Fenn implies that readers can cultivate Smith's 'impartial' spectator by imagining that the spectator is like Mamma, ready to affirm (or critique) one's actions. The conversational primer becomes a site where philosophical-economical ideals are modelled for textual characters and implied readers as the home becomes the place where children learn about the ethics of consumerism and the principles of generosity and benevolence. In this way, Fenn suggests that the home is an ideal site from which to induct children into the world of ethical commerce, under a mother's guidance.

Mitzi Myers suggested that Georgian 'Rational Dames' redefined power because they were 'barred' from 'Georgian sociopolitical life', and Barbauld, Trimmer and Fenn's deployment of the conversational primer suggests their use of genre in this project.[78]

[75] Fenn appears to concur with Pierre Bayle on the morality of an act being dependent on the giver's intentions (Saxton, p. 11).
[76] Adam Smith, *The Theory of Moral Sentiments* (London and Edinburgh: Millar and Kincaid, 1759), p. 43 §2; p. 49 §3; p. 219 §3; Part II, p. 249 §1.
[77] Fenn, *Cobwebs*, II, pp. 17–20.
[78] Mitzi Myers, 'Impeccable Governesses, Rational Dames, and Moral Mothers: Mary Wollstonecraft and the Female Tradition in Georgian Children's Books', *Children's Literature*, 14 (1986), 31–59 (p. 43).

By using the conversational primer's verisimilar conversations between middle- and upper-class mothers and their young children, Barbauld, Trimmer and Fenn used their pedagogic position as mother-teachers to pivot into the middle of social debates while promoting home education for the very young. Bringing concepts of tolerance, religious education and commercial ethics into the domestic space, *Lessons for Children, An Easy Introduction to the Knowledge of Nature* and *Cobwebs to Catch Flies* form an important part of the tapestry of British intellectual history. What Barbauld, Trimmer and Fenn present in their conversational primers is a claim for the right to participate in public national debates on the basis of their authority in the home over the education of the very young.

Works Cited

Primary

[Anon.], *The Infant's Miscellany: or, Easy Lessons, Extracted from Different Authors. On a New Plan. Intended to Facilitate the Attainment of the English Language to the Youngest Readers, by Teaching Them Not Only to Read, but Likewise to Understand Clearly What They Read* (London: Printed for the Author; sold by T. Beecroft, 1778)

[Anon.], 'Review of New Publications', July 1813, *The Gentleman's Magazine: and Historical Chronicle from July to December 1813*, volume 83, ed. by Sylvanus Urban (London: Nichols, Son, and Bentley, 1818)

Barbauld, Anna Letitia, *Lessons for Children Part I: For Children from Two to Three Years Old* (London: J. Johnson, 1788)

——. *Lessons for Children Aged Three Years Old: Part I* (London: Joseph Johnson, 1787)

——. *Lessons for Children of Three Years Old: Part II* (London: J. Johnson, 1788)

——. *Lessons for Children Aged Three to Four Years Old* (London: Joseph Johnson, 1788)

——. *Lessons for Children, in Four Parts* (London: J. Johnson, 1808)

——. 'Live Dolls', in *Evenings at Home: or, The Juvenile Budget Opened. Consisting of a Variety of Miscellaneous Pieces for the Instruction and Amusement of Young Persons. Fourteenth edition. Carefully revised and corrected throughout by Arthur Aikin, Esq. FLS., &c. And with some additional pieces, by the authors. The whole newly arranged. In 4 volumes*, ed. by Lucy Aikin (London: Baldwin, Cradock and Joy; Hunter; Longman, Rees and Co.; Booker; Harvey and Darton; Hamilton, Adams and Co.; and Simpkin and Marshall, 1826)

Descartes, René, 'Treatise on Man', in *Descartes: The World and Other Writings*, ed. by Stephen Gaukroger (Cambridge: Cambridge University Press, 1998), pp. 97–169

Diary and Letters of Madam D'Arblay, vol. 5 of 6, ed. by Charlotte Barrett (London: Macmillan, 1904–5)

Edgeworth, Mary and Richard Lovell, *Practical Education* (1801), 2nd edn, vol. 2 of 3 (New York: Woodstock Books, 1996)

Lamb, Charles and Mary, *The Letters of Charles and Mary Lamb*, vol. 2, ed. by Edwin W. Marrs, Jr. (New York: Cornell University Press, 1976)

Locke, John, *Some Thoughts Concerning Education and Of the Conduct of the Understanding* (1706 edn), ed. by Ruth W. Grant and Narthan Tarcov (Indianapolis and Cambridge: Hackett Publishing Company, 1996)

Lovechild, Mrs [Lady Ellenor Fenn], *Cobwebs to Catch Flies: or, Dialogues in Short Sentences, Adapted for Children from the Age of Three to Eight Years. In two volumes* (London: John Marshall, 1783)

Memoir of Mrs Barbauld, Including Letters and Notices of Her Family and Friends, ed. by Anna Letitia LeBreton (London: George Bell and Sons, 1874)

Smith, Adam, *The Theory of Moral Sentiments* (London and Edinburgh: Printed for Millar and Kincaid and Bell, 1759), digitized by *Eighteenth Century Collections Online*, Gale Document CW3320137306

Somerville, Elizabeth, *Lessons for Children of Three Years Old* (London: Sampson Low, 1800)

Trimmer, Sarah, *A Companion to the Book of Common Prayer of the Church of England: Containing a Comment on the Service for Sundays; Including the Collects Epistles, and Gospels* (London: Longman, G. G. J. and J. Robinson, and Johnson, 1791)

——. *An Easy Introduction to the Knowledge of Nature, and Reading the Holy Scriptures: Adapted to the Capacities of Children* (London: Printed for the Author and sold by Dodsley, Robson, Longman and Robinson, Johnson, Welles and Grosvenor, Shave, 1780)

——. *An Easy Introduction to the Knowledge of Nature, and Reading the Holy Scriptures: Adapted to the Capacities of Children. By Mrs Trimmer. The ninth edition, with considerable additions and improvements* (London, 1796), digitized by *Eighteenth Century Collections Online*, Gale Document Number CB3326809317

Secondary

Andrews, Robert M., *Lay Activism and the High Church Movement: The Life and Thought of William Stevens 1732–1804* (Brill's Series in Church History, Leiden and Boston: Brill, 2015)

Bulman, William J., *Anglican Enlightenment: Orientalism, Religion and Politics in England and Its Empire, 1648–1715* (Cambridge: Cambridge University Press, 2015)

Cole, G., 'Doctrine, Dissent and the Decline of Paley's Reputation 1805–1825', *Enlightenment and Dissent*, 6 (1987), 19–30

Delaney, Lesley Jane, 'Key Developments in the Nursery Reading Market 1783–1900' (unpublished doctoral thesis, University College London, 2012)

Eddy, Matthew D. and David Knight (eds), 'Introduction', in William Paley, *Natural Theology; or, Evidence of the Existence and Attributes of the Deity, collected from the appearances of nature* (Oxford: Oxford University Press, 2006), pp. ix–xix

Fyfe, Aileen, 'Reading Children's Books in Late Eighteenth-Century Dissenting Families', *Historical Journal* 43 (2000), 453–73

Hilton, Mary, *Women and the Shaping of the Nation's Young: Education and Public Doctrine in Britain 1750–1850* (Abingdon and New York: Ashgate, 2007)

Immel, Andrea, '"Mistress of the Infantine Language": Lady Ellenor Fenn, Her *Set of Toys*, and the "Education of Each Moment"', *Children's Literature*, 25 (1997), 214–28

Langford, Paul, *A Polite and Commercial People: England 1727–1783* (Oxford: Clarendon Press, 1989)

Levy, Michelle, 'Barbauld's Poetic Career in Script and Print', in *Anna Letitia Barbauld: New Perspectives*, ed. by William McCarthy and Olivia Murphy (Lewisburg, PA: Bucknell University Press, 2014), 37–58

Lim, Jessica W. H., 'Barbauld's Lessons: The Conversational Primer in Late Eighteenth-Century British Children's Literature', *Journal for Eighteenth-Century Studies*, 43 (2019) 101–20

McCarthy, William, *Anna Letitia Barbauld: Voice of the Enlightenment* (Baltimore: Johns Hopkins University Press, 2008)

Michals, Teresa, *Books for Children, Books for Adults: Age and the Novel from Defoe to James* (Cambridge: Cambridge University Press, 2014)

Myers, Mitzi, 'Impeccable Governesses, Rational Dames, and Moral Mothers: Mary Wollstonecraft and the Female Tradition in Georgian Children's Books', *Children's Literature*, 14 (1986), 31–59

Neale, Stephen, 'Questions of Genre', in *Approaches to Media: A Reader*, ed. by Oliver Boyd-Barrett and Chris Newbold (London: Arnold, 1995), pp. 460–72

Nockles, Peter, 'Church Parties in the Pre-Tractarian Church of England 1750–1833: The "Orthodox" – Some Problems of Definition and Identity', in *The Church of England c.1689–c.1833: From Toleration to Tractarianism*, ed. by John Walsh, Colin Haydon and Stephen Taylor (Cambridge: Cambridge University Press, 1993), 334–59

——. *The Oxford Movement in Context: Anglican High Churchmanship, 1760–1857* (Cambridge: Cambridge University Press, 1994)

Richardson, Alan, *Literature, Education, and Romanticism: Reading as Social Practice, 1730–1832* (Cambridge: Cambridge University Press, 1994)

Saxton, Teresa, 'Benevolent Intentions: Hospitality, Ethics and the Eighteenth-Century Novel' (unpublished doctoral dissertation, University of Tennessee, 2012)

Schnorrenberg, Barbara Brandon, 'Sarah Trimmer', *Oxford Dictionary of National Biography*, online edition <https://doi.org/10.1093/ref:odnb/27740> [accessed 18 June 2021]

Stoker, David, 'Establishing Lady Fenn's Canon', *Papers of the Bibliographical Society of America* (2009), 43–72

Wakely-Mulroney, Katherine, 'Isaac Watts and the Dimensions of Child Interiority', *Journal for Eighteenth-Century Studies*, 39 (2016)

Walsh, John and Stephen Taylor, 'Introduction: The Church and Anglicanism in the "Long" Eighteenth Century', *The Church of England c.1689–c.1833: From Toleration to Tractarianism*, ed. by John Walsh, Colin Haydon and Stephen Taylor (Cambridge: Cambridge University Press, 1993), pp. 1–66

Weir, Heather E., 'Reading Nature before Reading the Bible: Sarah Trimmer's Natural Theology', in *Breaking Boundaries: Female Biblical Interpreters Who Challenged the Status Quo*, ed. by Nancy Calvert-Koyzis and Heather Weir (New York: T & T Clark International), pp. 53–68

White, Daniel E., '"With Mrs Barbauld it is different": Dissenting Heritage and the Devotional Taste', in *Women, Gender and Enlightenment*, ed. by Sarah Knott and Barbara Taylor (Basingstoke: Palgrave Macmillan, 2005), pp. 474–92

Chapter 2

Reading *Poetry for Children* in the Long Eighteenth Century

Felicity James

We start with a silenced woman. In one of the most notorious discussions of Romantic children's literature, Charles Lamb's comments in his letter to Coleridge of 1802, his sister's voice is absent. Yet Mary Lamb is at the heart of the anecdote, with her attempt to purchase books for the infant Derwent Coleridge:

> Goody Two Shoes is almost out of print. Mrs. Barbauld['s] stuff has banished all the old classics of the nursery; & the Shopman at Newbery's hardly deign'd to reach them off an old exploded corner of a shelf, when Mary ask'd for them. Mrs. B's & Mrs. Trimmer's nonsense lay in piles about. Knowledge insignificant & vapid as Mrs. B's books convey, it seems, must come to a child in the *shape* of *knowledge*, & his empty noddle must be turned with conceit of his own powers, when he has learnt, that a Horse is an Animal, & Billy is better than a Horse, & such like: instead of that beautiful Interest in wild tales, which made the child a man, while all the time he suspected himself to be no bigger than a child. Science has succeeded to Poetry no less in the little walks of Children, than with Men. —: Is there no possibility of averting this sore evil? Think what you would have been now, if instead of being fed with Tales and old wives' fables in childhood, you had been crammed with Geography & Natural History.?[1]

Charles Lamb's vituperative comments are well known; Mary's presence in the scene is overlooked. Yet we might assume, from her specific request to the shopman, that she had her own opinions about the sort of literature which would be suitable for a child to learn to read. She had, after all, taught Charles, her junior by ten years; she

---

[1] Charles Lamb, letter no. 136 to S. T. Coleridge, 23 October 1802, *The Letters of Charles and Mary Lamb*, ed. by Edwin W. Marrs, Jr., 3 vols (New York: Cornell University Press, 1975–8), II, pp. 81–2.

would continue tutoring children until late in life, among them the
Shakespeare scholar Mary Cowden Clarke. But her voice is drowned
out by Charles' exuberant damnation of 'the cursed Barbauld Crew,
those **Blights & Blasts** of all that is **Human** in man & child'.[2] Partly,
this is misogynist bravado, as, after an uncomfortable rift of two
years, Charles Lamb re-establishes his friendship with Coleridge: he
aims to recall the homosociality of their young London years together, fuelled by tobacco and egg-hot in the *Salutation and Cat*.
His dismissal of Anna Letitia Barbauld, in particular, also serves to
mark his awareness of Coleridge's growth away from Dissenting allegiances. Yet it – perhaps deliberately – obscures the importance
of this Dissenting tradition in forming the Lambs' own approach
to children's literature, just as it silences Mary Lamb. Charles seeks
instead to tap into a powerful narrative Coleridge and Wordsworth
were helping to develop around childhood and the Romantic imagination.[3] Indeed, Charles' comments have traditionally been set
alongside Coleridge's celebrations of his own 'early reading of Faery
Tales' and Wordsworth's images of childhood freedom to support, as
Alan Richardson puts it, a persistent 'dualistic model – didacticism
and imagination, instruction and delight, reason and fantasy –
underlying most accounts of the development of children's literature'.[4]

But of course, as Richardson's own nuanced analysis suggests,
there are no easy polarities here. The move from Rationalism to
Romanticism, from the garden to the street, is not a linear one.[5]
For a start, the hyperbole of Charles' letter points up a certain tension around the power of 'wild' imagination. The Lambs walked a
tightrope, in their life and works, between the pleasures and dangers
of wildness, both keenly aware of the perilous nature of their own
mental health. Moreover, in publishing with the Godwins' Juvenile
Library, they were taking part in a much larger debate over the nature and purpose of educational literature for children. In closing,
this chapter will look closely at a single poem, 'What Is Fancy?' from

[2] Ibid., p. 82.
[3] For more on the Romantic concept of imaginative life and how it might feed
into pedagogic practice, past and present, see David Halpin, 'Pedagogy and the
Romantic Imagination', *British Journal of Educational Studies*, 56.1 (2008),
59–75.
[4] Alan Richardson, *Literature, Education, and Romanticism: Reading as Social
Practice, 1780–1832* (Cambridge: Cambridge University Press, 1994), p. 114.
[5] See Morag Styles' excellent study for an overview of the development of children's
poetry: *From the Garden to the Street: An Introduction to 300 Years of Poetry for
Children* (London: Cassell, 1997).

Poetry for Children, asking how it carefully negotiates the potential dangers of imagination against this backdrop. Moreover, the Lambs' interest in 'fancy' forms part of a much larger exploration by children's writers of the eighteenth century into the power of the imagination, and the work that poetry could do in prompting the child to consider larger imaginative possibilities. This awareness, as we will see, was balanced against the need to control the dangers of an over-active imagination, and to properly direct and educate the child reader: a balance negotiated most notably by women writers, including Barbauld and her niece Lucy Aikin, who were appropriating and revising a long tradition of Dissenting educational literature. We might usefully place Lucy Aikin's *Poetry for Children* (1801) alongside the Lambs' quite different volume of the same name, *Poetry for Children* (1809), to understand more fully the difficult and often fractious relationship between poetry and children's education through the long eighteenth century. In doing so, we can try to listen in to some of the – occasionally indistinct – women's voices behind the scenes.

Reading Children's Poetry through the Eighteenth Century

Our understanding of the rise of children's literature through the eighteenth century, Romantic and Victorian periods should be inflected by questions both of genre and of gender. The deep importance of children's literature in allowing women to claim cultural – and economic – power through the long eighteenth and nineteenth centuries has attracted much excellent critical discussion, building on the groundbreaking work of Mitzi Myers in the 1980s and 1990s. Children's *poetry*, however, has not attracted quite so much dedicated attention: Melissa Valiska Gregory goes so far as to call this a critical 'blind spot' in discussions of the long eighteenth century; similarly, Donelle Ruwe points out that the 'full history of children's poetry of the Romantic era – its practitioners, major genres and poetics – has yet to be written'.[6] The dedicated, archivally grounded,

---

[6] Donelle Ruwe, *British Children's Poetry in the Romantic Era: Verse, Riddle, and Rhyme* (Basingstoke and New York: Palgrave Macmillan, 2014), pp. 2, 16; also *The Aesthetics of Children's Poetry: A Study of Children's Verse in English*, ed. by Katherine Wakely-Mulroney and Louise Joy (Oxford and New York: Routledge, 2018).

scholarship of Gregory and Ruwe, alongside the pioneering work of Morag Styles, and recovery work on authors such as Barbauld, and the Taylors of Ongar, is helping to alter the terms of the debate. We are now beginning to be aware of how the 'rich legacy' of juvenile verse by women, in Gregory's words, 'can enhance our understanding of the ways in which such writers negotiated the relations between gender, genre and authorship'.[7] One of the aims of this chapter is to underscore how vital, and how complex, a part poetry has to play in the story of women's literary education in the long eighteenth century.

What role did poetry play in educating children? This is a complicated question, not least because of the sheer range of poetry for children in the period. The long eighteenth century was a time of variety, experiment and inventiveness in children's poetry. Within the broad generic categorisation of poetry, works for children ranged from nursery rhymes to hymns; from original verse written for, and in, the child's perspective, to schoolroom anthologies which gathered together extracts of classic works. Poetry for children, quite apart from any literary considerations, might have a commercial, religious or educational agenda – sometimes all three combined. Yet these different forms of children's verse were often motivated by a similar question: how could the particular qualities of poetry – rhyme, metre, sound – be best used to encourage children to learn?

Two very different collections of verse for children give a good insight into the generic diversity and richness of juvenile poetry in the eighteenth century, and some of the key debates over its purpose. The first is Isaac Watts' *Divine Songs Attempted in Easy Language for the Use of Children* (1715), one of the most heavily reprinted and influential volumes of children's poetry in the eighteenth century. The 'easy language' of the title demonstrates his loyalty to the Dissenting traditions of familiar worship, and the verses, with their comfortably regular metre and rhyme, show his skill as a popular hymnodist.[8] There is a strong sense of the child's perspective, as in the poem 'Praise for Mercies Spiritual and Temporal', where the

---

[7] Melissa Valiska Gregory, 'Women Writers, Nineteenth Century Nursery Rhyme and Lyric Innovation', *Literature Compass*, 12.3 (2015), 106–18 (p. 107).

[8] On this point, see J. R. Watson, 'The Hymns of Isaac Watts and the Tradition of Dissent', in *Dissenting Praise: Religious Dissent and the Hymn in England and Wales*, ed. by Isabel Rivers and David L. Wykes (Oxford: Oxford University Press, 2011), pp. 33–67.

child narrator looks at other, very different, 'Children in the Street', half-naked, begging and cold. This is an attempt to teach, in simple terms, the literate middle-class child about responsibilities and social duties. For Watts, there was a clear, divinely ordained link between poetry and education. His 'Preface', addressed to those in charge of children's education, emphasises the biblical imperative to 'teach and admonish one another by hymns and songs' (drawn from Ephesians 5:19).[9] Watts' lifelong preoccupation with education intersects with Lockean philosophy, and his comments in the 'Preface' borrow from Locke's advice on how best to introduce children to religious and moral concepts, in language adapted to the 'Capacity and Notions' of its intended audience, with the aim that '*Learning* might be made a Play and Recreation to Children'.[10] Watts emphasises the special connection between pleasure and instruction which poetry provides:

> There is a greater delight in the very learning of truths and duties this way. There is something so amusing and entertaining in rhymes and metre that will incline children to make this part of their business a diversion.[11]

Poetry, then, brings together 'delight' with 'duties': pleasure and instruction are embodied in its very form, because it is through the joy a child takes in 'rhyme and metre' that they will be educated. Didacticism and musicality go hand in hand. Yet the preface also betrays an anxiety about other forms of poetry, suggesting that a familiarity with *Divine Songs* will mean that the child will 'not be forced to seek relief for an emptiness of mind out of the loose and dangerous sonnets of the age'.[12] The power of poetry, warns Watts, needs to be carefully directed to proper moral ends.

A second example demonstrates the power of children's poetry in a quite different way. *Tommy Thumb's Pretty Song-Book* (1744) is an illustrated, child-sized commodity, its pages printed in alternate red and black.[13] It was produced by a woman printer-publisher,

[9] Isaac Watts, *Divine Songs Attempted in Easy Language for the Use of Children* (1715 edition), ed. by J. H. P. Pafford (London: Oxford University Press, 1971), 'Preface', n.p.

[10] John Locke, *Some Thoughts Concerning Education* (London: 1693), p. 176.

[11] Watts, 'Preface', n.p.

[12] Ibid.

[13] *Tommy Thumb's Pretty Song-Book* [An advertisement at the end is signed N. Lovechild, i.e. Nurse Lovechild.] (1744?): the book is extremely rare, and the copy consulted belongs to the British Library, shelfmark C.59.a.20.

Mary Cooper, and possibly also written or compiled by her; the author signs herself 'Nurse Lovechild'. This is one of the first extant collections of nursery rhyme, and many of the verses included are still reprinted today: 'Hickere Dickere Dock', 'Bah Bah, a black Sheep', 'Who Did Kill Cock Robin'. This boisterously scatological rhyme from the song-book nicely demonstrates its difference from the verse of Isaac Watts:

> Piss a Bed,
> Piss a Bed,
> Barley Butt,
> Your Bum is so heavy
> You cant get up.[14]

The recognisable tones of infant insult echo down the centuries to us, as does the joy of the sing-song game, the play of plosive 'p's and 'b's. Watts tries to harness the child's voice in verse to inculcate a sense of moral and social responsibility; *Tommy Thumb* echoes the child's game.[15] Watts' narrator looks at the children of the street; the nursery rhyme lets us listen in to their own lively language. Cooper's gleeful rhymes thus seem opposed to the social and moral imperatives of Watts, but *Divine Songs* and *Tommy Thumb* represent part of the same wider movement in the eighteenth century – the ways in which the burgeoning book market might be tailored to appeal to those buying for children, and how children's literacy could be encouraged. Both books are alert to the pleasures of verse: the effect of repetition, rhyme and metre, to soothe the child or to hold its attention. When reprinted, *Tommy Thumb* usually included a letter 'On Nursing' which describes the book as 'a Collection of Songs, so fit for the capacities of Infants, both in words and tunes, by which they are often lull'd to rest, when cross, and in great pain'.[16]

---

[14] *Tommy Thumb's Pretty Song-Book*, p. 34.

[15] Darton acknowledges the importance of the book – whose rhymes are 'old and dear friends', excepting a few 'coarse' and 'nasty' poems – but describes its originator as 'One Cooper, otherwise unknown'. F. J. Harvey Darton, *Children's Books in England: Five Centuries of Social Life* (Cambridge: Cambridge University Press, 1932), p. 101.

[16] The book is reprinted in countless editions; see, for example, *Tommy Thumb's Song Book, for All Little Masters and Misses, to Be Sung to Them by Their Nurses, until They Can Sing Themselves, by Nurse Lovechild, to Which Is added a Letter from a Lady on Nursing* (Glasgow: Lumsden and Son, 1814).

The end-piece to *Tommy Thumb* functions as an advertisement for one of Cooper's other titles, *The Child's New Play-Thing: Being a Spelling-Book Intended to Make the Learning to Read, a Diversion instead of a Task*, a compendium of fables, stories, songs and riddles which might unite entertainment with education:

> The Childs Plaything
> I recommend for Cheating
> Children into Learning
> Without any Beating.[17]

While not as explicitly as in Watts' careful engagement with pedagogical theories, Cooper's marketing of these rhyme books nevertheless shows traces of the ways in which Lockean concepts – the idea that '*Learning* might be made a Play and Recreation to Children'[18] – had filtered into broader culture, resulting in an attempt to bring together learning and pleasure.

Cooper's venture into the children's book business was probably not, however, prompted by educational or by literary motives: this was, above all, an important new market. Mary Cooper was the widow of Thomas Cooper, who had established himself as one of the major trade publishers in the period.[19] After he died in 1743, Mary Cooper continued the business successfully under her own name until her death in 1761: a growing body of scholarship recognises her tenacious business skills.[20] She is part of a long line of often forgotten women in the business of writing, producing, printing, circulating and revising children's poetry in the long eighteenth century, one of the predecessors of women booksellers such as Eliza Fenwick and Mary Jane Godwin. The rhymes of *Tommy Thumb*, at first glance ephemeral, speak to a much larger story of the ways in which women sought to accrue cultural power through writing flair or commercial expertise in the children's poetry market, and in educational practice in the period.

---

[17] *Tommy Thumb* (1744), p. 64.

[18] Locke, p. 176.

[19] Michael Treadwell, 'London Trade Publishers 1675–1750', *The Library*, 6th ser., 4.2 (June 1982), 99–134.

[20] See Beverly Schneller, 'John Hill and Mary Cooper: A Case Study in Eighteenth-Century Publishing', in *Fame and Fortune: Sir John Hill and London Life in the 1750s*, ed. by Clare Brant and George Rousseau (London: Palgrave Macmillan, 2018), pp. 107–20.

Barbauld, Aikin and *Poetry for Children* (1801)

Across the long eighteenth century, we see women writers of juvenile verse engaging with these complex legacies: rewriting Wattsian verse; seeking, in the footsteps of pioneers like Cooper, to profit from the children's book market; above all, trying to channel the power of poetic form for their own purposes. Two further examples demonstrate the different ways in which these ideas could manifest themselves in children's poetry: Anna Letitia Barbauld's *Hymns in Prose* (1781) and her niece Lucy Aikin's *Poetry for Children* (1801).

Barbauld was well aware of the pedagogic power of poetry. Her geographical poems, for instance, use 'lively strokes of description' to spark response in the child, evoking India, Constantinople, 'Lapland woods and hills of frost'.[21] Probably, as William McCarthy has noted, these were designed for her own geography classes at Palgrave Academy – lessons, as Lucy Aikin puts it, 'remembered by their auditors less among their tasks than their pleasures'.[22] In Aikin's account of her aunt's geography lessons, poetry becomes a means to bring together instruction and play – in Wattsian terms, delight and duties – as a serious educational purpose is turned into pleasure. Yet despite using poetry for her own teaching, Barbauld did not publish much poetry for children; her best-known pedagogic works are written in prose, such as the child-size reading primers *Lessons for Children* (1778–9), discussed elsewhere in the volume. While this children's work was highly successful, it was also persistently patronised and dismissed, as in Samuel Johnson's pompous exasperation, reporting her marriage to 'a little Presbyterian parson':

> all her employment now is 'To suckle fools, and chronicle small-beer'. She tells the children, 'This is a cat, and that is a dog, with four legs and a tail; see there! you are much better than a cat or a dog, for you can speak.'[23]

---

[21] *The Works of Anna Laetitia Barbauld, with a Memoir by Lucy Aikin*, 2 vols (London: Longman Hurst, 1825), I, p. xxvi, and *Poetry for Children: Consisting of Short Pieces, to Be Committed to Memory*, ed. by Lucy Aikin (London: Longman, Hurst, Rees, Orme, and Brown, 1801), p. 146.

[22] *The Poems of Anna Letitia Barbauld*, ed. by William McCarthy and Elizabeth Kraft (Athens and London: University of Georgia Press, 1994), p. 334; Lucy Aikin, *Memoir*, I, p. xxvii.

[23] James Boswell and Samuel Johnson, *Boswell's Life of Johnson Together with Boswell's Journal of a Tour to the Hebrides and Johnson's Diary of a Journey into*

Johnson's satire has several targets: Barbauld's Rational Dissent, here flattened into Presbyterianism; the maternal identity she adopts as a narrator, reduced to 'suckl[ing] fools'; and the simple prose of *Lessons for Children*, designed to encourage children as young as two or three to read. Compare Charles Lamb's satire: 'a Horse is an Animal, & Billy is better than a Horse, & such like'. This contempt runs alongside the comments towards 'Mrs Bare-bald' by other male Romantics – Southey, for example, imagined Charles Lamb might declare war on her, 'singe her flaxen wig with squibs, and tie crackers to her petticoats till she leapt about like a parched pea for very torture'.[24] There is a troubling association between older womanhood and pedagogy, as Southey imagines Barbauld immolated by the subversive spark of Charles Lamb's imaginative writing. But her uncertainties over the use of poetry for children are not a retreat into dull, dried-pea prose, but an attempt to work through larger pedagogical ideas.

Some reasons for her reluctance are foregrounded in the 'Preface' to *Hymns in Prose for Children* (1781). The collection explicitly acknowledges Watts as a predecessor, drawing, like him, from the metres of the psalms to produce pieces which 'are intended to be committed to memory, and recited'.[25] But unlike Watts, Barbauld steers away from verse; indeed, in an oft-quoted passage, she expresses doubt about whether

> poetry *ought* to be lowered to the capacities of children or whether they should not rather be kept from reading verse, till they are able to relish good verse.[26]

Perhaps poetry is simply too difficult for children to understand; the sort of poetry they *can* understand, too bad for us to tolerate. Might there, however, be some deeper anxieties behind this reluctance?

For Barbauld does have a deep commitment to encouraging the child's imagination, to spark them into thinking beyond the material.

North Wales, ed. by George Birkbeck Hill, rev. by L. F. Powell, 6 vols (Oxford: Clarendon Press, 1934), II, pp. 408–9.

[24] *The Life and Correspondence of Robert Southey*, ed. by Charles Cuthbert Southey, 6 vols (London: Longman, Brown, Green, and Longmans, 1850), II, p. 275.

[25] Anna Letitia Barbauld, *Hymns in Prose for Children* (London: Johnson, 1781), p. vi.

[26] Ibid., p. v.

This might be through teaching them to read for themselves; it might be through the sweeping landscapes of her geographical poems, or through the awe-inspiring imagery, the King James rhythms, of her *Hymns in Prose*, as in Hymn 4:

> COME, and I will shew you what is beautiful. It is a rose full blown. See how she sits upon her mossy stem, like the queen of all the flowers! her leaves glow like fire; the air is filled with her sweet odour; she is the delight of every eye.
>
> She is beautiful, but there is a fairer than she. He that made the rose, is more beautiful than the rose: he is all lovely; he is the delight of every heart.[27]

This is Barbauld's attempt to arouse 'devotional feelings', an imaginative response of wonder and awe, in a child reader. It is a form of prose poetry, involving the child's senses of sound and sight through the incantatory repetitions and cumulative echoes: 'rose'/'blown'/'flowers'/'glow'/'odour'. We move inward from the eye at the end of the first paragraph to the heart at the end of the second: the feelings of wonder at the sight of the flower are internalised to become a form of 'practical devotion' (p. v). Watts' religious appeal to the child reader has now been made into something rich and sensuous, in keeping with Barbauld's larger intent to imbue her own culture of Rational Dissent with a greater commitment to feeling.

Yet Barbauld is often simultaneously troubled by anxieties about what Christopher Stokes has termed the 'instability of that affect'.[28] Her best work often circles around the risky, speculative possibilities of poetry, as in 'A Summer Evening's Meditation' where the poet soars off into 'desarts of creation, wide and wild', before 'fancy droops'; 'thought astonish'd stops her bold career', and comes back down to earth.[29] Poetry, with its potentially dangerous capacity for ambiguity and emotion, has an ability to take both poet and reader off into imaginative flight. Instead, Barbauld grounds her published

---

[27] Ibid., pp. 21–2.
[28] Christopher Stokes, *Romantic Prayer: Reinventing the Poetics of Devotion, 1773–1832* (Oxford: Oxford University Press, 2021), p. 72; also Jon Mee, *Romanticism, Enthusiasm, and Regulation: Poetics and the Policing of Culture in the Romantic Period* (Oxford: Oxford University Press, 2003).
[29] 'A Summer Evening's Meditation', in *Poems*, ed. by McCarthy and Kraft, pp. 81–4.

work for children in prose: 'it will probably be found', she writes in the 'Preface' to *Hymns*, 'that the measured prose in which such pieces are generally written, is nearly as agreeable to the ear as a more regular rhythmus'.[30] Measured, here, seems to carry an ambiguity of its own, evoking a steady, regular rhythm, but also a double meaning of controlled, or restrained, a way of reining in the child's emotional and imaginative speculations. Barbauld's use of 'measured prose' for children suggests a heightened awareness – and uncertainty – about the possibilities of poetry, on which she nevertheless seems to have drawn in her own schoolroom.

A similar anxiety about the nature of imagination and the role of poetry in education is evident in the work of Barbauld's niece, Lucy Aikin, such as in her anthology *Poetry for Children: Consisting of Short Pieces, to Be Committed to Memory* (1801). The daughter of John Aikin, she was highly conscious of her position as heir to a powerful pedagogic legacy, both through her family and her Dissenting religion. But she also subtly contests these legacies: even as she overtly celebrates the influence of Barbauld and of Watts, she pushes back against them to create her own space for educational poetry. Her anthology features verse which can easily be learned by heart, recited, and which introduces the child to major writers – including Aikin's own family in that canon. Aikin is self-consciously following in the footsteps of previous educational anthologists, such as Vicesimus Knox. She was seeking to position her own work, with its wider range of poetry, as a more engaging and diverse, Dissenting competitor to these older volumes, including original poems by her aunt Barbauld alongside other eighteenth-century work. As in Barbauld's *Hymns in Prose*, emphasis is placed on startling images, repetition, metre and rhythm: Lucy Aikin, however, stubbornly makes the case for poetry. Her comments in the 'Preface' reveal her slightly fractious engagement with both her aunt and Isaac Watts. She begins by making a claim for the peculiar nature of poetry, just as Watts had done:

> The magic of ryme is felt in the very cradle – the mother and the nurse employ it as a spell of soothing power.[31]

---

[30] Barbauld, *Hymns in Prose*, p. v.
[31] Aikin, *Poetry for Children*, p. iii.

Her language, however, differs from that of Watts in its evocation of magic and spells, an odd contrast to the Dissenting emphasis on reason, rationality and familiar language:

> Since dragons and fairies, giants and witches, have vanished from our nurseries before the wand of reason, it has been a prevailing maxim, that the young mind should be fed on mere prose and simple matter of fact.[32]

Her comments mark both a family dispute and a larger debate. The 'prevailing maxim' is one which Barbauld herself might be seen as having helped to promote; her niece, instead, argues that poetry is a useful way to channel the child's love of 'the fanciful and marvellous'.[33] Her interest in the role of the imagination and the fairy tale, meanwhile, links her to other writers who, like her, were published by Tabart's Juvenile Library: among them, William Godwin, who worked alongside her in the early 1800s before leaving to start his own rival establishment. The 'Preface' to his 1801 *Bible Stories* offers a useful parallel to Aikin, condemning 'modern improvers' for focusing only on the intellect of children, and ignoring 'that most essential branch of human nature, the imagination'.[34] Both Aikin and Godwin are taking part in the same discussion concerning the pedagogic role of imagination. Moreover, Godwin was, from the early 1800s onwards, a frequent visitor to the Lambs. Might there be a faint echo of Lucy Aikin's 'Preface', and the questions it raises about what a young mind should be 'fed on' in Lamb's letter to Coleridge: a buried memory of a fireside conversation with Godwin, and a trace of another silenced female voice?

In contrast to Lamb's boisterous advocacy of 'Tales and old wives' fables', however, Aikin is awkward and defensive. That oxymoronic 'wand of reason', as Pete Newbon points out, 'ironically derives its power from the magic that it seeks to expunge', and the repeated

---

[32] Ibid.

[33] Ibid.

[34] See the preface to William Scolfield [William Godwin], *Bible Stories: Memorable Acts of the Ancient Patriarchs, Judges and Kings. Extracted from Their Original Historians for the Use of Children*, 2 vols (London: R. Phillips, 1803), discussed by John-Erik Hansson, '"To teach every principle of the infidels and republicans?": William Godwin through His Children's Books' (unpublished doctoral dissertation, Florence: European University Institute, 2018), p. 74. See also Matthew Grenby, 'Godwin's *Popular Stories* for the Nursery', in *New Approaches to William Godwin: Forms, Fears, Futures*, ed. by Eliza O'Brien, Helen Stark and Beatrice Turner (London: Palgrave Macmillan, 2021), pp. 185–213 (p. 189).

references to dragons, fairies, magic and spells suggest the ways in which poetry might retain something unpredictable or uncontrollable.[35] Where might the child's imagination, once unleashed, go? Aikin tries to neutralise this anxiety by returning to Watts' belief in the power of poetry as mental resource, 'a store of beautiful imagery and glowing sentiment' gathered in childhood to provide solace, and 'strengthen feelings of piety, humanity, and tenderness' in future years.[36] Her anthology is thick with 'beautiful imagery' and description: the child reader moves from the oriental visions of 'India' and 'Arabia' to the pastoral idylls of Shenstone in the 'First of April', and the frozen landscapes of Ambrose Philips, 'glaz'd' with ice. Works such as Barbauld's 'The Mouse's Petition', John Thelwall's description of 'The Orphan Boy' from the *Fairy of the Lake* and Frank Sayers' 'The Dying African' appeal to the child's social conscience. Poetry, hopes Aikin, might thus become a tool of moral education. There remains, however, an undercurrent of doubt around the proper direction of the child's imagination; Aikin emphasises the need to guard the child reader from both 'romantic sensibility' and 'wild, exalted fancy'. Indeed, some reviewers, such as the Dissenter James Plumptre, expressed dismay over the collection's inclusion of works such as 'The Fairy's Song'; *The Chace* by William Somerville, meanwhile, with its evocation of the 'sweet phrensy' of 'hunting the hare' seemed to Plumptre to contain 'ideas not proper to be put into the minds of school boys'.[37] Moreover, Aikin's own stance is as ambiguous as her image of the 'wand of reason'. Although she might at first seem to be advocating for poetry and the power of childish imagination, as opposed to her aunt's emphasis on 'mere prose', her anthology of extracts actually adheres to a more conventional pedagogic approach than Barbauld's supple rhythmic reinvention of the psalms in *Hymns in Prose*.[38] Nevertheless, these two different examples show us how women writers might use poetry both as a tool of education and to shape their own Dissenting inheritance, revising

---

[35] Pete Newbon, *The Boy-Man: Creativity and Masculinity in the Long Nineteenth Century* (London: Palgrave Macmillan, 2019), p. 184.

[36] Ibid., p. iv.

[37] James Plumptre, *Letters to John Aikin, M. D.: On His Volume of Vocal Poetry* (Cambridge: 1811), pp. 104–5.

[38] Aikin, whilst protective of the family intellectual legacy, also privately exhibited disapproval of her aunt's wild romantic streak: see William McCarthy, *Anna Letitia Barbauld: Voice of the Enlightenment* (Baltimore: Johns Hopkins University Press, 2008), pp. 135–6.

and rewriting Watts to promulgate a powerful domestic pedagogy. At the same time, they steer a cautious path through the sensual and imaginative pleasures – and perceived dangers – of poetry for children.

The Lambs and *Poetry for Children* (1809)

In 1809, the Lambs brought out their own *Poetry for Children*, a work primarily undertaken for financial motives, as their friend Robert Lloyd describes:

> It is *task* work to them, they are writing for money, and a Book of Poetry for Children being likely to sell has induced them to compose one.[39]

Yet they also clearly felt a good deal of pride in the work, the last of their collaborative commissions for the Godwins' 'Juvenile Library', which had published *Tales from Shakespeare* (1806) and *Mrs Leicester's School* (1809) alongside nursery rhyme chapbooks by Charles, and his *Adventures of Ulysses* (1808). The similarity in titles between the Aikin and Lamb volumes is probably no coincidence. As we have seen, the Godwins were well aware of Aikin's work, and of trends in the children's marketplace. They may have commissioned a book of children's poetry from the Lambs as a rival both to Aikin's anthology and to the Taylor group's *Original Poems for Infant Minds* (1804). Like the latter work, the Lambs' volume is also composed of original verses for children. However, in subsequent Juvenile Library republications, the verses by the Lambs would become part of schoolroom anthologies like Aikin's. The Lambs' *Poetry for Children* is very little known partly because it was not republished as a separate volume; instead, its poems were extracted to appear in other publications by the Godwins such as *The Junior Class Book: or, Reading Lessons for Every Day in the Year, in Prose and Verse* (1809), intended to help children practise skills in reading aloud. The Lambs' *Poetry for Children* thus nicely illustrates the ways in which children's poetry might be co-opted for educational purposes. For the Lambs themselves, and particularly for Mary Lamb, the struggle between didactic and imaginative writing had a special resonance.

[39] E. V. Lucas, *Lamb and the Lloyds* (London: Smith, Elder and Co., 1898), p. 161.

We began this chapter by noting Mary Lamb's absence from her brother's discussion of children's literature. Yet even when we try to hear her voice it proves a difficult task. The Lambs often wrote together, sharing the same table, as Mary describes it to her friend Sarah Stoddart:

> like Hermia and Helena in the Midsummer Night's Dream; or rather, like an old literary Darby and Joan, I taking snuff and he groaning all the while and saying he can make nothing of it, which he always says till he has finished, and then he finds out he has made something of it.[40]

There is no clear record, save in a handful of cases, of the authorship of the poems in the volume. Charles Lamb told his friend Thomas Manning 'the best you may suppose mine; the next best are my coadjutor's; you may amuse yourself in guessing them out; but I must tell you mine are but one-third in quantity of the whole'.[41] Manning did make a 'guess who wrote the Nonsenses in that little book of Child's poetry', but tellingly misidentified Charles' 'coadjutor' not as Mary, but as Coleridge and Wordsworth.[42]

Even contemporary readers found it difficult, then, to fully appreciate Mary's writing voice, and she remains a shadowy, equivocal figure whose status, both literary and social, is hard to define. On the one hand, she was an esteemed children's writer, whose calm, affectionate and tender relationship with her brother is noted by friends and early biographers. Thomas Noon Talfourd deemed her 'the most comfortable of advisers, the wisest of consolers'; for William Hazlitt, she was the only 'thoroughly reasonable' woman he knew.[43] Yet on the other, she is a figure of violence, wildness and unpredictability. The Lambs' lives were overshadowed by the events of 1796 when Mary, in a manic fit, killed their mother. She continued to experience mental crises intermittently throughout her life, often requiring periods of confinement in private asylums, but she was also able to lead

---

[40] *Letters*, II, p. 229.
[41] *Letters*, III, p. 35.
[42] In a letter of 27 August 1811 to George Leman Tuthill from Runjpore, Bengal; Royal Asiatic Society, Thomas Manning Archive, TM/2/3/7. My thanks to Dr Edward Weech for pointing me towards and discussing this letter.
[43] See Thomas Noon Talfourd, *Final Memorials of Charles Lamb*, 2 vols (London: Edward Moxon, 1848), II, p. 227.

an independent life, writing, occasionally tutoring, and living quietly with Charles. As Adriana Craciun has explored, Mary Lamb

> presents an intriguing set of problems for feminist scholarship because she embodies irreconcilable qualities of violence and gentleness, assertiveness and self-effacement, and because these irreconcilable differences she embodies are directly related to writing.[44]

Her authorship, after all, only comes about through her act of violence towards her mother, which releases her from her duties as caregiver and seamstress, and allows her a space where her writing identity can be set free, albeit constrained by social judgement, by her brother's watchfulness and by her own 'self-restraining' character.[45] She and Charles lived together until his death in 1834, he ensuring that she was mostly cared for at home, she taking care of him in the extremes of alcohol dependence and depression. It was a remarkably creative, loving relationship of 'double singleness', as Elia expresses it; this mutual dependence, however, had its nightmarish aspects of darkness and hopelessness.[46] Mary Lamb's is an imaginative life enabled, but also restrained, through collaboration, a wildness held firmly within bounds. Similarly, the poems in the collection often push at the boundaries of 'fancy' or 'make-believe', questioning how the child's imaginative play might be at once nurtured and also carefully directed.

One good example of this fractious relationship between imagination and education is offered by the poem 'What Is Fancy?', probably written by Mary, although no precise attribution evidence exists. Like many poems in the collection, it shows a brother and sister pairing, two children debating their writing task:

SISTER.
I AM to write three lines, and you
Three others that will rhyme.
There – now I've done my task.

---

[44] Adriana Craciun, *Fatal Women of Romanticism* (Cambridge: Cambridge University Press, 2002), p. 25.

[45] See Wordsworth's elegy for Charles Lamb; discussed by Craciun, p. 25.

[46] See 'Mackery End', in *The Works of Charles and Mary Lamb*, ed. by E. V. Lucas, 6 vols (London: Methuen, 1912), II, p. 75; the best discussion of this doubleness, and Mary Lamb's equivocal status, is Jane Aaron's *A Double Singleness* (Oxford: Clarendon Press, 1991). See also Alison Hickey, 'Double Bonds: Charles Lamb's Romantic Collaborations', *ELH*, 63.3 (1996), 735–71.

BROTHER.
Three stupid lines as e'er I knew.
When you've the pen next time,
Some Question of me ask.

SISTER.
Then tell me, brother, and pray mind,
Brother, you tell me true:
What sort of thing is *fancy*?

BROTHER.
By all that I can ever find,
'Tis something that is very new,
And what no dunces *can see*.

SISTER.
That is not half the way to tell
What *fancy* is about;
So pray now tell me more.

BROTHER.
Sister, I think 'twere quite as well
That you should find it out;
So think the matter o'er.

SISTER.
It's what comes in our heads when we
Play at 'Let's make believe',
And when we play at 'Guessing'.

BROTHER.
And I have heard it said to be
A talent often makes us grieve,
And sometimes proves a blessing.[47]

This is a riddle which enacts its own lesson, not only teaching children about fancy but encouraging its expression; offering a portrait
of children experimenting with rhyme in order to prompt a child
reader into response. The poem opens with a portrait of a child care-
lessly dashing off a homework task; there is a winning colloquial
immediacy to the brother's 'stupid lines' insult, which sparks his

---

[47] 'What Is Fancy?', *Poetry for Children, Entirely Original*, 2 vols (London: M. J.
Godwin, for the Juvenile Library, 1809), II, pp. 50–2.

sister into response. The siblings' conversation suggests the importance of peer learning, as the definition of fancy is produced through the back-and-forth of dialogue rather than from an authority figure: 'what comes in our heads when we [. . .] play at "Guessing"'. And indeed, the reader needs to guess at the overall meaning of the poem. Fancy, or imagination, is presented as an uncertain good: the sister's playful, pleasurable evocation of 'make believe' is followed up by the brother's note of warning, as he rhymes it with 'grieve'. We might recall Charles' brotherly care towards Mary, his one-time tutor, in the extremes of her illness: the necessary restraint of her 'fancy'. Yet the poem ends ambivalently, its final word one of 'blessing', so that the pleasurable possibilities of imagination remain open for the children. The brother has the last word, but it is an ambivalent, uncertain one; neither brother nor sister has authority in this poem, which represents a world of their own, separate from the maternal voice so often present in other writing for children. Moreover, the sibling dialogue – like the Lambs' collaboration itself – is equivocal; it is hard to know who was ultimately responsible for writing this poem, just as it is hard to know whether the brother or the sister has a better definition of 'fancy'.[48] As in many of the brother–sister dialogues of *Poetry for Children*, gender distinctions are humorously subverted: the sister shows herself, if initially uncertain, as adept as her brother at rhyme and riddle. This is underlined by the Miltonic echo of Adam instructing Eve in Book 5 of *Paradise Lost* about the strange power of 'mimic Fancy', following her troublesome dream. Adam, however, although assuming the position of educator, is himself beguiled by the 'wild work' of Eve's fancy in due course. This forms a neat parallel to the brother of the Lambs' poem, who is in reality no wiser than his sister.

Throughout this chapter, from Watts onwards, we have seen how poetry for children seeks to mirror their experience of the everyday world, drawing, as in Barbauld's work, on familiar language or domestic situations even as it incorporates broader literary allusions. The Lambs' poetry, too, is familiar verse – in the sense both of colloquial and informal, but also something familial and intimate, which seeks to open up the power of the fancy in the space of the everyday.

---

[48] For an interestingly gendered reading of the poem, see Darlene Ciraulo, 'Fairy Magic and the Female Imagination: Mary Lamb's *A Midsummer Night's Dream*', *Philological Quarterly* 78.4 (1999), 439–53.

Indeed, the earnestness of the brother and sister seeking to define 'fancy' might be read as a wry nursery take on Romantic debates – for example, by Coleridge – around the primacy of the imagination and its distinction from fancy. Both the Lambs were interested in the nature of the child's imagination: its power, and its dangers. The poem might be set alongside, say, Elia's later musings on the 'poverty of my dreams' in 'Witches and Other Night-Fears', an essay which dwells on the terrifying power of the child's fantasies, while at the same time satirising Romantic flights of fancy.[49] Mary Lamb's story 'The Young Mahometan', in which the child Margaret Green descends into delirium through a course of lonely reading, similarly carefully negotiates its way through an excess of imagination.[50]

This gently amusing riddle, with its appeal to the child's own power of make-believe and its teasing Miltonic echoes, speaks to a deeper effort to unite education and imaginative play through the long eighteenth century, right back to Watts' attempts to capture the child's attention through verse, tapping into 'something so amusing and entertaining in rhymes and metre'. We began with Charles Lamb's outburst against educational literature by women; this sly poem reminds us to enquire more sceptically into a brother's hasty dismissal, and to take seriously women's educational writing of the period, in all its diverse genres. *Poetry for Children* provides us with a playful example of the ways in which the educational task and imaginative fancy, far from being opposed, were in dialogue with one another in the period, and testifies to the imaginative force of women's educational writing through the eighteenth and into the nineteenth century.

Works Cited

Primary

Manuscript

Royal Asiatic Society, Thomas Manning Archive, TM/2/3/7.

---

[49] See Mary and Charles Lamb, *Works*, II, p. 69.
[50] 'The Young Mahometan', in *Mrs. Leicester's School* (London: M. J. Godwin at the Juvenile Library, 1809), pp. 94–109.

Printed Materials

[Anon.], *Tommy Thumb's Pretty Song-Book* (London: no publisher, 1744)

[Anon.], *Tommy Thumb's Song Book, for All Little Masters and Misses, to Be Sung to Them by Their Nurses, until They Can Sing Themselves, by Nurse Lovechild, to Which Is Added a Letter from a Lady on Nursing* (Glasgow: Lumsden and Son, 1814)

Aikin, Lucy, *Poetry for Children: Consisting of Short Pieces, to Be Committed to Memory* (London: Longman, Hurst, Rees, Orme and Brown, 1801)

Barbauld, Anna Letitia, *Hymns in Prose for Children* (London: Johnson, 1781).

——. *The Poems of Anna Letitia Barbauld*, ed. by William McCarthy and Elizabeth Kraft (Athens and London: University of Georgia Press, 1994).

——. *The Works of Anna Laetitia Barbauld, with a Memoir by Lucy Aikin*, 2 vols (London: Longman Hurst, 1825)

Boswell, James and Samuel Johnson, *Boswell's Life of Johnson Together with Boswell's Journal of a Tour to the Hebrides and Johnson's Diary of a Journey into North Wales*, ed. by George Birkbeck Hill, rev. by L. F. Powell, 6 vols (Oxford: Clarendon Press, 1934)

Lamb, Mary, 'The Young Mahometan', in *Mrs. Leicester's School* (London: M. J. Godwin at the Juvenile Library, 1809), pp. 94–109

Lamb, Mary, and Charles Lamb, *Poetry for Children, Entirely Original*, 2 vols (London: M. J. Godwin, for the Juvenile Library, 1809)

——. *The Works of Charles and Mary Lamb*, ed. by E. V. Lucas, 6 vols (London: Methuen, 1912)

——. *The Letters of Charles and Mary Lamb*, ed. by Edwin W. Marrs, Jr., 3 vols (New York: Cornell University Press, 1975–8)

Locke, John, *Some Thoughts Concerning Education* (London: 1693)

Plumptre, James, *Letters to John Aikin, M. D.: On His Volume of Vocal Poetry* (Cambridge: 1811)

Scolfield, William [William Godwin], *Bible Stories: Memorable Acts of the Ancient Patriarchs, Judges and Kings. Extracted from Their Original Historians for the Use of Children*, 2 vols (London: R. Phillips, 1803)

Southey, Robert, *The Life and Correspondence of Robert Southey*, ed. by Charles Cuthbert Southey, 6 vols (London: Longman, Brown, Green, and Longmans, 1850)

Talfourd, Thomas Noon, *Final Memorials of Charles Lamb*, 2 vols (London: Edward Moxon, 1848)

Watts, Isaac, *Divine Songs Attempted in Easy Language for the Use of Children* (1715 edition), ed. by J. H. P. Pafford (London: Oxford University Press, 1971)

Secondary

Aaron, Jane, *A Double Singleness* (Oxford: Clarendon Press, 1991)

Ciraulo, Darlene, 'Fairy Magic and the Female Imagination: Mary Lamb's *A Midsummer Night's Dream*', *Philological Quarterly* 78.4 (1999), 439–53

Craciun, Adriana, *Fatal Women of Romanticism* (Cambridge: Cambridge University Press, 2002)

Darton, F. J. Harvey, *Children's Books in England: Five Centuries of Social Life* (Cambridge: Cambridge University Press, 1932)

Gregory, Melissa Valiska, 'Women Writers, Nineteenth Century Nursery Rhyme and Lyric Innovation', *Literature Compass*, 12.3 (2015), 106–18

Grenby, Matthew, 'Godwin's Popular Stories for the Nursery', in *New Approaches to William Godwin: Forms, Fears, Futures*, ed. by Eliza O'Brien, Helen Stark and Beatrice Turner (London: Palgrave Macmillan, 2021), pp. 185–213

Halpin, David, 'Pedagogy and the Romantic Imagination', *British Journal of Educational Studies*, 56.1 (2008), 59–75

Hansson, John-Erik, '"To teach every principle of the infidels and republicans?": William Godwin through His Children's Books' (doctoral dissertation, Florence: European University Institute, 2018). Cadmus permanent link: <http://hdl.handle.net/1814/59870> [accessed 10 June 2022]

Hickey, Alison, 'Double Bonds: Charles Lamb's Romantic Collaborations', *ELH*, 63.3 (1996), 735–71

Lucas, E. V., *Lamb and the Lloyds* (London: Smith, Elder and Co., 1898)

McCarthy, William, *Anna Letitia Barbauld: Voice of the Enlightenment* (Baltimore: Johns Hopkins University Press, 2008)

Mee, Jon, *Romanticism, Enthusiasm, and Regulation: Poetics and the Policing of Culture in the Romantic Period* (Oxford: Oxford University Press, 2003)

Newbon, Pete, *The Boy-Man: Creativity and Masculinity in the Long Nineteenth Century* (London: Palgrave Macmillan, 2019)

Richardson, Alan, *Literature, Education, and Romanticism: Reading as Social Practice, 1780–1832* (Cambridge: Cambridge University Press, 1994)

Ruwe, Donelle, *British Children's Poetry in the Romantic Era: Verse, Riddle, and Rhyme* (Basingstoke and New York: Palgrave Macmillan, 2014)

Schneller, Beverly, 'John Hill and Mary Cooper: A Case Study in Eighteenth-Century Publishing', in *Fame and Fortune: Sir John Hill and London Life in the 1750s*, ed. by Clare Brant and George Rousseau (London: Palgrave Macmillan, 2018), pp. 107–20

Stokes, Christopher, *Romantic Prayer: Reinventing the Poetics of Devotion, 1773–1832* (Oxford: Oxford University Press, 2021)

Styles, Morag, *From the Garden to the Street: An Introduction to 300 Years of Poetry for Children* (London: Cassell, 1997)

Treadwell, Michael, 'London Trade Publishers 1675–1750', *The Library*, 6th ser., 4.2 (June 1982), 99–134

Wakely-Mulroney, Katherine, and Louise Joy, *The Aesthetics of Children's Poetry: A Study of Children's Verse in English* (Oxford and New York: Routledge, 2018)

Watson, J. R., 'The Hymns of Isaac Watts and the Tradition of Dissent', in *Dissenting Praise: Religious Dissent and the Hymn in England and Wales*, ed. by Isabel Rivers and David L. Wykes (Oxford: Oxford University Press, 2011), pp. 33–67

Chapter 3

Women Writing Geography Texts, 1790–1830

Michèle Cohen

Instructing the young in geography began in Britain in the eighteenth century. John Locke advised that it could be taught to young children in his treatise *Some Thoughts Concerning Education*.[1] As a new subject of instruction, geography was presented variously as a 'useful amusement for boys', a 'delightful and useful Amusement for Ladies', an 'accomplishment for gentlemen'. Like much science in the eighteenth century, geography was perceived as a polite subject, useful for contributing to conversation in the spaces of sociability of eighteenth-century culture.[2] According to a contemporary commentator, adults 'cannot well converse either with Men or Books [. . .] without some knowledge of geography'.[3] It was also thought the best subject 'to initiate [the Fair Sex] in the study of useful knowledge'.[4] The minds of both sexes were considered 'improvable', and 'to occasion an innate love of Virtue and Knowledge must be to increase human felicity [. . .] Science naturally tends to enlarge ideas, to give a benevolence of mind, to moderate the passions, and to render human

---

[1] See John Blair, *The History of the Rise and Progress of Geography* (London: T. Cadell, 1784); John Locke, *Some Thoughts Concerning Education*, in *The Educational Writings of John Locke*, ed. by John William Adamson (Cambridge: Cambridge University Press, 1922), Section 178, pp. 146–7.

[2] James A. Secord, 'How Scientific Conversation Became Shop Talk', *Transactions of the Royal Historical Society*, 17 (2007), 129–56; *Science and Spectacle in the European Enlightenment*, ed. by Bernadette Bensaude-Vincent and Christine Blondel (Aldershot: Ashgate, 2008).

[3] William Butler, *Exercises on the Globes: Interspersed with Some Historical, Biographical, Chronological, Mythological, and Miscellaneous Information; on a New Plan: Designed for the Use of Young Ladies* [1800] (London: T. Mawman, 1803), p. 73.

[4] *The Young Lady's Geography* (London: R. Baldwin; T. Lownds, 1765), Preface, n.p.

nature charming.'[5] Because of the moral necessity of improvement associated with the practice of politeness, geography texts often had a didactic objective.[6]

Taught by and to both sexes, geography instruction was largely not gendered. Although some texts were designed for 'Ladies', this did not mean their content was made easier than that taught to males. Rather, it meant avoiding the use of language or concepts females tended not to learn, such as Latin or geometry.[7] William Butler's *Exercises on the Globes Specifically for the Use of Young Ladies* (1803), for example, was not simplified but amplified. He required his pupils to learn definitions and technical terms and provided 'anecdotes from biography, and [. . .] facts from natural history and the annals of nations' to construct a wide cultural frame for dry designations. For instance, Butler's definition of longitude includes a reference to Hipparchus, who 'determined the longitude and latitude of places; which he effected by observing the stars, and thus, by connecting geography with astronomy, fixed that science on certain principles'.[8] Nor are the problems on the Globes simplified for female consumption; they are identical to those in other schoolbooks.

This chapter examines the construction and significance of geography works by women, a topic that has not been examined systematically, if at all. As geography was a new subject of instruction, no author or teacher of geography had been formally taught the subject. They might not even be geography specialists.[9] For instance, William Guthrie, late eighteenth-century author of the highly popular *A New Geographical, Historical, and Commercial Grammar* (1779), was a historian and political journalist.[10] Little is known about male or female author-practitioners, who reveal little about themselves in their works, placing the focus on the content of the geography books, rather than on the author-practitioners who wrote them.

[5] S. Harrington, *New and Elegant Amusements for the Ladies of Great Britain* (London: S. Crowder, 1772), dedication.

[6] John Clarke, *An Essay upon Study* (Dublin: Edward Exshaw, 1736), p. 106; *The Young Lady's Geography*, Preface, n.p.

[7] Harrington, dedication.

[8] Butler, pp. v, 24–5.

[9] Paul Stock points this out in *Europe and the British Geographical Imagination, 1760–1830* (Oxford: Oxford University Press, 2019).

[10] William Guthrie, *A New Geographical, Historical, and Commercial Grammar*, 6th edn (London: Edward and Charles Dilly, 1771); see Robert Mayhew, 'William Guthrie's Geographical Grammar, the Scottish Enlightenment and the Politics of British Geography', *Scottish Geographical Journal*, 115.1 (1999), 19–34.

Most eighteenth-century geography books for instruction and for the general public were compilations which 'set out to accumulate and disseminate conventional knowledge',[11] goals without explicit methods or structures. Since geography was a new subject, it lacked both an instructional tradition and pedagogical norms, so authors were free to innovate within the conventions dictated by the factual subject matter, but most books authored by men and women were constructed on a two-part model. The repeated use of this model helped codify the subject into a discipline. The first part featured 'general' or mathematical geography, and the second part featured 'particular' geography.[12] The 'general' part described the terraqueous globe in terms of the physical features of land and waters, including mountains, islands, bays, capes and promontories, lakes, oceans, rivers. It included a section on the use of globes, which explained the concepts relating to mathematical measurements of the artificial globe in terms of latitude, longitude, meridians, horizon etc. The 'particular' part consisted of 'discursive expositions' about the continents and their political divisions into countries, cities, ports, and might include any or all of the following: people, manners, language customs, religion and government, natural products, minerals and metals, and animals, curiosities, new geographical discoveries and unusual phenomena.[13] This chapter describes the approaches and specific methods that women deployed within this model to present geography, showing how the writings of female authors contributed to the consolidation of this new subject into a discipline.

'Local' Approaches to Teaching Geography

The 'local' approach to teaching geography begins with what children presumably know already, such as their surrounding area and its topography.[14] The women geography writers who developed the approach in the late eighteenth and early nineteenth centuries situated

---

[11] Stock, p. 37.

[12] The division of geography between 'general' and 'particular' has a long history. For the origin of the use of these terms to describe geography, see J. N. L. Baker, *The History of Geography* (Oxford: Basil Blackwell, 1963), p. 113.

[13] 'Discursive expositions' is a term used by Harry Robinson in 'Geography in the Dissenting Academies', *Geography*, 36.3 (1951), 179–86 (p. 185).

[14] A. S. Harrison et al., *Studies and Impressions, 1902–1952* (London: Institute of Education, 1952), p. 32.

the instruction in domestic spaces to encourage children's engagement. In *Geography and History, Written by a Lady for the Use of
Her Own Children* (1790), the author recommended that geography
instruction begin with showing the child

> the county he lives in, and a few adjacent ones; pointing out to him his
> own town; explaining to him that it appears but a speck, because the
> map is little [. . .] then shewing any other towns that are familiar to his
> ear, where any of his acquaintances come from, etc.[15]

At a time when instructing children was a matter of 'getting facts
into the child's mind and making them stick there', children's capacities for learning, this author argues, should make them active participants in their learning.[16] She recommends the use of play, especially
dissected maps, as a means of engaging the child in the subject.[17]
Even though the rest of her text follows the conventional structure
and content I have outlined above, she continues to engage the reader
by including occasional footnotes suggesting amusing exercises or
extra reading, an innovation no other author followed. This author's
use of footnotes suggests her awareness of the importance of differ-
entiating prescribed topics for the interests and abilities of individual
students.

   Similarly, Jane Marcet's *Conversations with Children: On Land
and Water* (1838) shapes its geography lessons within a domestic
narrative guided by Mrs B., the mother in the 'female mentorial tradition'.[18] The story begins with children who have been building sand

[15] *Geography and History Selected by a Lady for the Use of Her Own Children*
(London: B. Law, 1790), p. iv. The author signs her preface E.R. Linda Hannas
claims that E.R. is Elizabeth Roberts in *The English Jigsaw Puzzle, 1760–1890*
(London: Wayland Publishers, 1972), p. 61.

[16] J. E. Vaughan, 'Aspects of Teaching Geography in England in the Nineteenth
Century', *Paedagogica Historica*, 12.1 (2006), 128–47 (p. 135); *Geography and
History*, pp. iii–vi.

[17] Dissected maps were an instructive geography jigsaw puzzle invented in mid-
eighteenth-century England or France, writes Jill Shefrin in *Neatly Dissected for
the Instruction of Young Ladies and Gentlemen in the Knowledge of Geography:
John Spilsbury and Early Dissected Puzzles* (Los Angeles: Cotsen Occasional
Press, 1999); see also Hannas; Martin Norgate, 'Cutting Borders: Dissected
Maps and the Origins of the Jigsaw Puzzle', *Cartographic Journal*, 44.4 (2007),
342–50.

[18] Jane Marcet, *Conversations with Children: On Land and Water*, 3rd edn (London:
Longman, Brown, Green and Longman, 1843); Mitzi Myers, 'Impeccable
Governesses, Rational Dames, and Moral Mothers: Mary Wollstonecraft and

mountains in the garden. This prompts a lesson on mountains and springs and on the ways in which different physical manifestations of water relate to land, such as 'how rivers find their way to the sea', and how physical aspects of the earth relate to sociopolitical aspects, for example, considering 'why towns are usually built on Rivers'. Using a dialogic method of instruction, Mrs B. asks:

> cannot you guess any reason why the neighbourhood of a river should be preferred? Perhaps, that people may catch fish in it for their dinner, said Caroline, or perhaps, observed William, for the pleasure of bathing and swimming in summer, and sliding and skating in winter. There are much more important reasons than those to induce men to build towns on rivers, said their mother.[19]

The answers provided by the child characters rehearse experiences with rivers that will be familiar to the child, opening the possibility for the instructor-mother to prepare them for more abstract and scientific explanations. The conversational format gave fictional children a space to express their opinions or judgements. A key feature of this method was for the instructor or parent to 'draw' children out with questions to encourage them to think, so that their questions and comments had a role in the development of the text.[20] Significantly, the format also allowed child characters to translate the impersonal, scientific descriptions into familiar language and images which served to aid child readers' understanding. Thus, when Mrs B. explains that transporting goods via rivers is cheaper than transporting food and heavy materials on land, Sophy adds: 'that is true. When things are brought in a waggon, you must not only pay for the waggon but for the horses that draw it.'[21] Marcet uses Sophy's voice to make children recall their own first-hand experiences and relate the information presented to their everyday lives.

Papa and Mamma's Easy Lessons in Geography (1850) by Anna Maria Sargeant is also structured as a domestic narrative, showing the popularity of the technique of basing a local approach on familial education. Papa teaches his children geography because Kate,

---

the Female Tradition in Georgian Children's Books', *Children's Literature*, 14 (1986), 31–59 (p. 50).

[19] Marcet, p. 26.

[20] Michèle Cohen, 'The Pedagogy of Conversation in the Home: "Familiar Conversation" as a Pedagogical Tool in Eighteenth- and Nineteenth-Century England', *Oxford Review of Education*, 41.4 (2015), 447–63.

[21] Marcet, pp. 26, 62.

the youngest child, finds learning geography with her governess 'too hard'. Mr Goodwin uses a conversational method and a local approach which links abstract knowledge with what is already known to children through the evidence of their own bodies:

> 'Where will you sit, papa?' asked Kate
>   'Put me a chair to the south'
>   'South, papa! Oh, I do not know which is the south; you must tell me first, if you please.'

Mr Goodwin explains to the children how north and south can be identified in relation to the position of the sun by asking them where the sun rises and sets, and encouraging them to use their bodies for their orientation in space: 'If you stand with your face to the setting sun, that is, with your back to the east, your right hand will be north.'[22]

The 'local' approach was used primarily by female authors, suggesting that there may have been minor differences in the pedagogies implemented by women and by men. This approach to geography, a method designed and developed by late eighteenth- and early nineteenth-century women out of their experiences with children, was reinvented by geography author and teacher James Fairgrieve in the early twentieth century.[23]

Maps

Schoolmasters James Clarke and Vicesimus Knox assumed that maps interested boys but nowhere mention girls' engagement with maps.[24] Yet, from the 1780s, British schoolgirls spent hours stitching map samplers, thereby learning geography. Many of these exquisite samplers have survived and have been the subject of various exhibitions.[25]

---

[22] Anna Maria Sargeant, *Papa and Mamma's Easy Lessons in Geography* (London: Thomas Dean and Son, ?1850), p. 8.

[23] Harrison et al.

[24] John Clarke, *An Essay upon the Education of Youth in Grammar-Schools* (Dublin: Edward Exshaw, 1736); Vicesimus Knox, *Liberal Education* (London: no publisher, 1781).

[25] See Judith A. Tyner, *Stitching the World: Embroidered Maps and Women's Geographical Education* (London: Routledge, 2016); Carol Humphrey, *Sampled Lives: Samplers from the Fitzwilliam Museum* (Cambridge: Fitzwilliam Museum, 2017); Helen Wyld, *Embroidered Stories: Scottish Samplers* (Edinburgh: National

As far as we know, S. Harrington, who wrote *New Introduction to the Knowledge and Use of Maps*, designed for '*young gentlemen* and *ladies* who have a taste for *geography*' (1772), was the first female author and teacher of geography in the eighteenth century.[26] While most schoolbooks concerned with maps taught how to draw them, Harrington alone aimed to teach how to *read* them.[27] Her explanations evince a number of methodological initiatives. The first is her drawing of a prototypical, diagrammatic map to teach pupils to identify the signs and symbols used on maps to represent seas, mountains, rivers, towns. Her design is not a map *of* a specific place but a map to explain the concepts and symbols conventionally used to identify physical and sociopolitical features of the terraqueous globe.

Even though there were four editions of her text, her work on maps appears never to have been cited, not even in the *History of Women in Cartography* (2013).[28] Nevertheless, the uniqueness of her map is apparent when it is compared with the maps in conventional schoolbooks and authors' claims that 'the only successful mode of communicating a knowledge of maps is by making the pupil copy or draw them'. While Harrington taught how maps represented the features of the earth, copying maps repeatedly was, according to Goldsmith's *Geography*, 'the whole secret and business of teaching and learning geography'.[29] Harrington's skills-based education thus focused more on equipping her students to encounter new maps and gain new knowledge while avoiding wearisome repetition.

Another unusual feature of Harrington's text is her use of the pronoun 'we' and her address of the pupils as 'you', as if she is speaking to them personally instead of using the impersonal declarative form common in most geographies. She also uses informal language,

---

Museum of Scotland, 2018); Witney Antiques, *Samplers: Mapped and Charted* (Witney: Witney Antiques, 2005). See also Susan Schulten, 'Map Drawing, Graphic Literacy, and Pedagogy in the Early Republic', *History of Education Quarterly*, 57.2 (2017), 185–220.

[26] S. Harrington, *New Introduction to the Knowledge and Use of Maps*, 3rd edn (London: S. Crowder, 1774). Harrington indicated that she was female and a teacher of geography in the preface to *Amusements*, pp. viii–ix.

[27] See, for example, Thomas Keith, *Short and Easy Introduction to the Science of Geography*, 5th edn (London: no publisher, 1805); J. Goldsmith, *Geography for the Use of Schools* (London: Richard Phillips, 1803).

[28] Will C. van den Hoonaard, *Map Worlds: A History of Women in Cartography* (Waterloo, ON: Wilfrid Laurier University Press, 2013).

[29] Goldsmith, p. iv.

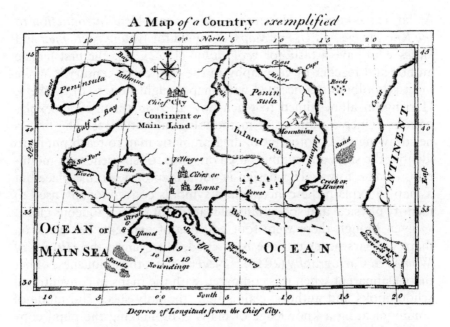

S. Harrison, *New Introduction to the Knowledge and Use of Maps* (1774). By Courtesy of the British Library.

when appropriate, making the subject feel more accessible and less institutionalised:

> Let us take notice by what Figures the various parts of Land and Water are described in a Map, and in what manner they are represented. [. . .] Rocks are sometimes made *like little pointed things sticking up* sharp in the Sea. (p. 30, emphasis added)

Harrington's method for teaching technical concepts such as latitude and longitude illustrates a further innovation. Having stated that 'latitude and longitude' are the 'very foundations of geography' (p. 39), she does not just provide definitions of the concepts, as most geography texts tended to do. Instead, she invites the pupil to imagine travelling 'from *London* to *Dover*', counting 'the miles as we travel and reckon them from *London*', asking them to calculate the longitude as they stop at towns along the way. Her method suggests that anyone could perform this mental operation, and provides the pupil with a means of understanding that longitude is not just an abstract concept. Only after she has paved the way with this illustration does she give a comprehensive definition of the concept (pp. 41–2), ensuring that when it comes, the learner already has a context for the information that is supplied.

In a similar way to Harrington, Mrs Wilkinson's work on maps avoids rote learning, and hence the implication that geography consists of fixed knowledge. Volume 1 of *Atlas for the Use of Schools* (1816) includes fourteen maps of the 'eastern and Western Hemisphere', including the continents and individual countries of Western and Southern Europe. The second volume comprises 'The Blank Duplicates' of the same maps, outlines for the pupil to recognise and fill in as required. The advantage of blank maps, explained Wilkinson, was that they allowed the study of 'a picture' with 'shape and tangibility' and avoided 'committing to memory the phrases of a science which they do not comprehend'. Wilkinson maintained that 'youth of both sexes could quickly learn to draw and imitate maps [. . .] for the Practice of the Hand speedily instructs the Mind, and strongly confirms the memory beyond any other Method whatever'.[30] Blank maps were also 'an easy method of learning [. . .] the situation of the countries of the earth and coasts of the sea' because they worked with 'a prepared plan'.[31] This method of geographic instruction proved popular: books of outlines of maps were sold by eighteenth-century publishers and were 'aggressively' marketed among the new consumer goods relating to education in general and geography in particular.[32]

Physical Geography

Geography was a highly popular modern subject for both males and females in the late eighteenth and early nineteenth centuries. As new information became available, geographical knowledge expanded and fragmented into different specialisms. Journalist and critic Elizabeth Rigby complained in 1844 that geography's 'ramifications into

---

[30] Miss Wilkinson, *Geographical Exercises: or, A New Method of Acquiring a Knowledge of Geography by Drawing Maps* (Stourport: no publisher, 1798), preface; Miss Wilkinson, *An Atlas for the Use of Schools: Part I. The Maps at Large, Part II. The Blank Duplicates* (Stourport: no publisher, 1816), preface.

[31] Robert Wilkinson, *An Easy Method of Learning Geography* (London: Robert Wilkinson, 1796), title page. He was a cartographer and publisher, and Miss Wilkinson's husband.

[32] Jill Shefrin, '"Make it a pleasure and not a task": Educational Games for Children in Georgian England', *Princeton University Library Chronicle*, 60.2 (Winter, 1999), 251–75 (p. 252).

"Civil Geography", "Historical Geography", "Political Geography", "Physical Geography", "Natural Geography", "Grammar of Geography" [. . .] gave good old *common* Geography" [. . .] but a slender chance'.[33] Schoolbook author Hugo Reid did not consider this fragmentation a problem. On the contrary, in his schoolbook, *Elements of Physical Geography* (1850), he maintained that 'Physical Geography or Natural Geography, Ordinary or Political Geography, Mathematical Geography, And Geology' together constituted 'the subject of Geography [. . .] meaning, a description of the earth'.[34] In the 1840s, two books titled *Physical Geography* were published by women: the first by Rosina Zornlin in 1840, the second by Mary Somerville in 1848.[35] Physical geography was a relative newcomer in nineteenth-century geography, its objects, according to Zornlin, having only recently been elevated to the 'dignity of a science'.[36] Earlier publications such as Goldsmith's *Grammar of Geography*, which included sections on physical geography, only described briefly the climate, winds, tides and earthquakes, mostly in relation to South and North America and Africa, and then focused on the human race, linking the origin of racial differentiation to the climate.[37]

Although there is no evidence that Somerville knew Zornlin's work, intriguingly, since physical geography was a new approach to the subject, both authors shared certain geographical perspectives. For example, both women focused on descriptions of the earth as God's creation rather than the political and social divisions of the earth created by humans. This approach stresses the physical and geological features of the earth, the great variety of animal and vegetal species, and the processes that underlie some of the variations: temperature, atmosphere, climate, evaporation. Both texts are structured thematically around features of the earth – land and water, lakes, rivers, springs, mountain ranges and valleys, volcanoes – illustrating them by reference to their occurrence and situations in different parts of the globe. According

[33] Elizabeth Rigby, 'Children's Books', *Quarterly Review*, 74 (June–Oct. 1844), 1–26 (p. 13).
[34] Hugo Reid, *Elements of Physical Geography, for the Use of Schools and Private Students* (Edinburgh: Oliver and Boyd, 1850), p. 5.
[35] Rosina Zornlin, *Recreations in Physical Geography: or, The Earth as It Is* (London: John W. Parker, 1840); Mary Somerville, *Physical Geography*, 2 vols (London: John Murray, 1848).
[36] Zornlin, p. 1.
[37] The 1829 edition of the *Grammar* is the first of the many editions of this text to have included a section on physical geography.

to Zornlin, physical geography 'directs our attention to the general structure of the terrestrial globe, to the atmosphere by which it is surrounded, and to the distribution of organized beings on its surface'. It also 'attempts to discover the laws by which the whole earth is governed' and to 'reduce' these laws to 'a few general principles'. The study of these laws, she reasons, fixes the mind 'on nature's Ruler', and on 'the Omnipotence and the Omnipresence of the deity' (p. 2). At the same time, Zornlin highlighted the 'considerable [. . .] practical advantages' of physical geography 'to a nation possessing extensive colonies' (p. 4) in different parts of the globe. She suggests that the geographer can help reconcile religion and commerce because its content encompasses both fields, describing the 'friendly intercourse' between 'barbarous people and Christian explorers and traders' as something that contributes to the employment of 'our manufacturing population' (pp. 407–8).

Somerville's text is more comprehensive than Zornlin's, as it includes descriptions of geological processes such as mineral veins and metalliferous deposits, and provides detailed descriptions of the global distribution of flora, insects, marine and land animals. Somerville defines physical geography as 'a description of the earth, the sea, and the air, with their inhabitants [. . .] and the distribution of these organized beings and the causes of that distribution'.[38] As her focus on the significance of the 'causes' of distribution implies, she saw the world through a unitary frame, 'structured by the Creator'.[39] One remarkable feature of Somerville's style is that she puts the reader in the position of a spectator observing the 'enormous prodigality' and beauty of the geology of the earth as well as its animal and plant life.[40] This stance of the detached observer corresponds with the way Somerville remained aloof from considerations of utility and commerce, contributing to the image of the scientist, a term coined in connection with her.[41]

---

[38] Somerville, *Physical Geography*, 2nd edn (1849), quoted in Mary Sanderson, 'Mary Somerville: Her Work in Physical Geography', *Geographical Review*, 64.3 (Jul. 1974), 410–20 (p. 410).

[39] Kathryn A. Neely, *Mary Somerville: Science, Illumination, and the Female Mind* (Cambridge: Cambridge University Press, 2001), p. 136.

[40] Somerville, II, p. 151.

[41] The term 'scientist' was first used in connection with Mary Somerville in the *Quarterly Review*, writes David Knight, *Natural Sciences Books in English 1600–1900* (Tiptree, Essex: Batsford, 1989), p. 202.

The Hand of the Almighty

Most of the women writing about the physical aspects of the terraqueous globe referred to its wonders as a manifestation of the Deity,
suggesting that geography was seen, at least by some, as a subset of
the branch of theology. Women's references to the Creator brought
together science and religion in language which 'employs the cadences
of both science and poetry'.[42] Somerville's *Physical Geography*, argues Kathryn Neely, 'blends science, nature and natural theology'
and uses a 'scientific sublime', which 'allows the reader "an encounter with the attributes of God revealed in nature by science"'.[43]

> The earthquake and the torrent, the august and terrible ministers
> of Almighty Power, have torn the solid earth and opened the seals of
> the most ancient records of creation, written in indelible characters on
> the 'perpetual hills and the everlasting mountains'. There we read of the
> changes that have brought the rude mass to its present fair state [. . .]
> Who shall define the periods of those mornings and evenings when God
> saw that his work was good? [. . .] These stupendous changes may be but
> cycles in those great laws of the universe, where all is variable but the
> laws themselves, and He who has ordained them.[44]

Somerville's dramatic language – terming natural features the 'terrible
ministers' of God – situates the geological practice of reading the age
of the earth through examining rock strata and composition within
the Judeo-Christian creation story by suggesting that the 'mornings'
and 'evenings' are poetic expressions of indefinite amounts of time.
Here, then, geography provides a means of reflecting on the work
and power of God.

Similarly, Mrs Sherwood's *Introduction to Geography, Intended
for Little Children* (1820) fused the definitions and descriptions of
geography with scripture to show them as united:

GEOGRAPHY

Geography is the description of the earth, and of the counties which it
contains. The earth is composed of land and water.

---

[42] Erin K. Johns Speese, '"Our feelings become impressed with the grandeur of omnipotence": Mary Somerville's Feminine Scientific Sublime', *Prose Studies*, 35.2
(2013), 171–88 (p. 172).

[43] Neely, p. 128; Speese, p. 173.

[44] Somerville, I, pp. 2–3. See J. N. L. Baker, 'Mary Somerville and Geography in
England', *Geographical Journal*, 111.4/6 (Apr.–June 1948), 207–22.

'And God said, Let the waters under heaven be gathered unto one place, and let the dry land appear: and it was so. And God called the dry land Earth; and the gathering together of the waters called he the seas: and God saw that it was good' (*Gen. i. 9, 10*).[45]

In some ways this merging is unsurprising: 'the sciences were routinely understood to be part of a theological understanding of nature'.[46] Yet very few geography texts written by men over the period even mention the Deity, including Hugo Reid's *Elements of Physical Geography* (1850), the only text on physical geography published by a man in that period. This suggests that women writing geography perceived fewer disciplinary boundaries between geography and theology, though the reasons for this are beyond the remit of this chapter to explore.

Geography and History

Geography, a new subject of instruction, was often linked with history, an old discipline, suggesting an attempt to justify the new discipline through an association to an established field of study. Some educationists considered geography to be necessary to the study of history, but only as an adjunct. In his *Essay on a Course of Liberal Education* (1765), Joseph Priestley promoted the study of geography because he thought it one of the 'eyes' of history (the other 'eye' is chronology), enabling readers of history to have 'clear and distinct' ideas of what happened and where. But he was not interested in the 'science of geography' as such, and did not discuss it. Headmaster Vicesimus Knox valued geography for a similar reason: boys 'engaged in reading [. . .] historians antient and modern' were 'travelling in the dark', as he put it, if they were unacquainted with geography.[47]

Several women author-practitioners titled their books 'geography and history', but the content of these books suggests that the addition of 'and history' acted chiefly to lend a measure of gravitas.

---

[45] Mrs [Martha] Sherwood, *An Introduction to Geography, Intended for Little Children*, 2nd edn (Wellington: F. Houlston and Son, 1820), p. 1.

[46] Aileen Fyfe, 'Science and Religion in Popular Publishing in 19th-century Britain', in *Clashes of Knowledge: Orthodoxies and Heterodoxies in Science and Religion*, ed. by Peter Meusburger, Michael Welker and Edgar Wunder (New York: Springer, 2008), pp. 121–32.

[47] Joseph Priestley, *An Essay on a Course of Liberal Education for Civil and Active Life* [1765], 3rd edn (Dublin: Luke White and P. Byrne, 1791), pp. 201–2; Knox, p. 166.

In *Geography and History* (1790), written by a Lady, and in Miss Kennedy's *Outlines of Geography and History* (1799), written for the pupils of her school, the geography sections are similar, but the history sections differ greatly. The geography section of *Geography and History*, as discussed earlier, is conventionally structured around the descriptions of the terraqueous globe. The section on history consists of a chronology, based on 'Extracts from Guthrie's Chronological Table of Remarkable Events, Discoveries, and Inventions, with some additions'. It begins with Homer in 907 BC and ends in AD 1789. It also includes Guthrie's 'Table of Men of Learning and Genius among the ancients', and provides lists of men of learning and celebrated artists associated with most countries of Europe. This global (rather than local) approach contrasts with Miss Kennedy's book. The geography section of Miss Kennedy's schoolbook uses a question-and-answer format to instruct about the physical and political geography of the continents, starting conventionally with Europe, its political divisions and its natural features. But she differs from conventional texts because she intends 'to make her pupils early acquainted with the history of their own country'. She introduces Ireland before Britain and devotes much more geographical and historical information to it than to any other country, including Britain. Her historical narrative is a mix of sacred and secular history: she begins both geography lessons and the biblical narrative in Asia, the birthplace of 'Our Saviour'. She also ornaments her history with imaginary details, suggesting that mankind learned the arts relating to food 'probably from his Creator'.[48] Kennedy's national historical focus, presumably designed to increase student engagement with the material, was echoed in other female-authored geography works: Ellin Devis, who ran a fashionable boarding school in Upper Wimpole Street in London, included a secular list of the kings of England in her very brief *Introduction to Geography* (c.1790).[49] It is not clear why these authors included history in their texts, especially as it was not linked to their geography section. In view of Priestley and Knox's comments, one possibility is that they thought it would add a degree of scholarliness to their texts, texts which in other respects revel in the freedom that geography authors could exercise in selecting what to include in their books.

---

[48] Miss Kennedy, *Outlines of Geography and History: Intended for the Use of Schools* (Dublin: D. Graisberry, 1799), pp. v, 129.

[49] [Ellin Devis], *Introduction to Geography: For the Use of Mrs Devis's Little Society* (London: no publisher, c.1790), pp. 164–86.

Geography and Travel

A few women travelled abroad and wrote accounts of their travels, such as Lady Hester Stanhope, who set out for the Middle East in 1810, but most female (and male) authors of geography books and schoolbooks stayed home and researched, read, compiled and imagined or translated travels. The lady author of *Geography and History*, whose pedagogical insight has already been mentioned, suggested that it would be 'amusing to children, and at the same time very instructive, to let them make an imaginary voyage through all the seas and straits of Europe', and describes how this could be done.[50] Priscilla Wakefield did more than this. She integrated the teaching of geography and travel stories. Although Wakefield is now best known for her *Reflection on the Present Condition of the Female Sex; with Suggestions for Its Improvement* (1798), in her time she was famous as an author of children's books. Her most popular publication in this genre was *The Juvenile Travellers: Containing the Remarks of a Family during a Tour through the Principal States and Kingdoms of Europe with an Account of Their Inhabitants, Natural Production, and Curiosities* (1801), a title which sums up the geographical content of the text.[51]

The story is constructed as a domestic fiction framing parental instruction of their children. Mr and Mrs Seymour take their children, Theodore, almost fourteen, and Laura, twelve, travelling through Europe, 'with the hope of increasing their knowledge, and promoting their general improvement' (p. 3). From the start, pedagogy is at the heart of the story. This was a frequent feature of books for children written between the late eighteenth and early nineteenth centuries. Instruction served to create the idealised family, involving the good parents or relatives who devote their time to teaching children about a variety of subjects.[52] Wakefield's book exploits geography for this

---

[50] *Geography and History*, p. 10. Geography author and instructor Joseph Ouiseau developed a similar idea in *Practical Geography* (1828).

[51] It reached nineteen editions by 1850 (*ODNB*). Bridget Hill notes that Wakefield's 'Library Journal covering the years 1805–08 gives some impression of how she systematically researched for every book she wrote and the breadth of her reading' in 'Priscilla Wakefield as a Writer of Children's Educational Books', *Women's Writing*, 4.1 (1997), 3–15 (p. 10); see also Ruth Graham, 'Juvenile Travellers: Priscilla Wakefield's Excursions in Empire', *Journal of Imperial and Commonwealth History*, 38.3 (2010), 373–93.

[52] Diana Bailey, *Employment, The True Source of Happiness* (London: John Harris, 1825) is one example.

purpose. On the boat taking them to Hamburg, the children's 'favourite amusement' is to trace 'on the map their route to Copenhagen' (p. 3), their first planned stop. When the mother asks, 'which of you can tell me where Hamburg stands?', Theodore immediately refers to the map and describes its situation 'in the duchy of Holstein, to the north of the river Elbe' (p. 6). As they pass by a few small islands, Mrs Seymour makes sure that the children have a good look at them, for they will get 'a juster idea of the properties of an island, than any map can do' (p. 5). Theodore agrees, adding that 'it would be much easier to learn geography if instead of being taught words only, it were possible to see a representation of the things described' (p. 5). Later, Theodore is expected to recite what his father has told him about 'the King of Denmark's dominions' because, Mr Seymour has reminded him, 'we do not travel merely for amusement: unless we gain knowledge as well as pleasure, we had better stay at home' (pp. 16–17).

Their itinerary mirrors the contents page of standard geography books and schoolbooks published at the time: it starts with Northern Europe and goes east and south, ending in Turkey. However, unlike these books, Wakefield's text is no impersonal description. The detailed experiences of the child characters fuse the didactic and the personal as the geographical narrative is developed through a variety of voices: third-person narrative and the didactic voices of Mr and Mrs Seymour; the voices of the local inhabitants who obligingly explain local, national, commercial and cultural practices; the children's voices in the letters Theodore writes Laura when he and his father travel more widely on their own, and in the letters that the brother and sister write to Laura's friend Sophia in England. Theodore and Laura's letters complement each other and conform only minimally to gendered expectations: both write about people, manners and places, although Theodore includes more history. One effect of presenting geography through the eyes and the voices of children is to present learning and knowing as a pleasure. This was a key feature of Wakefield's pedagogy: she wanted her instructive texts 'to be read rather from choice than from compulsion, and be sought by [her] young readers'.[53] Wakefield's construction of the didactic narrative as family saga also renders it 'familiar' and serves to engage child readers with the protagonists' adventures. A family drama ensures this engagement. Theodore drowns in a sea swell in Sicily.

[53] Priscilla Wakefield, *Mental Improvement*, 2 vols (London: Darnton and Harvey, 1794), I, p. ii.

Laura's deep despair does not, however, interfere with her continued enjoyment of instructive travel to Spain and France, and the story ends with the miraculous discovery that Theodore is alive and well despite having had to suffer a stint as a Christian slave in Turkey.

If only a few women travelled abroad and wrote accounts of their travel, the second half of the eighteenth century saw an expansion of domestic travel and writings by women.[54] Zoe Kinsley has argued that 'it became increasingly important [. . .] for the British to recognize and celebrate the virtues of their own land, and home tour travel was a means by which this could be reassuringly achieved'. At the same time, she points out, 'home tour narratives [. . .] share many of the features common to accounts of foreign tourism', in particular, in representing 'otherness'.[55] Miss Hatfield's *The Terra Incognita of Lincolnshire* (1816) displays both of these features. Her travel narrative purports to be letters written by a female friend to her brother Frederick, who then entrusted them to her. The narrator journeys with two other ladies by carriage to 'the very extremity of Lincolnshire'.[56] The letters are meant to demonstrate the 'alternate' pleasures of rural travel (p. v) and the beauty of local nature against the general tendency to seek 'the beauties of foreign climes' (p. 23). Because of its history, even in provincial England, travellers can encounter Roman ruins including an encampment and a 'Roman tumulus or burying ground' (pp. 69, 97). They can even encounter the 'otherness' of a foreign practice in their own land. What attracts the narrator's attention in the pretty village of Colby is not 'a relic of antient greatness' but something which 'exoticized' the local. Having already designated Lincolnshire as 'Terra Incognita', she finds that the local peasants are all cultivating the white poppy to get intoxicated:

> We may without doing much violence to fancy, suppose these to be the fields on Minor Asia. [. . .] I was not a little surprised to find that this stately flower was raised for the purpose of distillation; that the villagers had frequent recourse to its Lethean juices, as an inducer to stupefaction, the worse species of intoxication. (pp. 97–9)

---

[54] Alison Mary Stenton, 'Late Eighteenth-Century Home Tours and Travel Narratives: Genre, Culture and Space' (unpublished doctoral thesis, King's College London, 2003), p. 17.

[55] Zoe Kinsley, *Women Writing the Home Tour, 1682–1812* (Aldershot: Ashgate, 2008), pp. 2, 7.

[56] Miss [Sarah] Hatfield, *The Terra Incognita of Lincolnshire* (London: G. and S. Robinson, 1816), p. 8.

The narrator is also intent on evocatively describing the domestic landscapes waiting to be discovered as the local geographic explorations help codify national aesthetics of the sublime and the pastoral. At the river Trent, she encounters a 'stupendous hill' whose 'rugged features' hang 'indignantly terrific at those waves [of the river] whose tempests have for ages beaten and torn its lacerated bosom' (p. 60). Following this terrifying scenery is an 'enchanting [. . .] pastoral' landscape that may 'vie with that of the immortally famed Arcadia of the ancient Peloponnesus' (p. 61). The local area is full of picturesque landscapes such as the 'romantic' village of Alkborough with its 'verdant hedges of thick foliage' (p. 66) and 'village steeple [. . .] gilded by a transparent sun-beam, and azure sky, "tapering, pointing to heaven"' (p. 68), suggesting that travelling in Lincolnshire is a deeply aesthetic activity that can help people engage more deeply with art and better navigate classical references. Local travel, finally, offers the uniquely emotional experience of returning to the area of one's birth, looking 'upon objects that were once dear to [one's] young heart' (p. 71) and finding out what happened since one left the area. Hatfield, a schoolmistress who authored a text on education, *Letters on the Importance of the Female Sex* (1803), ends her book with a not always coherent disquisition on the importance of the local. Nevertheless, she created a convincing blueprint for local travel and its many and varied pleasures while showing how texts on local travel could contribute to geographical knowledge.

Women could also translate foreign explorers' accounts of their travel and discoveries, enabling them to enter debates about racial otherness through the guise of translating another's words. Elizabeth Helme, mainly a children's writer, translated a book of real travels, François Le Vaillant's account of his *Travels from the Cape of Good Hope during the Years 1780–1785* (1790).[57] Le Vaillant was an ornithologist and explorer who also described the encounter of South African peoples with colonialists. Although Megan Norcia argues that English female writers of geography for children 'struggled to construe their human data in a way that would support [British] domination of other races', Helme consciously chose to translate a book which enabled her to criticise British domination of other races. Her translation includes detailed descriptions of European colonists'

---

[57] Elizabeth Helme, *Travels from the Cape of Good-Hope, into the Interior Parts of Africa, Translated from the French of Monsieur Vaillant*, 2 vols (London: William Lane, 1790).

odious treatment of the native South African peoples.[58] The Caffree's reputation as 'barbarous and bloody' has been 'circulated' by colonists to justify their abuse (I, p. 353). This is what leads them to 'perpetual war, supposing vengeance is a natural right' (I, p. 286). Helme translates Vaillant's reports that the colonists pretended to have lost cattle to justify the invasion and genocide of Caffree settlements to take away the cattle, a method 'much easier than the slow method of breeding' cattle (I, p. 353). Since little is known about Helme, it is difficult to say why she chose to translate Vaillant's texts. It is possible that the description of birds was her main interest, but it enabled her to intervene in the ongoing debates about the justice of inter-racial interactions by translating the opinions of another.[59]

Geography as Amusement

Instructional geographical games abounded, such as the one invented by Abbé Gaultier, and Barbara Hofland's *Panorama of Europe: or, a New Game of Geography*, which further enabled explorations of attitudes towards other nations and cultures.[60] Hofland's book describes the game as played by the Davenport family and their nine children. Mr Davenport directs the children, a visiting friend and Mrs Davenport to engage in role play, each representing a different country in Europe. They are given two weeks to prepare an account of the situation, 'customs, character, production, and even history' of their chosen nation. They must also be dressed 'in some way emblematical of the country they mean to represent' (p. 10). Little Anne, representing Poland, appears 'dressed in a green robe, with a circlet of towers upon her head, over which was thrown a piece of sackcloth; she had beautiful bracelets on each arm, but they were fettered, and she advanced with a mournful step, holding an inverted crown and sceptre in her hand' (p. 47). As each child arrives upon the scene,

---

[58] Megan A. Norcia, *X Marks the Spot: Women Writers Map the Empire for British Children, 1790–1895* (Athens: Ohio University Press, 2010), p. 32.

[59] See Norcia for a discussion of these debates.

[60] *A Complete Course of Geography, by Means of Instructive Games, Invented by the Abbé Gaultier* (London: Abbé Gaultier, 1795); Mrs [Barbara] Hofland, *The Panorama of Europe* (London: A. K. Newman and Co., 1813); for the meaning of 'Panorama' at the time, see Ralph Hyde, *Panoramania!: The Art of Entertainment* (London: Trefoil in association with Barbican Art Gallery, 1988).

Mr Davenport asks the questions, and the answers that follow tell the history of each country:

> *Father*. I presume, sir, you represent European Turkey?
> *Emma*. I do, sir; my boundaries are Russia, Poland, and Sclavonia [. . .]
> *Father*. You represent, my child, the most interesting place in the world; can you tell me why it is such?
> *Emma*. I think I can, papa: the country abounds with natural advantages, possessing the finest climate, the most beautiful intermixture of mountains, plain, valleys, rivers, and seas that can be imagined; but that which renders it a place endeared to every person of intelligence, is the remembrance that this was Ancient Greece, the abode of freedom, the nurse of science, the emporium of art. (pp. 81–3)

Mr Davenport's questions require the role-players to articulate some of the usual information found in geography schoolbooks in their own words, avoiding formulaic repetitions and making it seem as if the child is giving his or her opinion, as Emma does. Aside from suspending disbelief about Mrs Davenport's ability to provide the imaginatively symbolic costumes, the game is entirely plausible, and encourages children to develop a critical and a personal engagement with the knowledge of countries and peoples of Europe.

Contrastingly, Mary Anne Venning's *Geographical Present* provides a series of disconnected 'facts' aimed at creating surprise, awe and even revulsion, constituting what Charles Withers has called the 'trope of astonishment'.[61] *Geographical Present* consists of short entries on countries, cities and islands throughout the world with several colourful illustrations of individuals wearing 'national' costumes or performing a 'national' activity or gesture. While the entries mention geographical facts such as major rivers, cities and manufactures, the information is not systematic and the 'writing is choppy at times', and the spatial arrangement of countries is ignored.[62] London is followed by the city of Strasburg in Alsace in eastern France, followed by the province of Normandy in western France. Paris is summed up in three sentences, and we move on to Bohemia, Austria and the

---

[61] Mary Anne Venning, *A Geographical Present, Being Descriptions of the Principal Countries of the World; with [. . .] Costumes, etc* (London: no publisher, 1817); Charles W. J. Withers, *Geography, Science and National Identity: Scotland since 1520* (Cambridge: Cambridge University Press, 2001), p. 91. For a different perspective on Venning's *Geographical Present*, see Norcia, ch. 1.

[62] Norcia, p. 34.

Ionian Islands in Greece. The focus is less on providing systematic knowledge than on shaping readers' attitudes towards the inhabitants of different countries. The 'Hungarians still resemble their uncivilized ancestors the Huns' (p. 28), the Senegalese 'are not destitute of understanding or address, but they employ it in theft' (p. 99), and the Jaggas of South Africa are 'ferocious in character, they kill and plunder all whom they meet with: they are cannibals, and often make war to obtain prisoners, whose flesh they devour' (p. 107).[63] Venning's cultivation of spatial disorder – her lack of system – suggests that she intended to distance herself from the order followed by geographies describing countries and their peoples. Some writers of 'amusing and instructive' texts for children in the late eighteenth to early nineteenth century claimed that lack of order in a text was 'more agreeable than a methodical arrangement'.[64] Venning's *Geography Present* was a gift designed to amuse and enjoy, not to be homework, and appears to have fulfilled its aims very successfully. Not only was it republished twice more in Britain, and in America as three separate volumes by the children's publisher William Burgess, but it launched her career 'as a scientific writer and [. . .] authority as an educator of the young'.[65]

Conclusion

Geography's character as a new, modern subject of instruction allowed women to explore a variety of ways for compiling and synthesising the information they collected from their sources. Again and again, the texts illustrate the range of female authors' innovations and, for a few, their ability to articulate complex ideas through images or the voices of textual children to render them comprehensible to child readers. Even though their instructive innovations have

---

[63] For a discussion of cannibalism, see Mark Stein, 'Who Is Afraid of Cannibals? Some Uses of the Cannibalism Trope in Olaudah Equiano's *Interesting Narrative*', in *Discourses of Slavery and Abolition: Britain and Its Colonies 1760–1838*, ed. by Brycchan Carey, Markman Ellis and Sara Salih (Basingstoke: Palgrave Macmillan, 2004), pp. 96–107.

[64] John Aikin and Anna Barbauld, *Evenings at Home* [1792–6] (London: James Cornish, 1846), p. 8.

[65] Norcia, p. 34.

mostly been overlooked in the history of geographical pedagogy, these women's writings have contributed to the construction of the science of geography as a discipline, and thus to the history of women's educational literature.

Works Cited

Primary

[Anon.], *Geography and History Selected by a Lady for the Use of Her Own Children* (London: B. Law, 1790)

[Anon.], *The Young Lady's Geography* (London: R. Baldwin; T. Lownds, 1765)

Aikin, John and Anna Barbauld, *Evenings at Home* [1792–6] (London: James Cornish, 1846)

Bailey, Diana, *Employment, the True Source of Happiness* (London: John Harris, 1825)

Blair, John, *The History of the Rise and Progress of Geography* (London: T. Cadell, 1784)

Butler, William, *Exercises on the Globes: Interspersed with Some Historical, Biographical, Chronological, Mythological, and Miscellaneous Information; on a New Plan: Designed for the Use of Young Ladies* [1800] (London: T. Mawman, 1803)

Clarke, John, *An Essay upon Study* (Dublin: Edward Exshaw, 1736)

——. *An Essay upon the Education of Youth in Grammar-Schools* (Dublin: Edward Exshaw, 1736)

[Devis, Ellin], *Introduction to Geography: For the Use of Mrs Devis's Little Society* (London: no publisher, c.1790)

[Gaultier, Aloisius Edouard Camille, Abbé] *A Complete Course of Geography, by Means of Instructive Games, Invented by the Abbé Gaultier* (London: Abbé Gaultier, 1795)

Goldsmith, J., *Geography for the Use of Schools* (London: Richard Phillips, 1803)

Guthrie, William, *A New Geographical, Historical, and Commercial Grammar*, 6th edn (London: Edward and Charles Dilly, 1771)

Harrington, S. *New Introduction to the Knowledge and Use of Maps*, 3rd edn (London: S. Crowder, 1774)

——. *New and Elegant Amusements for the Ladies of Great Britain* (London: S. Crowder, 1772)

Hatfield, Miss [Sarah], *The Terra Incognita of Lincolnshire* (London: G. and S. Robinson, 1816)

Helme, Elizabeth, *Travels from the Cape of Good-Hope, into the Interior Parts of Africa, Translated from the French of Monsieur Vaillant*, 2 vols (London: William Lane, 1790)

Hofland, Mrs [Barbara], *The Panorama of Europe* (London: A. K. Newman and Co., 1813)

Keith, Thomas, *Short and Easy Introduction to the Science of Geography*, 5th edn (London: no publisher, 1805)

Kennedy, Miss, *Outlines of Geography and History: Intended for the Use of Schools* (Dublin: D. Graisberry, 1799)

Knox, Vicesimus, *Liberal Education* (London: no publisher, 1781)

Locke, John, *Some Thoughts Concerning Education*, in *The Educational Writings of John Locke*, ed. by John William Adamson (Cambridge: Cambridge University Press, 1922)

Marcet, Jane, *Conversations with Children: On Land and Water*, 3rd edn (London: Longman, Brown, Green and Longman, 1843)

Priestley, Joseph, *An Essay on a Course of Liberal Education for Civil and Active Life* [1765], 3rd edn (Dublin: Luke White and P. Byrne, 1791)

Reid, Hugo, *Elements of Physical Geography, for the Use of Schools and Private Students* (Edinburgh: Oliver and Boyd, 1850)

Sargeant, Anna Maria, *Papa and Mamma's Easy Lessons in Geography* (London: Thomas Dean and Son, ?1850)

Sherwood, Mrs [Martha], *An Introduction to Geography, Intended for Little Children*, 2nd edn (Wellington: F. Houlston and Son, 1820)

Somerville, Mary, *Physical Geography*, 2 vols (London: John Murray, 1848)

Venning, Mary Anne, *A Geographical Present, Being Descriptions of the Principal Countries of the World; with [. . .] Costumes, etc* (London: no publisher, 1817)

Wakefield, Priscilla, *The Juvenile Travellers: Containing the Remarks of a Family during a Tour through the Principal States and Kingdoms of Europe with an Account of their Inhabitants, Natural Production, and Curiosities* (London: Darton and Harvey, 1801)

——. *Mental Improvement*, 2 vols (London: Darnton and Harvey, 1794)

Wilkinson, Miss, *An Atlas for the Use of Schools: Part I. The Maps at Large, Part II. The Blank Duplicates* (Stourport: no publisher, 1816)

——. *Geographical Exercises: or, A New Method of Acquiring a Knowledge of Geography by Drawing Maps* (Stourport: no publisher, 1798)

Wilkinson, Robert, *An Easy Method of Learning Geography* (London: Robert Wilkinson, 1796)

Zornlin, Rosina, *Recreations in Physical Geography: or, The Earth as It Is* (London: John W. Parker, 1840)

Secondary

Baker, J. N. L., *The History of Geography* (Oxford: Basil Blackwell, 1963)

——. 'Mary Somerville and Geography in England', *Geographical Journal*, 111.4/6 (Apr.–June 1948), 207–22

Bensaude-Vincent, Bernadette and Christine Blondel, eds, *Science and Spectacle in the European Enlightenment* (Aldershot: Ashgate, 2008)

Cohen, Michèle, 'The Pedagogy of Conversation in the Home: "Familiar Conversation" as a Pedagogical Tool in Eighteenth-and Nineteenth-Century England', *Oxford Review of Education*, 41.4 (2015), 447–63

Fyfe, Aileen, 'Science and Religion in Popular Publishing in 19th-century Britain', in *Clashes of Knowledge: Orthodoxies and Heterodoxies in Science and Religion*, ed. by Peter Meusburger, Michael Welker and Edgar Wunder (New York: Springer, 2008), pp. 121–32

Graham, Ruth, 'Juvenile Travellers: Priscilla Wakefield's Excursions in Empire', *Journal of Imperial and Commonwealth History*, 38.3 (2010), 373–93

Hannas, Linda, *The English Jigsaw Puzzle, 1760–1890* (London: Wayland Publishers, 1972)

Harrison, A. S. et al., *Studies and Impressions, 1902–1952* (London: Institute of Education, 1952)

Hill, Bridget, 'Priscilla Wakefield as a Writer of Children's Educational Books', *Women's Writing*, 4.1 (1997), 3–15

Hoonaard, Will C. van den, *Map Worlds: A History of Women in Cartography* (Waterloo, ON: Wilfrid Laurier University Press, 2013)

Humphrey, Carol, *Sampled Lives: Samplers from the Fitzwilliam Museum* (Cambridge: Fitzwilliam Museum, 2017)

Hyde, Ralph, *Panoramania!: The Art of Entertainment* (London: Trefoil in association with Barbican Art Gallery, 1988)

Kinsley, Zoe, *Women Writing the Home Tour, 1682–1812* (Aldershot: Ashgate, 2008)

Knight, David, *Natural Sciences Books in English 1600–1900* (Tiptree, Essex: Batsford, 1989)

Mayhew, Robert, 'William Guthrie's Geographical Grammar, the Scottish Enlightenment and the Politics of British Geography', *Scottish Geographical Journal*, 115.1 (1999), 19–34

Myers, Mitzi, 'Impeccable Governesses, Rational Dames, and Moral Mothers: Mary Wollstonecraft and the Female Tradition in Georgian Children's Books', *Children's Literature*, 14 (1986), 31–59

Neely, Kathryn A., *Mary Somerville: Science, Illumination, and the Female Mind* (Cambridge: Cambridge University Press, 2001)

Norcia, Megan A., *X Marks the Spot: Women Writers Map the Empire for British Children, 1790–1895* (Athens: Ohio University Press, 2010)

Norgate, Martin, 'Cutting Borders: Dissected Maps and the Origins of the Jigsaw Puzzle', *Cartographic Journal*, 44.4 (2007), 342–50

Rigby, Elizabeth, 'Children's Books', *Quarterly Review*, 74 (June–Oct. 1844), 1–26

Robinson, Harry, 'Geography in the Dissenting Academies', *Geography*, 36.3 (1951), 179–86

Sanderson, Mary, 'Mary Somerville: Her Work in Physical Geography', *Geographical Review*, 64.3 (Jul. 1974), 410–20

Schulten, Helen, 'Map Drawing, Graphic Literacy, and Pedagogy in the Early Republic', *History of Education Quarterly*, 57.2 (2017), 185–220

Secord, James A., 'How Scientific Conversation Became Shop Talk', *Transactions of the Royal Historical Society*, 17 (2007), 129–56

Shefrin, Jill, '"Make it a pleasure and not a task": Educational Games for Children in Georgian England', *Princeton University Library Chronicle*, 60.2 (Winter, 1999), 251–75

——. *Neatly Dissected for the Instruction of Young Ladies and Gentlemen in the Knowledge of Geography: John Spilsbury and Early Dissected Puzzles* (Los Angeles: Cotsen Occasional Press, 1999)

Speese, Erin K. Johns, '"Our feelings become impressed with the grandeur of omnipotence": Mary Somerville's Feminine Scientific Sublime', *Prose Studies*, 35.2 (2013), 171–88

Stein, Mark, 'Who Is Afraid of Cannibals? Some Uses of the Cannibalism Trope in Olaudah Equiano's *Interesting Narrative*', in *Discourses of Slavery and Abolition: Britain and Its Colonies 1760–1838*, ed. by Brycchan Carey, Markman Ellis and Sara Salih (Basingstoke: Palgrave Macmillan, 2004), pp. 96–107

Stenton, Alison Mary, 'Late Eighteenth-Century Home Tours and Travel Narratives: Genre, Culture and Space' (unpublished doctoral thesis, King's College London, 2003)

Stock, Paul, *Europe and the British Geographical Imagination, 1760–1830* (Oxford: Oxford University Press, 2019)

Tyner, Judith A., *Stitching the World: Embroidered Maps and Women's Geographical Education* (London: Routledge, 2016)

Vaughan, J. E., 'Aspects of Teaching Geography in England in the Nineteenth Century', *Paedagogica Historica*, 12.1 (2006), 128–47

Withers, Charles W. J., *Geography, Science and National Identity: Scotland since 1520* (Cambridge: Cambridge University Press, 2001)

Witney Antiques, *Samplers: Mapped and Charted* (Witney: Witney Antiques, 2005)

Wyld, Helen, *Embroidered Stories: Scottish Samplers* (Edinburgh: National Museum of Scotland, 2018)

Chapter 4

'What follows': Maria Edgeworth's Works for Older Children

Aileen Douglas

In the latter part of 1820, Maria Edgeworth, accompanied by her two much younger stepsisters, was on an extended visit to the Continent and staying in Pregny, close to Geneva. From Switzerland, Edgeworth directed a triangular correspondence, the other vertices of which were her 'dear Triumvirate Council of critics and friends' at home in the Irish midlands, and the publisher Rowland Hunter in London.[1] Manuscript, transcripts, critical opinions, proofs and views on marketing circulated between the three sets of participants. At issue was the preparation for the press of a work that Hunter would publish in 1821: *Rosamond: A Sequel to Early Lessons*. At one point in the correspondence, Edgeworth reassured those at home who had expressed doubts as to what was apparently Hunter's preferred title: 'Sequel does not exclusively mean *end*. It means also *Continuation* or *what follows*.'[2] Origins and beginnings are the stuff of myth and glamour; 'Continuation or *what follows*' attracts less notice, but it too can be venturesome. *Rosamond* occurs in that interstitial period between childhood and young adulthood, taking its young heroine from age eleven to fourteen, an age when girls are considered 'neither quite as children, nor quite as women'.[3] *Frank: A Sequel to Early*

---

[1] *Maria Edgeworth in France and Switzerland: Selections from the Edgeworth Family Letters*, ed. by Christina Colvin (Oxford: Oxford University Press, 1979, repr. 2014), p. 236. The 'Council' at home consisted of Frances Edgeworth (1769–1865), Richard Lovell Edgeworth's fourth wife; Honora Edgeworth (1791–1857), Maria Edgeworth's stepsister; and Mary Sneyd (1750–1841), sister of Honora and Elizabeth Sneyd, Richard Lovell Edgeworth's second and third wives.

[2] Colvin, *Maria Edgeworth*, p. 235.

[3] Maria Edgeworth, *Rosamond: A Sequel to Early Lessons*, 2 vols, 2nd edn (London: R. Hunter and Baldwin, Cradock and Joy, 1822), p. 74.

Lessons (1822) concerns a younger child, nine when the sequel begins and eleven at its close.[4] In spatial terms, both works broach new ground as their young protagonists encounter new social situations and challenges beyond the protected familial spaces in which Edgeworth's works for younger children, *Early Lessons* (1801) and *Early Lessons Continued* (1814), mainly occur. Edgeworth's sequels represent the receptive and expressive powers of older children as they acquire knowledge of the self and of the world, come to understand themselves as separate from the supportive family matrix and begin to establish themselves as gendered speaking subjects. Through continuation, through the process of imagining 'what follows', Edgeworth pushed into new spaces and contributed to an expanded understanding of what fiction might be.

The juncture of Edgeworth's literary career at which these fictions were written was one in which writerly acts of 'continuation' held especial resonance. With the death in 1817 of Richard Lovell Edgeworth, Maria lost not only a much-loved father but also a literary collaborator, one Edgeworth was inclined to credit as a moving force for her work: 'it was to please my father I first exerted myself to write, to please him I continued'.[5] Apart from *Memoirs of the Life of Richard Lovell Edgeworth* (1820), a work begun by her father and completed by Maria at his request, the works for older children considered in this chapter were the first she published after his death. As the correspondence with the female 'Triumvirate Council of critics and friends' shows, however, Edgeworth did not produce the sequels in isolation but rather in collaboration with her female relatives at home. In this way, the busy correspondence in 1820 initiated a new phase of the 'family authorship' in which various members of the Edgeworth household had continuously engaged since the 1790s.[6]

---

[4] There is a discrepancy as to Frank's age. The preface speaks of offering the history of Frank from seven to 'between ten and eleven', but very early in the sequel Mary, Frank's cousin, says he 'will be ten next July'; *Frank: A Sequel to Early Lessons*, 3 vols, 2nd edn (London: R. Hunter and Baldwin, Cradock and Joy, 1825), pp. x, 17. The older age is accepted here.

[5] Edgeworth to Étienne Dumont, September 1817, quoted in Marilyn Butler, *Maria Edgeworth: A Literary Biography* (Oxford: Clarendon Press, 1972), p. 289.

[6] Michelle Levy, *Family Authorship and Romantic Print Culture* (London: Palgrave Macmillan, 2008); Levy introduces her study of the 'conjunction of authorship and family life' with the example of the Edgeworths. On the later collaborative practices of the Edgeworth women see Frances R. Botkin, 'Finding Her Own Voice or "Being on Her Own Bottom": A Community of Women in Maria

Rosamond and Frank had first appeared as much younger children and had grown up over successive instalments of their respective histories. Rosamond first appeared in one of Edgeworth's earliest publications, *The Parent's Assistant* (1796), and Frank in the first instalments of *Early Lessons*. Both had also featured in *Continuation of Early Lessons*. In these works, Edgeworth followed the pioneering lead of Anna Barbauld, particularly her *Lessons for Children* (1778–9), one of the first works explicitly conceived and designed for children of a particular age: in this case, from two to three. In *Practical Education* (1798), a treatise that Maria Edgeworth co-wrote with her father, Richard Lovell Edgeworth, Barbauld is acknowledged as an important precursor.[7] The Edgeworths' influential study of education as an 'experimental science' understood learning as a process sparked by the child's observations of the world; developed through the child's curiosity; and further encouraged through dialogue with parents and other children. The mode of instruction promoted by *Practical Education* was intimately linked to the Edgeworths' own experiences in Edgeworthstown, an estate run upon progressive lines and an experimental space in which twenty-one Edgeworth children were educated. Maria Edgeworth's *Early Lessons* took up where Barbauld's volumes left off and were intended for older children who knew their letters and were beginning to read. Like *Practical Education*, *Early Lessons* came out of the shared work of teaching and entertaining the young in which all the Edgeworth adults participated. While the ten tiny volumes bore Maria's name, the first story had in fact been given to her by Richard Lovell Edgeworth and written many years before by Honora, his second wife.[8] In keeping with the views of *Practical Education*, Frank (aged six) and Rosamond (aged seven) in their early adventures learn from observation of what is going on around them, in the house, in the garden or on excursions

---

Edgeworth's *Helen*', in *New Essays on Maria Edgeworth*, ed. by Julie Nash (Farnham: Ashgate, 2008), pp. 93–108.

[7] On the relationship between Barbauld and the Edgeworths, see Joanna Wharton, *Material Enlightenment: Women Writers and the Science of Mind, 1770–1830* (Woodridge: Boydell Press, 2018), and Aileen Douglas, 'Maria Edgeworth and Anna Letitia Barbauld: Print, Canons, and Female Literary Authority', *European Romantic Review*, 31.6 (2020), 699–713.

[8] Richard Lovell Edgeworth claimed in the 'Address to Mothers' that prefaced *Continuation of Early Lessons* (1814) that he had written the first Harry and Lucy story. For the argument in favour of Honora's authorship, see Anne Markey, 'Honora Sneyd Edgeworth's "Harry and Lucy": A Case Study of Familial Literary Collaboration', *Eighteenth-Century Ireland: Iris an dá chultúr*, 34 (2019), 50–65.

further afield, and from discussing what they see with their older siblings or parents.

'It has [. . .] been my daughter's aim to promote, by all her writings, the progress of education from the cradle to the grave.'[9] In his preface to the first volume of Maria Edgeworth's *Tales of Fashionable Life* (1809), Richard Lovell stated that Maria's aim in her *Parent's Assistant* (1796), along with her *Moral Tales* (1801) and *Popular Tales* (1804), had been to 'exemplify the principles contained in *Practical Education*', while the current work endeavoured 'to disseminate, in a familiar form' the ideas of *Essays on Professional Education* (a work published under Richard Lovell Edgeworth's name in 1809, but in which Maria had played a considerable part). For Richard Lovell, all his daughter's fictions, whether written for children or adults, were understood as vessels to be valued for their important educational ideas. Indeed, as Marilyn Butler notes, Maria could occasionally represent herself as little more than her father's 'amanuensis', privileging content derived from her father and dismissing the importance of literary form: 'In the lighter works [. . .] I have only repeated the same opinions [i.e. R.L.E.'s] in other forms [. . .] A certain quantity of bullion was given to me and I coined it into as many pieces as I thought would be convenient for popular use.'[10] In her continuations of the stories of Rosamond and Frank, and in representing them as older children, however, Maria Edgeworth did more than simply narrativise pedagogical ideas. She also treated in fiction the engendering of subjectivity.

The 1820s have often been understood as a fallow period for Maria Edgeworth's career. In her biography of Edgeworth, written in the early 1970s, Marilyn Butler pondered why Edgeworth in her final three decades 'succeeded in publishing so little of importance'.[11] This double-edged query reflects Butler's esteem for Edgeworth's earlier achievement in works such as *Ennui* – one of the tales in the volume whose preface by Richard Lovell Edgeworth is cited above – and *The Absentee* (1812), novels rich in social documentation, the quality

---

[9] Richard Lovell Edgeworth, 'Preface', in Maria Edgeworth, *Castle Rackrent and Ennui*, ed. by Marilyn Butler (London: Penguin, 1992), p. 141.

[10] Butler, *Maria Edgeworth*, p. 272; Maria Edgeworth to Francis Jeffrey, 18 December 1806, quoted in Butler, p. 272. On Maria Edgeworth's acts of self-abnegation, see Catherine Gallagher, *Nobody's Story: The Vanishing Acts of Women Writers in the Marketplace 1670–1820* (Berkeley: University of California Press, 1995), pp. 257–328.

[11] Butler, *Maria Edgeworth*, p. 433.

which Butler sees as pre-eminent in Edgeworth's central contribution to the development of the novel as a genre.[12] Butler's question, however, also dismisses much of the writing that occupied Edgeworth from the 1820s onwards – including her stories for older children. In the half century since Butler's biography, the nature and status of children's literature, especially that written by women in the late eighteenth and early nineteenth centuries, has been newly assessed and recognised.[13] While the development of writing specifically for children has attracted more intense critical interest, the place of this pedagogical work in a wider literary history is also increasingly being explored. Frances Ferguson, for example, has recently argued for Anna Barbauld's contribution to the development of the realist novel. Connecting Barbauld's writing for children and her critical work in the editing of the fifty-volume *British Novelists* (1810), Ferguson sees the moment as one in which 'Literature Started Talking with Children' and identifies conversation – the mode of Barbauld's works for children – as central to Barbauld's criticism and 'key to her description of the novel as genre'.[14] Similarly, in the case of Edgeworth, there is the sustained work of Mitzi Myers, earliest among critics in arguing that Edgeworth's writing for children initiated subjects and forms that would become central to the novel as a genre. Myers offered particularly vigorous and passionate readings of the Rosamond stories in which she argued that Edgeworth's (sometimes maligned) didacticism fostered the writer's realism.[15] Contrasting the Rosamond sequence with marriage-plot novels such as Frances Burney's *Evelina* (1775), Myers saw Edgeworth's tales as 'a coherent reconceptualization of the female development plot'. Emphasising the autobiographical valences in the works, and the dialogic narratives between 'child and adult, daughter and mother', Myers pronounced the series a 'complex *Bildungsroman* which enacts its author's as well as its protagonist's coming of age – mothering writer, heroine, and reader

---

[12] Ibid., pp. 395–6.

[13] See, for example, in the valuable collection of essays *Opening the Nursery Door: Reading, Writing and Childhood 1600–1900*, ed. by Mary Hilton, Morag Styles and Victor Watson (London and New York: Routledge, 1997).

[14] Frances Ferguson, 'The Novel Comes of Age: When Literature Started Talking with Children', *Differences: A Journal of Feminist Cultural Studies*, 28.1 (2017), 37–63 (p. 43).

[15] Mitzi Myers, 'Socializing Rosamond: Educational Ideology and Fictional Form', *Children's Literature Association Quarterly*, 14.2 (1989), 52–8 (p. 55).

alike'.[16] For Myers, what Edgeworth produced in the Rosamond stories was a distinctly female *Bildungsroman*:

> Generic definitions of the *Bildungsroman* embody male maturational norms and linear plots directed towards separation and autonomy, though women's more interdependent sense of self has historically been organized around the weaving and maintenance of intimate relationships, especially those of childhood: female individualism tends towards the connected and the contextual.[17]

The present discussion traverses terrain marked out by Myers but, partly because it considers Edgeworth's boy protagonist, Frank, alongside Rosamond, and partly because it deliberately concentrates on the last stages of Rosamond's history, its arguments concerning gender and literary form are different. 'Separation' of the young protagonist from the familial matrix is an important and clearly gendered element in both stories, experienced by Rosamond and Frank alike. Psychology, emotion and the affective are notably absent from the fiction for adults which established Edgeworth's reputation in the period before 1820. It is in the stories for older children that Edgeworth begins to realise this aspect of character, work she would continue with remarkable effect in her last novel, *Helen* (1834).

Prefacing *Rosamond* with an address 'To Parents', Edgeworth stated: 'The same principles will here be found as in all the preceding Early Lessons, but applied to those new views of character, new thoughts, feelings, and objects, which present themselves at this time of life' (p. iv). Each of the works for older children is domestic fiction of a kind, each text made up of ordinary incidents as these occur in an affluent and enlightened gentry household: conversations with siblings and parents; reading books and viewing prints; a country house visit; some tourism and the exercise of philanthropy. *Early Lessons* and *Early Lessons Continued* had contained stories of a little group of protagonists, both boys and girls: Rosamond and Frank, along with Harry and Lucy. The dedication of the sequels to a single

---

[16] Mitzi Myers, 'The Dilemmas of Gender as Double-Voiced Narrative: or, Maria Edgeworth Mothers the Bildungsroman', in *The Idea of the Novel in the Eighteenth Century*, ed. by Robert W. Uphuas (East Lansing, MI: Colleagues Press, 1988), pp. 67–97 (pp. 67–8); see also Gillian Adams and Donelle Ruwe, 'The Scholarly Legacy of Mitzi Myers', in *Culturing the Child, 1690–1914: Essays in Memory of Mitzi Myers*, ed. by Donelle Ruwe (Lantham, MD: Children's Literature Association and Scarecrow Press, 2005), pp. 227–40 (pp. 223–4).

[17] Myers, 'Dilemmas of Gender', pp. 75–6.

girl and, later, a single boy expresses an understanding made explicit in the texts themselves: that is, that these are stories very concerned with defining womanliness and manliness for young readers. Both sequels place gender along with class as circumstances that shape the scope and nature of individual action, and represent their young characters, male and female, as they become aware of, and are marked by, the social ramifications of gender difference. As a consequence, there is a fundamental contrast between *Rosamond* and *Frank*. Frank's story is shaped by an anticipated rupture of the boy's domestic life owing to his imminent departure for public school. Rosamond, however, like many girls of her class, will complete her education at home, her future life and its exercise of 'female domestic virtues' being envisaged as a continuation of the present.[18]

Readers first meet Rosamond in 'The Purple Jar', Edgeworth's most divisive, and most anthologised, story for children. Little Rosamond is shopping with her mother for badly needed new shoes when she spies a beautiful purple jar. Her mother says she can have jar or shoes, but no further purchases will be made that month. Drawn by beauty, the little girl chooses the jar, only to discover that it is not coloured at all, merely filled with nasty liquid. Meanwhile her shoes disintegrate completely, literally hobbling the little girl for the remainder of the month. Her 'rational mother', obdurate, insists that Rosamond abide by the consequences of her choice. The early Rosamond stories are dominated by the girl's conversations with her mother, the dialogic narratives described by Myers. In 'The Hyacinth', one of the stories in *Early Lessons*, little Rosamond has yet again to make a choice, this time between flowers – lovely now – and roots – promising future gratification. When she looks anxiously into her mother's eyes for guidance, she meets with a rebuff:

> 'Don't consult my eyes, Rosamond,' said her mother, smiling: 'you shall see nothing in my eyes'; and her mother turned away her head. 'Use your own understanding, because you will not always have my eyes to see with.'[19]

In *Rosamond*, the narrative increasingly leaves the teenager to see with her own eyes: the conversations between mother and daughter

---

[18] *Rosamond: A Sequel to Early Lessons*, 2 vols, 2nd edn (London, 1822), II, p. 258. All further references are to this edition and will be given parenthetically in the text.

[19] *Early Lessons: Rosamond, Part II* (London: J. Johnson, 1809), pp.67–8.

continue, but less prominently, and are accompanied by the exchanges the girl has with others, many of them outside the home. Through the relative recession of the mother figure, Edgeworth signals that the heroine must independently make sense of what goes on about her, both within and outside the family.

As the events of *Rosamond* unfold in varied social settings, one of the most important lines of development is the girl's negotiation of speech and silence, of when to speak up and when to hold her tongue. Childhood choices between jars and shoes, flowers and roots, are now replaced with choices between different forms of social action.[20] In one of the early episodes, Rosamond is on a house visit and enjoying chat with some other girls when she hears a story of how a young servant has been mistreated by her mistress. The story is false, and Rosamond's repetition of it causes the young servant to lose her position, a serious consequence which Rosamond tries in vain to reverse. In a contrasting episode at the end of the first volume, Rosamond is attending a dance and sitting with a group of slightly older young people who intimidate her with their fashionable airs and confidence:

> Rosamond was just at that age when girls do not join in conversation, but when they sit modestly silent, and have leisure, if they have sense, to judge of what others say, and to form by choice, and not by chance, their opinions of what goes on in that great world, into which they have not yet entered. (I, p. 191)

The conversation turns to ridicule of Rosamond's friend, the old lady Mrs Egerton and her family, with Rosamond all the while becoming more self-conscious and embarrassed. Eventually, she is taunted for her silence, and does speak out:

> 'Silent only because I had not the courage to speak', said she. 'How I wish', added she, commanding her trembling voice, 'that I could be a judicious friend! Such a one as Mrs. Egerton has been to me.' (I, pp. 202–3)

The heroine willing to risk ridicule to defend unpopular positions is a trope in Edgeworth's adult fiction, but the representation differs in the case of Rosamond as the narrative realises the young girl's discomfort and hesitation before she finds the courage to speak. The exposition is as much concerned with Rosamond's uneasiness and

---

[20] A partial exception here is 'The Bracelet of Memory' in Volume II, where Rosamond is allowed to choose between a bracelet and a horse.

her feeling of being isolated in the group as it is with her eventual statement.

The opportunities that Rosamond enjoys in London 'of meeting, at different houses, many young companions' make her aware of diverse manners and ways of being agreeable: 'She became very desirous to please, and anxious about her appearance and manners' (I, p. 74). Some of the episodes in *Rosamond* deal with the heroine's misplaced efforts to be agreeable in the way she speaks and dances and with her fall into imitation and affectation. The desire to please strangers is, however, shown to be as nothing compared to the desire to please those closer to home. The most vivid episodes in *Rosamond* concern the girl's relationship with her brother Godfrey. Home from public school, Godfrey is irritated and jealous that his little sister has committed to spending an hour in the morning reading to the elderly Mrs Egerton. The 'pleasure of giving pleasure' (I, p. 138) has made Rosamond consistent in this practice, but Godfrey determines to test his power over Rosamond by making her miss a visit. Over a period of several days, Godfrey seeks to delay and distract his sister and to tempt her with alternative excursions such as going to see the Elgin Marbles in the British Museum. He even abuses her for becoming 'a prim Pattern-of-perfection-miss in her teens' (I, p. 156), and then sulks when asked if he were in earnest:

> 'Oh, don't plague me, Rosamond', said Godfrey, impatiently.
> 'Plague you! Oh brother! when you plague me for ever. What can I do to please you?' cried Rosamond.
> 'You don't want to please me', replied Godfrey. 'Go and please Mrs. Egerton.'
> 'But cannot I please you both?' said Rosamond; 'I am sure I love you both.'
> 'May be so, but you cannot please us both; so please yourself, I advise you: go, it's just time; go and read to your *new* friend, and leave me in peace to read to myself.' (I, p. 159)

Eventually, it is Godfrey who concedes, admitting that he knew all along that Rosamond was in the right, 'but my desire to show my power over you, and to gain my point, my foolish point, made me go on, from one step to another' (I, p. 207). At one family breakfast, the father articulates the conventional view that 'it is particularly amiable in a woman to be ready to yield, and avoid disputing about trifles' (I, p. 102). Among the 'new views of character, new thoughts, feelings, and objects' with which Rosamond is confronted in the continuation of her history, however, and a major theme in the book, is the complexity of the desire to please, and the occasional need not to be amiable or yielding to those one loves but to set oneself apart. Rosamond is able enough to puncture Godfrey's superiority, as when she answers his assertion that he has not 'been at school and learned logic for nothing' with the retort that 'Indeed, I see you have not been at school for nothing [. . .] you have learned to triumph over, and laugh at your poor little sister' (I, p. 86). Quick-wittedness has, however, limited usefulness in 'trials of power'.

As Godfrey himself comes to admit, his antics are 'foolish', but this does not mean that the difficulties in which they involve Rosamond are negligible. Edgeworth represents delicately and vividly the girl's emotional conflict as she painfully realises that the desire to please should not always be satisfied.

The struggles between Godfrey and Rosamond propel the first volume of *Rosamond*, but there were problems with the composition of Volume II. In the late summer and early autumn of 1820, work had proceeded on *Rosamond* in Pregny, Edgeworthstown and London. In July, Hunter had begun printing the work, and the 'dear friends' at home were organised to read the proofs.[21] In early September, Edgeworth herself had sent Hunter a 'tiny address' to the reader.[22] Then the process hit a snag: there was not enough copy. 'I received your letter about Rosamond late last night and I answer it early this morning.'[23] The belated discovery elicited a long letter from Edgeworth in which she denounced 'make-weight pages' and subjects 'foisted in to break the unity of the design'. Significantly, Edgeworth feared that 'instead of the gradual improvement and progress which appear in Rosamond's character there would be *a going backwards and forwards* or a repetition of examples of faults and follies which would tire the reader'.[24] Edgeworth's decisive eschewal of repetitive examples indicates the extent to which she conceived *Rosamond* in terms of forward motion and progress as far as the young protagonist's maturation was concerned. In the end, Edgeworth wrote two new episodes for Volume II, one 'The Bracelet of Memory' and the other 'Blind Kate'. In the second of these episodes, Rosamond successfully funds and manages a philanthropic project by which the poor, old, eponymous Kate is cured of her blindness. In other words,

---

[21] Colvin, *Maria Edgeworth*, p. 179.
[22] Ibid., p. 235.
[23] Maria Edgeworth to Honora Edgeworth, 1 October 1820, in Colvin, *Maria Edgeworth*, p. 255.
[24] Colvin, *Maria Edgeworth*, p. 255.

Rosamond, despite her youth, enacts exactly the kind of benevolent paternalism fundamental to Edgeworth's idealised views on class relations.

The chapter has to this point discussed how Edgeworth's representation of Rosamond's progress towards young adulthood broke new fictional ground, but that is not to imply that *Rosamond: A Sequel to Early Lessons* is uniformly successful. In particular, the awkwardness of the late addition, 'Blind Kate', reveals Edgeworth's experimentation with 'what follows' hitting an imaginative limit, one that is intimately related to elements of her views on class. Edgeworth's favoured class dynamic, in which gentry benevolence generates lower-class gratitude, permeates her adult fiction, but it is given especially direct expression in an early story for children, 'The Orphans', first published in the third edition of *The Parent's Assistant* (1800). Evicted by their landlord on the death of their mother, the orphans of the title make a home in a ruined castle and manage through hard work and ingenuity to get by. Their efforts, including the making of slippers, are admired and supported by the vicar's daughters who supply the children with some raw materials and help them market their goods. When the children discover some coins in the ruins, their friends in the vicarage help establish the coins' value, giving rise to the following comment from the narrator: 'It is not only by their superior riches, but it is yet more by their superior knowledge, that persons in the higher ranks of life may assist those in a lower condition.'[25] This class-based trickle-down view of enlightenment, central to Edgeworth's view of society, is not only repeated in 'Blind Kate' but also used to underpin the plot. On a visit to the country house of the Egertons, Rosamond becomes acquainted with a poor local woman, blind Kate. During her stay, Rosamond has listened carefully to the scientific and improving conversation of the other house guests and so she hears discussion of a pamphlet by 'the celebrated Genevese oculist' Maunoir, on the removal of cataracts (II, p. 174).[26] She realises that this knowledge may be useful in Kate's case and, after arranging a consultation, also organises and finances

---

[25] Maria Edgeworth, *The Parent's Assistant: or, Stories for Children*, 6 vols, 3rd edn (London: J. Johnson, 1800), V, p. 108.

[26] Jean Pierre Maunoir (1768–1861), *Mémoires sur l'organisation de l'iris et l'opération de la pupille artificelle* (1812).

Kate's trip to London (using with parental permission the 60 guineas which were to buy her a horse):

> 'Joy! Joy! For now it is all settled! All certain! And I will tell you how it is to be. You are to go to London directly.'
>
> 'Shall I?' said Kate, with a bewildered air, turning her head to the side from which Rosamond's voice came.
>
> 'Yes, you shall, good Kate; listen to me and I will explain it all.'
> (II, p. 188)

As a social ideology, eighteenth-century paternalism infantilised the labouring classes. Kate is doubly infantilised, as the individual from the 'higher ranks of life' who assists her is also a fourteen-year-old girl. The object of the story is to show how Rosamond progresses to effective philanthropic action outside her domestic circle, but the mix of elements deployed by Edgeworth, of ideology and plot, sit badly together: in the mismatched and poorly judged 'Blind Kate' episode, a lively narrative of individual development rubs uncomfortably against the representation of class. In Edgeworth's effort to reconcile the story of 'what follows' for Rosamond with the wider social views underpinning her adult fiction, the implausibility of the plot in fact reveals Edgeworth's impossible idealisation of class relations.

Rosamond concludes with a scene in the print gallery of Egerton Abbey, just prior to the family's return to their London home, in which the heroine is asked which of all the women in ancient and modern history she would rather have been. Rejecting ancient models, including the 'stabbed and stabbing' Roman women, Rosamond turns to modern history, where she again rejects queens and empresses, preferring to be a 'private person' (II, p. 249). Her ultimate choice is Rachel, Lady Russell (1636–1723), famed for her efforts to save the life of her husband, William, who was beheaded for his part in the Rye House Plot of 1683. The choice delights her auditors, pleased that 'Rosamond was not dazzled with the glare of historic greatness, but that she felt the full value of female domestic virtues' (II, p. 258). Significantly, though, domestic virtue includes female expressivity, as it is remarked that we know Lady Russell not merely through historians and biographers but 'from her own letters', which had first been published in 1777.

A year after Edgeworth brought Rosamond's history to a close with promises of the girl's 'future excellence' (II, p. 258), she published *Frank: A Sequel to Early Lessons*. Here, the workings of gender

become even more overt, as Frank's future masculinity is seen to depend on his departure for public school and the inevitable rupturing
of his domestic existence. As already noted, *Frank* is not exactly a
companion volume to *Rosamond*. To start with, the protagonist is
a younger child; additionally, the work is largely driven by a single
issue – the proper preparation at home of a male child for the experience of public school – and is quite programmatic. In this respect,
the volumes follow on from earlier stories involving Frank, which
are particularly heavily concerned with imparting certain kinds of information and knowledge to do with trades and processes. In *Frank*,
and in keeping with the boy's more advanced age, his sense of his
place, both geographically and in terms of narratives of civilisation,
is mediated through reading and discussing histories and accounts
of travel, as well as primers on natural history.[27] Butler indicates a
possible source for some of these differences when she notes that
Richard Lovell Edgeworth had left 'many unused notes [. . .] Maria
seems to have been left enough notes for a last series about Frank,
and she could handle Rosamond for herself.'[28] Certainly, of the two
sequels, *Frank* is more directly linked to the Edgeworths' treatises
on education, both of which had contributed to the long-running
late-eighteenth-century debate on the relative merits of public versus
private (that is, home) education for boys, a debate that 'contributed
to the articulation of gender difference and the conceptualization of
gendered modes of knowing'.[29] *Practical Education* had adjudicated
the relative merits of private and public education in a chapter dedicated to the issue. *Essays on Professional Education* (1809), as each
profession is discussed, makes a recommendation in favour of either private or public education.[30] *Frank*, however, assumes public

[27] This aspect of *Frank* deserves further study. The intertextuality of the work is
explored by Clíona Ó Gallchoir, '"A desert island is a delightful place": Maria
Edgeworth and *Robinson Crusoe*', *European Romantic Review*, 31.6 (2020),
715–29.
[28] Butler, *Maria Edgeworth*, p. 166.
[29] Michèle Cohen, 'Gender and the Private/Public Debate on Education in the Long
Eighteenth Century', in *Public or Private Education? Lessons from History*, ed.
by Richard Aldrich (London and Portland, OR: Woburn Press, 2004), pp. 15–35
(p.15); see also Sophia Woodley, '"Oh miserable and most ruinous measure":
The Debate between Private and Public Education in Britain, 1760–1800', in
Educating the Child in Enlightenment Britain: Beliefs, Cultures, Practices, ed. by
Mary Hilton and Jill Shefrin (Farnham: Ashgate, 2009), pp. 21–40 (p. 28).
[30] The later work declares private education to be best for clergymen but emphasises
it must 'never be thought of for a soldier. Every thing forbids it. The very love

education as the norm for boys; indeed, as the 'Preface to Parents' states, the very object of the book is to prepare boys for this stage in their lives:

> It is the object of the present little book, not only to contribute to the amusement and advantage of children, but to point out by what means every father, and still more every mother, may, by care in the previous education of their children at home, guard in a great measure against the danger which they fear at school: and by what means they may give to their boys the greatest chance of securing every advantage to be hoped from public education. (I, pp. ix–x)

Proper preparation for public school requires an acquisition and understanding of true manliness. The first marker of masculinity is the acquisition of Latin, with which Frank struggles. Other masculine pursuits he finds more congenial: learning to ride; going on a hunt; accompanying his father to drills and parades at the local barracks; and going on long country excursions with his father, leaving Mary, his little cousin and companion, at home with his mother. At one point, gender difference becomes a project for ten-year-old Frank:

> [I] shall ask mamma for two of the largest sheets of paper she has in her paper treasury; at the top of the one I will write, or I will print, in large letters, MAN, and, on the other, WOMAN; and I will rule lines very close, and on these two sheets of paper I will make two lists, one for myself, man; and the other for Mary, woman; and under these heads I will put every thing that we ought to know or learn, before we grow up to be man and woman. (I, p. 203)

For a while, the two children cooperate on the list before Frank tires of the exercise and goes off riding, leaving Mary to get on with the drudgery of transcription. Frank's managerial and fleeting interest in what distinguishes 'MAN' and 'WOMAN' contrasts with his female cousin's patient embodiment of those distinctions through her labour. In discussing her literary partnership with her father, Edgeworth, as we have seen, occasionally drew on understandings of writing which gendered conception as male and execution as female. It is appealing

---

of home, which he would acquire with domestic tastes, would become a source of unavailing regret. The necessity for resistance, and fortitude, the competition, the bodily and mental contests, which arise daily in public schools, force young men to exert themselves, and give them courage, and presence of mind among numbers and amidst the bustle of active life'; *Essays on Professional Education* (London: J. Johnson, 1809), pp. 84, 142.

to read the gentle irony of the list episode in *Frank: A Sequel* as Edgeworth's mature riposte to gendered attitudes towards creativity that she had herself earlier expressed.

Examining the role of gender in educational debates in the long eighteenth century, Michèle Cohen notes that a recurring objection to public schooling for girls was that it separated them from their families and threatened to weaken affective bonds: 'Yet, no educational or moral manual throughout the whole period even hinted that distancing boys from their families might be problematic.'[31] Parts of *Frank*, such as those in which his parents and other adults discuss the boy's future, may read like a manual, but Edgeworth uses fictional form to explore a topic that manuals left untouched: the emotional cost of 'distancing boys from their families'. That the acquisition of manliness requires distance from the feminine and the domestic is a matter of explicit comment in the book. As Frank's father explains the situation to little Mary:

> [Frank] would grow effeminate if he lived only with gentle girls and women. He must be roughed about among boys, or he will never be a man, and able to live among men. He is too much an object of our constant attention at home, and he would learn to think himself of too much consequence. (I, p. 54)

In *Frank*, as in *Rosamond*, a country house visit serves as a staging post for the movement from the intimacies of home to a wider social world. During the two-week visit to Bellombre, Frank is submitted to a kind of hazing by a group of 'men-boys' (III, p. 23), as Mary calls them, and toughened up for his future experiences at public school. Even though Frank is accompanied by his parents and Mary, the visit also separates him from them in an unprecedented way. On the first evening, 'Mary was carried off by one of the higher powers to some distant region, where, with the governess and the Miss Granvilles, she was to be invisible' (III, p. 26). Frank misses his companion, who now 'was never with him' (III, p. 64). His mother explains to him that she 'thought it was good for him to be separated from the friends with whom he had been used to live, especially from Mary, of whose kind and constant sympathy he would much feel the loss at school' (III, p. 66). The visit concluded, Frank and Mary are reunited and the drive home in the carriage is 'delightful': 'Mary, especially, enjoyed it for it has seemed to her very long since they had been all

---

[31] Cohen, p. 24.

together' (III, p. 279). On the journey, the young people chat with 'that unceasing flow of spirits, which the prospect of returning home and to their usual happy ways naturally excited' (III, p. 281). Their 'usual happy ways' will not, however, be of long duration, for within pages Frank is in the carriage again, and off to school, the separation of the cousins a physical manifestation of the different gendered roles they will come to occupy.

When Edgeworth, in Pregny, heard in October 1820 that she needed to supply more copy for *Rosamond: A Sequel to Early Lessons*, she reassured those in Edgeworthstown: 'It is by no means necessary for me to be *at home* or in any particular place to invent, or *write*.'[32] The earlier instalments of Rosamond and Frank's histories were closely linked to the Edgeworth home and to collaborative acts of teaching and entertaining the young that had, over a period of several decades, gone on there. They were also linked to, and exemplified the principles of, the pedagogical work Maria co-authored with her father, Richard Lovell. With that collaboration dissolved by Richard Lovell's death in 1817, it feels appropriate that Maria Edgeworth was not entirely '*at home*' when undertaking the sequels. Edgeworth's correspondence with her 'dear Triumvirate Council of critics and friends' as she worked in Switzerland on the sequel to *Rosamond* illuminates how she valued the contributions of her stepmother, stepsister and aunt. She trusted them to put the manuscript together, to deal with proofs and to liaise with the publisher. She listened to their advice and, in turn, put forward her own views. From the correspondence, we know why she thought 'sequel' could justifiably appear as part of the title, and, more importantly, what her aspirations for the sequel were, and that it would show Rosamond moving forward and developing. When Edgeworth says that she does not need to be in 'any particular place to invent, or write', she is being matter-of-fact, but she is also reserving to herself, and asserting, the distinctiveness of her own creative power.

A measure of authorial dislocation is also appropriate to Edgeworth's writing in the early 1820s because both sequels represent older children as they deal with separation and distance. The gendered nature of schooling in the long eighteenth century and the expectation that boys would complete their education at public school shapes the storyline of *Frank* as well as the emotional lives of

[32] Colvin, *Maria Edgeworth*, p. 256.

the young characters. The boy's experience of separation from the feminine and the domestic is most obviously represented externally, in a physical, spatial way, but Edgeworth's form nonetheless allows her to suggest the emotional costs of 'what follows' for the young boy. Unlike Frank, Rosamond will remain in her family home until maturity, and her experience of separation is not literal, but emotional, as she realises that moral autonomy can entail painful separation from loved ones. The 1820s have been seen as a relatively unproductive period for Edgeworth, and the significance of the works for older children she then wrote has been dismissed. Such views should be revised on two grounds. Edgeworth's attention to affect and emotional experience in her works for older children expanded the range of early-nineteenth-century fictional representation. These works also released energies, and apprehensions of emotional life, that would later characterise Edgeworth's final work of fiction for adults, *Helen* (1834).

Works Cited

Primary

Edgeworth, Maria, *Early Lessons: Rosamond, Part II* (London: J. Johnson, 1809)
——. *Frank: A Sequel to Early Lessons*, 3 vols, 2nd edn (London: R. Hunter and Baldwin, Cradock and Joy, 1825)
——. *The Parent's Assistant: or, Stories for Children*, 6 vols, 3rd edn (London: J. Johnson, 1800)
——. *Rosamond: A Sequel to Early Lessons*, 2 vols, 2nd edn (London: R. Hunter and Baldwin, Cradock and Joy, 1822)
Edgeworth, Richard Lovell, *Essays on Professional Education* (London: J. Johnson, 1809)
——. 'Preface', in Maria Edgeworth, *Castle Rackrent and Ennui*, ed. by Marilyn Butler (London: Penguin, 1992)

Secondary

Adams, Gillian, and Donelle Ruwe, 'The Scholarly Legacy of Mitzi Myers', in *Culturing the Child, 1690–1914: Essays in Memory of Mitzi Myers*, ed. by Donelle Ruwe (Lantham, MD: Children's Literature Association and Scarecrow Press, 2005), pp. 227–40
Botkin, Frances R., 'Finding Her Own Voice or "Being on Her Own Bottom": A Community of Women in Maria Edgeworth's *Helen*', in

New Essays on Maria Edgeworth, ed. by Julie Nash (Farnham: Ashgate, 2008), pp. 93–108

Butler, Marilyn, *Maria Edgeworth: A Literary Biography* (Oxford: Clarendon Press, 1972)

Cohen, Michèle, 'Gender and the Private/Public Debate on Education in the Long Eighteenth Century', in *Public or Private Education? Lessons from History*, ed. by Richard Aldrich (London and Portland, OR: Woburn Press, 2004), pp. 15–35

Colvin, Christina, ed., *Maria Edgeworth in France and Switzerland: Selections from the Edgeworth Family Letters* (Oxford: Oxford University Press, 1979)

Douglas, Aileen, 'Maria Edgeworth and Anna Letitia Barbauld: Print, Canons, and Female Literary Authority', *European Romantic Review*, 31.6 (2020), 699–713

Ferguson, Frances, 'The Novel Comes of Age: When Literature Started Talking with Children', *Differences: A Journal of Feminist Cultural Studies*, 28.1 (2017), 37–63

Gallagher, Catharine, *Nobody's Story: The Vanishing Acts of Women Writers in the Marketplace 1670–1820* (Berkeley: University of California Press, 1995)

Hilton, Mary, Morag Styles and Victor Watson, eds, *Opening the Nursery Door: Reading, Writing and Childhood 1600–1900* (London and New York: Routledge, 1997)

Levy, Michelle, *Family Authorship and Romantic Print Culture* (London: Palgrave Macmillan, 2008)

Markey, Anne, 'Honora Sneyd Edgeworth's "Harry and Lucy": A Case Study of Familial Literary Collaboration', *Eighteenth-Century Ireland: Iris an dá chultúr*, 34 (2019), 50–65

Myers, Mitzi, 'Socializing Rosamond: Educational Ideology and Fictional Form', *Children's Literature Association Quarterly*, 14.2 (1989), 52–8

——. 'The Dilemmas of Gender as Double-Voiced Narrative: or, Maria Edgeworth Mothers the Bildungsroman', in *The Idea of the Novel in the Eighteenth Century*, ed. by Robert W. Uphaus (East Lansing, MI: Colleagues Press, 1988), pp. 67–97

Ó Gallchoir, Clíona, '"A desert island is a delightful place": Maria Edgeworth and *Robinson Crusoe*', *European Romantic Review*, 31.6 (2020), 715–29

Wharton, Joanna, *Material Enlightenment: Women Writers and the Science of Mind, 1770–1830* (Woodridge: Boydell Press, 2018)

Woodley, Sophia, '"Oh miserable and most ruinous measure": The Debate between Private and Public Education in Britain, 1760–1800', in *Educating the Child in Enlightenment Britain: Beliefs, Cultures, Practices*, ed. by Mary Hilton and Jill Shefrin (Farnham: Ashgate, 2009), pp. 21–40

Part II

Acknowledging the Past

Chapter 5

Desire and Performative Masquerade in L.E.L's and E.B.B.'s Classical Translations

Jennifer Wallace

Generic Exceptionality

Letitia Elizabeth Landon (L.E.L.) and Elizabeth Barrett Browning (E.B.B.) achieved literary fame in the 1820s and 30s through their remarkable ability, despite educational obstacles, to imitate and translate ancient Greece. L.E.L. was renowned as the Brompton 'Sappho', performing in society soirées with her hair in ancient fashion like the lyric poet.[1] Published in weekly magazines, monthly journals and annual giftbooks, which were striking for their classical 'embellishments' and verses on Hellenic and Philhellenic topics, her poems were regathered in anthologies and collections under antique and antiquarian titles: 'Classical Sketches', 'Subjects for Pictures', 'Medallion Wafers'.[2] E.B.B., meanwhile, was lauded as a teenage prodigy, the 'author of the *Battle of Marathon*' (1820), published when she was aged fourteen, and *An Essay on Mind* (1826), her first collection which included many Philhellenic poems. She was to go on to produce two different translations of *Prometheus Bound*, in 1833 and 1850, as well as *Aurora Leigh* (1857) with its many classical allusions.[3]

The contemporary celebration of these two extraordinary classical 'poetesses' at a time when women were excluded from studying

[1] Benjamin Disraeli, *Letters*, ed. by J. A. W. Gunn et al., 10 vols (Toronto: University of Toronto Press, 1982), I, p. 247.

[2] Jennifer Wallace, 'Classics as Souvenir: L.E.L. and the Annuals', *Classical Receptions Journal*, 3.1 (2011), 109–28.

[3] Jennifer Wallace, 'Elizabeth Barrett Browning: Knowing Greek', *Essays in Criticism*, 50.4 (2000), 329–53; Clara Drummond, '"A Grand Possible": Elizabeth Barrett Browning's Translations of Aeschylus's *Prometheus Bound*', *International Journal of the Classical Tradition*, 12.4 (2006), 507–62.

ancient Greek in educational institutions might seem paradoxical. As many literary historians have pointed out, there was a sharp gender polarity in formal classical education in the eighteenth and nineteenth centuries.[4] Classics constituted a form of cultural capital offering access to positions of power in the establishment. Upper- and middle-class boys and men were schooled in Latin and Greek, while women and girls might have access to some Latin through home tutors or governesses but very rarely to ancient Greek. There was, of course, no university education for women in Britain until 1869. George Eliot satirised the prevailing attitude towards female classical learning in the first half of the nineteenth century in the voice of Mr Brooke, who warns Mr Casaubon that 'such deep studies, classics, mathematics, that kind of thing, are too taxing for a woman – too taxing, you know [. . .] there is a lightness about the feminine mind'.[5] Femininity seemed specifically to entail *not* knowing Greek. Exclusion from classical languages and a knowledge of ancient literature went hand in hand with political and social marginalisation.

However, in recent years, scholars have questioned historians' previous assumptions about classical reception being exclusively the privilege of one gender and one class. New research has revealed that, although women and lower-class men had very limited access to formal classical education, there was a larger number of female and working-class readers of Latin and Greek in the nineteenth century than previously estimated.[6] This is coupled with a widening understanding of what classical reception might mean: its sources, its

---

[4] Joan Burstyn, *Victorian Education and the Ideal of Womanhood* (London: Croom Helm Publishers, 1980), pp. 18–22; Christopher Stray, *Classics Transformed: Schools, Universities and Society in England, 1830–1960* (Oxford: Oxford University Press, 1998); Jennifer Wallace, '"Greek under the trees": Classical Reception and Gender', in *The Oxford History of Classical Reception in English Literature, 1790–1880*, ed. by Norman Vance and Jennifer Wallace (Oxford: Oxford University Press, 2015), pp. 243–6.

[5] George Eliot, *Middlemarch*, ed. by David Carroll (Oxford: Oxford University Press, 1986), I.vii, p. 64.

[6] See especially Isobel Hurst, *Victorian Women Writers and the Classics: The Feminine of Homer* (Oxford: Oxford University Press, 2006); Shanyn Fiske, *Heretical Hellenisms: Women Writers, Ancient Greece and the Victorian Popular Imagination* (Athens: Ohio University Press, 2008); Noah Comet, *Romantic Hellenism and Women Writers* (Basingstoke: Palgrave Macmillan, 2013); Jonathan Rose, *The Intellectual Life of the British Working Classes* (New Haven: Yale University Press, 2001), pp. 4–5, 7–8, 18–20; Edith Hall and Henry Stead, *A People's History of Classics: Class and Greco-Roman Antiquity in Britain and Ireland, 1689–1939* (London: Routledge, 2020).

mediations, its potentially 'fragmentary and fractured understanding' of ancient texts.[7] Rather than the lone male reader studying a
single classical author in his study and incorporating allusions or
'influences' into his writing, classical reception can now be traced
across a number of diverse contexts, genres and media both verbal
and non-verbal, extending the range of art forms that 'used or re-
figured classical material [. . .] to include popular culture' in what
Lorna Hardwick and Christopher Stray identify as the 'democratic
turn'.[8] Classical translation should no longer be defined narrowly
as solely linguistic or literal or indeed involving an education in,
and knowledge of, the ancient languages. Nineteenth-century writers might be considered to 'translate' a hybrid mixture of mediations, adaptations and embellishments, alongside their dusty copy of
Sophocles or Seneca.

It is in the context of a widening definition of classical reception
and translation, and the consequential rethinking of classical education in the nineteenth century, that we can understand the work
of L.E.L. and E.B.B. These writers challenged the binary pedagogical exclusions of gender by writing on ancient Greek subjects and
also characterised the new mediated, fractured and performative
approach to classical 'translation'. They introduced their female
readers to new topics and new texts from classical antiquity, thus
undertaking an educational role. More importantly, through the nature of their 'translations', which emphasised the body, the emotions
and linguistic elaboration and repetition, they drew attention to the
ambiguous, paradoxical desire for the past resulting from the contemporary educational prohibitions.

In her recent book *Ladies' Greek*, Yopie Prins notes the paradoxically 'generic [. . .] exemplarity' of female poets like E.B.B. who were
celebrated as 'exceptional':

> In their diaries, correspondence, autobiographies, biographies, and other
> narratives, we encounter again and again a narrative of desire for an-
> cient Greek that has its own predictable *topoi*: an early encounter with
> the Greek alphabet, a primal scene of falling in love with the language,

---

[7] Siobhan McElduff, 'Fractured Understandings: Towards a History of Classical
Reception among Non-Elite Groups', in *Classics and the Uses of Reception*,
ed. by Charles Martindale and Richard F. Thomas (Oxford: Blackwell, 2006),
pp. 180–91.

[8] Lorna Hardwick and Christopher Stray, 'Introduction: Making Connections',
in *A Companion to Classical Receptions*, ed. by Lorna Hardwick and
Christopher Stray (Oxford: Wiley, 2013), pp. 1–9 (p. 3).

a pedagogical experience that revolves around the pain and pleasure of learning to read Greek, an attempt to translate and incorporate Greek into a body of writing, an idea that the woman writer herself might be the very embodiment of Greek letters.[9]

E.B.B.'s extraordinary prodigiousness in classical learning, which marked her out for commendation and involved her in a strange dynamic of desire, prohibition and transgression, turns out to be repeated, according to Prins, across a range of other female examples.[10] But unlike E.B.B. and others, L.E.L. did not recall a 'primal scene of falling in love' with classical languages. Indeed, it is far from clear that she could read the Greek alphabet, much less study a large ancient corpus in the original language. So, on the face of it, the relation to the classical past which the two poets enjoyed and which cemented their reputations might seem quite different. However, I argue in this chapter that it was closer than we and indeed E.B.B. might admit. Both poets figured their classical imitations and translations as a kind of performance, one that played up to the wishes and desires of its audience and that also explored the ambiguities of masquerade. Both poets self-consciously used the performativity of their work to highlight the artifice, attenuation and reproducibility of the nineteenth-century representation of the classical past and to think about different forms of reading and engagement which alternative pedagogies might elicit. And, indeed, in L.E.L.'s sentimental and cynical verses on Greek and Latin subjects, which appear already imitative and imitated even as they are created, we can see the uncanny, repressed version of E.B.B.'s more overtly scholarly poems and translations, themselves performing their own citational and haunted qualities.

L.E.L.'s (Dis)allusion

L.E.L.'s education in classical and other languages, like so many other aspects of her life, remains somewhat unknown. 'The *Improvisatrice* of the incognito and spell-like initials', as her editor (and lover)

---

[9] Yopie Prins, *Ladies' Greek: Victorian Translations of Tragedy* (Princeton: Princeton University Press, 2017), p. 5.

[10] For my own work on Mary Shelley and others in this vein, see my '"Copying Shelley's Letters": Mary Shelley and the Uncanny Erotics of Greek', *Women's Studies*, 40.4 (2011), 404–28; and 'Greek under the Trees'.

William Jerdan described her, was similarly enigmatic about the extent of her scholarly attainments.[11] It seems to have been in her interests to play up her untaught and giddily feminine qualities so that she seemed the innocent ingénue. While she attended a girls' school from the age of five until seven in Hans Place, Brompton, and thereafter was educated at home by a governess (Elizabeth Landon, a cousin), it is not clear what exactly she learned or read during this time besides a large range of recently published Romantic poetry and sentimental and Gothic fiction. In her novel *Romance and Reality* (1831), one character describes the standard female schooling at the time in bitingly sarcastic terms:

> Talk of education! What course of Eton and Oxford equals the mental fatigues of an accomplished young lady? There is the piano and the harp – the hands and feet equally to be studied – one to be made perfect in its touch, the other in its tread – [. . .] French and Italian are indispensable – geography, grammar, histories ancient and modern; there are drawings, in crayons and colours – tables to be painted, and also screens – a little knowledge of botany and her catechism, and you have done your best towards giving your daughter that greatest of blessings [. . .] a solid education. [. . .] as soon as the great purpose of feminine existence, marriage, is accomplished, the labour and expense of years will be utterly forgotten and wasted; but you have not the less done your duty. Emerged from the dull school-room, the young lady comes out.[12]

Although her recent biographer, Lucasta Miller, deduces from this that L.E.L. found the schoolroom 'a place of pain and degradation', it does seem, from various clues, that the young Landon was drawn to her own private reading of more serious classical work, at least in translation.[13] She read the posthumous work of Elizabeth Smith, a self-taught remarkable linguist, who when she died at the young age of thirty, was claimed to have been conversant in French, Spanish, German, Welsh, Latin, Greek, Hebrew, and some Arabic and Persian. Smith's books, *Fragments of Prose and Verse* (1808) and *Memoirs of Fredrick and Margaret Klopstock, Translated from the German* (1808), with their highlighted 'use which she made of learning', 'every acquisition of science', 'extensive reading' and

---

[11] Laetitia Elizabeth Landon, *Romance and Reality: With a Memoir of the Author* (London: R. Bentley, 1852), p. vii.

[12] Ibid, p. 47.

[13] Lucasta Miller, *L.E.L.: The Lost Life and Scandalous Death of Letitia Elizabeth Landon, the Celebrated 'Female Byron'* (London: Jonathan Cape, 2019), p. 51.

'deep reflection', must surely have been an inspiration to L.E.L.[14] She describes 'a most literary looking table' with novels, treatises, 'two German volumes and three Latin, together with a scientific journal', which gives her heroine 'a cold chill' in *Romance and Reality*, but it might very well have been an accurate representation of her own writing desk.[15] Certainly, she references Arrian and Plutarch as the sources for one of her poems, 'The Deathbed of Alexander the Great', as well as Phylarchus, whose work, now lost, she could only have known through Polybius.[16]

Primarily, however, L.E.L.'s sources for her classical poems were mediated, either by more recent translations and adaptations or by visual material: paintings, sculpture, engravings. The 'Head of Tyrtaeus', for example, was indebted to Richard Polwhele's translation of the Spartan poet's lyric elegies as well as to the propagandistic imitation by the poet laureate Henry James Pye.[17] Landon's version actually subverts their militarism by adopting, at times, the perspective of 'the soldier cowered beneath his tent' who refused to fight while 'his comrades, who had dared to die' now lie 'unburied on the plain'.[18] But the immediate prompt for the poem was a 'wafer', a gummed paper sticker produced by Thomson of Wellington Street and marketed as a cheap alternative to a seal and wax for fastening a letter.[19] Each wafer was decorated with a scene from classical mythology; L.E.L. was commissioned by William Jerdan to provide verses to accompany the wafers to illustrate and promote them, and the resulting series of poems was collected as 'Medallion Wafers' and published in *The Literary Gazette* over a few weeks. In a hybrid mix

---

[14] Elizabeth Smith, *Fragments in Prose and Verse: With Some Account of Her Life and Character by H. M. Bowdler* (London: Cadell and Davies, 1811), pp. xi–xii.

[15] Landon, *Romance and Reality*, p. 61.

[16] *New Monthly Magazine, and Literary Journal* [hereafter NMM], ed. by Samuel Carter Hall et al. (London: Henry Colburn, 1821–54), 45 (1835), 302; *The Life and Literary Remains of L.E.L.*, ed. by Samuel Laman Blanchard, 2 vols (London: Henry Colburn, 1841), II, p. 242 [hereafter Blanchard].

[17] Richard Polwhele, *The Idyllia, Epigrams and Fragments of Theocritus, Bion and Moschus, with the Elegies of Tyrtaeus. Translated from the Greek into English Verse. To Which Are Added Dissertations and Notes* (Exeter: R. Thorn, 1786), pp. 305–19; Henry James Pye, *The War Elegies of Tyrtaeus, Imitated and Addressed to the People of Great Britain: With Some Observations on the Life and Poems of Tyrtaeus* (London: Cadell and Davies, 1795). See Norman Vance, 'Classical Authors, 1790–1880', in Vance and Wallace (eds), p. 34.

[18] *The Literary Gazette* [hereafter LG], ed. by William Jerdan et al. (London: Henry Colburn, 1817–63), 8 February 1823, p. 91.

[19] Miller, p. 151.

of high and low culture and mediation, her Tyrtaeus poem is thus the embellishment of a commodified image, inspired by a recent poetic adaptation, itself indebted to a translation, of a seventh-century BC lyric poet. Thus L.E.L.'s indirect access to the original, which creates what some traditionalist critics might deem the derivative effect of her work, becomes paradoxically the core of the poem's meaning: the mediation is not a sign of failure but a recognition of any educator's complicated access to an ancient text.

Classical reception becomes about the medium rather than the message because the message is inaccessible. 'Leander and Hero', for example, which retells a story which L.E.L. might have derived from Ovid, Marlowe, Shakespeare or Byron, recognises its own iterative origins:

> It is a tale that many songs have told,
> And old, if tale of love can e'er be old:
> Yet dear to me, this lingering o'er the fate
> Of two so young, so true, so passionate![20]

Indeed, the apparent source of the poem – 'the idol of my harp, the soul of poetry' – is invoked but not disclosed. It is as if the origin of the classical myth is an always-already narrative citation, the generic 'soul of poetry' itself. Similarly, 'Head of Ariadne' sets its narrative within a palimpsestic repeated story of love and betrayal. Classical 'translation' becomes a metaphor for the trafficking of used women down the centuries:

> Look back on each old history,
>   Each fresh remembered tale;
> They'll tell how often love has made
>   The cheek of woman pale; —
>
> Her unrequited love, a flower
>   Dying for air and light;
> Her love betrayed, another flower
>   Withering before a blight.[21]

Just as the experience of each woman seduced and abandoned is repeated over the centuries to generic banality, so each iteration of

---

[20] *LG*, 22 February 1823, p. 124; reprinted in Letitia Elizabeth Landon, *The Vow of the Peacock, and Other Poems* (London: Saunders and Otley, 1835), p. 133.

[21] *LG*, 1 March 1823, p. 139; reprinted in Landon, *Vow*, pp. 143–4.

classical myth has its originality tarnished by ubiquity. In this poem –
one of several on the story of Ariadne – L.E.L. emphasises the tired
clichés which her poem laments through her rhyme scheme: 'tale/
pale', 'light/blight', each couplet disfiguring its fresh hope.

Like John Keats before her, L.E.L. is unapologetic about the belated nature of her poems. Indeed, her 'Awakening of Endymion',
in the 'Subjects for Pictures' series, retells Keats' already derivative
tale. The sleeping Endymion is watched by the goddess ('midnight's
stately queen') and wakes up to clichés, 'red as the red rose towards
the morning turning'.[22] The poet declares that the frequently re-
counted story does not impede its sincerity:

> What is this old history but a lesson given,
> How true love still conquers by the deep strength of truth.[23]

But the repeated 'true', 'truth' here seems to profess too much. As
Lucasta Miller has perceptively put it, 'true and false are treacherous
words in Letitia Landon's lexicon, miniature bombs that threaten to
explode at any moment'.[24] For while Keats transformed his belated-
ness into a political act of radical defiance, L.E.L.'s becomes associated with cynical detachment and female exploitation.[25] Her poem
'Unknown Female Head', also in the Medallion Wafers series, points
to the enigmatic nature of the image and the degree to which we are
shut off from understanding the past: 'I know not of thy history, thou
sad / Yet beautiful faced Girl'. But it turns speculation, 'idle thought',
into a projected fantasy of continued imprisonment. Both the girl
and the poem must hide their own constraints and trafficked origins,
a performance which is only apparent to the 'idle thought' of another
performative artist:

> It may but be
> An idle thought, but I have dreamed thou wert
> A captive in thy hopelessness [. . .]
>   [. . .] I can see thee wasting,
> Sick for thy native air, loathing the light

---

[22] This repeated refrain has variations: 'silver', 'weary' and 'stately', Blanchard, II,
pp. 13–14.
[23] *NMM* 49 (1837), 73; reprinted in Blanchard, II, p. 214.
[24] Miller, p. 123.
[25] John Keats, *Endymion*, preface, in *The Poems of John Keats*, ed. by H. W. Garrod
(Oxford: Oxford University Press, 1956), p. 54.

And cheerfulness of men; thyself the last
Of all thy house, a stranger and a slave.[26]

In L.E.L.'s classical poems, imitation of ancient Greek and Latin culture is a tired cliché to be performed, a script to be animated by the
forced vivacity of the 'strang[e] and slav[ish]' marionette. Her poem
'Sappho' (1822) draws attention particularly to the need of the celebrated poet to please her audience. Even more than in Madame de
Staël's *Corinne*, there is a distinction between the public's 'love and
wonder' at L.E.L.'s Sappho and her inner 'melancholy tenderness'.
But even that inner feeling is itself a complicated series of memories
of past instances of unrequited love and betrayal, each one triggering
something experienced previously. It is as if, to coin a phrase from
the poem's prefatory quotation, 'woman's loving heart' is no more
than a 'transcript', a palimpsest of thoughts and feelings ascribed
to – and inscribed upon – her.[27] And as Yopie Prins has pointed out,
even the poet's public song, the 'words that died in utterance', is
echoed back both by the hills and by each individual auditor: 'every
heart / Found in itself some echo to her song'. The poem thus 'introduce[s] Sappho's song as a form of repetition rather than origina-
tion'.[28] To deepen the sense of reception as endless iteration of feeling
as text, L.E.L. draws from her own previous work in the opening
two quotations. It all adds to the citational quality of the poem and
her approach to translation as ironic performance.

Although, therefore, L.E.L. is traditionally associated with what
Isobel Armstrong identified as the 'gush of the feminine',[29] and was
thought to animate her subjects with sentimental feeling, one is repeatedly brought up, in her poems, against the enigmatic and endlessly reiterated cited text: 'The name of Greece is only another word'
('Bacchus and Ariadne'); 'the scorched footprints sorrow leaves in
passing' ('Unknown Female Head'); 'the heart clings to old idolatry, /
If not with true belief, with tenderness' ('The Thessalian Fountain').[30]
Text produces feelings rather than vice versa. So, while the well-
known couplet from L.E.L.'s 'Sappho's Song' would have it that 'It

---

[26] *LG*, 8 February 1823, p. 91; reprinted in Landon, *Vow*, p. 132.
[27] *LG*, 4 May 1822, p. 282; reprinted in Landon, *Vow*, p. 115.
[28] Yopie Prins, *Victorian Sappho* (Princeton: Princeton University Press, 1999),
p. 192.
[29] Isobel Armstrong, 'The Gush of the Feminine', in *Romantic Women Writers:
Voices and Countervoices*, ed. by Paula Feldman and Theresa Kelley (Hanover,
NH: University Press of New England, 1995), pp. 13–32.
[30] Landon, *Vow*, pp. 125, 131, 151.

was not song that taught me love / But it was Love that taught me song', the glib chiastic lines and the rest of her work would urge us to reverse this pedagogy.[31] Feeling is a commodity to be produced and purchased on commission, just like the classical gems and engravings and relics that were the prompts for L.E.L's contracted labour. The prefatory poem for her 'Subjects for Pictures' series makes this performative artifice clear:

> What seek I here to gather into words?
> The scenes that rise before me as I turn
> The pages of old times. A word – a name –
> Conjures the past before me, till it grows
> More actual than the present.[32]

As I have pointed out at greater length before, L.E.L. transforms and compresses classical subjects into souvenirs.[33] I mean this partly in the obvious sense that she published in giftbooks and annuals that were designed to serve the function of sentimental memorial keepsakes. But also, for her, the classical commodity becomes the object of longing which can be animated (or not) by desire. In Medallion Wafers, the fetishised object or 'slightest thing' is the decorative seal on the letters: 'I do so prize the slightest thing / Touched, looked, or breathed upon by thee'.[34] Classics are reduced to 'slight' things, to trivial embellishments, to empty ciphers for other significations and agendas. But there is also latently here the other connotation of 'slight' as denigration or disrespect. In 'Sappho', for example, the poetess knows that 'genius, riches, fame / May not soothe slighted love'.[35] 'Slight' things are already 'slighted', in L.E.L.'s work ('slight'/'blight'/'light'). The imitated is tarnished, trafficked, generic but also gemlike in its sentimental beauty.

E.B.B.'s Greek under the Trees

Unlike L.E.L., Elizabeth Barrett Browning's education was far more extensively and carefully documented. Initially she shared lessons

---

[31] Letitia Elizabeth Landon, *The Improvisatrice, and Other Poems* (London: Hurst, Robinson, 1824), p. 11.

[32] *NMM* 47 (1836), 175; Blanchard, II, p. 197.

[33] Wallace, 'Classics as Souvenir'.

[34] *LG*, 25 January 1823, p. 60.

[35] *LG*, 4 May 1822, p. 282, lines 71–2.

with her brother from his tutor, Mr McSwiney, learning Greek and Latin from the age of ten and reading 'Homer in the original with delight inexpressible together with Virgil'.[36] In her very early twenties, she exchanged letters on aspects of Greek metre, accent and pronunciation with Sir Uvedale Price, the by-then elderly landowner and theorist of the picturesque, who was their neighbour in Herefordshire and a family friend. Her queries and arguments, prompted by Price's *An Essay on the Modern Pronunciation of Greek and Latin* (1827), were so impressively erudite that they were subsequently published as *The Art of Scansion*.[37] Shortly after this exchange with Price, E.B.B. began her important relationship with another mentor, the blind scholar and translator of Aeschylus' *Agamemnon*, Hugh Stuart Boyd. For the next four or five years, she visited Boyd regularly, reading ancient Greek texts out loud to him and discussing classical literature. He tutored her in the minute technicalities of grammar as well as in extending her range of reading in the classical corpus. She confided in her diary on 15 June 1831 her passionate dependence upon his guidance:

> The Cliffes brought me the Seven Cheifs [*sic*; i.e. Aeschylus' *Seven against Thebes*] which Mrs Best had ordered from Worcester at my request; and I have been reading over again what I read with him [i.e. Boyd] yesterday & writing in the margins such remarks of his as I could remember. The last day's reading with him, must soon come, even if it be not past – but I can't bear to think that![38]

Despite these occasional tutors and mentors, E.B.B. felt she had been largely self-educated and intellectually isolated. She wrote to Boyd that 'my classical studies have been solitary and unassisted & I must necessarily be deficient in delicacies which are the subjects of investigation to critical scholars'.[39] Yet, though her lack of formal education in a public school meant that she believed herself 'deficient in delicacies', it also allowed her to read Greek and Latin differently, since, rather than being associated with the classroom and an

---

[36] *The Brownings' Correspondence*, ed. by Philip Kelley, Ronald Hudson et al., 27 vols (Winfield, KS: Wedgestone Press, 1984–), I, p. 352 [hereafter *BC*].

[37] Elizabeth Barrett Browning, *The Art of Scansion: With an Introduction by Alice Meynell* (London: Clement Shorter, 1916).

[38] Elizabeth Barrett Browning, *Diary by EBB: The Unpublished Diary of Elizabeth Barrett Browning 1831–1832*, ed. by Philip Kelley and Ronald Hudson (Athens: Ohio University Press, 1969), p. 17.

[39] *BC*, II, p. 35.

institutional passport to a career, classical reading conducted privately took on a somatic form of absorption, one associated with physical pain, pleasure and transgression. Years later, in 1843, she recalled to Richard Hengist Horne that she 'read Greek as hard under the trees as some of you Oxonians in the Bodleian; gathered visions from Plato and the dramatists, and eat [sic] and drank Greek and made my head ache with it'.[40] As Prins has shown, classical Greek learning was for E.B.B. a form of submission, a 'curious conflation of textual and physical torment', as she endeavoured to drum the grammar and vocabulary into her head.[41] 'Reading Aeschylus & learning the verb τυπτω!!', she wrote in June 1831, the verb '*tupto*' itself meaning 'I beat' or 'I strike'. And the next day: 'I sate down in my armchairs to put the verbs in μι in me', the Greek *mi*-verbs being particularly irregular and difficult.[42] This was, as Prins points out, a punishing process of 'internalisation', as she stuck to the determined 'incorporation of dead letters into her own living body'.[43]

But while self-education in this form was figured as a physical torment, it was also strangely pleasurable and even erotic. E.B.B. joined a small group of 'extraordinary' female readers of ancient Greek in investing both the literature from antiquity and their male guides into it with perverse attraction. Mary Shelley back in 1813 had associated her induction into classical reading with her elopement with Shelley.[44] George Eliot, later, in *Middlemarch*, was to explore Dorothea Brooke's strange erotic attraction to Casaubon's 'dried up pedant' because of the chance to learn Greek and to assist him in his scholarship which he seemed to offer her.[45] The relationship is figured partly through the myth of Ariadne, 'buried alive' (p. 216) in the labyrinth of her husband's claustrophobic and imprisoning mind, with Casaubon initially appearing to be Jason but in fact becoming more and more Minotaur.[46] In keeping with these other transgressive or masochistic couplings, E.B.B. indicated in her correspondence and

---

[40] *BC*, VII, p. 354.

[41] Prins, *Ladies' Greek*, p. 62.

[42] EBB, *Diary*, pp. 20–1.

[43] Prins, *Ladies' Greek*, p. 63.

[44] *The Letters of Mary Wollstonecraft Shelley*, ed. by Betty T. Bennett, 3 vols (Baltimore: Johns Hopkins University Press, 1980), I, p. 3; see Wallace, 'Copying Shelley's Letters'.

[45] *Middlemarch*, II.xxi, p. 199. This is the descriptive term used by Will Ladislaw, who 'was given to hyperbole'.

[46] Ariadne: *Middlemarch*, II.xix, pp. 183–4; Minotaur: *Middlemarch*, II.xxii, p. 215.

in her diary a certain sexual attraction to Hugh Stuart Boyd, located partly in his 'quenched and deadened eyes' and partly in his facility in a dead language.[47] The reading of Greek literature with him seemed to be conflated by the minute attention to the disposition of their bodies: his eyes, his voice, his limbs. 'Mr Boyd gave me Meleager's ode to Spring to read while he stretched his legs in the garden. Very, very happy! – Meleager's ode is beautiful, tho' monotonous'.[48]

So, although E.B.B.'s sense of her pedagogical induction into classical antiquity was associated especially with language – with Greek letters, verbs, grammar, literary texts – I want to suggest that it runs parallel with that of L.E.L. because of this strange association between access to the classical past, bodily desire and performative masquerade. Much has been written before about E.B.B.'s two translations of *Prometheus Bound*, the first under the influence of Boyd and the second while she was conducting her epistolary courtship with Robert Browning, and I do not wish to repeat it here.[49] E.B.B. confessed to Browning that she had previously 'translated or rather *undid* into English, the Prometheus of Aeschylus' and that now she was revisiting it to rebind it through their entangled, intellectual, mutual love.[50] The two of them discussed the text and their philosophy of translation (should it be liberating? Should it be faithful?) as they fell in love with one another. E.B.B. was due to escape from one form of metaphorical binding, at the hands of her Zeus-like tyrant father, only to become bound amorously to another – Browning – who was proving himself very ready to become chained. 'Do you hear the stroke of the riveting?', she playfully wrote to Browning. 'Now it is done – now you are chained – *Bia* has finished the work . . . I, Ba! – (observe the anagram!)'[51] As Prins has shown, E.B.B. and Robert Browning used *Prometheus Bound* as a 'script for the unfolding

---

[47] *BC*, II, p. 118.

[48] EBB, *Diary*, p. 98.

[49] Alice Falk, 'Elizabeth Barrett Browning and Her Prometheuses: Self-Will and a Woman Poet', *Tulsa Studies in Women's Literature*, 7.1 (1988), 69–85; Yopie Prins, 'Elizabeth Barrett, Robert Browning and the *Différance* of Translation', *Victorian Poetry*, 29 (1991), 435–51; Wallace, 'Elizabeth Barrett Browning', 332–3; Drummond; Isobel Hurst, 'Elizabeth Barrett Browning', in Vance and Wallace (eds), pp. 462–4; Prins, *Ladies' Greek*, pp. 31–2, 59–62, 65–84, 90–1.

[50] *BC*, X, p. 102.

[51] *BC*, XII, p. 132.

drama of their lives', drawing upon ideas of translation as a dynamic metaphor for reciprocal desire and the erotic appeal of difference.[52]

In addition to the Prometheus translations, however, E.B.B. revealed her association of classical translation with desire in a series of translations that she produced in 1845 for a classical album commissioned by Anne Thomson, a friend of her cousin John Kenyon. Thomson, whom E.B.B. describes as 'a Greek' and full of '"divine fury" for converting our sex into Greek scholarship', was proposing to produce a classical album, along the lines of *Winter's Wreath* or *The Amulet* or *The Keepsake*, complete with illustrations from the Poniatowski collection of neoclassical gems.[53] So, the album would mirror those for which L.E.L. wrote 'Medallion Wafers' in being driven by its visual images or embellishments and being designed as a commercial gift for female consumers, or, as Robert Southey described them, 'picture-books for grown children'.[54] But in contrast to the earlier annuals, Thomson, who went on to marry the scholar and archaeologist August Emil Braun, planned that her volume would contain translations from Greek texts rather than ornamented imitations. The project thus married interestingly the format of sentimental albums aimed at female readers with a potentially pedagogical exhibition of classical translation and therefore – it was hoped – 'converting [the female] sex into Greek scholarship'.

Despite her sceptical fears that Thomson's album might prompt a superficial 'fashion for scholarship', and make light of the 'year after year of studious life' necessary for the genuine classical translator, E.B.B. obliged her friend and produced translations from nine ancient authors: Homer, Hesiod, Anacreon, Euripides, Theocritus, Bion, Nonnus, Apuleius and Achilles Tatius.[55] A frequently recurring complaint at this time was that annuals had encouraged a form of surface reading of anthologised extracts, paralysing the 'invigorating power of books':

> The press has a constant issue of journals containing in many instances well written but short critiques, interspersed with copious extracts. To

---

[52] Prins, 'Elizabeth Barrett, Robert Browning and the *Différance* of Translation', p. 435 and *passim*.

[53] *BC*, X, p. 222.

[54] Anne Renier, *Friendship's Offering: An Essay on the Annuals and Gift Books of the Nineteenth Century* (London: Private Libraries Association, 1964), p. 12.

[55] *BC*, X, p. 222.

thousands of people these papers suffice; they go on tasting the cream that is skimmed off for them, and never once look upon the 'honest face' of a book [. . .] The knowledge – the mental ownership (if so we may phrase our meaning) – of a single genuine book freshly cast from a human mind is worth all the sweets that bees can gather together from out of a thousand flowers.[56]

But E.B.B. exploited these 'skimmed off', flowery expectations to their full potential in her translations, drawing attention to their compressed qualities as 'extracts' and their characteristic linguistic ornamentation in order to think about different kinds of classical reading.

Her translation of *Idyl* XI, by the Hellenistic poet Theocritus, for example, omits the first six lines, which in the original Greek discuss the difficulty of finding a cure for love, the only cure being poetry. Instead, E.B.B. cuts immediately to the Cyclops Polyphemus and his love song to the nymph Galatea, with a simple 'And so . . .', creating a gemlike self-containment through her ABAB tetrameter verse. Theocritus' poem is a comic grotesque of a love poem, the humour originating in the ridiculous image of a one-eyed giant going soppy about a beautiful but oblivious and inaccessible sea nymph. E.B.B. relishes this comic juxtaposition, taking on some of the ekphrastic ornamentation of Polyphemus' speech and extending it: 'Who with these / Would choose the **salt** wave of the **lukewarm** seas?' (61–2), or 'I wish / My mother had borne me finned **like a fish**' (70) or 'As I, who sing **out here my heart's emotion**, / Could sit **forever**' (84–5) (E.B.B.'s supplements to the original Greek highlighted in bold). E.B.B.'s Polyphemus is both a comically pompous and poignantly heartfelt Prufrock *avant la lettre*, thinking his feelings in the staccato lines of the dramatic monologue. His excess words, unattached to the Greek original and futile in their courtship of the nymph, are like the fantasy flowers which he would like to give Galatea but cannot:

That I might plunge down in the ocean near thee,
And [. . .]
          [. . .] I would bear thee
Each lily white, and poppy fair that bleeds
Its red heart down its leaves! – one gift, for hours
Of summer, – one, for winter; since to cheer thee,
I could not bring at once all kinds of flower.

[56] Alexander William Kinglake, 'The Rights of Women', *Quarterly Review*, 75 (1845), 94–125 (p. 119).

The classical extract in an anthology – literally a 'collection of flowers' – offers a fantasy bouquet to woo its readers which is just as ornamental and uprooted as Polyphemus' floral bunch here.

Idyl XI brings together sentiment and humour in a comic grotesque. Some of E.B.B.'s other album translations polarise these characteristics more starkly. Her translation of the episode in *Iliad* Book 6 in which Hector bids farewell to his wife and small son before heading back to the battlefield emphasises the tender emotions of the family unit even more than the Homeric original while it downplays the humour. In Homer, Hector and Andromache laugh when their son is scared of his father's helmet; in E.B.B. they 'could not choose but smile' (89–90).[57] In contrast, her (brief) translation of Hesiod's *Theogony*, recounting the story of the marriage of Bacchus and Ariadne, transforms the original, lyrical classical mythography into a quasi-limerick, complete with Byronic, comic rhymes:

> The golden-haired Bacchus did espouse
>   That fairest Ariadne, Minos' daughter,
> And made her wifehood blossom in the house;
>   Where such protective gifts Kronion brought her,
> Nor Death nor Age could find her when they sought her.

No longer the gloomy Ariadne in the labyrinth or the mournful heroine abandoned by her lover that L.E.L. explored, this Ariadne mocks the Victorian 'angel in the house' with witty, linguistic poise.

E.B.B.'s task for the classical album was to find passages from the Greek and Latin corpus which matched Thomson's illustrations and to produce translations. In other words, it was to perform an ekphrastic transformation, freed from the constraints that a man more formally educated might have felt bound to obey. In the pieces that she produced, she self-consciously performed other kinds of transformation, from one medium or genre to another. Her extracts from Apuleius, for instance, which she termed 'paraphrases', converted the original Latin prose into verse.[58] Her couplets and alternative rhymes turn the story of Cupid and Psyche into a series of lyric

---

[57] The Greek word, ἐγέλασσε, can mean both 'laughed' and 'smiled', but it is conventionally translated as 'laughed' here. E.B.B.'s word choice is in keeping with the more moral, socially conscientious, tone she adopts throughout this translation. See Wallace, 'Elizabeth Barrett Browning: Knowing Greek', pp. 334–5; Hurst, 'Elizabeth Barrett Browning', pp. 457–8.

[58] *BC*, X, p. 258.

episodes in bravura fashion.[59] Meanwhile her translation from Nonnus' *Dionysiaca*, on Bacchus and Ariadne, was considered so 'loose' an adaptation that a male scholar intervened with the proverbial red pen. She wrote to Robert Browning in August 1845:

> This correcting is a mania with that man! And then I, who wrote what I did from the Dionysiaca, with no respect for 'my author', and an arbitrary will to 'put the case' for Bacchus and Ariadne as well as I could, for the sake of the art illustrations, [. . .] and did it all with full liberty and persuasion of soul that nobody would think it worth while to compare the English with Greek and refer me back to Nonnus and detect my wanderings from the text!! But the critic was not to be cheated so! And I do not doubt that he has set me all 'to rights' from beginning to end; and combed Ariadne's hair close to her cheeks for me.[60]

George Burges, classical scholar and editor, expected a translation to bear a direct correlation to the original words. E.B.B., on the other hand, revels in the unruliness of her 'case', imaging her text as a body to be set free or carefully groomed and set 'to rights'.

So free, indeed, was E.B.B.'s text that, as I have argued before, her translations occasionally have a performative awkwardness, highlighting their foreign, alien or perverse qualities.[61] In her translation of the Hellenistic poet Bion's elegiac 'Lament for Adonis', E.B.B. twists the original Greek into an even more precious and grotesque aestheticism. The dead Adonis becomes as beautiful as a sculpture: 'While the black blood drips down on the pale ivory' (10). Through her prosody, which replicates as far as possible the Greek dactylic metre, and through the awkwardness of her syntax, her puns and linguistic ambiguities, she allows words to swim free of their origins, highlighting the quality of the poem as a clever piece of inauthentic masquerade. Hartley Coleridge's review of her 1833 *Prometheus Bound* translation complained about E.B.B.'s 'tendency to the over-strained and violent, which seems natural to her mind' and wished she had developed more of the 'discipline of art and sense of beauty

---

[59] As if to prove Yopie Prins' 'generic exceptionality' argument, the previous highly successful translation of Apuleius into verse was done by another 'lady' translator 'uniquely' educated in classical languages, Mary Tighe. See Mary Tighe, *Psyche: or, The Legend of Love* (London: Longman, 1811).
[60] *BC*, X, pp. 259–60.
[61] Wallace, 'Elizabeth Barrett Browning: Knowing Greek', pp. 339–44.

which a warmer study of Sophocles might probably have impart-
ed'.[62] But the 'Lament for Adonis' exhibited even more of the over-
strained violence of language, exaggerating Bion's highly polished
rhetoric to make a piece of foreignising artifice. This was, as I have
argued, 'a startling performance of translation which "makes visible", in Lawrence Venuti's terms, the gulf between her world and the
ancient one'.[63]

L.E.L.'s Last Question

When the news reached London of L.E.L.'s mysterious death at the
age of thirty-six in Ghana (then known as the Gold Coast), E.B.B.
wrote a poem in her memory. Over the years, she expressed mixed
opinions to her friend Mary Russell Mitford on the marginally older
poet, admiring her 'raw bare powers' while wishing that 'she had
been more intellectual' and done more than 'striking of one note'.[64]
Yet in the memorial poem, 'L.E.L.'s Last Question', published within
a couple of weeks in the *Athenaeum*, 26 January 1839, E.B.B. took
a line from the poet's final work – 'Do you think of me as I think of
you?' – and echoed back its already enigmatic self-reflexivity in reit-
erative, imitative verses:

> It seemed not much to ask – as I of you?
> We all do ask the same. No eyelids cover
> Within the meekest eyes, that question over,
> And little in the world the Loving do
> But sit (among the rocks?) and listen for
> The echo of their own love evermore –
> 'Do you think of me as I think of you?'[65]

E.B.B. was echoing back L.E.L.'s own 'one note' to form an ironic
harmony.

[62] Hartley Coleridge, 'Modern English Poetesses', *Quarterly Review*, 66 (1840),
374–418 (p. 383).
[63] Wallace, 'Elizabeth Barrett Browning: Knowing Greek', p. 344; see Lawrence
Venuti, *The Translator's Invisibility: A History of Translation* (London:
Routledge, 1995).
[64] *BC*, V, p. 74; III, p. 194.
[65] Elizabeth Barrett Browning, *The Poetical Works of Elizabeth Barrett Browning*,
ed. by Harriet Waters Preston (Boston: Houghton Mifflin, 1974), p. 178.

Reflection was a key trope of E.B.B.'s concept of translation. In the preface to her 1833 translation of *Prometheus Bound*, she had argued that there was more than one way to respond to past texts, observing that 'a mirror may be held in different lights by different hands; and, according to the position of those hands, will the light fall'.[66] E.B.B.'s 'mirror' could only reflect the text with which it was presented; translation was a form of echo or ventriloquism. Yet that 'mirror' could alter the angle of the light, could become a deflection as well as a reflection, a prism rather than a single note of illumination. Seeing the world prismatically through the work of other writers, rather than directly from experience, had, of course, become the necessary training that the sickly E.B.B. had had to endure. Confined to the house and with no prospect of 'ever passing the threshold of one room again', she lived vicariously in 'books and dreams'. Like Plato's prisoners in the cave, her world was formed from the 'lumbering, ponderous, helpless knowledge of books'. As a 'blind poet', like Homer, her life was lived 'inwardly', transforming the reflected experiences of others into imagined feeling and thought.[67] L.E.L.'s last question, from the Gold Coast, becomes another such vicarious glimpse to be analysed and refracted.

Despite their apparently different styles and educational attainments, E.B.B. and L.E.L. were connected in their performing, reflecting and deflecting of other voices, classical myths and past texts, a strangely collaborative pedagogical and experimental venture. George Henry Lewes complained that the literature of women was 'too much a literature of imitation', but both L.E.L. and E.B.B. subverted this criticism and turned 'imitation' into an awkward and feisty virtue.[68] Both drew attention to the artifice and wordplay of translation and to the paradoxical desire for the classical world which the prohibition on learning and the temporal distance of the ancient past produced. L.E.L.'s last question was yet another echo which E.B.B. incorporated into her complex palimpsest of translations and re-mediations and performances of the female poet, her symbol of

---

[66] Elizabeth Barrett Browning, *Prometheus Bound: Translated from the Greek of Aeschylus, and Miscellaneous Poems, by the Translator* (London: Valpy, 1833), p. 3.

[67] *BC*, X, p. 133.

[68] George Henry Lewes, 'The Lady Novelists', *Westminster Review*, 58 (July 1852), 129–41 (p. 132).

the receptive mind shaped by the public's imaginative desires and projections over the centuries:

> A palimpsest, a prophet's holograph
> Defiled, erased and covered by a monk's –
> The apocalypse, by a Longus! poring on
> Which obscene text, we may discern perhaps
> Some fair, fine trace of what was written once,
> Some upstroke of an alpha and omega
> Expressing the old scripture.[69]

Works Cited

Primary

The Amulet: or, Christian and Literary Remembrancer, ed. by S. C. Hall (London: Frederick Westley and A. H. Davis, 1826–36)

Browning, Elizabeth Barrett, *The Art of Scansion: With an Introduction by Alice Meynell* (London: Clement Shorter, 1916)

——. *Aurora Leigh*, ed. by Kerry McSweeney (Oxford: Oxford University Press, 1993)

——. *The Brownings' Correspondence*, ed. by Philip Kelley, Ronald Hudson et al., 27 vols (Winfield, KS: Wedgestone Press, 1984–)

——. *Diary by EBB: The Unpublished Diary of Elizabeth Barrett Browning 1831–1832*, ed. by Philip Kelley and Ronald Hudson (Athens: Ohio University Press, 1969)

——. *Poetical Works*, 10th edn, 5 vols (London: Smith, Elder and Co., 1873)

——. *The Poetical Works of Elizabeth Barrett Browning*, ed. by Harriet Waters Preston and with a new introduction by Ruth M. Adams (Boston: Houghton Mifflin, 1974)

——. *Prometheus Bound: Translated from the Greek of Aeschylus, and Miscellaneous Poems, by the Translator* (London: Valpy, 1833)

Coleridge, Hartley, 'Modern English Poetesses', *Quarterly Review*, 66 (1840), 374–418

Disraeli, Benjamin, *Letters*, ed. by J. A. W. Gunn et al., 10 vols (Toronto: University of Toronto Press, 1982)

Eliot, George, *Middlemarch*, ed. by David Carroll (Oxford: Oxford University Press, 1986)

---

[69] Elizabeth Barrett Browning, *Aurora Leigh*, ed. by Kerry McSweeney (Oxford: Oxford University Press, 1993), p. 28.

Keats, John, *The Poems of John Keats*, ed. by H. W. Garrod (Oxford: Oxford University Press, 1956)

The Keepsake, ed. by F. M. Reynolds et al. (London: Hurst, Chance and Co., 1828–56)

Kinglake, Alexander William, 'The Rights of Women', *Quarterly Review*, 75 (1845), 94–125

Landon, Letitia Elizabeth, *The Improvisatrice, and Other Poems* (London: Hurst, Robinson, 1824)

——. *The Life and Literary Remains of L.E.L.*, ed. by Samuel Laman Blanchard, 2 vols (London: Henry Colburn, 1841)

——. *Romance and Reality: With a Memoir of the Author* (London: R. Bentley, 1852)

——. *The Vow of the Peacock, and Other Poems* (London: Saunders and Otley, 1835)

Lewes, George Henry, 'The Lady Novelists', *Westminster Review*, 58 (London: John Chapman, 1852), 129–41

The Literary Gazette [LG], ed. by William Jerdan et al. (London: Henry Colburn, 1817–63)

New Monthly Magazine, and Literary Journal [NMM], ed. by Samuel Carter Hall et al. (London: Henry Colburn, 1821–54)

Polwhele, Richard, *The Idyllia, Epigrams and Fragments of Theocritus, Bion and Moschus, with the Elegies of Tyrtaeus. Translated from the Greek into English Verse. To Which Are Added Dissertations and Notes* (Exeter: R. Thorn, 1786)

Pye, Henry James, *The War Elegies of Tyrtaeus, Imitated and Addressed to the People of Great Britain: With Some Observations on the Life and Poems of Tyrtaeus* (London: Cadell and Davies, 1795)

Shelley, Mary, *The Letters of Mary Wollstonecraft Shelley*, ed. by Betty T. Bennett, 3 vols (Baltimore: Johns Hopkins University Press, 1980)

Smith, Elizabeth, *Fragments in Prose and Verse: With Some Account of Her Life and Character by H. M. Bowdler* (London: Cadell and Davies, 1811)

Tighe, Mary, *Psyche: or, The Legend of Love* (London: Longman. 1811)

The Winter's Wreath: or, A Collection of Original Contributions in Prose and Verse, ed. by George Smith (London: George Whittaker, 1828–32)

Secondary

Armstrong, Isobel, 'The Gush of the Feminine', in *Romantic Women Writers: Voices and Countervoices*, ed. by Paula Feldman and Theresa Kelley (Hanover, NH: University Press of New England, 1995), pp. 13–32

Burstyn, Joan, *Victorian Education and the Ideal of Womanhood* (London: Croom Helm Publishers, 1980)

Comet, Noah, *Romantic Hellenism and Women Writers* (Basingstoke: Palgrave Macmillan, 2013)

Drummond, Clara, '"A Grand Possible": Elizabeth Barrett Browning's Translations of Aeschylus's *Prometheus Bound*', *International Journal of the Classical Tradition*, 12.4 (2006), 507–62

Falk, Alice, 'Elizabeth Barrett Browning and Her Prometheuses: Self-Will and a Woman Poet', *Tulsa Studies in Women's Literature*, 7.1 (1988), 69–85

Faxon, Frederick W., *Literary Annuals and Gift Books: A Bibliography*, reprinted with supplementary essays by Eleanore Jamieson and Iain Bain (Pinner: Private Libraries Association, 1973)

Fiske, Shanyn, *Heretical Hellenisms: Women Writers, Ancient Greece and the Victorian Popular Imagination* (Athens: Ohio University Press, 2008)

Hall, Edith, 'Navigating the Realms of Gold: Translation as Access Route to the Classics', in *Translation and the Classics: Identity as Change in the History of Culture*, ed. by Alexandra Lianeri and Vanda Zajko (Oxford: Oxford University Press, 2008), pp. 315–40

Hall, Edith and Henry Stead, *A People's History of Classics: Class and Greco-Roman Antiquity in Britain and Ireland, 1689–1939* (London: Routledge, 2020)

Hardwick, Lorna and Christopher Stray, 'Introduction: Making Connections', in *A Companion to Classical Receptions*, ed. by Lorna Hardwick and Christopher Stray (Oxford: Wiley, 2013), pp. 1–9

Hurst, Isobel, 'Elizabeth Barrett Browning', in *The Oxford History of Classical Reception in English Literature, 1790–1880*, ed. by Norman Vance and Jennifer Wallace (Oxford: Oxford University Press, 2015), pp. 449–70

——. *Victorian Women Writers and the Classics: The Feminine of Homer* (Oxford: Oxford University Press, 2006)

McElduff, Siobhan, 'Fractured Understandings: Towards a History of Classical Reception among Non-Elite Groups', in *Classics and the Uses of Reception*, ed. by Charles Martindale and Richard F. Thomas (Oxford: Blackwell, 2006), pp. 180–91

Miller, Lucasta, *L.E.L.: The Lost Life and Scandalous Death of Letitia Elizabeth Landon, the Celebrated 'Female Byron'* (London: Jonathan Cape, 2019)

Prins, Yopie, 'Elizabeth Barrett, Robert Browning and the *Différance* of Translation', *Victorian Poetry*, 29 (1991), 435–51

——. *Ladies' Greek: Victorian Translations of Tragedy* (Princeton: Princeton University Press, 2017)

——. *Victorian Sappho* (Princeton: Princeton University Press, 1999)

Renier, Anne, *Friendship's Offering: An Essay on the Annuals and Gift Books of the Nineteenth Century* (London: Private Libraries Association, 1964)

Rose, Jonathan, *The Intellectual Life of the British Working Classes* (New Haven: Yale University Press, 2001)

Stray, Christopher, *Classics Transformed: Schools, Universities and Society in England, 1830–1960* (Oxford: Oxford University Press, 1998)

Vance, Norman, 'Classical Authors, 1790–1880', in *The Oxford History of Classical Reception in English Literature, 1790–1880*, ed. by Norman Vance and Jennifer Wallace (Oxford: Oxford University Press, 2015), pp. 29–55

Venuti, Lawrence, *The Translator's Invisibility: A History of Translation* (London: Routledge, 1995)

Wallace, Jennifer, 'Classics as Souvenir: L.E.L. and the Annuals', *Classical Receptions Journal*, 3.1 (2011), 109–28

——. '"Copying Shelley's Letters": Mary Shelley and the Uncanny Erotics of Greek', *Women's Studies*, 40.4 (2011), 404–28

——. 'Elizabeth Barrett Browning: Knowing Greek', *Essays in Criticism*, 50.4 (2000), 329–53

——. '"Greek under the trees": Classical Reception and Gender', in *The Oxford History of Classical Reception in English Literature, 1790–1880*, ed. by Norman Vance and Jennifer Wallace (Oxford: Oxford University Press, 2015), pp. 243–78

Chapter 6

'Wisdom consists in the *right use* of knowledge': Socrates as a Symbol of Quaker Pedagogy in Maria Hack's *Grecian Stories*

*Rachel Bryant Davies**

Introduction

Lucy Barton Fitzgerald, daughter of Quaker poet Bernard Barton, and briefly Edward Fitzgerald's wife, 'revelled' in '*Grecian Stories* when they first appeared [...] during the Christmas holidays' of 1819, when she was about eleven years old, and 'well remember[ed]' crying at Maria Hack's portrayal of Socrates' death.[1] This chapter examines how and why prolific children's author Maria Hack deployed the ancient Athenian philosopher Socrates as a role model of successful Christian pedagogy. Hack (1777–1844) and her near contemporary Priscilla Wakefield (1751–1832) were prominent children's authors from established Quaker families who published with Quaker firm Harvey and Darton. Both women exploited Greco-Roman antiquity to consolidate their pedagogic programmes: classical exemplars, particularly Socrates, facilitated both authors' modelling of age-appropriate and individually tailored familiar dialogue templates for moral and religious socialisation. Hack adapted Socratic dialogue to challenge contemporary maxims surrounding the moral and educational value of historical exemplars, and further transformed them by promoting ideals specific to the Dissenting religious Society of Friends: Socrates becomes a model for parental pedagogy and even a Christlike proto-Quaker, whose educational method is portrayed as a modern, accessible substitute for miracle-working.

* I am grateful to the editors, both for their patience when the research was delayed by ill health, and for their insightful suggestions on the draft. I am also indebted to Judy Nesbit and Kiera Vaclavik for reading and discussing drafts. Any mistakes are my own.
[1] Lawrence Darton, *The Dartons: An Annotated Check-List of Children's Books Issued by Two Publishing Houses, 1787–1876* (London: British Library, 2004).

Barton Fitzgerald's Christmas tears were prompted by the first edition of Hack's *Grecian Stories*.[2] In 1840, adverts for Hack's new, illustrated edition cited a review from the *East Anglian Circular* for 'prompt[ing] the youthful mind to the acquisition for itself of further knowledge [. . .] exercising its own judgement'.[3] The reviewer, quoting seventeenth-century French historian Charles Rollin, that 'history, when properly taught, becomes a school of morality, and shows, by thousand examples, more effectual than any reasoning, that virtue is man's real good', concludes: 'we have seldom seen a volume on the subject more calculated to attain so desirable an end, then Maria Hack's *Grecian Stories*'.[4]

What this reviewer omits is that Hack's achievement was her stated aim. To improve existing histories inspired by Rollin's expansion of Cicero's maxim 'history teaches life', Hack transformed the mode of delivery, familiar dialogue, innovatively 'prompting' child readers to an independent 'acquisition' of knowledge and ethical 'judgement'.[5] This reviewer, concerned with how Hack meets Rollin's criteria for historical education, fails to notice that this innovation is designed to supersede existing textbooks with more effective practical learning. Hack's focus on nuanced yet active moral reasoning, shaped by Quaker ideals, challenges Rollin's assertion that historical exemplars are 'more effectual than any reasoning'.[6] Hack is influenced by 'guarded education' practices which restricted curricula to promote Quaker ideals such as pacifism, while encouraging experimental and collaborative learning.[7] Hack identifies a 'massy chain' joining her ostensibly individual, yet chronologically ordered, 'links' (historical episodes): the 'right use of knowledge', illustrated in a series of pedagogical exemplars which culminate in Socrates' biography.[8]

---

[2] Maria Hack, *Grecian Stories: Taken from the Works of Eminent Historians. With Explanatory Conversations* (London, 1819).

[3] 'Interesting Works for Young People, Published by Harvey and Darton, Grace Church St. History and Biography', appended to [Margaret F. Tytler], *Hymns and Sketches in Verse* (London: Harvey and Darton, 1840), p. 225.

[4] Ibid.

[5] Ibid.

[6] Maria Hack, *Grecian Stories [. . .] Third edition* (London: Harvey and Darton, 1829), p. x.

[7] Stephen Ward Angell and Clare Brown, 'Quakers and Education', in *The Cambridge Companion to Quakerism*, ed. by Stephen Ward Angell and Pink Dandelion (Cambridge: Cambridge University Press, 2018), pp. 128–46.

[8] Hack, *Grecian Stories*, pp. x, 293.

Hack (and to a lesser extent, Wakefield) repurposed Socrates' own aim of transforming society through education, particularly the dialogic process of *elenchus*. Socrates exemplifies the possibilities of religious acculturation and pedagogy within a leisurely, familial context. Hack and Wakefield's Socrateses embody the perfectibility of children's characters through education, and especially dialogic pedagogy. This is most evident in Hack's *Grecian Stories*, her only full-length work explicitly focused on Greco-Roman antiquity. Hack's *Grecian Stories* present Socrates' elenctic model of dialogic education as superior to existing historical textbooks (such as Rollin's): engaging children's attention and their emotions to more successfully instil a moral education. History, for Hack, becomes a 'school of morality' when taught in a 'guarded' manner and through active listening, questions and debate. In this programme, Socrates exemplifies both model pupil and teacher whose dissenting beliefs (crucially presented as enlightenment rather than impiety) push educational reform and social justice.

Unpacking Socrates' role in Hack's *Grecian Stories* in light of her and Wakefield's other classical pedagogies involves juggling several disciplines which converge in the eighteenth and nineteenth centuries: historical and religious education, children's literature, and classical reception. Studies of familiar conversational education have shown the extent to which dialogue was modelled as the aspirational form of home education in the late eighteenth and early nineteenth centuries,[9] its role in disseminating specialist subjects,[10] and the key parts played by women authors.[11] Such conversational templates often

---

[9] Christina de Bellaigue, *Home Education in Historical Perspective: Domestic Pedagogies in England and Wales, 1750–1900* (Abingdon: Routledge, 2019); Jill Shefrin and Mary Hilton, *Educating the Child in Enlightenment Britain: Beliefs, Cultures, Practices* (Abingdon: Routledge, 2016).

[10] E.g. Eleanor Anne Peters, 'Observation, Experiment or Autonomy in the Domestic Sphere? Women's Familiar Science Writing in Britain, 1790–1830', *Notes and Records of the Royal Society of London*, 71.1 (2017), 71–90; Melanie Keene, 'Familiar Science in Nineteenth-Century Britain', *History of Science*, 52.1 (2014), 53–71.

[11] E.g. Rebecca Davies, *Written Maternal Authority and Eighteenth-Century Education in Britain: Educating by the Book* (Abingdon: Routledge, 2014); Mary Hilton, Morag Styles and Victor Watson, *Opening the Nursery Door* (Abingdon: Routledge, 2012); Frances Ferguson, 'The Novel Comes of Age: When Literature Started Talking with Children', *Differences*, 28.1 (2017), 37–63; Matthew Orville Grenby, *The Child Reader, 1700–1840* (Cambridge: Cambridge University Press, 2011).

promoted specific moral, religious and social agendas.[12] Domestic instruction and familial conversation flourished from Barbauld onwards.[13] Maria Hack and Priscilla Wakefield were prolific, bestselling authors who expanded this trend with subject-specific content for older children, incorporating specifically Quaker views.

Three main strands of research explore Wakefield and Hack as female pedagogues, Quaker authors, and science popularisers and geography teachers.[14] Hack and Wakefield's presentation of ancient empires has been mentioned in these contexts;[15] however, their longlasting significance for children's encounters with Greco-Roman antiquity has fallen through disciplinary cracks. This is partly because their extensive classical content is scattered throughout books ostensibly on other topics. Moreover, despite the growing body of scholarship on Greco-Roman antiquity in children's curricula and culture, as well as eighteenth- and nineteenth-century classical reception, the place of Classics in domestic, leisurely and playful pedagogy is still relatively unexplored. Eighteenth- and nineteenth-century women have been the welcome focus of recent scholarship,[16] yet British

[12] Michelle Levy, 'The Radical Education of Evenings at Home', *Eighteenth-Century Fiction*, 19.1/2 (2006), 123–50; Donelle Ruwe, 'Guarding the British Bible from Rousseau: Sarah Trimmer, William Godwin, and the Pedagogical Periodical', *Children's Literature*, 29 (2001), 1–17; *New Critical Studies on Early Quaker Women, 1650–1800*, ed. by Lise Michele Tarter and Catie Gill (New York: Oxford University Press, 2018); Aileen Fyfe, 'Reading Children's Books in the Late Eighteenth-Century Dissenting Families', *The Historical Journal*, 43.2 (2000), pp. 453–73.

[13] E.g. Jessica W. H. Lim, 'Barbauld's Lessons: The Conversational Primer in Late Eighteenth-Century British Children's Literature', *Journal for Eighteenth-Century Studies*, 43.1 (2019), 101–19.

[14] E.g. Camilla Leach, 'Religion and Rationality: Quaker Women and Science Education 1790–1850', *History of Education*, 35.1 (2006), 69–90; Bridget Hill, 'Priscilla Wakefield as a Writer of Children's Educational Books', *Women's Writing*, 4.1 (1997), 3–15; Elizabeth Bouldin, '"The Days of Thy Youth": Eighteenth-Century Quaker Women and the Socialization of Children', in Tarter and Gill (eds), pp. 202–20; 'Introduction', in Tarter and Gill (eds), pp. 1–19.

[15] Norcia highlights that their 'genealogy of past empires' often presents contemporary British imperialism in a benevolent light. Megan A. Norcia, *X Marks the Spot: Women Writers Map the Empire for British Children, 1790–1895* (Athens: Ohio University Press, 2010), pp. 167, 214.

[16] E.g. Yopie Prins, *Victorian Sappho* (Princeton: Princeton University Press, 1999); Yopie Prins, *Ladies' Greek: Victorian Translations of Tragedy* (Princeton: Princeton University Press, 2017); *Women Classical Scholars: Unsealing the Fountain from the Renaissance to Jacqueline de Romilly*, ed. by Rosie Wyles and Edith Hall (Oxford: Oxford University Press, 2016); Caroline Winterer, *The Mirror*

girls' classical encounters and how they fit into female educational traditions and the history of pedagogical reform remain largely uncharted. Studies of Socrates' eighteenth- and nineteenth-century afterlives have focused on adult culture.[17]

Hack and Wakefield's early examples of classical education aimed at girls as well as boys are test cases of how classical antiquity promoted the acculturation of children into future citizens through family conversation. Female classical pedagogy, and Dissenting Quaker versions of Classics, overturn assumptions – based on the predominance of elite male institutional educational texts, and later nineteenth-century material – about how Classics was experienced in children's daily lives. In the eighteenth and early nineteenth centuries, mothers and fathers (and visiting friends and relations) are shown in dialogue with sisters and brothers. Although more boys than girls in 1819 would have subsequently read the ancient texts in Greek rather than the cited translations, girls actively participate. Contemporaneous female authors who produced children's classical resources included prominent figures such as Sarah Trimmer, Anna Barbauld, Catherine Sinclair and Maria Budden, as well as Hack and Wakefield.

Understanding the central role Hack assigns to Socrates reveals the significance of uncovering hitherto overlooked receptions embedded in these everyday resources. Focusing on Hack's *Grecian Stories*, I outline her vision of the best 'History' to teach. This chapter then shows how Socrates' elenctic method (with qualifications) constitutes what is 'properly taught' through informal family dialogue: dissenting moral and religious values are embodied in Socrates to such an extent that he becomes almost a pre-Christian disciple or martyr (as in Wakefield's *Leisure Hours* (1796)), an idealised pre-Quaker. Greco-Roman antiquity, presented in this way, is designed to capture

---

of Antiquity: American Women and the Classical Tradition, 1750–1900 (Ithaca, NY and Bristol: Cornell University Press, 2007); P. Perkins, '"Too Classical for a Female Pen"? Late Eighteenth-Century Women Reading and Writing Classical History', *Clio*, 33.3 (2004), 241–64; Jennifer Wallace, Chapter 5 of the present volume.

[17] See *Socrates in the Nineteenth and Twentieth Centuries*, ed. by Michael Trapp (London: Taylor and Francis, 2016); Carol Poster, 'Heathen Martyrs or Romish Idolaters: Socrates and Plato in Eighteenth-Century England', in *Late Antique Epistemology: Other Ways to Truth*, ed. by Panayiota Vassilopoulou and Stephen R. L. Clark (London: Palgrave Macmillan, 2009), pp. 273–88; *Brill's Companion to the Reception of Socrates*, ed. by Christopher Moore (Leiden and Boston: Brill, 2019).

children's enthusiasm so that they absorb educational content while apparently at leisure – the most effective route to 'a school of morality'. In encouraging children's active listening and prompting independent conclusions, Hack models how identifying elements of the 'Inner Light'[18] within ancient characters inspires practical ethics and the application of wisdom in society: a female, Quaker response to Rollin's view of historical education.

'History': Socrates as Ideal Pedagogue and Religious Dissenter

Hack's preface to *Grecian Stories* explores 'in what manner History should be first presented'.[19] Spread over eighteen evenings, the conversation spans famous paintings, poems and current affairs, as well as historical narrative, and is led by children's questions; the interested children are rewarded with further reading, such as Plutarch's biographies in translation.[20] As the mother hands the book (understood to be *Grecian Stories* itself) to her children, she justifies why they should learn about 'the actions of famous men'.[21] Socrates' starring role in Hack's educational programme becomes clear by the end of the first edition. The ratio of images in later editions also highlight Socrates' importance: the 1840 edition of *Grecian Stories* illustrates Socrates' story with five of thirty new images, while the 1877 edition features Socrates' 'poison draught' as the only image of eight to illustrate a character or episode (rather than views of ruins).

Hack's 1819 epigraph provided an earlier clue to her Socratic focus: Akenside's poem asks the 'Genius of ancient Greece!' to 'Guide my way / Through fair Lycéum's walk [. . .] oft inchanted with Socratic sounds'. Extolling 'springs of ancient wisdom' as exemplars,

> to my compatriot youth
> I point the high example of thy sons,
> And tune to Attic themes the British lyre.[22]

---

[18] <https://quaker.org/the-inner-light/> [accessed 31 March 2022].
[19] Hack, *Grecian Stories*, p. v.
[20] Ibid., p. 346.
[21] Ibid, p. 4.
[22] Mark Akenside, *The Pleasures of the Imagination: And Other Poems* (New York: R. and W. A. Bartow, 1819), I, ll. 567–604, pp. 40–2.

Akenside here echoes Horace's *Odes*, a collection framed as an experiment in using Greek poetic form in Latin. This hints that Hack identified with transplanting 'living blossoms' from Greece to England by reworking Socratic dialogue and classical exemplary biographies for her pedagogical Quaker context.[23]

Socrates is not an unexpected character in a classical textbook, but his extensive and specific role for Hack is significant. Socrates is most familiar as the protagonist in Plato's many literary dialogues.[24] He is named both by early Church Fathers as an honorary Christian, and by Protestant apologetics as the antithesis of Christ.[25] Socrates appealed as a model of religious dissent: charges for Socrates' execution included his questioning of the conventions of fifth-century BC Athens, and his sense of a personal 'daimon' (divinity) (impiety against the city-state's gods). Socrates is a recurrent character in Plutarch's writings,[26] which were frequently exploited for the moral education of eighteenth- and nineteenth-century children. Most exemplary biographical selections omit the *Life* in which Socrates most features: despite Socrates' teaching, Alcibiades is more cautionary tale than role model. Hack's choice of Xenophon's 'eyewitness' accounts as her favoured primary sources makes Socrates key to her focus on practical education and civic justice.

Socrates figures in several contemporaneous children's works: he is mentioned in Aikin and Barbauld's *Evenings at Home* as 'wiser and better than his fellow citizens'.[27] At the climax of *Grecian Stories* – the finale of Socrates' defence – Hack uses Sarah Fielding's influential eighteenth-century translation of Xenophon, in which Fielding renders the 'good' (*agathon*) that Socrates claims to have taught as

---

[23] Horace, *Odes*, 1.1.33–6; 2.1.37–40; 3.1.4.

[24] For accessible analysis of sources and interpretations, particularly on the differences between Plato's and Xenophon's Socrates, see Debra Nails, 'Socrates', in *The Stanford Encyclopedia of Philosophy*, ed. by Edward N. Zalta (2020) <https://plato.stanford.edu/archives/spr2020/entries/socrates/> [accessed 28 March 2022].

[25] E.g. Justin Martyr, 1st Apology, 46; Greg L. Bahnsen, 'Socrates or Christ: The Reformation of Christian Apologetics', in *Foundations of Christian Scholarship: Essays in the Van Til Perspective*, ed. by Gary North (Vallecito, CA: Ross House, 1976), pp. 191–239.

[26] E.g. *On the Daimonion of Socrates* (in *Moralia*). See Christopher Pelling, 'Plutarch's Socrates', *Hermathena*, 179 (2005), 105–39.

[27] John Aikin and Anna Letitia Barbauld, *Evenings at Home: or, The Juvenile Budget Opened*, ed. by C. Hartley (New York: C. S. Francis and Co., 1852), p. 288.

'wise and happy'. [28] This fittingly references the eighteenth-century educational publishing catchphrase: *Merry and Wise* was a children's magazine,[29] and Fielding's Socrates had exemplified the phrase 'merry and wise' in seventeenth- and earlier eighteenth-century adult texts too.[30] Here Hack appears to apply Socratic etymology to the phrase's importance for children's literature by capitalising 'WISE AND HAPPY':[31] its recurrence underscores Hack's overarching message that true wisdom, brought about by education that establishes ethics, leads to real happiness.

Explaining that 'philosopher' means 'lover of wisdom', Hack sets up Socrates' biography to 'consider his claim to that title'.[32] Surprisingly, given her pacificist ideals, Hack rejects cliches of 'a sage with a long white beard' to establish Socrates' military prowess.[33] Ten pages describe 'the courage of Socrates in the field of battle',[34] his prowess in rescuing Alcibiades and Xenophon (both episodes illustrated), and his embodiment of the phrase 'wise and happy': 'Our philosopher not only surprised the soldiers by his hardiness, but delighted them by his wit and gaiety.'[35] This militaristic Socrates surprises the reader expecting a 'guarded' pacifist textbook. Hack does not avoid depicting warfare: this is expected historical content. Rather, by describing, not repressing, battle scenes, to depict character and 'the evils of war', she disseminates more subtly her pacifism among a broader readership.[36]

[28] *Grecian Stories* (1840), p. 313; *Grecian Stories* (1819), p. 381. Xenophon, *Apology of Socrates*, 27, trans. 'teaching them [. . .] whatever could make them wise and happy': Xenophon, *The Whole Works of Xenophon*, trans. by Maurice Ashley Cooper et al. (Philadelphia: T. Wardel, 1845), p. 378.

[29] Brian Alderson and Felix de Marez Oyens, *Be Merry and Wise: Origins of Children's Book Publishing in England, 1650–1850* (London: British Library, 2006).

[30] E.g. Abraham Tucker, *The Light of Nature Pursued* (Cambridge: Hilliard and Brown, 1831), p. 44; Robert Burton, *Melancholy Anatomised* (London: Chatto and Windus, 1881)."plainCitation":"Robert Burton, Melancholy Anatomised: Showing Its Causes, Consequences, and Cure with Anecdotic Illustrations Drawn from Ancient and Modern Sources, Principally Founded on the Larger Work Entitled Burton's Anatomy of Melancholy (London: Chatto and Windus, 1881

[31] Hack, *Grecian Stories*, p. 308.

[32] Ibid., p. 267.

[33] Ibid., p. 266.

[34] Ibid., p. 280.

[35] Ibid., p. 273.

[36] Ibid., p. 75.

Hack's citations encourage readers 'to compare our Stories with the authorities from which they were taken'.[37] She gleans from modern histories,[38] but, notably, rather than writing a 'juvenile Plutarch', Hack draws on works attributed to Xenophon, a career soldier and Socrates' pupil. Hack's deliberately 'numerous references' use historical 'authorities' rather than philosophical dialogue to establish her material as 'eyewitness' accounts rather than anecdotes.[39] Plato's Socratic dialogues, such as *Crito*, inform Hack's portrayal of Socrates' death, but are distanced from 'history': they appear under the unexpected header of 'Plato's embellishments', and when Harry requests 'Xenophon's account', he explains: 'I like to hear the truth'. Despite presenting daily episodes, rather than a single chronological narrative, Hack avoids designating her stories 'abridgements': she labels abridged versions a misleading 'conceit', which conceal incompleteness as 'superficial knowledge'.[40] This moral judgement that historical eyewitness sources such as Xenophon's equate to 'truth' emphasises her selection and manipulation of the ancient sources (Hack does explain Xenophon was abroad when Socrates died). Despite the informal family context that Hack models, her overall aim, influenced by Quaker 'guarded education', is to foster moral integrity.

Hack's other works appear to draw on her establishment of Socrates as a proto-Quaker pedagogical figure in *Grecian Stories*.[41] Priscilla Wakefield, another prolific Quaker children's author published by

---

[37] Ibid., p. xi.

[38] E.g. Hack cites 'Cooper's *Life of Socrates*', pp. 14, 16, 22, 53. She does not specify an edition, but may have used John Gilbert Cooper, *The Life of Socrates* (London: R. Dodsley, 1750), p. 16. The second and third editions share the same publisher and year.

[39] Hack, *Grecian Stories*, p. xi. On Plutarch's 'anecdotes' in nineteenth-century children's literature, see Rachel Bryant Davies, 'True Stories from Ancient History? History Repeating Itself" in Plutarchian Exemplary Biography for Nineteenth-Century British Children', in *Our Mythical History: Children's and Young Adults' Culture in Response to the Heritage of Ancient Greece and Rome*, ed. by Katarzyna Marciniak (Warsaw: University of Warsaw Press, forthcoming).

[40] Hack, *Grecian Stories*, p. viii.

[41] Maria Hack, *Familiar Illustrations of the Principal Evidences and Design of Christianity* (London: Harvey and Darton, 1824); Maria Hack, *Oriental Fragments* (London: Harvey and Darton, 1828); Maria Hack, *English Stories, Illustrating Some of the Most Interesting Events and Characters, between the Accession of Alfred and the Death of John* (London: Harvey and Darton, 1820); Maria Hack, *Harry Beaufoy: or, The Pupil of Nature* (London: Harvey and Darton, 1821).

Quaker firm Harvey and Darton, had previously presented Socrates as an example of character perfectibility in *Mental Improvement* (1794) and as a martyr in *Leisure Hours* (1796), traits which Hack incorporates.[42] These briefer versions of Socrates are not sufficiently lengthy to unpack the interwoven strands of characterisation evident in *Grecian Stories*: their very brevity suggests both the fruitfulness of this reception of Socrates, and the interconnectedness of these works.[43] While the various titles have different objectives, Hack and Wakefield share a primary concern: perfecting individual characters and thereby wider society through educational dialogue supported by religious conviction. Socrates is, as we shall see, the corrective to established educational models. Hack's Socrates, particularly, can be seen as not only a response to previous textbooks (such as Rollin's, or *Sandford and Merton*), but even as a logical extension to her and Wakefield's other portrayals of ancient education.

Grecian Stories emphasises Socrates as the ideal character for an ancient history textbook, and the success of its Socratic dialogue format in holding the children's attention. To conclude Hack's 1819 edition, the mother meditates on her children's reactions to 'the character and fate of Socrates', which the family had explored over three evenings: 'she was rather surprised at the interest with which Harry had listened to a story containing less of action and variety than those he had before heard'.[44] The narrator even reports that Harry 'could not go to sleep'[45] because he was so immersed in Socrates' biography, and demanded further discussion at breakfast. Harry wants reassurance concerning Socrates' dying wish of a sacrifice to Asclepius. The key problem is of Socrates as Christian role model: Harry's question is key to unpacking a potential sticking point in the suitability of ancient characters as role models for Christian children, extensively justified by Anglican authors of 'juvenile Plutarchs' such as William Mavor and Catherine Sinclair.[46] Harry's delayed sleep over this problem is not interpreted as concerning, but as evidence

---

[42] Priscilla Wakefield, *Leisure Hours: or, Entertaining Dialogues [. . .] Designed as Lessons of Morality for Youth* (London: Harvey and Darton, 1796), p. 22.

[43] See Poster; Priscilla Wakefield, *Mental Improvement: or, The Beauties and Wonders of Nature and Art, Conveyed in a Series of Instructive Conversations*, 2 vols (London: Harvey and Darton, 1794).

[44] Ibid., p. 317.

[45] Ibid., p. 318.

[46] E.g. William Fordyce Mavor, *A Selection of the Lives of Plutarch Abridged [. . .] for the Use of Schools. By William Mavor* (London: R. Phillips, 1800); Catherine Sinclair, *The Lives of the Caesars: or, The Juvenile Plutarch* (London, 1847).

that Hack's tailored dialogic method has successfully awakened his enthusiasm. As the following sections explore, Hack and Wakefield's conversations instilled educational and moral content through enjoyment of the ancient content, often through presenting ancient characters in terms relevant to children's own experiences.

'Properly Taught': Socratic *Elenchus* as Familiar/Maternal Conversation and Playful Pedagogy

When *Grecian Stories* was reissued with illustrations in 1840, Hack's new epigraph was Bunyan's defence of dialogue:

> I find that men as high as trees will writ
> Dialogue-wise, yet no man doth them slight
> For writing so.[47]

Hack explains that a scarcity of books made 'discourse' in ancient Athens 'the usual method of instruction'.[48] Hack's detailed account of Socrates' success in teaching Xenophon, her source author, promotes the Socratic *elenchus* as a means to inculcate Socratic virtues and as template for familiar conversation where the interlocutor is often the parent. Both Wakefield and Hack show familiar dialogue as especially powerful when led by maternal interlocutors.

Hack introduces 'the story of Socrates' as one of successful 'instruction [which] contributed to form the character which you admire[d]'.[49] Xenophon's 'first meeting' with Socrates illustrates the progression of educational dialogue from everyday domestic contexts to philosophical questions: 'Mamma' describes how Socrates barred Xenophon's way to ask, firstly, where to buy food, and secondly, 'In what place do men learn virtue?' Hack's application of Socratic dialogue fostered practical 'virtue' through interactive, question-led learning as a corrective to dominant (male, traditional) educational models, both ancient and modern.

Hack frequently cites 'venerable Rollin' and occasionally *Sandford and Merton* as examples of such modern educational models.[50] Rollin's detailed chronological narration is broken only by

---

[47] Hack, *Grecian Stories*, title page.
[48] Ibid., p. 269.
[49] Ibid., p. 267.
[50] E.g. Ibid., p. xiv.

subheadings; he identifies his own flaws of 'dry sterility' and 'tedious accuracy'.[51] Thomas Day's three-volume *History of Sandford and Merton* (1783–9) is more similar to *Grecian Stories*. Also published by Harvey and Darton, this was an abolitionist and Rousseau-inspired collection of stories which Day considered suited 'to the faculties of children' and connected 'by a continued narration'.[52] Hack's Mrs B. admits to enjoying Day's stories as a girl, and allows Lucy to read an episode, but discusses with her children at length why she considers it unsuitable and 'unjust'.[53] Day's educational discursions were not intended for children,[54] and the stories, separated from the framing dialogue by subheadings, have minimal ancient content (eliding Socrates). Crucially, Day's framing dialogue features a farmer's son, Sandford, and an aristocrat's son, Merton. The vicar teaches both boys after Merton's father realises that his son is spoiled by an indulgent mother: the antithesis of Hack's Mrs B. Hack uses the children's reactions to her familial conversation format to draw comparisons with these predecessors. Harry explains that reading books such as *Sandford and Merton* confuses him, but 'Nothing pleases me better than histories that I *do* understand.'[55] His mother, explaining that 'a connected history [such as Rollin's] was not suited to their age', instead selects stories each evening, but, unlike Day, guides her children through Socratic-style conversation to form their own opinions. Hack proves the success of her method when the children demand sequels,[56] for example, because 'Xenophon is [Harry's] favourite' he 'want[s] to know how they will get out of their difficulties'.[57]

Hack agrees with Socrates that 'instruction of youth' is essential to transform society.[58] She applauds Lycurgus' recognition that

---

[51] Charles Rollin, *The Ancient History by Charles Rollin [...] Containing an Account of the Egyptians, Carthaginians, Assyrians, Babylonians, Medes and Persians, Macedonians, and Grecians*, 8th edn (Edinburgh, G. Robertson and London: John Murray, 1789), p. 17.

[52] Hack, *Grecian Stories*, p. 90. See Margaret Maxwell, 'The Perils of the Imagination: Pre-Victorian Children's Literature and the Critics', *Children's Literature in Education*, 5 (1974), 45–52.

[53] Hack, *Grecian Stories*, pp. 107–9.

[54] See further: <http://hockliffe.dmu.ac.uk/items/0092.html> [accessed 4 April 2022].

[55] Hack, *Grecian Stories*, p. 90.

[56] Ibid., p. 150.

[57] Ibid., p. 276.

[58] Ibid., p. 291.

'The surest means of securing a lasting adherence to his institutions, was to educate the children.'[59] However, Hack's pacifist, abolitionist and pedagogical convictions all censure the aims of Spartan education, a dominant ancient educational model, as 'calculated to make them [. . .] endure labour, to fight and to conquer',[60] while kept in 'cruel bondage to the spirit of ambition depending [. . .] on the labour of others'.[61] The 'disgrace' of the Helot slavery system renders their educational system a failure: Wakefield had criticised the Spartans' 'chief care [. . .] to educate every boy a soldier';[62] Hack concludes, 'it is impossible not to be struck with the great *waste of power* [. . . Lycurgus] educated them for no useful purpose.' The priority of social justice as educational aim compounds Hack's lengthy denunciation of the 'selfish' Spartans.[63] The narrative progression of *Grecian Stories* therefore presents the Spartans, and other ancient pedagogical exemplars such as the Persian Cyrus,[64] as ultimately failed pedagogical exemplars. Socrates' devotion to 'scattering seeds of virtue in a soil where he thought there was more probability of their taking root and flourishing' corrects the mistakes of Lycurgus and other ancient pedagogues: both effective dialogue and ethical motivation are required to successfully educate children and transform society. Both Hack and Wakefield show familiar conversation, led by moral mothers teaching a 'guarded' curriculum in an enjoyable manner, to be superior to the more formal, usually male-dominated, textbooks that preceded them.

The essence of the Socratic method is formulating opinions through question-and-answer discussion. Hack's *Grecian Stories* shows that the acquisition and right use of knowledge is strengthened by conversation. The mother's assumption of the Socratic role is key: she guides the dialogue and incorporates learning aids such as atlases, poems and paintings, rather than rote questions or memorisation. All resources should, Hack implies, be mediated by the adult guiding the dialogue. Hack enacts the use of such resources: 'we will compare the ancient Atlas [Wilkinson's *Atlas Classica*] with the modern' because 'the names of places have been altered since the time

---

[59] Ibid., p. 64.
[60] Ibid., p. 65.
[61] Ibid., pp. 71–2.
[62] Wakefield, *Leisure Hours*, p. 42.
[63] Hack, *Grecian Stories*, p. 67.
[64] Subject of Xenophon's treatise *On the Education of Cyrus*.

of the ancient Greeks'.[65] Maximising learning through enjoyment emerges, almost 200 pages later in *Grecian Stories*, as a key aspect of Hack's innovative interpretation of what it means to be 'properly taught'. The children thank their mother 'for lending us this nice Atlas: there would not be half the pleasure in reading without it'.[66] Both children also relate how *Grecian Stories* itself helped them become independent learners, understanding references encountered in everyday reading without consulting their mother. Harry explains, 'I do not wish to be told everything, mamma; for there is a great deal of pleasure in finding out what once puzzled us.'[67]

Hack and Wakefield agree that women's education leads to better educated children, and therefore a fairer society. A metaliterary portrayal is the first illustration of *Grecian Stories*, depicting 'domestic instruction' of children at home with their mother.[68] In light of this key role of contemporary maternal educators, the lack of ancient female role models appears surprising. Hack and Wakefield's ancient female characters more often fall into stereotypical didactic moulds: Socrates' and Darius' wives are 'bad influences'. Nevertheless, in Wakefield's *Leisure Hours: or, Entertaining Dialogues*, Coriolanus' mother and Cornelia, mother of the Gracchi brothers, exemplify maternal education.[69] These women are important exceptions for Wakefield: even when women are supposedly her subject, as in *Variety*, ancient women are conspicuous by their absence.[70] The ancient woman who does appear – Atossa, wife of the Persian ruler Darius – Wakefield credits with destroying his empire.[71] Perhaps famous women such as Boudicca or Cleopatra are perceived as too complex for the young target audience, or as (failed) female leaders, they are not positive role models.[72] Nevertheless, Wakefield enacts the importance of maternal 'illustrious models' of pedagogy.

[65] Hack, *Grecian Stories*, p. 5; Robert Wilkinson, *Wilkinson's Atlas Classica, Being a Collection of Maps of the Countries Mentioned by the Ancient Authors* (London: Robt Wilkinson, 1823).
[66] Hack, *Grecian Stories*, p. 187.
[67] Ibid., p. 24.
[68] Ibid., p. 1.
[69] Wakefield, *Leisure Hours*, pp. 41–5 (Agesilaus); pp. 46–55.
[70] Priscilla Wakefield, *Variety: or, Selections and Essays, Consisting of Anecdotes, Curious Facts [. . .] with Occasional Reflections* (London: Darton, Harvey and Co., 1809; 3rd edn 1830), preface.
[71] Ibid., p. 158.
[72] Wakefield, *Mental Improvement*, p. 70. Pliny's description of Cleopatra's pearl earring is her only mention.

Her series of dramatised lives in *Leisure Hours*, explicitly intended for reading aloud to 'blend instruction with pleasure', opens with 'Cornelia and Campagnian Lady' [*sic*].[73] Wakefield's introductory stage-setting explicitly 'place[s] the chaste matron, occupied in forming the minds of her children, in a very superior point of view, to the mere woman of fashion'. Cornelia, 'a lady of distinguished rank among the Romans', is credited with the social reforms of her sons, Tiberius and Gaius Gracchus. Cornelia changes the course of history: 'By the noble principles of freedom and true patriotism with which she inspired them, [the Gracchi] became defenders of the liberty of the people.'[74] Wakefield emphasises Cornelia's educational role, describing her children as Cornelia's metaphorical jewels which shame her visitor's ornamental jewellery: 'My time, my attention, my best faculties are all occupied in the delightful task of forming their young minds to the practice of virtue, and the love of knowledge [. . .] will one day render them illustrious citizens.'

Wakefield also depicts banished Roman leader Coriolanus as an example of 'Filial love [. . .] a powerful instrument' (and a common feature of emblem books).[75] Wakefield dramatises his change of heart when begged by his mother not to lead the enemy army. In demonstrating the effectiveness of the Gracchi's family dialogue and the power of maternal speech, Wakefield argues that female education can achieve social justice. The importance of educating girls as well as boys is clearly linked to the central role of mothers in such home education, in leisurely contexts as well as schoolrooms. While the more usual attention to the education of kings and leaders implies upper-class boy readers, here the role of wives and mothers is emphasised as crucial to Hack and Wakefield's female Quaker agenda: promoting the '*right use* of knowledge'.[76]

Hack's *Grecian Stories* adds Socrates to these powerful models of maternal speech as a corrective to pre-Socratic models of education and to previous classical history textbooks, which failed to promote social justice values and instead gloried in military prowess. Hack's maternal interlocutor is shown in the process of successfully educating children who would become 'illustrious citizens' like Wakefield's Gracchi, also possessed of the ethical, religious 'wisdom' held up as *Grecian Stories'* goal. Hack and Wakefield's success is grounded

[73] Wakefield, *Leisure Hours*, pp. v–vi.
[74] Ibid., p. 1.
[75] Ibid., p. 62.
[76] Hack, *Grecian Stories*, p. 293.

in their application of Socratic didactic methods, a domesticated *elenchus*, combined with Socrates' exemplary biography which reinforced Quaker ideals of pacificism and social justice to become a superior version of Rollin's envisaged 'school of morality'.

A Quaker 'School of Morality': The 'Right Use of Knowledge' and Social Change

Hack argues throughout *Grecian Stories* for the superiority of education that upholds 'principles of justice'.[77] Agreeing with Rollin (and Cicero) that 'virtue is man's real good',[78] her adaptation of Socratic dialogue fostered a more interactive 'school of morality' which 'prompt[s] the youthful mind to acquire further knowledge for itself; to put it on the method of exercising its judgment; to cherish the growth of moral and religious principle'.[79] On their first encounter, Socrates invites Xenophon to 'Follow me, and thou shalt discover [virtue].'[80] The New Testament echoes of this exchange are reinforced by Hack's description of Xenophon and Plato as Socrates' 'disciples'.[81]

Hack and Wakefield's receptions of Socrates explicitly addressed how a pagan could function as a Christian role model. Exemplary biographies and histories, often known as 'juvenile Plutarchs', after Plutarch's *Parallel Lives of the Greeks and Romans*, were foundational for children's literature and culture. Many promoted ancient biography.[82] Ironically for a genre predicated on parallelism, many written from evangelical, Anglican and missionary perspectives wrestled with justifying the relevance of pre-Christian characters for Christian children. Writing from the Dissenting Quaker tradition, Hack and Wakefield are prime examples of how religious viewpoints shaped, or could be shaped by, children's encounters with antiquity. Their radically different presentations of antiquity feature a key intersection between 'guarded education' and religious socialisation.

[77] Hack, *Grecian Stories*, pp. 103, 111.
[78] Ibid., p. viii.
[79] Ibid., p. x.
[80] Echoes of 'Come, follow me, and I will make you fishers of men': Matthew 4:18–22; Mark 1:16–20; Luke 5:2–11; John 1:40–2.
[81] Hack, *Grecian Stories*, p. 279.
[82] See Bryant Davies, 'True Stories from Ancient History?'

Focusing on education, ethics and social justice provides a solution to the apparent oxymoron of a pre-Christian religious exemplar.

Hack's pedagogical adoption of Socrates' *elenchus* emphasises active listening and debate, measured judgement and practical application of knowledge: these skills are all informed by the Quaker concept of 'Inner Light', although Hack does not name this in *Grecian Stories*. Foreshadowing her conversion to the Church of England in 1837 over a controversy among evangelical Quakers about the relative significance of Inner Light, scripture and sacraments,[83] Hack frequently emphasises the Bible: Harry states 'The Bible is our Oracle',[84] and emphasises daily reading when asking for ancient history sequels: 'you know I can read [. . .] my own little Bible'.[85]

The value of the ancient exemplars is not so much as models of virtue but as templates of character potential and perfectibility, which children are guided to assess. Hack's introduction of Socrates reconceives this sort of interactive pedagogy as an artistic process. Socrates' 'great proficiency' in sculpture[86] is applied to his experience of philosophical education: 'as he had hitherto admired proportion and order [. . .] in carving, he now began to feel the beauty of regularity in the characters and manners of men'.[87] Dialogue as artistry emphasises ongoing perfectibility of character: a sculpting process. Discussion between Hack's mother and children clarifies that Socrates' attention is turned first to 'his own heart', i.e. character, although not selfishly.[88] Hack later describes Socrates as 'father of the republic, so attentive was he to the welfare and happiness of all'.[89]

Wakefield's unexpected cameo of Socrates in *Mental Improvement*, during a discussion of 'Tea and Chocolate', invokes another metaphor for the perfectibility of character through education: horticulture.[90] When Mrs Harcourt introduces the lesson 'never to despair of attaining any degree of perfection in virtue or knowledge', her husband adds: 'The possibility of overcoming vicious inclinations is

---

[83] See further: Rosemary Mitchell, 'Hack [Née Barton], Maria (1777–1844), Educational Writer', *Oxford Dictionary of National Biography*, online edition <https://doi.org/10.1093/ref:odnb/11834> [accessed 4 April 2022].

[84] Hack, *Grecian Stories*, p. 53.

[85] Ibid., p. 141.

[86] Ibid., p. 268.

[87] Ibid., p. 269.

[88] Ibid., p. 270.

[89] Ibid., p. 291.

[90] Wakefield, *Mental Improvement*, pp. 46–8.

finely exemplified in the story of Socrates and the physiognomist.'[91] The physiognomist, invited to observe Socrates 'without knowing the philosopher', concluded 'that he was a drunkard and a glutton, passionate, and a slave to vice'. While 'the company ridiculed his want of discernment', Socrates agreed with the physiognomist's assessment. Mr Harcourt's moral is that Socrates' 'resolution and perseverance had enabled him to overcome' innate faults.[92]

Hack addresses Socrates' domestic flaws, although this complicates his function as a Christian role model and proto-Quaker. Hack explains Socrates' faults as husband and father by his pre-Christian context. The ensuing discussion and explanation forms part of her wider programme to avoid condemning historical characters – a result of the Quaker attempt to discern Inner Light which also provides an optimistic space for educational outcomes. Socrates' wife, Xanthippe, 'a most capricious and passionate woman', was a notorious illustration of the letter X on alphabets. Hack is critical of Socrates' supposedly admirable choice to perfect his character through marriage to this anti-exemplar, especially his failure to educate his wife to become 'a better woman'.[93] Socrates is also criticised as a father: Lucy is shocked at his children's 'uncomfortable lives [. . .]!', which prompts her mother's only criticism of 'the best and the wisest of heathen philosophers': Socrates misguidedly 'treated [Xanthippe's] sallies of temper with derision'.[94] Lucy judges that Socrates' contradictory words and actions, in 'laugh[ing] at Xanthippe's faults', would have taught their son 'ingratitude of children towards parents'.[95] The mother endorses this critique, noting that Xenophon does not relate 'whether the excellent advice of Socrates made the desired impression on his son'.[96] Hack genders the siblings' disagreement; Harry considers it 'more surprising that Socrates should have had so many virtues, than that he should have been mistaken in one point of behaviour towards his wife'.[97] However, Harry's praise does restore Socrates as a proto-Christian exemplar, reinforced by Hack's conclusion to *Grecian Stories*: 'I have often told you that wisdom

[91] Ibid., pp. 46–7.
[92] Ibid., p. 48.
[93] Hack, *Grecian Stories*, p. 296.
[94] Ibid.
[95] Ibid., p. 298.
[96] Ibid., p. 297.
[97] Ibid., p. 301.

consists in the *right use* of knowledge.'[98] Earlier, the children questioned their mother's distinction between knowledge, 'a heap of logs and stones', and wisdom, 'a pleasant convenient house [built] from this heap of materials'.[99] Crucial to the children's overall approval of Socrates is that he acted on the fruits of his religious meditation, undertaking civic (including military) service as well as teaching their favourite character, Hack's primary source Xenophon. Socrates' dialogic education therefore exemplifies Hack's imperative to put education into action.

Socrates' story epitomised tangible outcomes from meditation combined with pedagogy and self-improvement. The links between knowledge, wisdom and practical ethics were ideal for Quaker 'guarded education'. Over seventy years later, the impact of Hack's Socrates was still striking: *The Humanitarian* even printed an excerpt in which Hack's discussion of democracy illustrates how Socrates sought political justice via conscientious voting in an unjust trial.[100] Socrates enabled a Quaker reworking of ancient history through familiar dialogue, adapting the Platonic model of the *elenchus*. Rather than eliminating hypotheses to conclude in a state of *aporia*, or not-knowing, Hack's guided dialogue is presented as an optimistic method: space for divergent opinions and nuanced suspension of judgement which leads to knowledge. In place of Socrates' famous wisdom through ignorance, Hack situates wisdom in learning, from the past, how to apply knowledge guided by religious ethics. Socratic teaching is presented as akin to miracle-working, so historical education is a more achievable goal for social change, accessible through the universal 'Inner Light'.

Conclusion: Classical Education as Evangelism

In April 1882, 'A Conversation on Books' in Charlotte Yonge's *Monthly Packet* examined different approaches to historical education.[101] The characters Arachne and Spider highlight Rollin's account

---

[98] Ibid., p. 293.

[99] Ibid., p. 19.

[100] Maria Hack, 'A Sketch from the Life of Socrates, Quoted from Maria Hack's *Grecian Stories*', *The Humanitarian*, 1.1 (1892), 7–8; Hack, *Grecian Stories* (1840), pp. 280–5.

[101] 'A Conversation on Books', *The Monthly Packet*, 1 April 1882, 22–412.

of Socrates in his *Ancient History*.[102] Arachne has also, to Spider's surprise, read Hack's *English History* for her 'own amusement'.[103] Hack
is not one of the newer authors that Yonge recommends; however,
Arachne's 'old-fashioned' opinion is clearly expressed: 'correspondence classes, lectures and essay societies', while valuable, cannot
replace family conversation. Spider and Arachne's conversational
format owed much to authors such as Hack and Wakefield, who
modelled 'family reading together [. . .] and discussing the book', so
it is unsurprising that they judged Hack's familial dialogue, aimed at
'well-educated children of ten years old', more suited than Rollin's
prose for children aged five to ten.[104]

Hack and Wakefield's focus on ancient pedagogy often appears
aimed at encouraging parental assessment of dialogic and interactive styles of education, rather than directly addressing ostensible
child readers.[105] This reinforces the idealised importance of real, un-
scripted, familial conversation (although their books could also substitute conversation for an individual) in drawing out the significance
and application of ancient examples. This communal aim further
supports Hack's depiction in *Grecian Stories* of the ultimate goal of
historical and religious education: social justice. Their purpose is 'the
right use of knowledge': all ancient examples are tailored towards
evaluation of characters' practical ethics.

While Hack and Wakefield's Quaker beliefs inform the content
chosen, and the dialogic presentation, these writings appear judged
to appeal to a wider range of (largely middle-class) Protestant consumers. Hack's child characters in *Grecian Stories* are taught about
the importance of meditation and prayer (via Socrates). They also
read the Bible: Harry and Lucy are inspired to read about the apos-
tle Paul's visits to Athens in light of their new knowledge about
Athens.[106] In addition to the geographical and historical connection
to *Grecian Stories*, Acts of the Apostles fits with Hack's emphasis on
social reform and practical Christianity. Such content is a form of

---

[102] Charles Rollin, *The Ancient History of the Egyptians, Carthaginians, Assyrians,
Babylonians, Medes and Persians, Macedonians and Grecians [. . .] Translated
from the French*, 2nd edn (London: Knapton, 1738).

[103] Maria Hack, *Stories from English History, during the Middle Ages*, ed. by D. M.
Smith (London: Virtue and Co., 1872).

[104] Hack, *Grecian Stories* (1829), p. x.

[105] Ibid., p. x.

[106] Ibid., pp. 331, 340–4.

evangelism, integrating the Dissenting ideals of the Society of Friends into the mainstream – largely Anglican – context of British-published history textbooks, when religious nonconformists were unable to receive university degrees in England.

Hack's pedagogical programme, then, not only illumines, but *itself constitutes*, religious education. In evangelical Anglican texts, which judge chronology and significance on a religious rather than historical plane, scriptural events tend to outshine ancient history. In contrast, Hack's *Grecian Stories* feels more rooted in the present through practical social awareness, and more inclusive. While characters are often evaluated according to nineteenth-century values, their relevance is perceived in the unchanged nature of God, nature and mankind.

This modern pertinence further enabled Hack to ground classical knowledge in contemporary ethical challenges. When the mother explains 'why [she] chose Grecian stories' during the first evening's conversation,[107] she describes ancient Greece as 'a brave and free people, who excelled all the surrounding nations'. The ancient Persian Wars, with Greece, are seen alongside the Ottoman Empire's occupancy of modern Greece and the Greek Wars of Independence. Hack's 1840 edition includes revisions in light of Greece's newly established monarchy.[108] Such parallels between ancient and modern – common at the time – often coexisted with imperialism, xenophobia and racism. Although Hack avoids any explicit mention of historically paralleled *translatio imperii* here, her perspective is, as has been shown of her other works, coloured by benevolent views of empire as a 'family of man'.[109]

Consequently, ancient history has the power to shape contemporary moral decisions, a concept made clearer by Hack's 1840 edition of *Grecian Stories*. Here, she explicitly sets the parallel between ancient and modern in the context of Quaker 'guarded education', which promoted values of liberty. Where her first edition ended with a description of Socrates' pupil Xenophon, the 'Philosophic

---

[107] Ibid., p. 4.

[108] See further, Rachel Bryant Davies, '"Our Mind Strives to Restore the Mutilated Forms": Nineteenth-Century Virtual Museum Tours in Children's Periodicals', in *Intersectional Encounters in the Nineteenth-Century Archive: New Essays on Power and Discourse*, ed. by Rachel Bryant Davies and Erin Johnson-Williams (London: Bloomsbury, 2022).

[109] Norcia, p. 22.

warrior',[110] her 1840 edition quotes William Haygarth's poem 'from the writings of Xenophon', and describes Xenophon's military retirement in the same terms as Hack's idealised educational programme: 'in the society of his own family, in the quiet pleasures of knowledge, and in the practice of virtue'.[111] In the 1840 edition, after the liberation of Greece from the Ottoman Empire, the children's desire to see Greece segues into discussions about modern travellers' or museum visitors' responses to ancient ruins. The children's absorption of practical morals is demonstrated in their approval of the repatriation of the Parthenon Sculptures from the British Museum.[112]

Hack and Wakefield's classical receptions thus offer a fresh perspective on familiar dialogue and female Quaker writing, in which girls' participation in historical education is relevant to contemporary and future social ethics. Their classical exemplars reinforce their message that educating women is even *more* important than Socrates' mission to educate the Athenian youth: aside from trailblazing equal educational convictions, girls are presented as the mothers and wives of the next generation – and also their teachers. Hack and Wakefield's mixture of genres – largely conversational, with collections of anecdotes and letters, and combining text with image even to the extent of Hack's toy-theatre-inspired *Panorama* – entwine modern experiences with ancient history and geography alongside morality and religion. Both authors exploit the pleasure associated with sightseeing, and the interactivity of consulting atlases, to breathe life, as well as educational detail, into their narratives. Primarily marketed at middle-class families, these texts are somewhat aspirational, describing – even replacing – the Grand Tour or museum visits for families, and modelling home teaching by educated mothers.

Both Hack and Wakefield demonstrate that the modern relevance and cultural currency of Greco-Roman antiquity is central to children's engagement with, and therefore enjoyment of, historical content: it is this active participation in familial debate which ensures moral efficacy. Practical interactive learning, shown in Hack's *Grecian Stories* through dialogue modelled on Socratic *elenchus*, promotes children's investment in the educational process and guides participants (and readers) to reach their own conclusions (with the

---

[110] William Haygarth, *Greece, a Poem* (London: W. Bulmer and Co. Cleveland-Row, 1814).

[111] Hack, *Grecian Stories* (1840), pp. 330, 325; Hack, *Grecian Stories* (1819) pp. 388–403.

[112] See further Bryant Davies, 'Our Mind Strives'.

narrator's direction) on modern, ethical, applications of the historical lessons – and the social value of female classical education.

Hack began *Grecian Stories* by quoting Rollin's paraphrase of the Ciceronian maxim 'History, properly taught, becomes a school of morality.'[113] Hack and Wakefield's adoption of Socrates as a model of dissenting pedagogy rebuilds historical education to a Quaker design, presenting Socrates' wisdom in proto-Quaker terms: divinely guided meditation, self-improvement and tangible social justice. Where Plato's idealises Socrates' paradoxical *aporia* in which lack of knowledge is portrayed as the first step to knowledge ('I neither know nor think I know'),[114] *Grecian Stories* teaches that 'Wisdom consists in the *right use* of knowledge.'[115] Ancient exemplary biography, written by Quaker women and delivered by moral mothers in dialogue with their children, fosters practical ethics. The Socratic *elenchus* model and Quaker experiential reasoning entails children's active participation in *Grecian Stories*, epitomised by both fictional and real reactions to Hack's Socrates' death, in Harry's loss of sleep, and Lucy Barton Fitzgerald's tears.

Works Cited

Primary

[Anon.], 'A Conversation on Books', *The Monthly Packet of Evening Readings for Younger Members of the English Church*, 1 April 1882, 22–412

[Anon.], 'Interesting Works for Young People, Published by Harvey and Darton, Grace Church St. History and Biography', appended to [Margaret F. Tytler], *Hymns and Sketches in Verse* (London, Harvey and Darton, 1840), p. 225

Aikin, John, and Anna Letitia Barbauld, *Evenings at Home: or, The Juvenile Budget Opened*, ed. by C. Hartley (New York: C. S. Francis and Co., 1852)

Akenside, Mark, *The Pleasures of the Imagination: And Other Poems* (New York: R. and W. A. Bartow, 1819)

Burton, Robert, *Melancholy Anatomised: Showing Its Causes, Consequences, and Cure with Anecdotic Illustrations Drawn from Ancient and Modern*

[113] Hack, *Grecian Stories*, p. x.
[114] Plato, *Apology*, 21d.
[115] Hack, *Grecian Stories*, p. 293.

Sources, Principally Founded on the Larger Work Entitled Burton's Anatomy of Melancholy (London: Chatto and Windus, 1881)

Cooper, John Gilbert, *The Life of Socrates* (London: R. Dodsley, 1750)

Hack, Maria, *English Stories, Illustrating Some of the Most Interesting Events and Characters, between the Accession of Alfred and the Death of John* (London: Harvey and Darton, 1820)

——. *Familiar Illustrations of the Principal Evidences and Design of Christianity* (London: Harvey and Darton, 1824)

——. *Grecian Stories [. . .] Third edition* (London: Harvey and Darton, 1829)

——. *Grecian Stories [. . .] with Thirty-Nine Illustrations by Gilbert, etc.* (London: Harvey and Darton, 1840)

——. *Grecian Stories: Taken from the Works of Eminent Historians. With Explanatory Conversations* (London, 1819)

——. *Harry Beaufoy: or, The Pupil of Nature* (London: Harvey and Darton, 1821)

——. *Oriental Fragments* (London: Harvey and Darton, 1828)

——. 'A Sketch from the Life of Socrates, Quoted from Maria Hack's Grecian Stories', *The Humanitarian*, 1.1 (1892), 7–8

——. *Stories from English History, during the Middle Ages*, ed. by D. M. Smith (London: Virtue and Co., 1872)

Haygarth, William, *Greece, a Poem [. . .] with Notes, Classical Illustrations, and Sketches of the Scenery* (London: W. Bulmer and Co. Cleveland-Row, 1814)

Mavor, William Fordyce, *A Selection of the Lives of Plutarch Abridged: Containing the Most Illustrious Characters of Antiquity; for the Use of Schools. By William Mavor* (London: R. Phillips, 1800)

Rollin, Charles, *The Ancient History of the Egyptians, Carthaginians, Assyrians, Babylonians, Medes and Persians, Macedonians and Grecians [. . .] Translated from the French*, 2nd edn (London: Knapton, 1738)

——. *The Ancient History by Charles Rollin [...] Containing an Account of the Egyptians, Carthaginians, Assyrians, Babylonians, Medes and Persians, Macedonians, and Grecians*, 8th edn (Edinburgh: G. Robertson and London: John Murray, 1789)

Sinclair, Catherine, *The Lives of the Caesars: or, The Juvenile Plutarch* (London, 1847)

Tucker, Abraham, *The Light of Nature Pursued* (Cambridge: Hilliard and Brown, 1831)

Wakefield, Priscilla, *Leisure Hours: or, Entertaining Dialogues; between Persons Eminent for Virtue and Magnanimity, the Characters Drawn from Ancient and Modern History. Designed as Lessons of Morality for Youth* (London: Harvey and Darton, 1796)

——. *Mental Improvement: or, The Beauties and Wonders of Nature and Art, Conveyed in a Series of Instructive Conversations*, 2 vols (London: Harvey and Darton, 1794)

———. *Variety: or, Selections and Essays, Consisting of Anecdotes, Curious Facts [. . .] with Occasional Reflections* (London: Darton, Harvey and Co., 1809; 3rd edn 1830)

Wilkinson, Robert, *Wilkinson's Atlas Classica, Being a Collection of Maps of the Countries Mentioned by the Ancient Authors, Both Sacred and Profane. With Their Various Subdivisions at Different Periods* (London: Robt Wilkinson, 1823)

Xenophon, *The Whole Works of Xenophon*, trans. by Maurice Ashley Cooper et al. (Philadelphia: T. Wardel, 1845)

Secondary

Alderson, Brian and Felix de Marez Oyens, *Be Merry and Wise: Origins of Children's Book Publishing in England, 1650–1850* (London: British Library, 2006)

Angell, Stephen Ward and Clare Brown, 'Quakers and Education', in *The Cambridge Companion to Quakerism*, ed. by Stephen Ward Angell and Pink Dandelion (Cambridge: Cambridge University Press, 2018), pp. 128–46

Bahnsen, Greg L., 'Socrates or Christ: The Reformation of Christian Apologetics', in *Foundations of Christian Scholarship: Essays in the Van Til Perspective*, ed. by Gary North (Vallecito, CA: Ross House, 1976), pp. 191–239

Bellaigue, Christina de, *Home Education in Historical Perspective: Domestic Pedagogies in England and Wales, 1750–1900* (Abingdon: Routledge, 2019)

Bouldin, Elizabeth, '"The Days of Thy Youth": Eighteenth-Century Quaker Women and the Socialization of Children', in *New Critical Studies on Early Quaker Women, 1650–1800*, ed. by Michele Lise Tarter and Catie Gill (Oxford: Oxford University Press, 2018), pp. 202–20

Bryant Davies, Rachel, '"Our Mind Strives to Restore the Mutilated Forms": Nineteenth-Century Virtual Museum Tours in Children's Periodicals', in *Intersectional Encounters in the Nineteenth-Century Archive: New Essays on Power and Discourse*, ed. by Rachel Bryant Davies and Erin Johnson-Williams (London: Bloomsbury, 2022)

———. 'True Stories from Ancient History? History Repeating Itself" in Plutarchian Exemplary Biography for Nineteenth-Century British Children', in *Our Mythical History: Children's and Young Adults' Culture in Response to the Heritage of Ancient Greece and Rome*, ed. by Katarzyna Marciniak (Warsaw: University of Warsaw Press, forthcoming)

Darton, Lawrence, *The Dartons: An Annotated Check-List of Children's Books Issued by Two Publishing Houses, 1787–1876* (London: British Library, 2004)

Davies, Rebecca, *Written Maternal Authority and Eighteenth-Century Education in Britain: Educating by the Book* (Abingdon: Routledge, 2014)

Ferguson, Frances, 'The Novel Comes of Age: When Literature Started Talking with Children', *Differences*, 28.1 (2017), 37–63

Fyfe, Aileen, 'Reading Children's Books in the Late Eighteenth-Century Dissenting Families', *The Historical Journal*, 43.2 (2000), 453–73

Grenby, Matthew Orville, *The Child Reader, 1700–1840* (Cambridge: Cambridge University Press, 2011)

Hill, Bridget, 'Priscilla Wakefield as a Writer of Children's Educational Books', *Women's Writing*, 4.1 (1997), 3–15

Hilton, Mary, Morag Styles and Victor Watson, *Opening the Nursery Door* (Abingdon: Routledge, 2012)

Keene, Melanie, 'Familiar Science in Nineteenth-Century Britain', *History of Science*, 52.1 (2014), 53–71

Leach, Camilla, 'Religion and Rationality: Quaker Women and Science Education 1790–1850', *History of Education*, 35.1 (2006), 69–90

Levy, Michelle, 'The Radical Education of Evenings at Home', *Eighteenth-Century Fiction*, 19.1/2 (2006), 123–50

Lim, Jessica W. H., 'Barbauld's Lessons: The Conversational Primer in Late Eighteenth-Century British Children's Literature', *Journal for Eighteenth-Century Studies*, 43.1 (2019), 101–19

Maxwell, Margaret, 'The Perils of the Imagination: Pre-Victorian Children's Literature and the Critics', *Children's Literature in Education*, 5 (1974), 45–52

Mitchell, Rosemary, 'Hack [Née Barton], Maria (1777–1844), Educational Writer', *Oxford Dictionary of National Biography*, online edition <https://doi.org/10.1093/ref:odnb/11834> [accessed 4 April 2022]

Moore, Christopher, ed., *Brill's Companion to the Reception of Socrates* (Leiden and Boston: Brill, 2019)

Nails, Debra, 'Socrates', in *The Stanford Encyclopedia of Philosophy*, ed. by Edward N. Zalta (2020) <https://plato.stanford.edu/archives/spr2020/entries/socrates/> [accessed XX Month YEAR]

Norcia, Megan A., *X Marks the Spot: Women Writers Map the Empire for British Children, 1790–1895* (Athens: Ohio University Press, 2010)

Pelling, Christopher, 'Plutarch's Socrates', *Hermathena*, 179 (2005), 105–39

Perkins, P., '"Too Classical for a Female Pen"? Late Eighteenth-Century Women Reading and Writing Classical History', *Clio*, 33.3 (2004), 241–64

Peters, Eleanor Anne, 'Observation, Experiment or Autonomy in the Domestic Sphere? Women's Familiar Science Writing In Britain, 1790–1830', *Notes and Records of the Royal Society of London*, 71.1 (2017), 71–90

Poster, Carol, 'Heathen Martyrs or Romish Idolaters: Socrates and Plato in Eighteenth-Century England', in *Late Antique Epistemology: Other Ways to Truth*, ed. by Panayiota Vassilopoulou and Stephen R. L. Clark (London: Palgrave Macmillan, 2009), pp. 273–88

Prins, Yopie, *Ladies' Greek: Victorian Translations of Tragedy* (Princeton: Princeton University Press, 2017)

——. *Victorian Sappho* (Princeton: Princeton University Press, 1999)

Ruwe, Donelle, 'Guarding the British Bible from Rousseau: Sarah Trimmer, William Godwin, and the Pedagogical Periodical', *Children's Literature*, 29 (2001), 1–17

Shefrin, Jill and Mary Hilton, *Educating the Child in Enlightenment Britain: Beliefs, Cultures, Practices* (Abingdon: Routledge, 2016)

Tarter, Michele Lise and Catie Gill, eds, *New Critical Studies on Early Quaker Women, 1650–1800* (New York: Oxford University Press, 2018)

Tarter, Michele Lise and Catie Gill, 'Introduction', in *New Critical Studies on Early Quaker Women, 1650–1800* (New York: Oxford University Press, 2018), pp. 1–19

Trapp, Michael, ed., *Socrates in the Nineteenth and Twentieth Centuries* (London: Taylor and Francis, 2016)

Winterer, Caroline, *The Mirror of Antiquity: American Women and the Classical Tradition, 1750–1900* (Ithaca, NY and Bristol: Cornell University Press, 2007)

Wyles, Rosie and Edith Hall, eds, *Women Classical Scholars: Unsealing the Fountain from the Renaissance to Jacqueline de Romilly* (Oxford: Oxford University Press, 2016)

Chapter 7

Bluestocking Epistolary Education: Elizabeth Carter and Catherine Talbot

Jack Orchard

I have another Obligation to [Charles Rollin] far superior to all the Others: for to him I owe the Happiness of the greatest part of my Life, since He in a manner began our acquaintance. Had it not been for Rollin, we should perhaps never have known enough of each other to enjoy the pleasures of Friendship, but might have been just so much acquainted as to Curtsy cross a Room. [H]ave each Others name down in a long List of Visits instead of at the Bottom of a Hundred Letters.[1]

Let Education's moral mint
The noblest images imprint;
[. . .]
But 'tis thy commerce, Conversation,
Must give it use by circulation;
That noblest commerce of mankind,
Whose precious merchandize is MIND![2]

These two extracts frame what might be considered 'the Bluestocking moment' which emerged in the 1760s until the conservative response to the French Revolution in the 1790s.[3] The first is a 1741 letter from Jemima Yorke, Marchioness Grey (1723–97) to the essayist and poet Catherine Talbot (1721–70), describing the sociable pleasure and intellectual fulfilment she receives in their mutual reading of Charles Rollin's *Histoire Romaine* (1739–50). The second is from Hannah More's *Bas Bleu: or, Conversation*, her 1786 manifesto for

---

[1] Jemima Grey to Catherine Talbot, September 1741, Bedfordshire and Luton Archives, Lucas Papers [hereafter LP], L30/9a/3, f.7.

[2] Hannah More, *Florio: A Tale, for Fine Gentlemen and Fine Ladies. And, The Bas Bleu: or, Conversation: Two Poems* (London: Printed for T. Cadell, 1786), ll. 243–51, pp. 82–3.

[3] Virginia Woolf, *A Room of One's Own* (London: Hogarth Press, 1935), p. 97.

Bluestocking conversation, blending the languages of commerce, patriotism and intellectual and moral growth. This chapter focuses on the ways in which shared reading was essential in providing the early Bluestocking writers with access to novel ideas, an avenue for sociocultural critique and a vehicle for self-fashioning as an unprecedented generation of public female intellectuals.

The concept of Bluestocking self-education through mutually developmental epistolary friendships has long formed a central concern of Bluestocking scholarship. Sylvia Harcstark Myers famously associated the movement with 'chosen friendship' between elite women outside of the family unit. She saw these friendships as a proto-feminist 'supportive structure' in which intellectual activity establishes a shared sense of feminine community.[4] This theory has been extended by Elizabeth Eger and Deborah Heller, who identify Bluestocking friendships with the neoclassical models of self-improvement, Socratic dialogue, Stoic rational community and Aristotelian 'virtue friendship'.[5] Heller defines virtue friendship, originally articulated in Aristotle's *Nichomachean Ethics* and carried into the eighteenth century via humanist education, as a model of simultaneous self-fashioning and community formation which is affective, rational and grounded in virtue. Heller takes Aristotle's statement that 'a friend is another self' and combines it with Jürgen Habermas' argument in *The Structural Transformation of the Public Sphere* that eighteenth-century bourgeois community was defined by the attempts of 'privatized individuals' to enter into '"purely human" relations with one another', separate from their status as economic subjects.[6] In *Nicomachean Ethics*, extending a selfhood parallel with your own to a friend equates to an argument that true friendship enables the mutual pursuit of *eudaimonia*, the ideal of rational and affective completion which is the core of Aristotelian virtue ethics.

[4] Sylvia Harcstark Myers, *The Bluestocking Circle: Women, Friendship and the Life of the Mind in Eighteenth-Century England* (Oxford: Clarendon Press, 1990), p. 153.

[5] Elizabeth Eger, *Bluestockings: Women of Reason from Enlightenment to Romanticism* (London: Palgrave Macmillan, 2010), p. 102; Elizabeth Eger, 'Paper Trails and Eloquent Objects: Bluestocking Friendship and Material Culture', *Parergon*, 26.2 (2009), 109–38 (p. 121); Deborah Heller, 'The Bluestockings and Virtue Friendship: Elizabeth Montagu, Anne Pitt, and Elizabeth Carter', *Huntington Library Quarterly*, 81.4 (2018), 469–97.

[6] Heller, p. 473; Aristotle, *Nicomachean Ethics*, trans. David Ross (Oxford: Oxford University Press, 2009), p. 178; Jürgen Habermas, *The Structural Transformation of the Public Sphere* (Cambridge, MA: MIT Press, 1989), p. 48.

Reading this into the Habermassian valorisation of the category of 'human, pure and simple', a common gloss on Bluestocking sociability, Heller finds the Bluestockings participating in the mutual 'develop[ment] through friendship [of] their essential human natures as rational, moral, and social beings'.[7] This chapter explores the unique opportunities of this kind of virtue friendship, reflected in discussions of reading between two of the first generation of Bluestocking thinkers, Catherine Talbot and the poet and translator of Epictetus, Elizabeth Carter (1717–1806). It then argues that the same practices of critical reading allowed the Bluestockings to situate themselves in the wider political nation. Having established a community of mutual support and moral rectitude, they exchanged letters reflecting a critical and creative reading of classical history to recast themselves as public moralists in contemporary Britain.

The familiar letter has long been recognised as a genre uniquely suited to moral and intellectual pedagogical exchange. As Susan Whyman argues, standards of epistolary writing informed the evolution of women's literary creativity and political self-fashioning in the eighteenth century. Letter-writing 'offered a narrative template to lay over random events, giving order and, sometimes, meaning, to life', establishing a space in which social hierarchies and preconceived ideas could be deconstructed.[8] Leonie Hannan has extended this idea, arguing that 'letter-writing [was] [. . .] an instrument for self-education and self-fashioning and provided the writer with the space to rehearse critical skills', aligning the cultivation of a creative voice with the type of moral and intellectual self-actualisation Heller associates with virtue friendship.[9] Ultimately, the text of the familiar letter is a conceptual space in which personal and collective interpretations can be practised, and from this space new interpretative frameworks can be drawn. This offered figures like Elizabeth Carter and Catherine Talbot opportunities to practise the theological and

---

[7] Heller, p. 470; Habermas, pp. 55–6; for examples of Bluestocking scholarship's engagement with Habermas, see Harriet Guest, 'Bluestocking Feminism', *Huntington Library Quarterly*, 65.1/2 (2002), 59–80; Harriet Guest, *Small Change: Women, Learning Patriotism: 1750–1810* (Chicago: University of Chicago Press, 2000); Eger, *Bluestockings*, p. 62.

[8] Susan Whyman, *The Pen and the People: English Letter Writers, 1660–1800* (Oxford: Oxford University Press, 2009), p. 10.

[9] Leonie Hannan, *Women of Letters: Gender, Writing and the Life of the Mind in Early Modern England* (Manchester: Manchester University Press, 2016), p. 70.

philosophical dispute and historiographical critique which informed their later published works.

Virtue Friendship: Carter and Talbot's Letters on Madame de Sévigné

Talbot and Carter's virtue friendship self-consciously establishes the familiar letter as a vehicle for communal spiritual improvement. Their readings of the letters of seventeenth-century socialite Madame de Sévigné (1626–96), the *Pensées* of her contemporary, Pascal, and their discussion of these figures form a vehicle for negotiating the affective and theological dimensions of their form of virtue friendship.

The seventeenth-century French *salonnière* Marie de Rabutin-Chantal, Marquise de Sévigné, was recognised in eighteenth-century Britain as one of the most significant letter-writers of the modern age. The series of over 1,000 letters she wrote to her daughter between 1671 and 1696, mingling court gossip and expressions of maternal longing, was translated into English in three separate editions between 1720 and 1800.[10] Horace Walpole referred to her as the 'sainte de Livry', and marshalled a transnational literary network, including Thomas Gray and Madame du Deffand, to conduct his 'Sévigné-researches'.[11] Tobias Smollett, Lord Chesterfield and Hugh Blair recognised her as the pinnacle of French letters, and Samuel Richardson even made Harriet Byron, his paragon of virtuous femininity, refer to one of her friends as 'a perfect Sévigné in correspondence' in

---

[10] *Letters of Madame de Rabutin Chantal, Marchioness de Sévigné*, trans. anon., 2 vols (London: Printed for N. Blandford, 1727; reprinted in 1745 by J. Hinton); *Court Secrets*, trans. by Edmund Curll (London: no publisher, 1727); *Letters from the Marchioness de Sévigné*, trans. anon., 10 vols (London: Printed for J. Coote, 1763–8).

[11] Horace Walpole to Thomas Gray, Saturday, 25 January 1766, *Electronic Enlightenment Scholarly Edition of Correspondence*, ed. by Robert McNamee et al., vers. 3.0 (University of Oxford, 2017) <http://dx.doi.org/10.13051/ee:doc/graythOU0030911a1c> [accessed 9 February 2018]; Horace Walpole to Lady Mary Coke, 14 December 1769, in *Yale Edition of Horace Walpole's Correspondence*, ed. by W. S. Lewis, 48 vols (New Haven: Yale University Press, 1937–83), XXXI, pp. 142–3 (p. 143); Horace Walpole to Lady Ossory, 26 November 1789, Ibid., XXXIV, pp. 80–4 (pp. 81–2); Jean-Yves Huet, 'Madame de Sévigné en Angleterre: Horace Walpole et Madame du Deffand', *Revue d'histoire littéraire de la France*, 96 (1996), 404–35 (p. 404); Madame du Deffand to Horace Walpole, Monday, 21 April 1766, *Electronic Enlightenment* <http://dx.doi.org/10.13051/ee:doc/vichmaHP0010342a1c> [accessed 9 February 2018].

Sir Charles Grandison (1753).[12] Sévigné's British legacy tended to centre on praise for her epistolary style as emotionally expressive and eloquent, and a consequent suspicion of the ways in which affective excess in such expressions is made a vehicle for intense maternal feeling.

Elizabeth Carter and Catherine Talbot were well aware of these associations. Markman Ellis' study of the reading practices of Elizabeth Montagu characterises Bluestocking reading as primarily framed around close attention to 'biography and [. . .] characteristic style', with the ultimate aim of 'assess[ing] the right of the writer to speak'.[13] Such a practice makes the Bluestockings invested in the epistolary expression of character. Carter and Talbot's translation of Sévignéan intimacy into their own letters makes it into a principle of moral and intellectual self-education, via the mechanism of virtue friendship. Their engagement with Madame de Sévigné's letters bears many similarities with that of Horace Walpole: they kept each other abreast of the developments of editions of her works, cultivated an empathic relationship with the projected image of their author and, in Carter and Talbot's case, critically discussed her philosophy and status as a paragon of sensibility. Their simultaneous embrace of, and superstition towards, their epistolary forebear indicates their respective approaches to the affective potential of the familiar letter. Exploring the ways in which Carter and Talbot incorporate Sévignéan tropes of epistolary intimacy, particularly the imagined presence of the correspondent, reveals how, at the same time, they find the moral philosophy of Jansenism underpinning Sévigné's declarations of affectivity to be ultimately hollow.

Initially, for Talbot, Sévigné's letters act as synecdoches for pure sensibility: the former's correspondence with Jemima Grey and their appreciation of Sévignéan epistolary style provides opportunities to

---

[12] Tobias Smollett, *Travels through France and Italy*, 2 vols (London: Printed for R. Baldwin, 1766), I, p. 78; Philip Dormer Stanhope, Lord Chesterfield to Philip Stanhope, 20 July 1747, *Letters Written by the Late Right Honourable Philip Dormer Stanhope, Earl of Chesterfield*, 2 vols (London: Printed for J. Dodsley, 1774), I, p. 267; Hugh Blair, *Lectures on Rhetoric and Belles-Lettres*, 3 vols (London: Printed for W. Strahan and T. Cadell, 1785), III, p. 75: Samuel Richardson, *The History of Sir Charles Grandison*, 6 vols (London: Printed for S. Richardson, 1753), I, p. 150.

[13] Markman Ellis, 'Reading Practices in Elizabeth Montagu's Epistolary Network of the 1750s', in *Bluestockings Displayed: Portraiture, Performance and Patronage, 1730–1830*, ed. by Elizabeth Eger (Cambridge: Cambridge University Press, 2013), pp. 213–32 (pp. 225–6).

display and celebrate their own sensibility, and each other's capacity for fine feeling. This celebratory acknowledgement of shared emotion is intensified by the affective intimacy with which Talbot draws the subjects of their shared reading into an imagined conversation, presenting Sévigné as an immediate presence, and her letters as a third member in their epistolary conversation:

> There are some real Authors whom I cannot help looking upon as still living, Mme Sevigne, Marcus Antoninus, [. . .] those who from time to time are to spend or a week or a fortnight with me, & can look upon many little incidents with a kind of reference to them, as if we were to talk them over & make our reflections upon them together.[14]

Talbot's empathic engagement with Sévigné extends to the point of conflating their identities into one another. If we take into account Dror Wahrman's conception of early modern selfhood as 'a set of positions' which are 'relational' and 'collective rather than individual', Talbot's ventriloquism of Sévigné's thoughts becomes a literal image of identity formation as she mixes Sévigné's mind with her own, adding a new strand to her own sense of self.[15] The parallel that this letter invites between Marcus Aurelius and Madame de Sévigné is indicative of the function that Talbot sees Sévigné fulfilling in terms of Talbot's identity construction. Aurelius' *Meditations*, by virtue of their first-person perspective and Stoic philosophical argument, invite self-reflection and engagement. Talbot's affective identification elevates the reading of Sévigné to something analogous to corresponding with her and experiencing the same 'self-affirm[ation]' which Leonie Hannan identifies as one of the central functions of correspondence for early modern women.[16] In these examples, we see the Bluestockings cultivating epistolary intimacy through shared sentimental experiences, and developing their intellectual communities of self-improvement through moral self-reflection and documentation. Madame de Sévigné's letters formed an opportunity and a framework for these practices.

---

[14] Catherine Talbot to Jemima Grey, 15 November, 1744, LP, L30/9a (1), 70.

[15] Dror Wahrman, *The Making of the Modern Self* (New Haven: Yale University Press, 2004), p. 168. The collapse of female selfhood into an affective identification with fictional characters was a danger eighteenth-century-conservatives observed, but reading memoirs or accounts of real historical figures was understood to mitigate this danger; Abigail Williams, *The Social Life of Books* (New Haven: Yale University Press, 2017), pp. 210–11, 257.

[16] Hannan, p. 64.

For Carter, however, Sévigné represented a more problematic model of moral and intellectual companionship. While Talbot was sharing in a playful affective identification with Sévigné in her correspondence with Grey in 1744, she and Carter were engaging in a more sober, critical assessment. Carter offers the following view of Sévigné in a 1744 letter, written in French, as both an intellectual exercise and imitation of Sévigné's own style:

> [L]es lettres de Madame de Sévigné elles m'ont toujours charmées. On y trouve tout ce qu'il y a de poli, et de spirituel dans la langue Françoise. Il me semble aussi qu'elles donnent aussi un portrait très naturel du coeur de l'auteur, qui à vrai dire, à quelques égards vaut mieux que sa tête, sur tout quand elle parle de la religion dont elle se forme des idées assez ridicules [. . .] Pour la traduction de ces lettres, je crois qu'on y réussiroit fort mal. Il y a un infinité de tours d'expression qui dependent entierement du genre de la langue Françoise et feroit une fort mauvaise figure dans la nôtre.[17]

Like Talbot, Carter is acutely conscious of the *salonnière*'s British reception, focusing on Sévigné as a paradigm of maternal sensibility, a journalist of Louis XIV's court, and a paragon of French epistolary style. Considering her as the paradigm of 'tout ce qu'il y a de poli, et de spirituel dans la langue Françoise', one whose letters embody all of the 'spiritual' and 'polite' virtues of the French language, Carter openly acknowledges the nationalistic conception of Sévigné implicit in the comparisons made by figures like Boyle and Smollett. Carter's reading deviates from the standard in her lack of suspicion regarding Sévigné's maternal sentiments, and in the distinction between

---

[17] Elizabeth Carter to Catherine Talbot, 9 October 1744, in *A Series of Letters between Elizabeth Carter and Catherine Talbot, 1741–1770, with Letters from Elizabeth Carter to Mrs. Vesey*, ed. by Montagu Pennington, 4 vols (London: Printed for F. C. and J. Rivington, 1809), I, p. 73; [As for Madame de Sévigné's letters, I have always found them charming. Within them, one reads everything that is polite and witty about the French language. It seems to me they also paint a very natural image of the author's heart which, if truth be told, is worth more than intellect in some respects, especially when she talks about religion, about which she has some quite preposterous ideas . . . As for the translation of these letters, I am unsure of any success. There are an infinite number of turns of phrase which depend entirely on the nature of the French language and which would appear poorly in our language.] English translation by students in the Translation Work Experience module from the Dept. of Modern Languages, Translation and Interpreting, Swansea University, 2018.

'spiritual' and 'religion', which Carter's analysis implies. The 'religion of which [Sévigné] forms rather ridiculous ideas', to which
Carter refers, can be loosely defined as a conservative, aristocratic
mode of Catholicism, which nevertheless bears a strong affinity
with the seventeenth-century neo-Augustinian movement known as
Jansenism, epitomised by Pierre Nicole's *Port Royal Logic* (1662)
and the works of Blaise Pascal.[18] While Carter does not directly address her issues with Sévigné's philosophy, her correspondence with
Talbot on Pascal in July and August 1748 sheds some light on the
Bluestocking critique of Sévigné's faith for failing to provide the ultimate foundation for the spiritual and transcendent model of friendship to which the two of them aspire.

One of the central tenets of Pascal's austere Jansenism lay in the
absolute rejection of earthly interests in favour of a total concern for
the afterlife. In her letter of 26 July 1748, Talbot quotes a passage
from Pascal's *Pensées* (1648), which encapsulates this theme:

> Il est injuste qu'on s'attache, quoi qu'on le fasse avec plaisir, et volo-
> ntairement: je tromperois ceux en qui je ferai naître ce desir, car je ne
> suis la fin de personne, et n'ai de quoi le satisfaire. Ne suis je pas prête à
> mourir? et ainsi l'objet de leur attachemont [*sic*] mourra donc?[19]

Where Talbot is initially seduced by Pascal's argument, calling him a
'saint' and a 'genius' for his admirable disdain of the material world,
she finds the intensity of his asceticism dangerously severe, identifying its troubling inhumanity with 'popery':

> To shut one's eyes on all the fair beauties of this world, was the way
> to raise our love, and gratitude to the beneficent author! Yet this is the

---

[18] John J. Conley, 'Marie de Rabutin-Chantal, Marquise de Sévigné (1626–1696)',
The Internet Encyclopedia of Philosophy (2018) <http://www.iep.utm.edu/
sevigne> [accessed 29 January 2018], §3.b.

[19] Catherine Talbot to Elizabeth Carter, 26 July 1748, *Series of Letters*, I, pp. 281–2.
This is excerpted from Fragment 14 of Pascal's *Pensées*, *Pensées de Pascal Online*,
ed. by D. Descotes and G. Proust (2011) <http://www.penseesdepascal.fr/I/I14-
moderne.php> [accessed 25 February 2018]; [It is not fair that we form attachments, even though they are done happily and willingly: I would mislead those
in whom I generate this desire, as I am not the be-all and end-all for anyone,
and I am not capable of satisfying it. Am I not about to die? and thus the object
of their attachment will die?] English translation by students in the Translation
Work Experience module from the Dept. of Modern Languages, Translation and
Interpreting, Swansea University, 2018.

comfortless horrid doctrine of strict popery, and those good hearts that
have been awed by it into error and wretchedness, deserve equal compassion and esteem.[20]

This rejection nuances Carter and Talbot's Christianisation of
Roman Stoicism in *All the Works of Epictetus* by suggesting that
an awareness of 'fair beauties of this world' may enable individuals
to grow in their Christian faith. Among the letters which Montagu
Pennington includes in his *Memoirs of Mrs Elizabeth Carter* (1807)
as background to the publication of *Epictetus*, there is a letter from
Talbot to Carter on the pitfalls of Epictetus' Stoic doctrine: 'He
bids us by our own strength root out every passion and feeling
implanted in our nature. Christianity teaches us how to obtain that
Divine assistance by which we may regulate and surmount them
all.' Implicit within this philosophy is the Stoic rejection of metaphysical, spiritual reality and the perfectibility of nature. Talbot
sums up: 'Epictetus treats us like perfect creatures, Christianity like
fallen and redeemed ones, and teaches us at once our disease and
our remedy.'[21] Carter closely responds to Talbot's concern in her
'Preface' to *Epictetus*, acknowledging that Stoic materialism is 'flat-
tering Man with false and presumptuous Ideas of his own Power
and Excellence', and arguing that its virtue lies in its 'Excellent rules
of Self-government, and of social behaviour, of a noble Reliance on
the Aid and Protection of Heaven, and of a perfect Resignation and
Submission to the divine Will'.[22] Carter and Talbot's collaboration
in the production of *Epictetus*, in short, presents an argument that
Christian spirituality provides the capacity for moral perfection,
where Stoic material self-analysis is ultimately hampered by its belief that humans are capable of total self-mastery without divine
intervention.

Carter is even more critically inclined against the French philosopher's argument than Talbot. In a lengthy critique levelled at Pascal's
discussion of attachment, Carter argues that while the material

[20] Catherine Talbot to Elizabeth Carter, 26 July 1748, *Series of Letters*, I, p. 282.
[21] Catherine Talbot to Elizabeth Carter, [1755], in Montagu Pennington, *Memoirs of Miss Elizabeth Carter*, 2 vols (London: Printed for F. C. and J. Rivington, 1807), I, p. 132.
[22] *All the Works of Epictetus, Which Are Now Extant*, trans. by Elizabeth Carter (London: Printed by S. Richardson, 1758), pp. ii, xxvi.

world should not be taken as the foundation of morality, the spiritual community which underpins social relationships facilitates divinely ordained moral self-mastery:

> Mais ils ne content pas que c'est a cette même nature humaine tout miserable, et chétife qu'elle soit, qu'on est obligé pour toutes ces belles speculations qu'on tourne contre elle. La meilleure representation que nous pouvons nous faire des perfections morales de Dieu, se tire de leur images dans l'esprit de l'homme – 'Mais il est injuste que l'on s'attache, par ce que nous mourrons!' – cela se repond fort naturellement par – nous revivrons.[23]

In her repudiation of Pascal's Jansenism, Carter postulates a spiritualised vision of sociability in which the worldly concerns of emotional affect and community are validated by the ultimately spiritual aim of true friendship. Having developed and concretised this model of virtuous, developmental community through their correspondence, Talbot articulates these concepts in her more formal essays. Whilst they remained unpublished in her lifetime, they are written in a self-consciously pedagogic style, such as 'On True Friendship', which argues that 'our friendship will probably be extended through the whole society of the blessed', and 'Angels themselves will not disdain to admit us to their friendship.'[24] Talbot offers this form of community as a corrective to materialism and worldly interests, 'the slight connections of a trifling world', affirming the alignment of affectivity and spirituality in social connections.[25]

Talbot's 'Letters to a Friend on a Future State' is her fullest attempt to elucidate the concept of paradisiac community. Her three

[23] Elizabeth Carter to Catherine Talbot, 5 August 1748, *Series of Letters*, I, pp. 286–7. [But, they do not recount that it is to this same human nature, however miserable and wretched it might be, that we owe all of these beautiful speculations that we turn against her. The best representation that we can make for ourselves of God's moral perfections, is drawn from the way the spirit of man depicts them – 'But it is unfair that we form attachments, as we will die!' – a natural response to which is – we will be reborn.] English translation by students in the Translation Work Experience module from the Dept. of Modern Languages, Translation and Interpreting, Swansea University, 2018.

[24] Catherine Talbot, *The Works of the Late Miss Catherine Talbot*, ed. by Montagu Pennington (London: F. C. and J. Rivington, 1819), pp. 168–9.

[25] Ibid., p. 169.

epistolary essays combine endlessly repeated reminders of divine ineffability with a vision of community in paradise:

> But where, you ask, are those companions of your former years, whose time of trial is over [. . .] Why equally in the divine presence as yourself – recollect you not the time, in former days of fancy, when you fondly delighted to contemplate the moon because a favourite distant friend might possibly at the same time be gazing on the same bright object? This fancy seemed to cancel distance, and bring you near together. Think then that not the waning moon but the source of glory shines on them with the same gracious beam, that in mercy extend even to you.[26]

God, in Talbot's theology, actualises the imaginative projection inherent in familiar correspondence. When she describes Sévigné's feeling as 'too lively for [this] world', she is identifying it with the paradisiac affection that can actualise the beloved into true intimacy. This affective proximity is replicated in the temporal flattening of Talbot's language in this letter, which moves from the past tense, 'delighted', 'seemed', into the present 'shines'. God can literalise the imagined intimacy of shared experience described in the letter, collapsing time as well as space. However, as Talbot's bittersweet remark indicates, Sévigné's inescapable worldliness waylaid this divine intimacy. Her heavenly sympathy might have been tempered into a moral philosophy, had she benefited from a community like that of Carter and Talbot. Instead, it falls foul on two counts: her inability to distinguish between divinely mandated friendship and the dangerous sociability of material distraction, and secondly, the absence of reasoned restraint, which causes Sévigné to become lost in her mortal experience. Carter's ultimate verdict on Sévigné in her discussion with Talbot is therefore one of tragically missed opportunity:

> The natural turn of her temper does not seem to have met with any restraint from a regular education [. . .] it is extremely difficult for such very lively people to keep themselves in some instance or other from running mad. [. . .] where the object is innocent, and the affection itself carries a moral appearance, a quick imagination is too much engaged by the first pleasing view to look any further, or consider the ill effects that often arise from a too great attention to even the best particular attachments.[27]

[26] Ibid., p. 266.
[27] Elizabeth Carter to Catherine Talbot, 4 December 1744, *Series of Letters*, I, pp. 81–2.

In a gesture which anticipates Mary Wollstonecraft's argument that the insubstantiality of women's education leads to them becoming incapable of philosophical discernment and moral consciousness, Carter lays the blame for Sévigné's inability to bind her affectivity to a coherent moral system on the lack of 'a regular education'.[28]

In their differing responses to Sévigné and her legacy, Carter and Talbot, as well as Jemima Grey, use Sévigné as a vehicle for articulating a vision of virtue friendship which combines rational and moral self-development with spiritual community. The shared reading of Sévigné's letters and Pascal's philosophical works, themselves acts of rational self-education, are an early example of the broader Bluestocking project of education through epistolary conversation and self-improvement via virtue friendship.

Critical Reading: Carter and Talbot on the Classics

If virtue friendship represents one method by which the early Bluestockings used reading and epistolary self-education to build a sense of themselves as individual moral beings and as a collective of ethical intellectuals, then their approach to classical historiography represents another. A critical reappraisal of well-known Greek and Roman historians and their eighteenth-century followers gave Carter and Talbot opportunities to hone their skills as critical readers and to carve out a public role for themselves as cultural commentators on modern Britain.

As Jacqueline Pearson and Penelope Wilson have both observed, women's reading of classical texts across the first half of the eighteenth century was accompanied by a variety of prejudices and expectations. Whilst reading in Latin and Greek represented 'the core of male scholastic upbringing', it continued to be 'discouraged rather than encouraged throughout [the eighteenth century] for most women'.[29] Women who learnt the classical languages anyway, or read the texts in English translation, were confronted with a discipline from

---

[28] Mary Wollstonecraft, *A Vindication of the Rights of Woman, with Strictures on Political and Moral Subjects*, 2 vols (London: Printed for J. Johnson, 1792), *passim*, esp. I, pp. 113–15, 129–30.

[29] Penelope Wilson, 'Women Writers and the Classics', in *The Oxford History of Classical Reception in English Literature*, ed. by David Hopkins and Charles Martindale, 4 vols (Oxford: Oxford University Press, 2012), III, pp. 495–518 (p. 496).

which they were alienated, whether by 'its predilection for martial heroism and indulgence to paganism', or by the fact that in doing so they 'risk[ed] criticism for vanity and pedantry'.[30] However, Carter, Talbot and Montagu all benefited from early education under supportive tutors who encouraged their acquisition of languages, dead and living. Catherine Talbot was raised in the house of Thomas Secker (1693–1768), Bishop of Oxford (1738–50) and Archbishop of Canterbury (1750–68), and had access to his libraries at Cuddesden and Lambeth, as well as his support and encouragement.[31] Elizabeth Carter received a classical education from her father, Nicolas Carter (1688–1774), curate of Deal in Kent. By age seventeen, Carter was fluent in Greek, submitting classical translations to the *Gentleman's Magazine*, and by her early twenties was providing a classical education to her stepsiblings in preparation for their Cambridge University degrees.[32]

Far from taking a conservative, conventional approach to the classics, which preparing her relatives for their education as gentlemen might imply, Carter's readings of Greek and Roman history were often arrestingly iconoclastic. Comparing Thucydides' *History of the Peloponnesian War* with David Hume's *History of England* (1759–62) in a letter to Montagu in 1774, she assessed Greek 'civilization' as one in which 'polish', the trapping of polite society, is eclipsed by an image of savage barbarism:

> Modern compilers give us a fine picture of the manners of heathen antiquity; but their own historians are more honest, and from them one discovers as high instances of barbarity even among the polished and enlightened Greeks as could be practised by the most savage parties of scalping Indians.[33]

[30] Wilson, p. 497; Jacqueline Pearson, *Women's Reading in Britain, 1750–1835* (Cambridge: Cambridge University Press, 1999), p. 69; See also Williams, pp. 258–9; for discussions of Carter's conscious articulation of her identity as a female classicist, see Eger, *Bluestockings*, p. 101; Melanie Bigold, *Women of Letters: Manuscript Circulation and Print Afterlives in the Eighteenth Century* (Basingstoke: Palgrave Macmillan, 2013), p. 194.

[31] Harcstark Myers, pp. 63–4; For more on the role of Anglican clergymen in the development of Bluestocking ideology, see Susan Staves, 'Church of England Clergy and Women Writers', *Huntington Library Quarterly*, 65.1/2 (2002), 81–103.

[32] Judith Hawley, 'Carter, Elizabeth (1717–1806)', *Oxford Dictionary of National Biography* (2009), online edition <http://www.oxforddnb.com/view/article/4782> [accessed 20 March 2019]; Bigold, pp. 172–3.

[33] Elizabeth Carter to Elizabeth Montagu, 20 August 1774, in *Letters from Mrs. Elizabeth Carter, to Mrs. Montagu, between the Years 1755 and 1800,*

As for the Romans, Carter interprets the conventional neoclassical discourse of the Roman Empire as an ideal state, of which Britain was a modern parallel, as woefully misguided:

> In reading the History of the Romans, considered as a people, can one help reflecting on that retributive justice of heaven, by which those who had been so remarkably distinguished by a general invasion of the liberty of mankind, at last sunk into such a deplorable condition of slavery to tyrants of their own raising; a slavery perhaps the most disgraceful that ever was suffered [. . .] endured with the most unmanly dejection, and encouraged by the vilest and most abject flattery that ever idolized the cruel and capricious demon of despotic power.[34]

Carter's provocative declarations reveal two major themes in her critique of contemporary neoclassicism. Firstly, there is the historiographical interest in the bleeding of state immorality into the characteristics of the individuals within that society, as identifiable infrastructural and cultural changes blur into private corruption and moral decline. J. G. A. Pocock describes this trope as 'corruption of the republic [. . .] entail[ing] the corruption of the individual'.[35] Secondly, there is the conviction that the canonisation and celebration of histories misrepresents the classical world to suit an agenda. This misinformation raises the possibility of alternative narratives that can be drawn from these normative texts. The interpretative mechanisms behind the Bluestocking rereading of the classics serve their goals of community formation and identities as public intellectuals.

Carter's key correspondences with her Bluestocking friends on the subject take place in the early 1740s and the 1770s. The above-quoted 1774 letter to Montagu contains Carter's articulation of a theory of Greek manners which informs her wider critique of classical historiography:

> Contemplating the last setting glories of the Athenian State. [. . .] there seemed to be no regular system of government; but all was hurried on by the rash impulse of a giddy populace, which irreparably gave decisions in one day, for which they were often ready to hang themselves the

---

ed. by Montagu Pennington, 3 vols (London: Printed for F. C. and J. Rivington, 1817), I, p. 267.

[34] Elizabeth Carter to Elizabeth Montagu, 9 August 1765, *Letters*, I, pp. 268–9.

[35] J. G. A. Pocock, 'Between Machiavelli and Hume: Gibbon as Civic Humanist and Philosophical Historian', in *Edward Gibbon and the Decline and Fall of the Roman Empire*, ed. by G. W. Bowerstock and John Clive (Cambridge, MA: Harvard University Press, 1977), pp. 103–20 (p. 103).

next [. . .] Plato and Xenophon must have been deeply imprest by a sense of the miseries flowing from this wild democracy, to lead them to such a strange admiration of the Spartan government, which they seem to have considered merely in the single point of opposition to the inconveniences of their own; without reflecting that the general system was a contradiction to the natural laws of humanity.[36]

Literalising the metaphor of national character as personal morality, Carter explores the way in which an irrational populace, comprised of violently impassioned individuals, deforms the apparatus of state. The need for universal consent forms the basis of Carter's critiques of the Greek democratic system and its national emotional character. The two divergent models of the *polis* enable Carter to negotiate an implicit *via media* of good governance. Athens offers a hedonistic model in which the state bends to the whims of its capricious citizenry, while Sparta, with its draconian system of social control, in 'contradiction to all the laws of humanity', offers a model in which human nature is subjected to the state. The former does not allow for the development of rational sociability; the latter supresses the citizen's individuality, and therefore capacity to evolve a private moral sense at all.[37] Carter explicitly highlights this binary of excessive individualism in Athens and systematic self-suppression in Sparta three years later: 'I have no other partiality for the Athenians than that it appears, I think, that their faults were more from sudden impulse, and less upon principle, than those of the Lacedemonians.'[38] While reflecting on the abundance of named Athenian figures in the history of the Peloponnesian War, compared with the scarcity of Spartan ones, Carter extends her discussion of this binary:

[It is] a necessary consequence, I suppose, of the difference between mere institution, and a natural exertion of the powers of the mind. Sparta was a single machine, wound up and regulated by clock-work springs.

[36] Elizabeth Carter to Elizabeth Montagu, 20 August 1774, *Letters*, II, pp. 237–8.
[37] Implicit in Carter's charge of inhumanity against the Spartan state is an attack on Jean-Jacques Rousseau's ardent laconism; see his claim in *Emile* (1762) that Spartan women produced the healthiest offspring, and his praise of the Spartan education system, in 'Discourse on the Moral Effects of the Arts and Sciences' (1750). Carter and Montagu loathed Rousseau; Carter suggested that Rousseau should 'pursue his own favorite scheme, of running wild, and grazing among the animals, whose morals would be in no danger of being relaxed by his stories', Elizabeth Carter to Elizabeth Montagu, 20 August 1774, *Letters*, II, p. 268.
[38] Elizabeth Carter to Elizabeth Montagu, 20 July 1777, *Letters*, III, p. 25.

Athens was all alive, and running into various directions by voluntary motion.[39]

Behind Carter's metaphors lies the principle of the golden mean, the political, religious and social maxim which governed much of the Bluestockings' sense of their roles within these various fields.[40] Just as the Bluestockings themselves steer the middle way between city and court, and the perfect conversation steers the middle course between pedantry and insipidity, so the perfect state steers a path between individualism and social accountability. It is the irreconcilability of individual emotion and civil discipline which always tainted the classical world for the Bluestockings.

The other major theme of Carter's response to Hume is the presumption of a historiographical duty incumbent on the modern historian to misrepresent the classical world in pursuit of one's own sociopolitical agenda. Carter, who, as we have seen, sarcastically took issue with the celebratory neoclassicism of her contemporaries, depicts contemporary historical scholarship as whitewashing. As she put it in her discussion of Hume: 'Modern compilers give us a fine picture of the manners of heathen antiquity, but their own historians are more honest.' Talbot and Carter parody the 'submissive' reading of history advocated by eighteenth-century conduct literature, based as it was on the engagement with history as a succession of models of appropriate behaviour.[41] They instead postulate this conceit of standard historiographical whitewashing as a means of exploring alternative, potentially dissident, historical narratives. Talbot's most defiantly critical approach to Thucydides, and through him, ancient Athens itself, emerges through such a dissident narrative. In January of 1745, Talbot wrote to Carter, bringing both the themes of counter-narrative and comparative history of manners to bear on a particularly difficult-to-justify portion of Thucydides' text, Pericles' famously dismissive speech to the wives of Athens:

> In my poor opinion, who am so prudent that I would fain make Pericles and Thucydides speak civilly to me, and to do them justice, have courage enough to oppose the sentiment of this venerable pedant, [the admonition has a much more delicate meaning,] and a very just one. Gentleness

[39] Ibid., p. 28.
[40] For a comprehensive definition of the 'golden mean', see Emma Major, *Madam Britannia: Women, Church, and Nation, 1712–1812* (Oxford: Oxford University Press, 2012), p. 214.
[41] Pearson, p. 50.

and reserve are such becoming qualities, that it is perhaps no inconsiderable privilege of our sex to be placed amongst *fair Virtue's silent train.* The well-bred Pericles did not mean to say, Go mind your spinning and hold your tongues – but what he did mean to say I will leave it to you to tell me.[42]

Talbot's incredulity at Pericles' dismissive tone towards the Athenian wives is represented as the product of a lack of mixed company, leading to a failure of manners. The moral failure of the Athenian state is encapsulated in its citizens' inability to display the appropriate behaviours towards one another which constitute a morally developed state like modern Britain. Pericles' rudeness and status as a 'venerable pedant' who fails to 'speak civilly' to her are more than mere social faux pas; they signify an empathic failure indicative of a failed society. Talbot's allusion to Alexander Pope's 1714 *Temple of Fame*, 'Fair Virtue's Silent Train', intensifies her critique by applying it to ancient Greece as a whole. Pope's poem applies this term to Socrates, an unostentatious figure of quiet heroism. Talbot deftly aligns the silencing of the Athenian women with Socrates' execution, aligning the modern social failure of Pericles' 'rudeness' with the ancient national tragedy of the death of Socrates. If we return to her analysis of Pericles' speech, with its dismissive dehumanisation and alienating tone, what initially appears a tongue-in-cheek piece of contrarian anti-classicism is, in fact, a diagnosis of moral bankruptcy akin to that which put Socrates to death. Though Talbot maintains the pose of disbelief, claiming to want Carter to explain away the more troubling implications of Pericles' words, here more than ever it appears more as a satirical gesture towards the pose of passive mimetic interpretation than a genuine doubt of her own interpretative skill. Between them, Carter and Talbot systematically trouble the waters of the certainty which underpins contemporary co-opting of classical ideals, arguing that the realities of the ancient world were far from the utopian ideal on which its eighteenth-century legacy depends.

Through their reading of classical history, Carter and Talbot evolve a framework for critical reading which highlights an awareness of the continuities and discontinuities between historical narratives of

---

[42] Catherine Talbot to Elizabeth Carter, 5 January 1745, *Series of Letters*, I, pp. 86–7; for Pericles' speech see Thucydides, *The History of the Grecian War: In Eight Books*, trans. by Thomas Hobbes, 2 vols (London: B. Motte, 1723), II, p. 106; for a comparable critique of the style of Thucydides, see Elizabeth Carter to Catherine Talbot, 5 December 1744, *Series of Letters*, I, p. 80.

the male-dominated public sphere and language of political participation, and which engages with the preconceptions of the justice
of such structures which inform contemporary and ancient historical narratives. This chapter now looks at the ways in which Carter
and Talbot's collaborative production of *All the Works of Epictetus*
(1758) marshals critical reading to combat the threat of philosophical movements like Deism and Scepticism in mid-century Britain.
Carter and Talbot's use of critical interpretation as a moral weapon
allows them to define their role, and, implicitly, the Bluestocking
project generally, as one of cultural critique and ethical reform.

Educating the Public: Elizabeth Carter's *Epictetus* and Elite Stoicism

Carter's translation of *All the Works of Epictetus* (1758), according to Montagu Pennington's biased and selective *Memoirs of the
Life of Elizabeth Carter*, was a coterie academic project that evolved
into a revisionist neoclassical manifesto to combat the moral threat
of an imagined Deist plot to undermine English Christianity. Talbot
initially proposed the project in 1743, casually hinting 'there is no
translation' of Epictetus' *Discourses* and suggesting she was 'vastly
curious' to see it.[43] Once the project commenced in earnest, however,
and Carter was systematically sending the completed pages to Talbot
and Secker in the mid-1750s, Talbot anxiously considered the danger
of publishing a translation of Epictetus in 'this infidel age':[44]

> [I]ts having been at first my own suggestion, has made me consider it the
> more attentively, and will, I own, give me very great and very lasting un-
> easiness, if this excellent translation [. . .] is not guarded in such a man-
> ner with proper notes and animadversions, as may prevent its spreading
> a mischief that I tremble to think of.[45]

The misinterpretation of which Talbot is so frightened is the reading of Epictetus by Philip Dormer Stanhope, Earl of Shaftesbury
and his circle, which she refers to in a later letter as 'Shaftesburian

---

[43] Catherine Talbot to Elizabeth Carter, 11 November 1743, *Series of Letters*, I,
p. 42.
[44] Catherine Talbot to Elizabeth Carter, March 1755, *Memoirs*, I, p. 127.
[45] Catherine Talbot to Elizabeth Carter, 1755, *Memoirs*, I, p. 131.

heathens'.[46] As Betty Schellenberg has argued, Talbot's role in the construction of *Epictetus* was 'strongly orientated towards potential ameliorative effects' it could have as part of a wider project of the reform of aristocratic manners.[47] Her anxiety that an insufficiently 'guarded' edition of Epictetus could provide a justification for aristocratic libertinism seems to have been founded primarily on her 1754 engagement with the *Essays on the Characteristics* (1754) by the Anglican clergyman John Brown (1715–66). *Essays* refutes Shaftesbury's magnum opus, *Characteristics* (1714), which argued against an ethics based on doctrinal religion. Brown's *Essays* explicitly attacks Shaftesburian libertinage and takes Shaftesbury's philosophy to task for its Stoic materialism. On the charge of libertinism, Brown quotes Shaftesbury's claim that 'the liberal, polish'd, and refin'd part of Mankind' do not 'apply [. . .] the Notion of a future Reward or Punishment to their immediate Behaviour in Society'. Brown glosses this as Shaftesbury claiming that 'Men of Sense should stand clear of the Fears of a Futurity'.[48] Talbot's engagement with *Characteristics* and Brown's essay anticipate her anxieties over Shaftesbury's use of the Stoics. Not only does Talbot repeat Brown's charges of arrogance and immortality, she also critiques the libertine seductiveness of Shaftesbury's 'elegant' and 'fair' style:

> I have only looked into the first volume, [of the *Characteristics*] to compare it as I went on with Mr. Browne's very ingenious and elegant answer, but I have met with so many things that offend me excessively as to leave me little inclination to look further. Arrogance, bitterness, prejudice, and obscurity, the falsest reasoning, the absurdest pride, the vilest ingratitude, the most offensive levity, disgrace whatever there was

[46] Catherine Talbot to Elizabeth Carter, 1755/6, *Memoirs*, I, p. 132. Whilst Stoicism underpins much of Shaftesbury's personal philosophy, his explicit discussion of the movement is primarily in the *Askemata*, or notebook, published in 1900; see John Sellars, 'Shaftesbury, Stoicism, and Philosophy as a Way of Life', *Sophia*, 55.3 (2016), 395–408 (p. 395).

[47] Betty Schellenberg, 'Catherine Talbot Translates Samuel Richardson: Bridging Social Networks and Media Cultures in the Mid-Eighteenth Century', *Eighteenth Century Fiction*, 29.2 (2016), 201–20 (p. 218).

[48] Anthony Ashley-Cooper, 3rd Earl of Shaftesbury, *Characteristicks of Men, Manners, Opinions, Times*, 3 vols (London: Printed for John Darby, 1714–15), III, pp. 177–8; John Brown, *Essays on the Characteristics* (London: Printed for C. Davis, 1754), pp. 273–4.

of elegant, and fair, and honest in some of the ideas, and whatever is easy and genteel in some parts of his style.[49]

Responding to Talbot's concerns, Carter adopted two strategies to address the dangers of libertine misinterpretations of Epictetus. Firstly her preface reminds readers that those 'who profess to admire *Epictetus*, unless they pursue that severely virtuous Conduct which he every-where prescribes, will find themselves treated by him, with the utmost Degree of Scorn and Contempt', directly combating the assumption that the absence of the divine is a licence to hedonism.[50] Secondly, and more famously, she 'devoted much of her introduction to a detailed and judicious demonstration of the superior merits of Christianity'.[51] See, for example, her comment in the introduction that 'the several Sects of Heathen Philosophy serve, as so many striking Instances of the Imperfection of human Wisdom; and of the extreme Need of a divine Assistance, to rectify the mistakes of depraved reason and replace natural Religion on its true Foundation'. Through reflections like this, Carter counters the aristocratic exclusivity of her libertine opponents by using a rhetoric of universality.[52] Betty Schellenberg and Jennifer Wallace postulate a clear division between Talbot's concern with moral amelioration and Carter's 'intellectual exercise of the accurate transmission of Epictetus' ideas'. However, I would contest that Carter, as a pious Anglican classicist, provides an alternative to the elite co-opting of Stoicism into nonconformity through her scholarly annotations and commentary.[53]

Carter critiques Shaftesbury's proposal that a closed circle of classically educated gentlemen is a model of virtuous community. Carter's critical apparatus instead asserts the superiority of Christianity over Epictetus' heathen morality and depicts Epictetus as a pale anticipation of Scripture. An example of the former is her reflection on Epictetus' famous doctrine that one should not mourn a dead child: 'Stoicism carries Truth into Absurdity; while Christian Philosophy

---

[49] Catherine Talbot to Elizabeth Carter, 26 November 1754, *Series of Letters*, II, p. 187.

[50] *All the Works of Epictetus*, pp. xxvi–xxvii.

[51] Gillian Wright, 'Women Reading Epictetus', *Women's Writing*, 14.2 (2007), 321–37 (p. 333).

[52] *All the Works of Epictetus*, pp. xxv, xv.

[53] Schellenberg, p. 218; Jennifer Wallace, 'Confined and Exposed: Elizabeth Carter's Classical Translations', *Tulsa Studies in Women's Literature*, 22.2 (2003), 315–34 (p. 327).

makes all Truths coincide, uniting Fortitude with Tenderness and Compassion.'[54] Her footnote for Epictetus' reflection that 'a Cynic [. . .] must be beat like an Ass, and when he is beat, must love all those who beat him' represents a typical example of the latter:

> Compare this with the Christian Precepts, of Forbearance and Love to Enemies, *Matth. V. 39–44.* The Readers will observe, that Christ specifies higher Injuries and Provocations than Epictetus doth; and requires of all his Followers, Epictetus describes only as the Duty of one or two *extraordinary* Persons, as such.[55]

In both cases, Carter diagnoses the Stoic doctrine as limited to a material epistemology, incapable of recognising universal truths of 'Tenderness' and 'Compassion', and guilty of social exclusivity, in which truth is accessible only to the Stoic sage and his inner circle. Whilst this language of universality and materiality generally characterises Hellenic philosophy, Carter uses it to extend the moral and social argument for her own translation. When this universality is placed alongside Carter's focus on 'plain' speech throughout the process of translating Epictetus, her translation assumes a subversive aspect. Carter wrote to Thomas Secker that 'the Enchiridion is merely plain common sense', stating her intention to 'make [Epictetus] speak such a language as will make him appear natural and easy to those with whom he is taught to converse'.[56] By distinguishing between the 'extraordinary persons' who form Epictetus' readership, and 'all' the followers of Christ, Carter deftly argues that Christian doctrine supersedes Epictetus in its universality and hints that the readers best placed to appreciate Christianised Stoicism are not 'those with whom [Epictetus] is taught to converse', but the speakers of 'plain common sense'. In short, the aristocratic 'Deists' are limited to Epictetan Stoicism in its immoral, pagan, form, while the Anglophone audience of ordinary people, to whom she has opened the book by her translation, can access the elevated, Christian form of Epictetus, by reading him through Scripture.

Carter's *Epictetus* is the most public face of her classical revisionism. It represents another case of establishing the terms of Bluestocking participation while cultivating public virtue and asserting the Bluestockings' place within the public sphere. Wilson finds in *Epictetus* 'a conveniently conservative model of support for women,

---

All the Works of Epictetus, p. 448, n. (m).
Ibid., p. 293, n. (o).
Elizabeth Carter to Thomas Secker, [1748], *Memoirs*, I, pp. 112–13.

encouraging them to collude with, as well as assisting them in facing, the limitations of their opportunities', focusing on the pragmatic value of Roman Stoicism for an imagined female audience.[57] Wallace, meanwhile, places it in the broader context of Carter's 'own distinct classical heritage', which she sees as defined by the same concepts of 'resignation and patent suffering'.[58] Whilst these concepts have a bearing on Carter's *Epictetus*, affecting the horizons of expectation which she brings to bear on her engagement with the classical world in general, the epistolary background to *Epictetus* suggests that, consciously at least, Carter and Talbot were also invested in cultivating roles of female moral and social reformers against the threat of Francophile libertinism.

To return to the two epigraphs with which this chapter opened, the case studies here dramatise a transition from the private hermeneutic practice of 'Shared Reading' to the public, national vision of conversation as 'the noblest Commerce of mankind'. The former, with its closed circle and informal encouragement of private morality, evolves over time into the active, pedagogical force of moral authority embodied in *All the Works of Epictetus* (1758). Through the processes of building affective rational ties and interrogating their literary forebears, familiar letters acted as tools for self-fashioning. They allowed a generation of mid- to late-eighteenth-century women writers to conceive of a polite public femininity which combined a respectable nationalism with the quiet radicalism of an intellectual community dedicated to transforming the presence and role of women on the British literary landscape.

Works Cited

Primary

Archive Collections

Lucas Papers, (L30) Bedfordshire and Luton Archives, Bedford

Digital Sources

Unless otherwise noted, texts published 1700–1800 were consulted on *JISC Historical Texts*.

---

[57] Wilson, p. 510.
[58] Wallace, p. 323.

Burney Collections of Seventeenth and Eighteenth Century British Newspapers (British Library, 2007–)
Electronic Enlightenment Scholarly Edition of Correspondence, ed. by Robert McNamee et al., vers. 3.0 (University of Oxford, 2017–)
Internet Encyclopedia of Philosophy, ed. by James Fieser and Bradley Dowden (1995–)
JISC Historical Texts (2014–)
Pensées de Pascal Online, ed. by D. Descote and G. Proust (2011–)

Print Sources

Aristotle, *Nicomachean Ethics*, trans. by David Ross (Oxford: Oxford University Press, 2009)
Blair, Hugh, *Lectures on Rhetoric and Belles-Lettres*, 3 vols (London: Printed for W. Strahan and T. Cadell, 1785)
Brown, John, *Essays on the Characteristics* (London: Printed for C. Davis, 1754)
Carter, Elizabeth, *Letters from Mrs. Elizabeth Carter, to Mrs. Montagu, between the Years 1755 and 1800*, ed. by Montagu Pennington, 3 vols (London: Printed for F. C. and J. Rivington, 1817)
Carter, Elizabeth and Talbot, Catherine, *A Series of Letters between Elizabeth Carter and Catherine Talbot, 1741–1770, with Letters from Elizabeth Carter to Mrs. Vesey*, ed. by Montagu Pennington, 4 vols (London: Printed for F. C. and J. Rivington, 1809)
Chesterfield, Philip Dormer Stanhope, Lord, *Letters Written by the Late Right Honourable Philip Dormer Stanhope, Earl of Chesterfield, to His Son, Philip Stanhope*, 2 vols (London: Printed for J. Dodsley, 1774)
Epictetus, *All the Works of Epictetus, Which Are Now Extant*, trans. by Elizabeth Carter (London: Printed by S. Richardson, 1758)
More, Hannah, *Florio: A Tale, for Fine Gentlemen and Fine Ladies. And, The Bas Bleu: or, Conversation. Two Poems* (London: Printed for T. Cadell, 1786)
——. *Poems* (London: Printed for T. Cadell, 1816)
Pennington, Montagu, *Memoirs of Miss Elizabeth Carter*, 2 vols (London: Printed for F. C. and J. Rivington, 1807)
Richardson, Samuel, *The History of Sir Charles Grandison*, 6 vols (London: Printed for S. Richardson, 1753)
Rousseau, Jean-Jacques, *Discours qui a remporté le prix a l'Academie de Dijon, en l'anée 1750* ['Discourse on the Moral Effects of the Arts and Sciences'] (Geneva: Chez Barillot et fils, 1751) <https://gallica.bnf.fr/ark:/12148/bpt6k10543566> [accessed 13 June 2022]
——. *Émile: ou, De l'éducation*, 3 vols ([La Haye]: Chez Jean Néalme, 1762) <https://gallica.bnf.fr/ark:/12148/btv1b8614553x> [accessed 13 June 2022]

Sévigné, Marie de Rabutin Chantal, Marchioness de, *Letters of Madame de Rabutin Chantal, Marchioness de Sévigné, to the Comtess [sic] de Grignan, Her Daughter, in two volumes, translated from the French*, trans. anon., 2 vols (London: Printed for N. Blandford, 1727)

——. *Court Secrets: or, The Lady's Chronicle Historical and Gallant [. . .] Extracted from the Letters of Madam de Sévigné*, trans. by Edmund Curll (London: no publisher, 1727)

——. *Letters of Madame de Rabutin Chantal, Marchioness de Sévigné, to the Comtess [sic] de Grignan, Her Daughter, in two volumes, translated from the French*, trans. anon., 2 vols (London: Printed for J. Hinton, 1745)

——. *Letters from the Marchioness de Sévigné, to Her Daughter the Countess de Grignan. Translated from the French of the last Paris edition*, trans. anon., 10 vols (London: Printed for J. Coote, 1763–8)

Shaftesbury, Anthony Ashley-Cooper, 3rd Earl of, *Characteristicks of Men, Manners, Opinions, Times*, 3 vols (London: Printed for John Darby, 1714–15)

Smollett, Tobias, *Travels through France and Italy: Containing Observations on Character, Customs, Religion, Government, Police, Commerce, Arts, and Antiquities*, 2 vols (London: Printed for R. Baldwin, 1766)

Talbot, Catherine, *The Works of the Late Miss Catherine Talbot*, ed. by Montagu Pennington (London: F. C. and J. Rivington, 1819)

Thucydides, *The History of the Grecian War: In Eight Books*, trans. by Thomas Hobbes, 2 vols (London: B. Motte, 1723)

Wollstonecraft, Mary, *A Vindication of the Rights of Woman, with Strictures on Political and Moral Subjects*, 2 vols (London: Printed for J. Johnson, 1792)

Woolf, Virginia, *A Room of One's Own* (London: Hogarth Press, 1935)

Secondary

Bigold, Melanie, *Women of Letters: Manuscript Circulation and Print Afterlives in the Eighteenth Century* (Basingstoke: Palgrave Macmillan, 2013)

Conley, John J., 'Marie de Rabutin-Chantal, Marquise de Sévigné (1626–1696)', *The Internet Encyclopedia of Philosophy* (2018) <http://www.iep.utm.edu/sevigne> [accessed 29 January 2018]

Eger, Elizabeth, *Bluestockings: Women of Reason from Enlightenment to Romanticism* (London: Palgrave Macmillan, 2010)

——. 'Paper Trails and Eloquent Objects: Bluestocking Friendship and Material Culture', *Parergon*, 26.2 (2009), 109–38

Ellis, Markman, 'Reading Practices in Elizabeth Montagu's Epistolary Network of the 1750s', in *Bluestockings Displayed: Portraiture, Performance and Patronage, 1730–1830*, ed. by Elizabeth Eger (Cambridge: Cambridge University Press, 2013), pp. 213–32

Guest, Harriet, 'Bluestocking Feminism', *Huntington Library Quarterly*, 65.1/2 (2002), 59–80

——. *Small Change: Women, Learning Patriotism: 1750–1810* (Chicago: University of Chicago Press, 2000)

Habermas, Jürgen, *The Structural Transformation of the Public Sphere* (Cambridge, MA: MIT Press, 1989)

Hannan, Leonie, *Women of Letters: Gender, Writing and the Life of the Mind in Early Modern England* (Manchester: Manchester University Press, 2016)

Harcstark Myers, Sylvia, *The Bluestocking Circle: Women, Friendship and the Life of the Mind in Eighteenth-Century England* (Oxford: Clarendon Press, 1990)

Hawley, Judith, 'Carter, Elizabeth (1717–1806)', *Oxford Dictionary of National Biography* (2009), online edition <http://www.oxforddnb.com/view/article/4782> [accessed 20 March 2019]

Heller, Deborah, 'The Bluestockings and Virtue Friendship: Elizabeth Montagu, Anne Pitt, and Elizabeth Carter', *Huntington Library Quarterly*, 81.4 (2018), 469–97

Huet, Jean-Yves, 'Madame de Sévigné en Angleterre: Horace Walpole et Madame du Deffand', in *Revue d'histoire littéraire de la France*, 96 (1996), 404–35

Major, Emma, *Madam Britannia: Women, Church, and Nation, 1712–1812* (Oxford: Oxford University Press, 2012)

Pearson, Jacqueline, *Women's Reading in Britain, 1750–1835* (Cambridge: Cambridge University Press, 1999)

Pocock, J. G. A., 'Between Machiavelli and Hume: Gibbon as Civic Humanist and Philosophical Historian', in *Edward Gibbon and the Decline and Fall of the Roman Empire*, ed. by G. W. Bowerstock and John Clive (Cambridge, MA: Harvard University Press, 1977), pp. 103–20

Schellenberg, Betty, 'Catherine Talbot Translates Samuel Richardson: Bridging Social Networks and Media Cultures in the Mid-Eighteenth Century', *Eighteenth Century Fiction*, 29.2 (2016), 201–20

Sellars, John, 'Shaftesbury, Stoicism, and Philosophy as a Way of Life', *Sophia*, 55.3 (2016), 395–408

Staves, Susan, 'Church of England Clergy and Women Writers', *Huntington Library Quarterly*, 65.1/2 (2002), 81–103

Wahrman, Dror, *The Making of the Modern Self* (New Haven: Yale University Press, 2004)

Wallace, Jennifer, 'Confined and Exposed: Elizabeth Carter's Classical Translations', *Tulsa Studies in Women's Literature*, 22.2 (2003), 315–34

Whyman, Susan, *The Pen and the People: English Letter Writers, 1660–1800* (Oxford: Oxford University Press, 2009)

Williams, Abigail, *The Social Life of Books* (New Haven: Yale University Press, 2017)

Wilson, Penelope, 'Women Writers and the Classics', in *The Oxford History of Classical Reception in English Literature*, ed. by David Hopkins and Charles Martindale, 4 vols (Oxford: Oxford University Press, 2012), III, pp. 495–518

Wright, Gillian, 'Women Reading Epictetus', *Women's Writing*, 14.2 (2007), 321–37

Part III

Responding to the Present

Chapter 8

Laughing to Learn:
Sarah Fielding's Life Lessons

Rebecca Anne Barr

Literary history has tended to underplay the comic and the humorous in eighteenth-century women's writing. While Restoration women wits are granted some licence to amuse, and late-eighteenth-century authors such as Frances Burney, Maria Edgeworth and the caustic Jane Austen are admitted as decorous representatives of 'comic feminism', both scholarship and university curricula conspire to consign the women novelists of mid-century to a dull didacticism. Women writers associated with Samuel Richardson tended to be regarded, like him, as didactic or sentimental, rather than amusing or (heaven forbid) *funny*. Sarah Fielding, author of *The Governess: or, The Little Female Academy* (1749), has long been recognised as an educational writer. But Fielding's work is also distinguished by a singular sense of humour. Fielding's witty satires ironise and calibrate moral actions and mental thoughts; her fictions activate and reform their readers – educating through fable, allegory, anecdote and droll commentary. Though sometimes characterised as a mid-century modification of Augustan satire, a 'calm and subdued' form which 'involves self-doubt' in its efforts to instruct and improve readers, Fielding's humour can also be sceptical, caustic and even crude.[1] With her collaborator, the irreverent satirist Jane Collier, Fielding planned a work entitled *The Laugh*, designed as a companion piece to their experimental prose work *The Cry* (1754).[2] Both works aim to 'laugh

---

[1] Mika Suzuki, 'The "true use of reading": Sarah Fielding and Mid-Eighteenth-Century Literary Strategies' (unpublished doctoral thesis, Queen Mary and Westerfield University, 1998), pp. 146–7.

[2] Michael Londry, quoting Collier's commonplace book, 'Our Dear Miss Jenny Collier', *TLS* (5 March 2004), pp. 13–14.

[readers] out of [. . .] absurdities', educating through amusement, drollery and fun.³ In contrast to the baleful critical commonplace of the downtrodden woman writer, Fielding displays a trenchant sense of humour in the face of gendered adversity – a keen grasp of the ridiculous equal to that of her rambunctious male peers. Such qualities would have been essential for withstanding what is increasingly conceptualised as an unsentimental eighteenth century: nasty, brutish and long.

This chapter argues that by focusing on the sombre, grave and serious aspects of the educational mode, critics have missed its comic strains, and ignored the instructive power of mirth in women's writing. I explore the ways in which Sarah Fielding uses humour to educate and reform her readers, and to inform them about their relative powerlessness in the world. Though *The Governess* is the most explicitly didactic of Fielding's works, her entire corpus uses 'narrative techniques, episodes, and themes *all* directed towards moral education'.⁴ Such didacticism is directed primarily (though not exclusively) towards women: all of her writings provide a 'female-oriented' perspective designed to equip intelligent women for a decidedly unideal world.⁵ While *The Governess* deploys moderated ridicule as a means of moral pedagogy within an enlightened matriarchy, with shared laughter inculcating individual humility, self-control and conformity to social bonds, in Fielding's final work, *The History of Ophelia* (1760), satiric laughter delivers women a bleaker moral. *Ophelia*'s humour illuminates the injustices of patriarchal society, highlighting women's vulnerability to exploitation and humiliation at the hands of the cruel and the ignorant, but simultaneously mobilises a Juvenalian ridicule to disabuse women of self-indulgent fantasies of victimisation. In Fielding's work, humour provides an unsentimental lesson in the 'challenges and limitations of eighteenth-century women's lives'.⁶

---

³ Sarah Fielding, *The Cry: A New Dramatic Fable*, ed. by Carolyn Woodward (Lexington: University of Kentucky Press, 2021), p. 57.

⁴ Sylvia Kasey Marks, 'Sarah Fielding's *The Governess*: A Gloss on Her "Books upon Education"', in *Women, Gender, and Print Culture in Eighteenth-Century Britain*, ed. by Temma Berg and Sonia Kane (Bethlehem: Lehigh, 2013), pp. 59–78.

⁵ Mary Anne Schofield, 'Introduction', in Sarah Fielding, *The Cry* (Delmar, NY: Scholars Facsimiles and Imprints, 1986), pp. 5–12 (p. 5).

⁶ Gillian Skinner, 'Introduction', in Sarah Fielding, *The History of the Countess of Dellwyn* (Abingdon: Routledge, 2022), pp. vii–xxv (p. x).

Education and the Proper Use of Laughter

The Governess is a watershed work in the literature of education. A text which 'has no direct precedents in English Literature', it takes seriously the task of entertaining and directing the intellects and passions of young women, treating them *as* children rather than miniaturised adults and redirecting the pedagogic aims of Locke's *Some Thoughts Concerning Education* towards girls.[7] Superintended by the benign Mrs Teachum, the handful of schoolgirls in the 'female academy' listens and responds to twenty micro-narratives (both fairy tales and personal histories). Their supervised intellectual progress is designed to inculcate 'habits' of rational analysis, female self-control and moral responsibility. Fielding's preface aims 'to cultivate an early Inclination to Benevolence, and Love of Virtue, in the Minds of Young Women [. . . showing them] that their True Interest is concerned in cherishing and improving those amiable Dispositions into Habits, and in keeping down all rough and boisterous Passions'.[8] Mental development and the exercise of individual reason are at the heart of Fielding's vision: education assists young women in regulating the unruly passions often ascribed to them in the period, granting them, at the very least, emotional empowerment and self-control.

Recent critical response to Fielding's *The Governess* has been varied, suggesting its educational ethos is not as straightforward as previously thought. While critics such as Rebecca Davies see it as typical of Fielding's 'conservative feminism', Christopher Johnson argues that it extends Lockean ideas of 'limited monarchy and personal liberty' into the domestic sphere.[9] Yet laughter, or humour, is rarely considered as an integral part of Fielding's literary repertoire. It is even more seldom related to her interrogation of 'Lockean and later Scottish Enlightenment epistemologies of the self', despite the fact that such philosophies frequently considered laughter in relation

---

[7] Linda Bree, *Sarah Fielding* (New York: Twayne, 1996), p. 59.

[8] Sarah Fielding, *The Governess: or, Little Female Academy. Calculated for the Entertainment and Instruction of Young Ladies in Their Education*, ed. by Candace Ward (Peterborough, ON: Broadview, 2005), p. 45. Further references are to this edition and are cited parenthetically in the text.

[9] Rebecca Davies, *Written Maternal Authority and Eighteenth-Century Education: Educating by the Book* (Farnham: Ashgate, 2016), p. 62; Christopher Johnson, *A Political Biography of Sarah Fielding* (London: Routledge, 2007), p. 115.

to human nature and social relations.[10] This is a gendered omission. While eighteenth-century philosophers were silent on the subject of women's laughter, conduct literature counselled against women's mirth as immodest, licentious and disruptive of domestic harmony.[11] There were class-based parameters for women's risibility, too, so that too 'boisterous kind of Jollity' 'throweth a Woman into a lower Form, and degradeth her from the Rank of those who are more re-fined'.[12] The stakes of the eighteenth-century laughter debate were raised for women. This does not mean that women were perpetu-ally sombre, fearful of raising a smile lest they be cast out of polite society. Yet critics more commonly insist that these women writers' affinities with Pope, Addison, Swift, Richardson and Henry Fielding are *moral* rather than *satirical*. Though Carolyn Woodward allows a 'note of teasing irony' in one of their co-authored letters to James Harris, she is at pains to refute notions that their deferential self-styling as 'little children' might convey anything other than sincere gratitude.[13] Moralism without satire; sincerity without playfulness. The qualities of wry and caustic wit attributed to male writers of the period are supposedly absent from their female peers.

But laughter was the Fielding family business. Her brother Henry wrote extensively in the comic mode, and on theories of humour, participating in one of the century's core debates about the moral content and social meaning of laughter. And Sarah was as well versed as he in both philosophical theories of laughter from Hobbes to Shaftesbury and in humorous fiction. Even Fielding's literary criti-cism was attuned to the comic: he notes that the tragic *Clarissa* was

[10] Misty Anderson, *Imagining Methodism in Eighteenth-Century Britain: Enthusiasm, Belief and the Borders of the Self* (Baltimore: Johns Hopkins University Press, 2012), p. 12.

[11] See Soile Ylivuori, *Women and Politeness in Eighteenth-Century England* (London: Routledge, 2019), 'Disciplining the Female Tongue', pp. 218–25.

[12] Marquess of Halifax (George Savile), *The Lady's New Year's Gift: or, Advice to a Daughter*, 3rd edn (London: Gillyflower and James Partridge, 1688), p. 108.

[13] Carolyn Woodward, 'Introduction', in Sarah Fielding, *The Cry: A New Dramatic Fable* (Lexington: University of Kentucky Press, 2021), p. 11. Peter Sabor reads the same letter as ironic and 'hyperbolically deferential' in his introduction to Sarah Fielding, *The Adventures of David Simple and Volume the Last* (Lexington: University Press of Kentucky, 1998), p. xv. I concur that 'the worn stereotype of female ignorance is treated with sardonic self-effacement and heavily ironized by the letter writers' considerable erudition', '"Barren Desarts of Arbitrary Words": Language and Communication in Collier and Fielding's *The Cry*', *Women's Writing*, 23.1 (2016), 87–105 (p. 87).

'judiciously interspersed with Scenes of comic Humour [. . .] calculated to relieve the Mind from fixing too long on mournful melancholy Ideas'.[14] Sarah's collaborative work *The Cry: A New Dramatic Fable* (1754) presents extended disquisitions on the relationship between humour, sentiment and morality, in which women characters critique the Hobbesian conception of laughter as a cynical generalisation, decry 'taunting ridicule' and defend their idiosyncratic position as 'Innocent mirth and real good-humour': their learned wit is an example of 'Fine countrefeasance [imitation] and unhurtful sport, / Delight and laughter deck'd in seemly sort'.[15] In *The Governess*, Fielding imagines the gentle reproof of social laughter as a persuasive tool for educating young women against affectation. *The Governess*' Teachum is a good-natured foil to *Tom Jones*' vicious tutor, Thwackum. She never resorts to violence, and encourages happiness in her charges, who run about 'laughing, talking, and singing', enjoying the freedom of play. This lack of bodily restraint accords with Locke's strictures on the development of robust children.

But while *Some Thoughts* conveys a mistrust of mirth typical of its period, Fielding's didactic fiction embraces the disciplinary capacity of good-natured humour in early years education. Locke warns against laughing at children's inquisitiveness and nascent reasoning, but sanctions mockery as a means of enforcing learning:

> [If] softer application prevails not, try to shame him out of [laziness], by laughing at him for it [. . .] expose and turn him into ridicule for it [. . .] put on a pretty cold brow towards him, and keep it till he reform; and let his mother, tutor, and all about him do so too.[16]

For Locke, laughing *at* children is more extreme than corporal punishment. If a child is secure and well loved, they can bear physical disciplining: he has seen one 'run away laughing, with good smart blows of a wand on his back, who would have cried for an unkind word, and have been very sensible of the chastisement of a cold look from the same person'.[17] Raillery is a 'nice and ticklish [. . .] business', a 'refined' mode of correction 'done with wit and good language', but one which risks incivility, since entertaining 'the rest of

---

[14] Sarah Fielding, *Remarks on Clarissa* (London: J. Robinson, 1749), p. 45.

[15] Fielding, *The Cry*, pp. 101–2; p. 148, quoting Spenser's *Tears of the Muses* (1591).

[16] John Locke, *Some Thoughts Concerning Education*, in *The Works of John Locke in Nine Volumes*, 12th edn, vol. 8 (London: Rivington, 1824), pp. 1–210 (p. 120).

[17] Ibid., p. 111.

the company is at the cost of that one [. . .] set out in their burlesque colours, who [. . .] is not without uneasiness'.[18] Youths should therefore generally avoid raillery. Rather than co-opting humour into his educational manifesto, then, Locke remains suspicious of laughter as a 'malicious passion' generated by 'the humiliation of one of the parties' and classed alongside 'derision, contempt and shame'.[19]

Locke's wariness of raillery's exacerbation of painful power dynamics testifies to the influence of Hobbes' *Leviathan* (1651), where laughter is the '*Sudden Glory*' of perceived superiority.[20] *The Governess*' same-sex environment safeguards against the potential harms of corrective mirth, its mild forms of feminine risibility part of a cultural rehabilitation of laughter as sociable, polite and benevolent rather than antagonistic, uncivil and hostile. Teachum's 'principal aim' is 'to improve [young women's] minds in all useful knowledge' but also 'to render them obedient to their superiors, and gentle, kind, and affectionate to each other'. Narrative pleasure and maternal laughter sweeten this inherently conservative disciplinary project: *The Governess* recognises that mirth is essential for juvenile readers. At one point, the diminutive Miss Polly Suckling requests improving reading, since 'fairy-tales were fit only for little children': 'it would be better if they were to read some true history, from which they might learn something' (p. 110). 'Such an objection coming from the little dumpling' provokes a smile in Jenny Peace, the eldest girl. She delivers a riposte in which gentle motherly mockery models the very instruction she delivers to her classmate. As a small child, Jenny too decided that 'it was beneath my wisdom to see raree-shows' and refused the chance to see one with her friends. But Jenny's self-denial was affectation: a chance 'to boast of my own great sense, in that I was above such trifles' (p. 111).

> When my mamma asked me, why I would not see the show, when she had given me leave? I drew up my head, and said, 'Indeed I did not like raree-shows. That I had been reading; and I thought that much more worth my while, than to lose my time at such foolish entertainments.' My mamma, who saw the cause of my refusing this amusement was only a pretence of being wise, laughed, and said, 'She herself had seen it, and

---

[18] Ibid., pp. 136, 135.

[19] Rebecca Anne Barr, 'Pathological Laughter and the Response to Ridicule: Samuel Richardson, Sarah Fielding and Jane Collier', *RSÉAA XVII–XVIII* 70 (2013), 223–44 (p. 223).

[20] Thomas Hobbes, *Leviathan*, ed. by Richard Tuck (Cambridge: Cambridge University Press, 1996), p. 43.

it was really very comical and diverting.' On hearing this, I was heartily vexed to think I had denied myself a pleasure, which I fancied was beneath me, when I found even my mamma was not above seeing it. This in a great measure cured me of the folly of thinking myself above any innocent amusement. And when I grew older, and more capable of hearing reason, my mamma told me, 'She had taken this method of laughing at me, as laughing is the proper manner of treating affectation; which of all things, she said, she would have me carefully avoid; otherwise, whenever I was found out, I should become contemptible.' (p. 111)

Polly, 'the very picture of health and good-humour', (p. 159) is chided for her seriousness because Fielding recognises laughter as 'a child's native state – symptomatic, even, of childish innocence'.[21] Risibility ought not to be supplanted by joyless didacticism. Instead, Jenny 'laughs to shame, all Follies, and insinuates Virtue, rather by familiar Examples, than by the severity of Precepts'.[22] A swift and effective dose of maternal ridicule 'is the proper manner of treating affectation' in little girls who are as yet incapable of reasoning. Unlike the lachrymose Harry Campbell, who at seven years old reportedly read Richardson's *Pamela*, so that he has 'half her Sayings by heart, talks in no other Language but hers: and [. . .] has become fond of his Book', Fielding's *The Governess* prefers infant levity to a 'gravity [that] is of the very essence of imposture'.[23] Jenny's lesson in humility crucially forestalls any allegation that Teachum's educational programme would produce 'affected' girls who might grow into the 'unnatural' women scholars (or pedants, so-called) so reviled at the time. Women's gentle laughter thus regulates the girls' behaviour, creating habitual forms of self-governance which ensure the reproduction of dominant norms.

---

[21] Louise Joy, 'The Laughing Child: Children's Poetry and the Comic Mode', in *The Aesthetics of Children's Poetry: A Study of Children's Verse in English*, ed. by Katherine Wakely-Mulroney and Louise Joy (London: Routledge, 2017), pp. 111–26 (p. 122).

[22] John Dryden, *Discourse Concerning the Original and Progress of Satire*, in *Poems, 1693–1696*, ed. by A. B. Chambers, William Frost and Vinton A. Dearing, in *The Works of John Dryden*, vol. 4, ed. by H. T. Swedenberg (Berkeley: University of California Press, 1974), pp. 3–90 (p. 63).

[23] Samuel Richardson, *Pamela: or, Virtue Rewarded*, ed. by Tom Keymer and Alice Wakely (Oxford: Oxford University Press, 2000), p. 51; Lord Shaftesbury, 'A Letter Concerning Enthusiasm to my Lord *****', in *Characteristics of Men, Manners, Opinions, Times*, ed. by Laurence Klein (Cambridge: Cambridge University Press, 2000), pp. 4–28 (p. 8).

In *The Governess'* tender-hearted pedagogy, laughter is a gentle but effective corrective of infant follies. Within the bounds of propriety (a brief moment rather than an extended episode of mockery), it reproves faults and helps moderate excessive, potentially antisocial, feeling. This laughter '*conducted by good nature*' is 'a great occasion of pleasure', consolidating communal bonds rather than causing faction.[24] That not Teachum but *Jenny* laughs at Polly, and does so through telling a story in which she laughs *at herself*, reduces the potential unpleasantness of power asymmetry – minimising the kind of direct raillery that Locke worries pains the child mocked.[25] Jenny's joviality sees her 'merry easy mind [. . .] diffuse a like disposition over all [. . .] in company', readying the audience for a fairy tale which preaches that true obedience 'consists in submission'.[26] Polite, gentle and corrective: even the smallest child can learn from such laughter.

The Governess' accommodation of levity suggests that *both* Fielding siblings (not solely Henry) are resistant to 'over-refinement and moralizing humourlessness', ridiculing those who would purge amusement of innocent pleasure and turn diversion into tedious lessons.[27] A comparable critique of killjoy tendencies is found in *Tom Jones'* puppet-show episode, where Tom finds that rather than perform a popular Punch-and-Judy, the company will instead present a version of Colley Cibber's *The Provoked Husband* (1728). The manager's rationale is didactic: 'every puppet show' ought to 'principally aim' at conveying 'good and instructive lessons', he proclaims.[28] Innocent, laughing pleasure (Henry laments) has been exchanged for a 'grave and solemn entertainment, without any low wit or humour, or jests; or, to do it no more than justice, without anything that could provoke a laugh'.[29] This dismal substitution is approved by 'a grave matron' who promises to 'bring [her] two daughters the next

---

[24] Francis Hutcheson, *Reflections upon Laughter, and Remarks upon the Fable of the Bees* (Glasgow: Printed by R. Urie for D. Baxter, 1750), p. 32. The work was originally published in 1725. My emphasis.

[25] In *The Cry*, Fielding partly concurs with Locke's mistrust of raillery, noting: 'Inexorable hatred hath [. . .] oftener arisen from a biting, taunting jest, than from any other cause whatever', p. 149.

[26] Ibid.

[27] Simon Dickie, *Cruelty and Laughter: Forgotten Comic Literature and the Unsentimental Eighteenth Century* (Chicago: University of Chicago Press, 2011), p. 169.

[28] Henry Fielding, *Tom Jones*, ed. by John Bender and Simon Stern (Oxford: Oxford University Press, 1998), p. 556.

[29] Ibid., p. 555.

night' so that they might benefit from this 'rational entertainment'. The novel contrasts the traditional 'low stuff' 'that did very well to make folks laugh; but was never calculated to improve the morals of young people' to critique the tediously virtue-signalling performance which has replaced it.[30] As Henry ridicules po-faced moral superiority, so Sarah also counsels guardians against depriving their wards of fun. In *The Governess*, '*laughing at*' moulds the malleable child and models a community of like-minded women capable of sharing a joke. Both a crucial moderator of wayward passions and corrector of affectation, mirth produces a harmonious conformity amongst rational reading women.

Sarah Fielding's Rape Joke

Fielding's pedagogic progressivism is challenged by the disillusionments of the next decade. Increasingly experimental and often coruscating in its moral acerbity, its context is that of a 'deepening sense of national malaise, stimulated by xenophobia and tinged by sharpening anti-aristocratic sensibilities': a state of affairs pungently described by Paula Backscheider as 'Mid-Century Anger'.[31] Mid-century fictions reflect what was *felt* to be the tenor of the time – bleak, amoral, ruthlessly cruel – expressing outrage at 'the horrible treatment of fellow humans' which indicted Britain's moral economy.[32] Anger would have been entirely reasonable for both Fielding and her collaborator Jane Collier, given the brutal indifference with which single women were treated at the time. Both their 'lives were shaped by poverty and literary friendships', Collier dying in her early forties, following

---

[30] Ibid., p. 556. Cibber's version of Vanbrugh's unfinished drama makes significant deviations from the original's satirical targets. Cibber defended his changes by arguing that 'such violent measures, however just they might be in real life, were too severe for comedy' ('To the Reader', in *The Provoked Husband*, ed. by Peter Dixon (Lincoln: University of Nebraska Press, 1973), ll. 23–34. Henry's contempt for Cibber's unfunniness may well have been augmented by his irritation at his performative piety.

[31] Kathleen Wilson, 'Empire of Virtue: The Imperial Project and Hanoverian Culture, c.1720–1785', in *The Imperial State at War: Britain from 1689–1815*, ed. by Lawrence Stone (London: Routledge, 1994), pp. 128–64 (p. 145); Paula R. Backscheider, 'Literary Culture as Immediate Reality', in *A Companion to the Eighteenth-Century English Novel and Culture*, ed. by Paula R. Backscheider and Catherine Ingrassia (Blackwell: Oxford, 2005), pp. 504–38 (p. 513).

[32] Backscheider, p. 523.

the depredations resulting from years of rootlessness and precarious finances; Fielding writing to supplement a meagre income drained by paternal profligacy, producing fiction and scholarship during years of reduced circumstances and declining health.[33] Fielding's unsparing *Volume the Last* (1754) systematically strips her hero, David Simple, of the bare comforts of earthly life, as friends and family reveal their base self-interest and cruelty. By the early 1750s, even Fielding's brother, Henry, was beginning to shift his opinion on mirth, denouncing 'all humour that lacked a corrective purpose and entirely abandoning his old conviction that laughter [. . .] could be an end in itself'.[34] In his preface to *Familiar Letters between Characters of David Simple and Others* (1747), Henry notes that Fielding's representation of the struggle between 'Nature and Habit, Truth and Hypocrisy' in women's behaviour introduced 'much Humour in their Characters'.[35] Rather than incidental, such humour was fundamental to the improving efficacy of a work expressly 'calculated for [women's] improvement and instruction [. . .] [which acts as] a Glass, by which they may dress out their Minds'.[36] Henry's praise is tinged with disdain at the lack of wider recognition that his sister's literary virtues have won. These 'excellent pictures of Virtue and Vice' will hopefully accrue 'more Advantage to the Reader [. . .] than the Good-Nature and Sensibility of the Age have, to their immortal Credit, bestowed on the Author'.[37] This sense of unfair neglect and profound moral disgust at an audience (of women) unwilling to be educated hardens into a conviction that superior insight, subtle penetration and moral discernment remain unacknowledged and unrewarded by an intellectually obtuse and fundamentally degraded reading public.

In Fielding's later fiction, such moral pessimism becomes a consistent undertone, as narrative arcs are increasingly unsettled by disappointment, bitterness and anger – a satiric despair at the incorrigibility of human nature that is frequently distilled in bleak comedy. Dark

---

[33] Isobel Grundy, 'Collier, Jane (bap. 1715, d. 1755), novelist', in *Oxford Dictionary of National Biography* (Oxford: Oxford University Press, 2010), online edition <https://www.oxforddnb.com/view/10.1093/ref:odnb/9780198614128. 001.0001/odnb-9780198614128-e-37302> [accessed 28 April 2021].

[34] Dickie, p. 167.

[35] Sarah Fielding, *Familiar Letters between the Principal Characters in David Simple, and Some Others. To Which Is Added, A Vision*, 2 vols (London: A. Millar, 1747), I, p. xvii.

[36] Ibid., I, p. xx.

[37] Ibid., I, p. xxii.

humour and rage combine in these works. *The History of Ophelia* has been described by Peter Sabor as a 'good-humoured novel, lighter than any other of [her] works', and perhaps for this reason it was 'amongst the most popular'.[38] Linda Bree is more circumspect, acknowledging that *Ophelia* has 'a vein of humour unexpectedly robust for what is known of Sarah'.[39] Indeed, *Ophelia* is responsible for 'the most unexpected rape joke in eighteenth-century women's writing'.[40] Rape jokes crystallise cultural misogyny: their punchlines retail scepticism at women's testimonies of sexual violence, insinuating their complicity and pleasure, or implying physical unattractiveness which disqualifies them from the sexual overtures they report, or the incapacity of the men accused of the crime. As a genre, rape jokes inculcate mistrust of women's words and women's motivations: they tend to connive with patriarchal power and consolidate its prerogatives. But we should not be surprised by humour in a novel which reworks the 'Richardsonian situation of a virgin abducted and threatened with violence', given the propensity for Richardson's own fictions to turn trauma into comedy, to sublimate rape into pastoral humour.[41] Like Clarissa Harlowe, Fielding's Ophelia escapes one confinement to another. Initially seized by the besotted Lord Dorchester, she is subsequently abducted by the Marchioness of Trente, who views her as a love rival. Accompanied by her jailer, the aged and obsequious Mrs Herner, Ophelia is spirited away to the country. Staying overnight at an inn, the protagonist is woken by distressed cries issuing from the room of her travelling companion. She finds Mrs Herner in a state of shock and déshabillé, wearing little other than a tattered nightgown, which is grasped at its corner by an unknown male intruder. No icon of female virtue in distress, Mrs Herner is a laughable grotesque. Her visage is a Swiftian assemblage of epidermal emollients, a skin-care regime which hints at ludicrous vanity. Her 'lips greased with Tallow; her Eyes done thinly over with a dark coloured Ointment and the Rest of her Face covered with thick Cream not quite dry [. . .] her yellow Skin [. . .] resplendent' through the

---

[38] Sabor, p. xxi.
[39] Bree, p. 149.
[40] Dickie, p. 212.
[41] Ibid. See Rebecca Anne Barr, 'Richardsonian Fiction, Women's Raillery, and Heteropessimist Humour', *Eighteenth-Century Fiction*, 33.4 (Summer 2021), 575–600.

rents in her gown.[42] Fielding's laughter brings Mrs Herner close for the purpose of irreverent scrutiny, drawing her 'into a zone of crude contact' which enables familiarity in order to 'break open its external shell, look into its centre, doubt it, take it apart, dismember it, lay it bare and expose it, examine it freely and experiment with it'.[43] Lacking Swift's tendencies towards scabrous sexual dismemberment, Fielding's laughter is nonetheless similarly irreverent: it 'demolishes fear and piety before an object, before a world'.[44] Rather than making Mrs Herner an object of pure feminine pathos, the novel ridicules her vanity at a time of life when courtship is out of the question.

Despite having broken into Herner's room, the drunken Squire (and Justice of the Peace) outrageously claims that *she* invited *him* into *her* bed, but now that he realises her age, he would rather sleep with his dog or horse than with such an ugly 'Hag' and 'Succubus'. In Dickie's reading, the attempted rape produces little sympathy in the female narrator, who cannot 'restrain a Smile' at Mrs Herner's humiliation by her would-be assailant (p. 166). The episode, Dickie argues, shows the novelistic persistence of coarse and misogynist tropes, distilled in jestbooks, but which permeate an eighteenth-century culture in thrall to male power. Fielding thus 'indulges in and elaborates' on such tropes, Mrs Herner's description resembling 'something out of Smollett – a strikingly unsympathetic depiction of female aging from an author who was herself a spinster of fifty'.[45] Notwithstanding his assumptions about the undifferentiated sorriness (and presumed solidarity) of post-menopausal unmarried women, Dickie locates genuine resonances between Smollett's dyspeptic humour and Fielding's supposedly more sympathetic feminine style. Fielding's bleak satire on male sexual entitlement reminds women readers that male misdemeanours tend, then as now, to go unpunished. That *Ophelia*'s lecherous squire is a Justice of the Peace underlines the text's social critique, reminding us of that other would-be rapist, Richardson's Mr B, who is *also* the local magistrate.

---

[42] Sarah Fielding, *The History of Ophelia*, ed. by Peter Sabor (Peterborough, ON: Broadview Press, 2004), pp. 165–6. All further references are given parenthetically in the text.

[43] Mikhail Bakhtin, *The Dialogic Imagination: Four Essays*, ed. by Michael Holquist, trans. by Caryl Emerson and Michael Holquist (Austin: University of Texas Press, 1981), p. 23.

[44] Ibid.

[45] Dickie, p. 213.

Despite her youth and beauty, for Pamela Andrews to allege rape would be as farcical as poor Mrs Herner. Such humour provides a starkly de-idealising corrective to the sexual pieties of *Pamela I*, where appeals to mercy and morality are only partly absorbed by imperfect male authority figures. If *Ophelia*, like Fielding's other works, acts as 'a guide for meaningful living in a hugely imperfect world', it does so by subjecting the sentimental consolations of narrative to the depredations of satire.[46]

Yet the novel's idiosyncratic humour cannot be entirely flattened into rape-culture complicity. The episode is brutal and bleak, but by delineating Mrs Herner's history and the subsequent behaviour of the Squire, the novel grants her allegation credence and sympathy. The narrative voice does not seamlessly align with the Squire's mockery. By including the history of Mrs Herner's predicament, the text balances comedy with quotidian tragedy, and teaches readers the risks that minor missteps and mischances may expose them to. That is, it laughs them into an awareness of female precarity: once unmoored from family and financial security, *any* gentlewoman may become the object of ridicule. Fielding's risibility does not preclude pity but packages astringent self-awareness into its comic vision of *things as they are*. Resolutely quiet throughout Ophelia's journey, Mrs Herner is nonetheless 'not void of Sweetness [. . .] Dejection and Humiliation appeared in her whole Aspect' (p. 163). The contrast between her mien and her frosty attitude towards her charge is explained by her background. Mrs Herner's financial generosity enabled her friend, the Marchioness of Trente, to make an advantageous marriage. Outliving her means, once Mrs Herner's fortunes are exhausted, the Marchioness absorbs her into her household, not as a friend and equal, but as a 'humble companion': a domestic inferior who will furnish a 'new subject of power'.[47] Mrs Herner's story thus provides a grim instance of the ways in which 'ungrateful returns are sometimes made for real favours', contrary to the utopian hopes of sentimentalists.[48] She 'exchanges poverty for Wretchedness [. . . and] for a Subsistence, sold herself to the most abject Slavery' (p. 164).

---

[46] Johnson, p. 52.
[47] Jane Collier, *The Art of Ingeniously Tormenting*, ed. by Katharine A. Craik (Oxford: Oxford University Press, 2006), p. 21.
[48] Ibid.

Mrs Herner is a toadeater. Fielding's long-standing interest in the toadeater can be seen in *David Simple*, where the heroine, Cynthia, explains the meaning of the term as

> a metaphor taken from a Mountebank's Boys eating Toads, in order to shew his Master's Skill in expelling Poison: It is built on a Supposition (which I am afraid is generally too true) that People who are so unhappy as to be in a State of Dependance, are forced to do the most nauseous things [. . .] to please and humour their Patrons [. . .] most people have so much the Art of tormenting, that every time they have made the poor Creatures they have in their power *swallow a Toad*, they give them something to expel it again, that they may be ready to swallow the next they think proper [. . .] they grow soft and good to them again, on purpose to have it in their power to *plague them the more*. The *Satire* of the Expression, in reality, falls on the Person who is mean enough to act in such a manner; but as it is no uncommon thing for People to make use of Terms they don't understand, it is generally used, by way of *Derision*, to the unfortunate Wretch who is thrown into such a miserable Situation.[49]

Conscious of 'derision's' tendency to follow power, Fielding is quick to forestall mindless mockery: the toadeater may seem the object of scorn but is in fact its victim. In a characteristically analytical move, satirical complicity is exposed and the laugh turned against those too quick to mock the unfortunate. Moreover, this is a role generated by 'unmitigated self-interest, financial opportunism, and pervasive gender inequalities'.[50] Fielding's fictions repeatedly invoke the toadeater as the potential fate for unmarried women of good family and slender means. Genteel women, especially those who are amiable, tender and impecunious, are ripe for the discreet emotional torture of such domestic dependency. The narrative's grasp of Mrs Herner's circumstances is painfully lucid. 'From continual servile Compliance with the Will of another, she lost all Liberty of Thought', finally bereaved of the very 'Method of pronouncing the Word No; [Mrs Herner's] Language was composed of nothing but Expressions of Assent and Affirmatives' (p. 164). As in *The Cry*, habits of language affect modes of thought. It is 'custom that corrupts' her, rather than vicious disposition. Mrs Herner is a woman whose moral autonomy

---

[49] Fielding, *The Adventures of David Simple*, Book II, p. 89.

[50] James Bryant Reeves, 'The Limits of Self: Sarah Fielding', in *Godless Fictions in the Eighteenth Century: A Literary History of Atheism* (Cambridge University Press, Cambridge, 2020), pp. 105–36 (p. 123).

is first compromised by rank vanity and self-indulgence.[51] Since self-control is a key tenet of Fielding's writings, the recurrent figure of the toadeater acts as a limit case of feminised submission which warns women against mindless conformism: against confusing necessary compromise with totalising submission. Though Mrs Herner's situation deserves sympathy, the novel is clear that *she* is responsible for her foolish choice to live beyond her means, and for her complicity with the Marchioness' scheme. By refusing to depict Mrs Herner as simply a sentimental victim, converting her into a 'satiric instrument', *Ophelia*'s satire insists that women's 'Liberty of Thought' – no matter how limited – makes women morally accountable for their actions.[52]

In the case of Mrs Herner's near-rape, Fielding's humour probes the proximity between the comic grotesque and the feminine pathetic and the delusional superiority (or autonomy) produced by thoughtless laughter. The moral risk of thinking oneself above another woman is clear in the outcome of the smile that Ophelia 'cannot restrain' at Mrs Herner's ridiculousness. 'Perceiv[ing]' the young woman's smile, the would-be rapist redirects his unwarranted attentions to her. 'Looking at me [. . . he] said [you] look good-natured and merry. I love a hoddy Girl hugely, that will make one laugh, and laugh with one [. . .] I will have [you] instead' (p. 166). By allowing herself to become susceptible, albeit momentarily, to the sense of superiority afforded by ridicule, Ophelia's apparent 'good-nature' is read as probable acquiescence to sexual high jinks. Ophelia seems 'merry' – 'laughing; loudly cheerful; gay of heart' – but the term suggests a moral carelessness, too, a propensity to indulge in promiscuous pleasure.[53] In such circumstances, women's laughter is risky. The Squire's pursuit becomes a Benny Hill-esque chase: a madcap race to escape, with the nimble and youthful Ophelia overtaken by the partially clad (and comically speedier) Mrs Herner. While Dickie is right to categorise this episode within the 'rape joke' genre, the detail of Fielding's narrative is more complex than that category. Mrs Herner's pride *is* laughable, but it is *also* insistently pathetic.

---

[51] Skinner, p. xix.

[52] Lynn Festa, 'Satire to Sentiment: Mixing Modes in the Later Eighteenth-Century British Novel', in *The Oxford Handbook of Eighteenth-Century Satire*, ed. by Paddy Bullard (Oxford: Oxford University Press, 2019), pp. 645–60 (p. 658).

[53] 'Merry, adj.', in Samuel Johnson, *A Dictionary of the English Language* (1755) <https://johnsonsdictionaryonline.com/1755/merry_adj> [accessed 8 February 2021].

Like the toadeaters described in Sarah Scott's *Millenium Hall*, she clings to 'advantages of birth, education, or natural talents; any thing will serve for a resource to mortified pride'. Even while exploiting risibility, Fielding's narrative does not let us forget that 'the pride which reduces many to be [. . .] toad-eaters, does not render them unworthy of compassion'.[54] The tatters of affectation are pitiable, as well as ridiculous. *The History of Ophelia* recalibrates the temptations to ridicule Mrs Herner by reference to Ophelia as a moral focus – both are impoverished, both the object of unwanted sexual attentions, both have limited agency, and both are the prisoners of the Marchioness. As Ophelia's jailer, Mrs Herner 'leads as melancholy a life as the Prisoner, and she longed, almost as much to be dismissed from her Charge, as I did to be out of her Power' (p. 186). Women's power, as Jane Collier's *Art of Ingeniously Tormenting* (1753) shows, is so vanishingly small that it breeds vicious competition for the slim pleasures of getting one over on each other. But the difference between women who win and women who lose is often a matter of mere happenstance. The novel's anger at women's capacity for petty cruelty is thus less *ad feminam* than bleak bemusement tempered with an awareness that 'enforced submission' – the systemic demands for female compliance with power structures – creates a comic and contorted desperation in women compelled to abase themselves to survive.[55]

Ophelia indicts women's vanity and fantasies of autonomy, affirming the status quo while holding gentlewomen to moral account. Its black humour, unedifying though it may be to modern readers more sympathetic to the constraints on women and less forgiving of violent misogyny, nonetheless acts as a 'mortal enemy of sentimentality' that increasingly rendered women passive by-products of male narratives.[56] Directing her 'satirical gaze on the structural defects, injustices and hypocrisies of society', Fielding's slapstick refuses to let women off the hook.[57] Laughter *at* Mrs Herner is unsettled by the realisation that this predicament could be Ophelia's, could be any woman's, creating 'a queasy movement between revulsion and

---

[54] Sarah Scott, *Millenium Hall*, ed. by Gary Kelly (Peterborough, ON: Broadview Press, 1995), pp. 82–5.

[55] Betty Schellenberg, *Companions without Vows: Relationships among Eighteenth-Century British Women* (Athens: University of Georgia Press, 1994), p. 21.

[56] André Breton, *Anthology of Black Humour*, trans. by Mark Polizzotti (London: Telegram, 2009), p. 10.

[57] Skinner, p. xxv.

unwilling self-recognition, identification and self-critical displacement'; women readers are forced to wonder: 'do I get the joke, or am I part of the joke?'[58] Lashing systemic injustice along with female fallibility, and mixing social critique with unforgiving mirth, *The Governess'* maxim that 'laughing is the proper manner of treating affectation' remains true in Fielding's final novel. *Ophelia*'s motley mode teaches gentlewomen pre-emptive humility, lest the startling selfishness, rapacity and brutishness of the world take them by surprise. Mrs Herner's story exposes the consolations of gentility and propriety as cold comfort when unaccompanied by the love and reciprocal respect provided by true friends or family. Respectability does not guarantee affection and care: women need the combined resources of sympathy and emotional self-knowledge to endure such harsh conditions.

While *Ophelia*'s abduction narrative deconstructs the reformation-by-love plot popularised by *Pamela*, the novel's happy conclusion insists that the trial of the heroine and her marriage-averse suitor has earned them a love match. Yet Ophelia's sage Aunt, a kind of super-annuated and romantically disillusioned Teachum, remains sceptical of Dorchester's moral worth. Why, she asks, should she believe him reformed when 'the Innocence and unfeigned Piety' of the heroine 'could not change your Heart?' (p. 271). Chastened, with 'a doleful Face and a simple Sheepishness' he listens 'with all the Humility of a School-boy to his Monitor, and gave her no Interruption' (p. 272). Comically (and unrealistically) silent, Dorchester's admission of guilt is a fantasy of male repentance and (perhaps) an amusing sop for the reader. Ophelia marries him, despite his egregious behaviour, and so (as in *Pamela*) the irrational generosity of love – or self-preservation within patriarchy – wins out. The engrafting of marital resolution onto a picaresque narrative gives women readers a brisk training in pragmatism. Reason, self-control and goodness *are* to be developed, but *Ophelia*'s comedy preaches that we resign ourselves to the ridiculous. Women are counselled to surrender their affectations and 'make the best of what eighteenth-century British society offers them' – which is not a great deal.[59] The novel's irreverent energy also reminds us of the ways in which gendered norms of laughter are more flexible than conduct orthodoxies allow. Recent stylometric analysis has suggested that the first volume of *Ophelia* may be

[58] Festa, pp. 646, 652.
[59] Johnson, p. 206.

partly the work of Fielding's sibling, Henry.[60] But the Herner episode and its 'robust' humour is in the *second* volume of the novel, which means that if the novel *is* collaborative, it is Sarah Fielding who is most likely responsible for the comedy. Considering Sarah as the author of this darkly amusing novel enables us to better understand women's sense of humour in the bleak mid-century. Uncovering the consistency of humour in writing from this period also provides us with a genealogical bridge which helps account for the re-emergence of women's comedy in the latter part of the century. Laughing to learn in the eighteenth-century novel may not deliver the most palatable of lessons, but in a society still more comfortable with women's subordination and their silence, Fielding's caustic satire teaches us about the ways in which black humour can indict social cruelties while sustaining the very habits of compliance upon which patriarchy depends.

Works Cited

Primary

Collier, Jane, *The Art of Ingeniously Tormenting*, ed. by Katharine A. Craik (Oxford: Oxford University Press, 2006)

Dryden, John, *Discourse Concerning the Original and Progress of Satire*, in *Poems, 1693–1696*, ed. by A. B. Chambers, William Frost and Vinton A. Dearing, in *The Works of John Dryden*, vol. 4, ed. by H. T. Swedenberg (Berkeley: University of California Press, 1974), pp. 3–90

Fielding, Henry, *Tom Jones*, ed. by John Bender and Simon Stern (Oxford: Oxford University Press, 1998)

Fielding, Sarah, *The Adventures of David Simple and Volume the Last*, introduction by Peter Sabor (Lexington: University Press of Kentucky, 1998)

——. *The Cry: A New Dramatic Fable*, ed. by Carolyn Woodward (Lexington: University of Kentucky Press, 2021)

---

[60] John Burrows, 'Sarah and Henry Fielding and the Authorship of *The History of Ophelia*: A Computational Analysis', *Script and Print*, 30.2 (2006–7), 71–92. Christopher Johnson believes the novel to be a genuine 'found manuscript' edited by Sarah Fielding. This is a controversial argument, and I concur with Peter Sabor and others that the narrative and its preoccupations are consistent with her authorship.

——. *Familiar Letters between the Principal Characters in David Simple, and Some Others. To Which Is Added, A Vision*, 2 vols (London: A. Millar, 1747)

——. *The Governess: or, Little Female Academy. Calculated for the Entertainment and Instruction of Young Ladies in Their Education*, ed. by Candace Ward (Peterborough, ON: Broadview, 2005)

——. *The History of Ophelia*, ed. by Peter Sabor (Peterborough, ON: Broadview Press, 2004)

——. *Remarks on Clarissa* (London: J. Robinson, 1749)

Halifax, Marquess of (George Savile), *The Lady's New Year's Gift: or, Advice to a Daughter*, 3rd edn (London: Gillyflower and James Partridge, 1688)

Hobbes, Thomas, *Leviathan*, ed. by Richard Tuck (Cambridge: Cambridge University Press, 1996)

Hutcheson, Francis, *Reflections upon Laughter, and Remarks upon the Fable of the Bees* (Glasgow: Printed by R. Urie for D. Baxter, 1750)

Johnson, Samuel, *A Dictionary of the English Language* (1755) <https://johnsonsdictionaryonline.com/1755/> [accessed 8 February 2021]

Locke, John, *Some Thoughts Concerning Education*, in *The Works of John Locke in Nine Volumes*, 12th edn, vol. 8 (London: Rivington, 1824), pp. 1–210

Richardson, Samuel, *Pamela: or, Virtue Rewarded*, ed. by Tom Keymer and Alice Wakely (Oxford: Oxford University Press, 2000)

Shaftesbury, Lord, 'A Letter Concerning Enthusiasm to my Lord *****', in *Characteristics of Men, Manners, Opinions, Times*, ed. by Laurence Klein (Cambridge: Cambridge University Press, 2000)

Scott, Sarah, *Millenium Hall*, ed. by Gary Kelly (Peterborough, ON: Broadview Press, 1995)

Vanbrugh, John and Colley Cibber, *The Provoked Husband*, ed. by Peter Dixon (Lincoln: University of Nebraska Press, 1973)

Secondary

Anderson, Misty, *Imagining Methodism in Eighteenth-Century Britain: Enthusiasm, Belief and the Borders of the Self* (Baltimore: Johns Hopkins University Press, 2012)

Backscheider, Paula R., 'Literary Culture as Immediate Reality', in *A Companion to the Eighteenth-Century English Novel and Culture*, ed. by Paula R. Backscheider and Catherine Ingrassia (Blackwell: Oxford, 2005), pp. 504–38

Bakhtin, Mikhail, *The Dialogic Imagination: Four Essays*, ed. by Michael Holquist, trans. by Caryl Emerson and Michael Holquist (Austin: University of Texas Press, 1981)

Barr, Rebecca Anne, '"Barren Desarts of Arbitrary Words": Language and Communication in Collier and Fielding's *The Cry*', *Women's Writing*, 23.1 (2016), 87–105

——. 'Pathological Laughter and the Response to Ridicule: Samuel Richardson, Sarah Fielding and Jane Collier', *RSÉAA XVII–XVIII* 70 (2013), 223–44

——. 'Richardsonian Fiction, Women's Raillery, and Heteropessimist Humour', *Eighteenth-Century Fiction*, 33.4 (Summer 2021), 575–600

Bree, Linda, *Sarah Fielding* (New York: Twayne, 1996)

Breton, André, *Anthology of Black Humour*, trans. by Mark Polizzotti (London: Telegram, 2009)

Burrows, John, 'Sarah and Henry Fielding and the Authorship of *The History of Ophelia*: A Computational Analysis', *Script and Print*, 30.2 (2006–7), 71–92

Davies, Rebecca, *Written Maternal Authority and Eighteenth-Century Education: Educating by the Book* (Farnham: Ashgate, 2016)

Dickie, Simon, *Cruelty and Laughter: Forgotten Comic Literature and the Unsentimental Eighteenth Century* (Chicago: University of Chicago Press, 2011)

Festa, Lynn, 'Satire to Sentiment: Mixing Modes in the Later Eighteenth-Century British Novel', in *The Oxford Handbook of Eighteenth-Century Satire*, ed. by Paddy Bullard (Oxford: Oxford University Press, 2019), pp. 645–60

Grundy, Isobel, 'Collier, Jane (bap. 1715, d. 1755), novelist', in *Oxford Dictionary of National Biography* (Oxford: Oxford University Press, 2010), online edition <https://www.oxforddnb.com/view/10.1093/ref:odnb/9780198614128.001.0001/odnb-9780198614128-e-37302> [accessed 28 April 2021]

Johnson, Christopher, *A Political Biography of Sarah Fielding* (London: Routledge, 2017)

Joy, Louise, 'The Laughing Child: Children's Poetry and the Comic Mode', in *The Aesthetics of Children's Poetry: A Study of Children's Verse in English*, ed. by Katherine Wakely-Mulroney and Louise Joy (London: Routledge, 2017), pp. 111–26

Londry, Michael, 'Our Dear Miss Jenny Collier', *TLS* (5 March 2004), pp. 13–14

Marks, Sylvia Kasey, 'Sarah Fielding's *The Governess*: A Gloss on Her "Books upon Education"', in *Women, Gender, and Print Culture in Eighteenth-Century Britain*, ed. by Temma Berg and Sonia Kane (Bethlehem: Lehigh, 2013), pp. 59–78

Reeves, James Bryant, *Godless Fictions in the Eighteenth Century: A Literary History of Atheism* (Cambridge: Cambridge University Press, 2020)

Schellenberg, Betty, *Companions without Vows: Relationships among Eighteenth-Century British Women* (Athens: University of Georgia Press, 1994)

Schofield, Mary Anne, 'Introduction', in Sarah Fielding, *The Cry* (Delmar, NY: Scholars Facsimiles and Imprints, 1986), pp. 5–12

Skinner, Gillian, 'Introduction', in Sarah Fielding, *The History of the Countess of Dellwyn* (Abingdon: Routledge, 2022), pp. vii–xxv

Suzuki, Mika, 'The "true use of reading": Sarah Fielding and Mid-Eighteenth-Century Literary Strategies' (unpublished doctoral thesis, Queen Mary and Westerfield University, 1998)

Wilson, Kathleen, 'Empire of Virtue: The Imperial Project and Hanoverian Culture, c.1720–1785', in *The Imperial State at War: Britain from 1689–1815*, ed. by Lawrence Stone (London: Routledge, 1994), pp. 128–64

Ylivuori, Soile, *Women and Politeness in Eighteenth-Century England* (London: Routledge, 2019)

Chapter 9

Emotional Regulation: Jane Austen, Jane West and Mary Brunton

Katie Halsey and Jennifer Robertson

I often wonder how *you* can find time for what you do, in addition to the care of the House; – And how good Mrs West cd have written such Books & collected so many hard words, with all her family cares, is still more a matter of astonishment! Composition seems to me Impossible, with a head full of Joints of Mutton & doses of rhubarb.

Jane Austen to Cassandra Austen, 8–9 September 1816[1]

I am looking over [Mary Brunton's] Self Control again, & my opinion is confirmed of its' being an excellently-meant, elegantly-written Work, without anything of Nature or Probability in it. I declare I do not know whether Laura's passage down the American River, is not the most natural, possible, every-day thing she ever does.

Jane Austen to Cassandra Austen, 11–12 October 1813[2]

Jane Austen's remarks about her contemporaries Mary Brunton and Jane West are characteristically double-edged, and in both cases tinged with admiration and professional jealousy. *Self Control*, not Austen's *Sense and Sensibility*, was, as Anthony Mandal reminds us, the runaway success of 1811, while 'good Mrs. West's' *Letters to a Young Lady*, published in the same year, immediately went through four editions in 1811 alone.[3] In the competitive literary marketplace of the 1810s, Austen's success was much more modest. Perhaps the more overtly didactic work of West and Brunton had a more

---

[1] All references to Jane Austen's letters are from *Jane Austen's Letters*, ed. by Deirdre Le Faye, 3rd edn (Oxford: Oxford University Press, 1995) [hereafter, *Letters*]. *Letters*, p. 321.

[2] *Letters*, p. 234.

[3] Anthony Mandal, 'Introduction', in Mary Brunton, *Self Control*, ed. by Anthony Mandal (London: Pickering and Chatto, 2014), p. xiii. This will be the edition cited for the remainder of this essay.

immediate and obvious appeal to the readership; perhaps their publishers simply did a better job at marketing their works. In West's case, of course, she was already a known name by 1811, in the genres of both conduct literature and the novel, and that, in itself, might have been enough to guarantee greater success than could be expected for the debut novel of an anonymous Hampshire lady. But the key point to note is that all three writers were competing for a share of the same market and readership, and that they were benefiting from a particular kind of anti-Jacobin public feeling that, by the 1810s, had come to associate sensibility and emotional freedom with the French Revolution and its terrifying aftermath, and reason, sense and emotional regulation with its opposition. Matthew Grenby identifies the popularity of the anti-Jacobin novel in the 1790s and 1800s as an expression of 'the almost hegemonic political conservatism that characterised Britain from the mid 1790s until after Waterloo', and suggests that 'in a fiercely competitive market there was no alternative' to an anti-Jacobin stance for a writer who wished to sell novels.[4]

In this political atmosphere, emotional regulation – in particular emotional *self*-regulation – had both a political and a personal dimension, allowing writers such as West, Brunton and Hannah More to conflate the national and patriotic with the personal and domestic, in the process arguing forcefully for the importance of a female education that emphasised rigour, regulation and self-control to avoid the excesses and the ravages caused, as they saw it, by the emotional volatility and laxity of the French. As Hannah More suggested, the role of 'women of rank and fortune' in a 'moment of alarm and peril' was to 'oppose a bold and noble *unanimity* to the most tremendous confederacies against religion, and order, and governments, which the world ever saw'.[5] The 'patriotism at once firm and feminine' that More advocated was rooted in 'propriety' and 'discretion' – synonyms for emotional self-regulation – and in this she was typical.[6] In this chapter, we will consider Austen, West and Brunton as authors within this context, focusing on their treatment of the theme of emotional regulation. Our discussion will centre on Austen's *Mansfield Park* (1814) and *Sense and Sensibility*, considering the ways in which these two works constitute conversations with those of West and

---

[4] Matthew Grenby, *The Anti-Jacobin Novel: British Conservatism and the French Revolution* (Cambridge: Cambridge University Press, 2001), pp. 169, 171.

[5] Hannah More, *Strictures on the Modern System of Female Education*, 9th edn, 2 vols (London: Cadell and Davies, 1801), I, pp. 4–6.

[6] Ibid., I, pp. 6–8.

Brunton on the subjects of self-control, self-discipline and regulation of the emotions. All four novels deal to some extent with the problems arising from the tension that can exist between an individual's attempts at emotional self-regulation and their reception in an imperfect world.

Much has, of course, been written on Austen's politics, and it is important to state at the outset that in suggesting that her works should be considered within an anti-Jacobin context, we are not characterising her as a straightforwardly conservative author, in the line of, for example, Marilyn Butler.[7] Nor, on the other hand, would we endorse the suggestion of a 'radical Austen' recently proposed by Helena Kelly.[8] Instead, in this chapter we will attempt to show the ways in which Austen's treatment of the theme of emotional self-regulation takes its place in a much more dynamic, nuanced and important conversation between women writers of educational fiction than has usually been recognised. In so doing, we hope to demonstrate both her congruences with and differences from her more straightforwardly evangelical or didactic contemporaries.

For women, frequently characterised as a softer and more 'naturally' emotional sex, a political and philosophical environment that rejected the value of sensibility had a particular, and particularly personal, resonance. And across the political spectrum, women writers engaged with the question of the role of the emotions in a woman's character, temper and education. Writers as superficially different as Mary Wollstonecraft, Mary Hays and Hannah More agreed on the fundamental importance of regulating the emotions in their didactic works. The necessity for emotional self-regulation became, in fact, one area in which women writers, whatever their political affiliation, could agree. Wollstonecraft, for example, describes the best education as 'such an attention to a child as will slowly sharpen the senses, form the temper, regulate the passions as they begin to ferment, and set the understanding to work before the body arrives at maturity'.[9] From the opposite end of the political spectrum, Hannah More devotes an entire chapter of her *Strictures on the Modern System*

[7] See, for example, Marilyn Butler, *Jane Austen and the War of Ideas* (Oxford: Clarendon Press, 1975), *passim*.

[8] See Helena Kelly, *Jane Austen the Secret Radical* (London: Icon Books, 2016), *passim*.

[9] Mary Wollstonecraft, *A Vindication of the Rights of Woman* [1792], in *A Vindication of the Rights of Woman and A Vindication of the Rights of Man* (Oxford: Oxford World's Classics, 1994; repr. 2008), p. 86.

of Female Education (1799) to the inculcation of habits of self-regulation, arguing that 'she who has been accustomed to have an early habit of restraint exercised over all her appetites and temper; she who has been used to set bounds to her desires as a general principle' will be able to direct 'all the faculties of the understanding, and all the qualities of the heart, to keep their proper places and due bounds, to observe their just proportions, and maintain their right station, relation, order, and dependence'.[10]

As Louise Joy has pointed out, however, the form of the novel was particularly suited not to the regulation of emotion, but to the subjective expression of emotion.[11] Anti-Jacobin didactic fiction therefore struggles with an inherent tension between the appeal of a character's emotional self-revelation to a novel's readers, and the need to provide a didactic message which checks or counters emotional excess. Hence the large number of novels of the 1790s and afterwards which make use of a pair of contrasting heroines – one sensible, virtuous and rewarded; one passionate, sensitive and punished. This structure allows a writer both to appeal to and gratify a reader's wish for vicarious passionate emotion (via access to the internal workings of the mind of a 'heroine of sensibility'), and to ensure that such emotion is regulated (via the contrasted example of the virtuously self-regulating behaviour of a 'heroine of sense'). Such is the structure of Elizabeth Inchbald's *A Simple Story* (1791), of Jane West's *A Gossip's Story* (1796), and at first glance, of Jane Austen's *Sense and Sensibility* (1811), which, as Janet Todd reminds us, in its very title recalls the polarised philosophical debates of the 1790s during which it was written.[12] Austen did not, however, as Brian Southam rightly says, title the novel *Sense and Sensibility* until it was revised from its original epistolary form in 1797 – the earlier version was in fact called 'Elinor and Marianne'. It does not seem impossible to imagine that, as Austen revised her earlier work, she deliberately retitled and recast it in a seemingly more didactic, and thus saleable, form. Our contention is that in doing so, she was making a deliberate, and, to her contemporary readers, recognisable, allusion to other didactic works, and in particular to *A Gossip's Story*, published the

[10] *Strictures*, I, pp. 158, 166.

[11] See Louise Joy, 'Novel Feelings: Emma Courtney's Point of View', *European Romantic Review*, 21.2 (2010), 221–34.

[12] Janet Todd, *The Cambridge Introduction to Jane Austen* (Cambridge: Cambridge University Press, 2015), pp. 50–64.

previous year, with its pointed and explicit endorsement of 'sense' and rejection of 'sensibility'.

A number of critics, among them Marilyn Butler, Devoney Looser, Melinda O'Connell and Caitlin Kelly, have pointed out the similarities in structure, plot, names and theme in *A Gossip's Story* and *Sense and Sensibility*.[13] Both works, for example, feature a pair of contrasting sisters, one of whom is a paragon of sensibility named Marianne, and the other who embodies rationality and emotional control. Both make use of an accident to bring their Mariannes into contact with the men with whom they fall in love, and who eventually prove unworthy as either suitor or husband. Both of the heroines of 'sense' (Louisa Dudley in *A Gossip's Story* and Elinor Dashwood of *Sense and Sensibility*) are rewarded with happy marriages, and both of these marry suitors who were previously in love with other women. Both authors also share, it seems, a belief in the importance of emotional self-regulation. These similarities are enough to suggest, as J. M. S. Tompkins does, that *A Gossip's Story* is 'not exactly the source but the starting-point of *Sense and Sensibility*'.[14] The differences in the two works, however, are substantial enough to imply that *A Gossip's Story* suggested various ideas to Jane Austen with which she disagreed vigorously enough to wish to rewrite the novel in her own way. Support for this assertion comes not only from internal evidence in the novels, but also from Austen's letters, in which she tells her niece, Anna Lefroy, in a letter of 28 September 1814, 'I am quite determined, however, not to be pleased with Mrs. West's "*Alicia De Lacy*", should I ever meet with it, which I hope I shall not. I think I *can* be stout against anything written by Mrs. West.'[15] It also chimes with what we know about Austen's creative practice, in which the impetus for creation is often a critical or parodic view of another author's work which gives rise to a comedic and sometimes deeply critical treatment of that work.[16] This is manifested most obviously in her juvenile works, but is still evident even in her final

[13] Butler, pp. 100–1; Devoney Looser, Melinda O'Connell and Caitlin Kelly (eds), 'Introduction', in Jane West, *A Gossip's Story* (Richmond, VA: Valancourt Books, 2016), pp. xi–xii. This edition will be the one cited throughout the remainder of this essay.

[14] J. M. S. Tompkins, '*Elinor and Marianne*: A Note on Jane Austen', *Review of English Studies* 16.61 (Jan. 1940), 33–43 (p. 33).

[15] *Letters*, pp. 277–8.

[16] See Olivia Murphy, *Jane Austen the Reader: The Artist as Critic* (Basingstoke: Palgrave Macmillan, 2013) for a full articulation of the integration of critical and creative practice in Austen's works.

work – the twelve chapters of *Sanditon* written on her deathbed in 1817.

Perhaps the most important differences between *Sense and Sensibility* and *A Gossip's Story* are the extent to which the straightforwardly didactic aim of West's work is complicated in *Sense and Sensibility*, and the ways in which each author uses the structural device of a pair of superficially contrasting heroines. The epigraph to *A Gossip's Story* announces to its readers that 'The following pages intended, under the disguise of an artless History, to illustrate the Advantages of CONSISTENCY, FORTITUDE, and the DOMESTICK VIRTUES; and to expose to ridicule CAPRICE, AFFECTED SENSIBILITY, and an IDLE CENSORIOUS HUMOUR'.[17] *A Gossip's Story* goes on to associate its two heroines fairly straightforwardly with these characteristics – Louisa is emblematic of consistency, fortitude and the domestic virtues, while Marianne displays caprice and affected sensibility in high measure. Throughout *A Gossip's Story*, West consistently presents Louisa as the epitome of emotional self-regulation, with 'a disposition to improve both in moral and mental excellence', and 'an informed, well-regulated mind' (pp. 15, 17), and Marianne as the opposite ('tremblingly alive to all the softer passions' and 'peculiarly unfit to encounter even those common calamities humanity must endure' (p. 17)). It is important to note that both Louisa and Marianne feel deeply; their difference is in how they manage to control and regulate passionate emotion. However, West consistently emphasises their differences rather than their basic similarity, in order to show fortitude rewarded and unregulated sensibility punished. Austen, on the other hand, is at pains from the first pages of *Sense and Sensibility* to comment on the similarities between Elinor and Marianne, as well as their differences. Elinor, for example, has *both* 'strength of understanding and coolness of judgment' *and* 'an excellent heart'.[18] Like her sister, Marianne, Elinor's 'disposition was affectionate, and her feelings were strong' (p. 7). Marianne, like Elinor, is 'sensible and clever' (p. 7); the difference between them is that Elinor can (and does) regulate her emotions, while Marianne has resolved not to do so. Here we see a key and important difference between West's characterisation and Austen's – in West's novel, Marianne *cannot* regulate her emotions; in Austen's, Marianne *will* not. *Sense and Sensibility*, then, presents us with a possibility which

---

[17] *A Gossip's Story*, p. 2.
[18] Jane Austen, *Sense and Sensibility*, ed. by Edward Copeland (Cambridge: Cambridge University Press, 2006), p. 7.

is effectively denied to West's Marianne Dudley: the possibility that a character of deep sensibility might develop and change.

As the two novels play out, another key difference appears: Marianne Dashwood conquers herself because of, not in spite of, her strong emotions. These two differences come to define the fates of the two 'heroines of sensibility'. Marianne Dashwood begins to regulate her emotional life when she recognises, understands and comes to respect her sister Elinor's painful attempts at emotional control. Her love for Elinor, and for her mother, enables this understanding, and her capacity for emotion is the means of her eventual happiness: 'Marianne found her own happiness in forming his [her husband, Colonel Brandon's] [. . .] Marianne could never love by halves; and her whole heart became, in time, as much devoted to her husband, as it had once been to Willoughby' (p. 430). Marianne Dudley, on the other hand, although quite as generous, sincere and charming as her Austenian counterpart, is denied either a second chance or a happy ending because her author is determined to show, as her epigraph demonstrates, that an overly passionate disposition, and a belief in romantic notions, must end badly. Austen agrees with West that sensibility can be dangerous to its possessor, but for her, it is also necessary. This is demonstrated not only in Marianne's happy ending, but in the creation of characters such as Fanny Dashwood and Lucy Steele, who are totally devoid of sensibility or feeling, and are treated with devastating irony. Where West demonstrates the disastrous effects of sensibility, then, *Sense and Sensibility* shows us that without true sensibility – that is, the ability to feel with and for others – the world is a cold and alarming place.

West presents the solution to the ills arising from sensibility as an explicitly religious one. Christianity, she reminds her readers, teaches us 'to *curb* our passions, and to *moderate* our desires; to expect with diffidence, enjoy with gratitude and resign with submission' (p. 31; italics West's). Throughout *A Gossip's Story*, Louisa fully lives up to these precepts, even under the most extreme emotional pressure, while Marianne is regularly cast down by the most trivial of emotional hardships. Louisa reaps the rewards of piety, as we see when, leaving her father's deathbed, she takes refuge in the library of the house in which he is staying:

> She returned the books to their places and after a minute's pause sunk upon her knees. Grief has been termed the parent of eloquence; – it is peculiarly so in an informed well-regulated mind. She raised her eyes, the feelings of her agitated soul animated every impassioned feature.

> Her snowy hands remained clasped in anguish, and regardless of the tears which fell copiously upon them. In the warm flow of unstudied elocution her lips expressed the piety of a seraph, chastised by the humble awe of a weak dependent mortal. She supplicated Heaven to spare her father, her only friend and comfort; but she asked with submission. She painted an orphan's sorrows; but not with the dark colourings of despair. Her mind appeared to gather strength from her divine employment; her tears ceased to flow; a serene sweetness beamed in her countenance, and when she rose from her knees to retire, her whole form seemed inspired with supernatural intelligence, and expressed the most lively resemblance of superior beings which the human imagination can form. (pp. 218–19)

Louisa's piety comforts and inspires her to an almost angelic transformation, and West rewards her heroine not only with the delights of religion, but with a husband, who, on seeing this scene in the library, forgets his earlier unsuccessful love for her sister, and determines to marry Louisa. Since she has secretly loved him from when she met him, it is clear that her Christian virtue and 'informed well-regulated mind' are being rewarded with both spiritual and earthly happiness – Mr Pelham is extremely rich, kindly and devoted, and 'her own prospects were peculiarly brilliant', we are told (p. 228). Her sister, Marianne, on the other hand, ends the book 'entirely broken'. 'Her early and severe disappointment preyed upon her heart; she no longer felt any inclination for amusement, or any desire to excel, and her thoughts continually wandered within the gloomy pale of her own calamity' (p. 227). West's didactic message could hardly be clearer: emotional self-regulation will be rewarded, while failing to regulate one's emotions will be severely punished.

Austen's treatment of the theme of self-regulation is significantly different. Where West presents us with a clear-cut exaltation of 'sense' and a denigration of 'sensibility', Austen's text eventually endorses the need for a balance between the two. As we have already seen, *her* Marianne ends up rich, happy and adored by her husband. While she does, to some extent, learn to regulate her emotions, she never does so completely ('Marianne could never love by halves' (p. 430)). So Austen's 'heroine of sensibility' retains both the capacity and the practice of passionate feeling until the end, and she is not punished for it. Rather the reverse, in fact. And, while her 'heroine of sense', Elinor, does of course get her own happy ending with Edward Ferrars, there is no blinding moment of near-angelic transfiguration for her. Instead, Austen shows us the painful cost of emotional regulation throughout *Sense and Sensibility*, most memorably in the scene where Elinor has to reveal her prior knowledge of Lucy and Edward's engagement to Marianne. Here, she speaks eloquently of the suffering she has endured:

> I have known myself to be divided from Edward for ever, without hearing one circumstance that could make me less desire the connection. – Nothing has proved him unworthy; nor has any thing declared him indifferent to me. – I have had to contend against the unkindness of his sister and the insolence of his mother; and have suffered the punishment of an attachment, without enjoying its advantages. – And all this has been going on at a time, when, as you too well know, it has not been my only unhappiness. – If you can think me capable of ever feeling – surely you may suppose that I have suffered *now*. The composure of mind with which I have brought myself at present to consider the matter, the consolation that I have been willing to admit, have been the effect of constant and painful exertion [. . .] I was *very* unhappy. (p. 299; italics Austen's)

Even in the happiest moment of the novel, when Edward proposes to her, we learn that Elinor 'was oppressed, she was overcome by her own felicity [. . .] it required several hours to give sedateness to her spirits, or any degree of tranquility to her heart' (p. 412). Unlike West's novel, which triumphantly demonstrates the rewards of emotional self-regulation, in *Sense and Sensibility* Austen is at pains to show its costs without ever explicitly commending its rewards. If we consider the means by which Austen brings about the marriage, we might realise that Elinor's happy union with Edward owes nothing to her own emotional control, and everything to Lucy Steele's amoral pursuit of wealth, suggesting Austen's rejection of self-regulation as a consistent method by which to secure personal happiness.

This is not to say that Austen rejects the idea that emotional self-regulation is important or necessary – indeed the narrative voice, which so often presents us with Elinor's worldview, encourages us to see the world as Elinor does, and to see Elinor's own self-control as both admirable and, to some extent, exemplary. But on the level of the structure and the plot – which is where Austen is so markedly in conversation with West – we can perceive a criticism of West's binary oppositions, and by extension of any kind of morality that sees the world so simply in black and white. Instead, in Austen's work, we find an attempt to use the form of the novel to present a more nuanced view of the world, one which recognises both the need for emotional self-regulation and the capacity to feel strongly and express emotion.

Although Austen never again presented her readers with a plot so strikingly like that of a predecessor, in *Mansfield Park* she entered into a second conversation with another author on the subject of emotional regulation, this time with Mary Brunton. Evidence in the letters demonstrates that Austen had read Brunton's *Self Control* at least twice, and probably three times by the time she embarked upon writing *Mansfield Park*.[19] Notably, as with *A Gossip's Story*, the evidence in Austen's letters suggests a critical engagement with *Self Control*, which manifested itself in a desire to improve on the original. In 1813, Austen had found Brunton's novel 'an excellently-meant, elegantly-written Work, without anything of Nature or Probability in it'.[20] By November of 1814, the year of *Mansfield Park*'s publication, she was joking ironically to her niece Anna that she hoped to write 'a close Imitation' of *Self Control*.[21] It seems within the realms of possibility that her joking allusion was to a work she had in fact *already* written, and which was in the forefront of her mind in 1814, and thus that *Mansfield Park* challenges some of the things that she found unpalatable in *Self Control*. *Mansfield Park*'s repeated emphasis on the painful cost of emotional self-regulation harks back to Elinor Dashwood's heartfelt outburst in *Sense and Sensibility*, but it also goes further than that novel in questioning the tenets that are confidently proposed as universal truths in *Self Control*.

In *Self Control*, the reader is presented with a heroine in whom both sentiment and reason coalesce in the perfect form of Laura Montreville. Despite her occasional lapses into intense sensibility, Laura is a paragon of virtue, never (consciously) allowing her emotions to overpower her superior sense. Laura is taught the importance of self-regulation by her friend and mother-manqué, Mrs Douglas. The latter compensates for the educational failings of her actual, ill-tempered and dissatisfied mother, who is more concerned with making her daughter accomplished than rational.

From the outset, it is clear that Mrs Douglas' instruction is of an orthodox Protestant tenor, combining love and fear:

> By degrees she taught [Laura] to know and to love the Author of her being, to adore him as the bestower of all her innocent pleasures, to seek his favour, or to tremble at his disapprobation in every hour of her life. (*Self Control*, p. 7)

---

[19] *Letters*, pp. 186, 234, 283.
[20] Ibid., p. 234.
[21] Ibid., p. 283.

Laura also has, by nature, a 'grave and contemplative turn of mind' and is easily schooled in the 'habit of self-examination' (p. 8). The reader is assured that Laura's occasional propensity for sentimental enthusiasm is always kept in check by her own superior rationality. Throughout the novel she is often on the brink of being overwhelmed by her feelings, only to pull herself back through the exertion of her own reason. Tears are checked just as they are about to fall; feelings are suppressed the very instant they are felt. It is only when feelings are so unbearably strong that they affect her ability to function physically that they overpower her completely, usually resulting in a temporary loss of consciousness. When, for example, she encounters her suitor, Hargrave, in London (having believed him to have forgotten her), she faints against him as she is 'weakened by the fatigue and emotion of the two preceding days, [and] overcome by the sudden conviction that she had not been willfully neglected' (p. 122). Although she later recalls her behaviour with regret, she consoles herself that 'her weakness had been merely that of body, to which the will gave no consent' (p. 129). The text thus excuses its heroine's loss of sense and reason by blaming it on an overwhelmingly powerful physical reaction to mental stress. Similarly, as we have seen, Elinor Dashwood is overcome with such intense emotion that it becomes a physical as much as a mental phenomenon.

Throughout the course of *Self Control*, Laura has recourse to fainting as a desperate solution to a situation that she finds impossible to negotiate successfully through self-regulation. The faint in this context can be read as a means of creating a kind of emotional hinterland where the application of reason is impossible and therefore its absence is not a moral failure on Laura's part. *Self Control* thus tacitly acknowledges the idea that self-regulation is, at best, a highly problematic means by which a woman might negotiate an imperfect, patriarchal world as it shows us circumstances in which female emotional self-regulation is simply not enough. Where *A Gossip's Story*, for example, strongly suggests that Louisa's emotional self-regulation is all that is needed to achieve both earthly and spiritual satisfaction, *Self Control* shows that unless others (in this case, men) can also control themselves, a woman's self-control may be rendered useless. Through Hargrave's relentless pursuit of Laura, the novel betrays its obvious debt to Richardson's *Clarissa*; in particular in its reduction of the heroine's field of experience to a claustrophobic microcosm of male sexual aggression. The novel therefore posits (albeit unintentionally) the idea that self-regulation is useless as a form of self-defence when a woman is faced with the intractable force of ruthless male sexual aggression.

Laura is further tormented by the fact that her aggressor's pursuit appears to be sanctioned. Laura's father chastises Laura for her continued resistance. As they face the grim reality of poverty, he tells her that it is no time for her 'frivolous scruples' (p. 142). Laura responds that 'reason and religion alike condemn' a marriage to Hargrave (p. 142). Montreville responds by admonishing her that

> in this instance you forge shackles for yourself, and then call them the restraints of religion and reason. It were absurd to argue the reasonableness of preferring wealth and title, with the man of your choice, to a solitary struggle with poverty, or a humbling dependence of strangers. And now, my dear girl, can any precept of religion be tortured into a restriction on the freedom of your choice? (p. 143)

The paternal concern that prompts Montreville's advice is not, in and of itself, unacceptable. In *A Gossip's Story*, we see that even the kindly – and equally impecunious – Mr Dudley urges Louisa to consider carefully the proposal of the morally ambiguous Sir William Milton. As we shall see, both scenes find an echo in *Mansfield Park* when Fanny is urged constantly and by various parties to overcome her scruples and marry Henry Crawford. However, as we will later demonstrate, Austen explores in a more nuanced way the great cost of personal conviction in the face of socially sanctioned bullying – particularly when it is disguised as benign patriarchal guidance. *Self Control* fails to sustain any genuine interrogation of the consequences to the individual in the face of this kind of pressure. In this context, Laura's fainting might be read in terms of a narrative failure; Laura's lack of consciousness signals not only her inability to resolve a situation with reason, but also the text's inability (or refusal) genuinely to confront the potential redundancy of self-regulation in the face of greater, socially endorsed male power.

Hargrave's failure to overcome Laura's moral repugnance leads him to abduct her and ship her to the wilds of Canada, where, like *Clarissa*'s Lovelace, he intends to have her by any means necessary. Laura famously – or infamously – escapes in a canoe (this was the adventure that Austen found so improbable in 1813) but she finds no real resolution to her troubles when she returns home until her fiendish and unprincipled suitor clears her name in his deathbed confession. In a rather chilling final assertion of his real power over Laura, Hargrave writes in his confession that 'he who was her [Laura's] murderer, was her avenger too' (p. 355). This suggests, as when the text excuses Montreville, that the power of patriarchal society is such that even when it is wrong, it is still unassailable. Again, we will see that *Mansfield Park* comes to a similar conclusion about the intransigency of male power in a more subtle way, via its representation of Sir Thomas Bertram's 'absolute power'.[22] Where Hargrave is evidently a villain, whose melodramatic abduction of Laura leaves the reader in no doubt of his wickedness, Austen's subtlety manifests itself in the fact that Sir Thomas' villainy is both more insidious and much less obvious. *Self Control*'s central message about the importance of self-regulation as a way of negotiating the world successfully is seriously undermined but remains uninterrogated, with the result that the novel's explicit didactic purpose is also undermined.

Brunton was resolutely clear in her intention that *Self Control* should be read as an endorsement of self-regulation. In her dedication to the poet and playwright Joanna Baillie, Brunton wrote that

> The regulation of the passions is the province, it is the triumph of RELIGION. In the character of Laura Montreville, the religious principle is exhibited as rejecting the bribes of ambition; bestowing fortitude in want and sorrow; as restraining just displeasure; or overcoming constitutional timidity; conquering misplaced affection; and triumphing over the fear of death and of disgrace. (p. 2)

Laura certainly does exert herself admirably throughout her various trials. The narrative is at pains to stress that Laura also strives constantly to conquer her clearly 'misplaced affection' for Hargrave through ceaseless self-reflection and mastery not only of her emotions, but of a strong physical attraction to him. She struggles, for example, 'in an evil hour for her resolution' when she encounters 'the fine eyes of Hargrave suffused with tears' (p. 125). Laura is not blind to her fault and readily admits to Hargrave that she might 'not always be able to listen to reason and duty rather than to you' (p. 135). By admitting the force of her physical attraction, the narrative emphasises the equal force of her emotional self-regulation.

However, the issue of self-regulation as a form of self-defence is complicated as Hargrave's pursuit grows increasingly aggressive. Despite Brunton's clearly stated intention, the narrative betrays her, as emotional regulation fails hopelessly in its purpose in the face of

---

[22] Jane Austen, *Mansfield Park*, ed. by John Wiltshire (Cambridge: Cambridge University Press, 2005), p. 326.

sexual aggression. Furthermore, Laura's attraction to Hargrave is finally killed not by her mastery of her emotions, but by the fact that
his brutality turns her love to hatred and fear. We can draw a parallel
here with Elinor Dashwood's experience: just as Elinor's happy outcome is the result of Lucy Steele's social climbing rather than her own
stoicism, so Laura's final escape from Hargrave is the result of a happily placed canoe on the St Lawrence river rather than her own emotional restraint. By the end of the novel, Laura's suffering is cast not
as an unfortunate consequence of existing in an imperfect world, but
rather as a route to eternal happiness in the next. Here Brunton and
West are clearly aligned. In a scene not dissimilar to that described
earlier in which Louisa Dudley emerges beatified from a period of
intense prayer, Laura finds more than mere comfort in religion:

> The raptures of faith beamed on her soul [. . .] Her countenance elevated
> as in hope; her eyes cast upwards; her hands clasped; her lips half open
> in the unfinished adoration; her face brightened with a smile [. . .] she
> was found by her attendant. Awe-struck, the woman paused, and at a
> reverend distance gazed upon the seraph. (p. 343)

Laura is beatified through suffering, and this is her true reward. It
is interesting to contrast this portrait of ecstatic religious experience with the tempered one in which her ultimate worldly reward –
marriage to DeCourcy – is described. Although Laura receives her due
share of earthly contentment, the moment of intense spiritual ecstasy
brought on by deep suffering offers the true climax of her experience.
There is a palpable sense of anti-climax in the final lines, in which
emotion has been regulated almost to the point of non-existence.

The rather drastic *deus ex machina* of the canoe, together with a
hurried adumbration of Laura's worldly reward, could suggest the
narrative's possible uneasiness with its own conclusion. Alternatively,
it might suggest the opposite – complete confidence in the inevitabil-
ity of a reward for continued self-control, even in the most trying
of circumstances. If this latter supposition is true, the sudden and
truncated ending would imply to the novel's readers that the rewards
of self-regulation are so inevitable as to hardly warrant much explanation or interrogation. Either way, for all Brunton's assurance of
purpose, *Self Control* raises more questions than it answers, and it
is via the gaps of these unexamined questions that *Mansfield Park*
inserts itself into a debate about the purpose and cost to women
of emotional self-regulation. Our contention is that Austen's novel
further explores the hints identified in *Self Control* that women are

powerless and cannot assert regulated selves against an entrenched patriarchal system. Through Fanny, *Mansfield Park* interrogates the sad irony that regulating the self, far from being a beatifying experience, comes at great cost to the individual.

Like *Self Control* and *A Gossip's Story*, *Mansfield Park* ostensibly endorses the need for emotional regulation in order for women to navigate an often hostile world. Fanny Price, like Laura Montreville and Louisa Dudley, is apparently temperamentally predisposed to introspection, religiosity, self-examination and self-regulation. However, Fanny is a far more complex embodiment of self-regulation than either Louisa Dudley or Laura Montreville, partly because she must pit her moral integrity against a much more nuanced depiction of society's attempts to overwhelm it.[23] Fanny may be temperamentally suited to the rigours of constant emotional vigilance, but it is also ultimately forced on her by circumstances beyond her control; as a poor dependent on wealthy relations, she cannot afford to give vent to her emotions. Her value to the Bertrams is based on her usefulness as an uncomplaining drudge. She is useful to her cousins Julia and Maria when their games 'were sometimes of a nature to make a third very useful, especially when that third was of an obliging, yielding temper' (p. 19). She functions as a kind of lady-in-waiting to Lady Bertram, and she is infamously treated almost as a servant by Mrs Norris, who despises Fanny for no better reason than the fact that she is poor and timid. Self-regulation is therefore essential to sustain her role as a quiet and uncomplaining household help. However, unlike those by West and Brunton, Austen's novel is more keenly aware that self-regulation, although necessary, is by no means an uncomplicated or painless process. It is through Fanny's relationships with Henry Crawford and Sir Thomas Bertram in particular that *Mansfield Park* concerns itself with the questions of gendered power dynamics revealed, but uninterrogated, by *Self-Control*.

Henry Crawford is an apparently charming young man of taste and education. Fanny's strong and instinctive dislike is the result of her own superior moral judgement that leads her to believe that there is real moral laxity beneath his seemingly harmless flirtations with her cousins Maria (who is engaged to marry Mr Rushworth) and Julia. Henry claims genuinely to fall in love with Fanny eventually,

---

[23] For an excellent analysis of the ways in which *Mansfield Park* interrogates the structures of patriarchal power, see Claudia Johnson's *Jane Austen: Women, Politics and the Novel* (Chicago: Chicago University Press, 1990), in particular pp. 94–120.

230 Katie Halsey and Jennifer Robertson

but his pursuit of her begins with a calculated decision prompted by boredom in the wake of Maria Bertram's marriage and Julia's departure. He declares to his sister Mary that he shall 'amuse' himself (p. 267) by making her fall in love with him. He cannot be 'satisfied [. . .] without making a small hole in Fanny Price's heart', and so he plans a campaign that will last

> but for a fortnight [. . .] and if a fortnight can kill her, she must have a constitution which nothing could save. No, I will not do her any harm, dear little soul! I only want her to look kindly on me, to give me smiles as well as blushes, to keep a chair for me by herself wherever we are and be all animation when I take it and talk to her; to think as I think, be interested in all my possessions and pleasures, try to keep me at Mansfield, and feel when I go away that she shall be never happy again. I want nothing more. (p. 269)

Despite his bantering tone, Henry's words are chilling, as they express clearly that his pursuit will be aggressive and his goal will be total dominance over his romantic prey. In some ways, his unfeeling pursuit of Fanny is more sinister than Hargrave's is of Laura. Where Hargrave is supposedly fired by burning passion (clearly reflected in his flamboyant declarations to Laura), Henry is initially driven by a cold-blooded determination to 'amuse' himself.

Henry's moral laxity repels Fanny, but to the rest of Mansfield society, he is a charming and welcome guest, and a friend. Henry Crawford is, in the words of Sir Thomas, a suitor 'with every thing to recommend him; not merely situation in life, fortune and character, but with more than common agreeableness, with address and conversation pleasing to every body' (p. 364). It is precisely the fact that Henry is 'pleasing to every body' that makes him so dangerous an adversary for Fanny, and far more threatening a villain than Hargrave. Hargrave's violent declarations are arguably designed to repel the reader as much as the heroine. Henry's pleasing manners and his 'moral taste' (p. 274), however, allow him an almost chameleon-like ability to transform himself into the kind of suitor who might appeal to Fanny's fastidious taste. Henry's eloquence, his ability appropriately to moderate and modulate his desires and his expression of them, is in marked contrast to Hargrave's impassioned outbursts; where Hargrave assaults, Henry insinuates, and his threat to Fanny may not seem so great precisely because it is so cleverly disguised.

Where Fanny sees distressingly insidious encroachment, however, everyone around her sees merely the attentive behaviour of a highly eligible young man in love. The fact that everyone is allied with Henry makes his courtship feel intensely claustrophobic. At one point, Fanny exclaims in desperation, 'If Mr. Crawford would but go away!' (p. 359). Henry is 'determined [. . .] to have the glory, as well as the felicity, of forcing her to love him' (p. 376). For this reason, 'he would not despair; he would not desist' (p. 376). What is possibly most frightening about Henry is the fact that, unlike Hargrave's, his relentless pursuit is endorsed and encouraged by everyone who claims to have Fanny's best interests at heart. We see how Lady Pelham's promotion of Laura's aggrandisement and her wicked machinations are here absorbed and normalised into acceptable and supposedly benign societal pragmatism that dictates that an impoverished young woman ought not to reject an eligible man. Fanny's rejection of Henry Crawford may be governed by the emotional regulation (and its attendant moral acuity) demanded of her by society, but her actions are simultaneously condemned as stubborn wrong-headedness. Even her supposed ally – the equally religious Edmund – applauds Fanny for having been 'upright and disinterested' in her rejection of Crawford, but urges her to reconsider her feelings:

> the matter does not end here. Crawford's is no common attachment, he perseveres, with the hope of creating that regard which had not been created before. This, we know, must be a work of time. But (with an affectionate smile), let him succeed at last, Fanny, let him succeed at last. *You have proved yourself upright and disinterested, prove yourself grateful and tender-hearted*; and then you will be the perfect model of a woman, which I have always believed you born for. (pp. 401–2; italics ours)

Edmund, with no apparent awareness of the irony of his words, voices the terrible bind in which Fanny finds herself: she must maintain control of her emotions while simultaneously allowing them to be overcome. Fanny's troubles illustrate how impossible a standard 'the perfect model of a woman' is to maintain.

Fanny rejects Henry's proposal because she does not and cannot love him, but Sir Thomas is confounded:

> I know he spoke to you yesterday, and (as far as I understand), received as much encouragement to proceed as a well-judging young woman could permit herself to give. I was very much pleased with what I collected to have been your behavior on the occasion; it shewed a discretion highly to be commended. But now, when he has made his overtures so properly, and honourably – what are your scruples *now*? (p. 363)

Fanny is adamant that she gave Henry no encouragement, and the exchange that follows illustrates clearly the gulf that exists between Fanny's sense of what is right and society's expectations of a young woman of what Sir Thomas calls 'mediocrity of condition' (p. 361). There is a darkly comedic tone to their conversation as each fails to fathom the other's interpretation of Henry's proposal. Sir Thomas claims that Henry has made his overtures 'properly and honourably' (p. 363) and that Fanny cannot, therefore, have any real objection. Fanny is rightly disturbed by the fact that Henry, according to Sir Thomas, found encouragement in her absolute rejection. Her rejection is taken here as a kind of subterfuge, or a tacit agreement to enter into a courtship game in which a decent young woman must respond to a proposal with such extreme circumspection that her answer cannot be taken at face value. In other words, Henry, like Hargrave, refuses to take no for an answer. Fanny must contend not only with the obtuseness of one man, but with the accumulated weight of opinion of a society that does not believe in the rationality of women, even while it urges its dictates upon them.

For all Hargrave's aggression, *Self Control* does not posit an all-pervading sense of threat to the morally superior heroine in quite the same way that *Mansfield Park* does, for two reasons. First, Fanny cannot escape from persecution because of her position as a dependent relative at Mansfield Park, whereas both Laura Montreville and Louisa Dudley have much more freedom of movement. Secondly, both Laura and Louisa are empowered by their intense religious feeling to the extent that they are occasionally capable of subduing and overpowering those around them. Fanny is not so empowered. Laura's religious faith also lend her a degree of confidence in her own convictions that allows her to defy her suitor more openly than Fanny can. For example, Laura frequently refuses to meet Hargrave, while Fanny has no alternative but to see Henry whenever he chooses to visit. The fact that she has no option for privacy, retreat or escape is perfectly highlighted when Sir Thomas invades what is meant to be her own private room in the attic in order to speak to her of Henry's proposal. Fanny's entrapment may not be as dramatically portrayed as Laura's kidnapping by Hargrave, but it is no less threatening. And it is far more difficult to escape, because of Fanny's lowly, dependent status. *Mansfield Park* throws the ludicrous nature of Laura's escape by canoe into sharp relief by showing that Fanny's experience is far closer to the deadly reality of life for many women.

For Fanny, unlike Laura, there is no alternative, like-minded family into which she can be absorbed through marriage; Fanny can be rewarded only by marriage into the very family who have made her suffer. This absorption is ostensibly presented to the reader as a happy ending. In the final chapter, the narrative appears to endorse the idea that Fanny has at last found her just reward:

> My Fanny indeed at this very time, I have the satisfaction of knowing, *must* have been very happy in spite of everything. She *must* have been a happy creature of all that she felt or *thought she felt*, for the distress of those around her. She had sources of delight that *must* force their way. She was returned to Mansfield Park, she was useful, she was beloved; she was safe from Mr Crawford. (p. 533; italics ours)

However, the apparent certainty of Fanny's well-deserved happy ending is undermined by the very language that seems to endorse it: that she 'must' be happy leaves room for the possibility that she is not. That there is a distinction made between what she feels and what she thinks she feels suggests that the text is very aware that Fanny's return to Mansfield is not quite such an unqualified reward for her moral integrity as the reader might suppose it to be. In *Self Control*, Laura's true reward is the beatification earned through her intense earthly suffering; *Mansfield Park* eschews such spiritual reward. Furthermore, where *Self Control* seems to posit earthly contentment as a real and legitimate reward for spiritual suffering, *Mansfield Park* offers no such consolation. Just as Laura's escape from Hargrave relies on the *deus ex machina* of a convenient canoe, so Fanny's escape from Henry relies on his sexual incontinence. Had he not run away with Maria Rushworth, had he 'persevered, and uprightly, Fanny must have been his reward' (p. 540).

Austen's insistence on this alternative ending encourages a nervousness about the actual ending of *Mansfield Park*. She reminds her readers once again of the potential costs of emotional self-regulation and the ambivalent nature of its rewards. Just as in *Sense and Sensibility*, where she rejects the straightforward dichotomy of sense rewarded and sensibility punished, in *Mansfield Park* she similarly rejects the idea that emotional self-regulation brings an inevitable prize. In Austen's conversations with Brunton and West, then, we see at least as much interest in the negative consequences of emotional self-regulation as in its oft-trumpeted rewards. Like Wollstonecraft, Austen recognises the necessity of emotional self-regulation as a protective mechanism for vulnerable women in a patriarchal world, but she cannot fully endorse it in the ways that West and Brunton attempt to do. For her sister novelists, suffering is transformative, and emotional self-regulation not only politically necessary, but proof of spiritual excellence. But for Austen, verisimilitude always trumps didacticism, and her novels suggest instead that the costs of emotional self-regulation do not always bring commensurate rewards in this world, whatever may happen in the next. In her *Strictures*, Hannah More suggests that 'a judicious unrelaxing, but steady and gentle curb on [girls'] tempers and passions can alone ensure their peace and establish their principles', arguing that only 'an early habitual restraint' will ensure the 'future character and happiness of women'.[24] Austen, on the other hand, reminds us that rather than necessarily ensuring their 'peace' and 'happiness', women's emotional regulation comes instead at the price of 'constant and painful exertion'.[25] Herein lies Austen's central and important contribution to her contemporaries' conversations about emotional regulation. Rather than taking for granted the fact that emotional self-regulation will empower women as Wollstonecraft, West, More and Brunton all, in their different ways, do, Austen instead interrogates this assumption by testing it out in what we might now think of as a series of 'real-world' scenarios. In so doing, she finds it lacking.

Works Cited

Primary

Austen, Jane, *Jane Austen's Letters*, ed. by Deirdre Le Faye, 3rd edn (Oxford: Oxford University Press, 1995)

——. *Mansfield Park*, ed. by John Wiltshire (Cambridge: Cambridge University Press, 2005)

——. *Sense and Sensibility*, ed. by Edward Copeland (Cambridge: Cambridge University Press, 2006)

Brunton, Mary, *Self Control*, ed. by Anthony Mandal (London: Pickering and Chatto, 2014)

More, Hannah, *Strictures on the Modern System of Female Education*, 9th edn, 2 vols (London: Cadell and Davies, 1801)

West, Jane, *A Gossip's Story*, ed. by Devoney Looser, Melinda O'Connell and Caitlin Kelly (Richmond, VA: Valancourt Books, 2016)

Wollstonecraft, Mary, *A Vindication of the Rights of Woman*, in *A Vindication of the Rights of Woman and A Vindication of the Rights of Man* (Oxford: Oxford World's Classics, 1994; repr. 2008)

---

[24] *Strictures*, I, p. 181.
[25] *Sense and Sensibility*, p. 299.

Secondary

Butler, Marilyn, *Jane Austen and the War of Ideas* (Oxford: Clarendon Press, 1975)

Grenby, Matthew, *The Anti-Jacobin Novel: British Conservatism and the French Revolution* (Cambridge: Cambridge University Press, 2001)

Johnson, Claudia, *Jane Austen: Women, Politics and the Novel* (Chicago: Chicago University Press, 1990)

Joy, Louise, 'Novel Feelings: Emma Courtney's Point of View', *European Romantic Review*, 21.2 (2010), 221–34

Kelly, Helena, *Jane Austen the Secret Radical* (London: Icon Books, 2016)

Murphy, Olivia, *Jane Austen the Reader: The Artist as Critic* (Basingstoke: Palgrave Macmillan, 2013)

Todd, Janet, *The Cambridge Introduction to Jane Austen* (Cambridge: Cambridge University Press, 2015)

Tompkins, J. M. S., '*Elinor and Marianne*: A Note on Jane Austen', *Review of English Studies* 16.61 (Jan. 1940), 33–43

Staging Women's Education in Two Anti-Jacobin Novels: More's *Coelebs in Search of a Wife* (1809) and Hawkins' *Rosanne: or, A Father's Labour Lost* (1814)

Laura White

Among the phalanx of anti-Jacobin British novels written in the decades after the French Revolution, two late offerings by notable women proffered a social and political attack on what French ideas had wrought, seemingly, on British soil: republicanism, rationalism, sentiment and religious laxity. Written to repudiate French revolutionary notions, both Hannah More's *Coelebs in Search of a Wife* (1809) and Laetitia Matilda Hawkins' *Rosanne: or, A Father's Labour Lost* (1814) focus on female education within the private domestic realm, in particular by highlighting scenes of reading, both cautionary and exemplary, as a guard for British virtues. More was the most important evangelical writer of the post-Revolutionary period; her voluminous literary output, including *Cheap Repository Tracts* (1795–8), acted as one of 'the chief agenc[ies] in checking the flood of philosophy, infidelity, and disrespect for inherited privilege that poured fearfully across the Channel from 1790 on'.[1] *Coelebs*, which employs the Latin for 'bachelor' as the name of its hero, was More's singular attempt to use the form of the novel to carry out her life's work of reform, employing fiction to argue for conservative politics, evangelical theology and the proper education for women. Hawkins, her contemporary, was equally prolific if less influential, publishing anonymous novels in the 1780s and continuing under her own name in the 1790s and beyond with travel writing, memoirs, conduct books, 'sermonets', translations and more novels (her last was *Heraline* in 1822). Hawkins was the daughter of Sir John

---

[1] Ford K. Brown, *Fathers of the Victorians: The Age of Wilberforce* (Cambridge: Cambridge University Press, 1961), p. 123.

Hawkins, author of the first important history of Western music (1776) and the unenviable author of the first biography of Dr Johnson (1787), a work occluded rather spectacularly in the public regard by Boswell's, published four years later.[2] Hawkins was brought up within the Twickenham sect and was on familiar terms with figures such as David Garrick, Dr Johnson and Oliver Goldsmith, the last of whom taught her finger games with paper.[3] Hawkins, like More, used the vantage of her cultural authority and superior education (both women, for instance, knew Latin, Greek, French and Italian; Hawkins also knew Hebrew) to conduct conservative polemical instruction, though both deplored women's direct intervention into the political sphere.

Hawkins and More joined the throng of female conservative writers who filled the bookstalls with attacks on French politics, irreligion and violence. As Mary Poovey has argued, this intervention served to make women essential to national security: 'As superintendents of "religious principle" and exemplars of "public morals", women [had] the opportunity to inaugurate a spirit of reform that [would . . .] make women saviors of all that is valuable in England'.[4] Neither Hawkins nor More, however, employs the strategy of many anti-Jacobin writers of fiction, that of depicting the horrors of the Terror directly, partly because they both dreaded the infection of French ideas more than the threat of physical violence. As More herself noted in 1793, 'it is not so much the force of French bayonets, as the contamination of French principles, what ought to excite our apprehensions'.[5] More thus takes a different approach than that of the many anti-Jacobin tales of the period set in revolutionary Paris where the tumult of the times takes centre stage. As M. O. Grenby notes, several polemical tales – Mary Robinson's

[2] As a child, Laetitia hated being forced to visit Johnson: she writes, 'I never heard him say, in any visit, six words that could compensate for the trouble of getting to his den, and the disgust of seeing such squalidness as I saw nowhere else'; *Anecdotes, Biographical Sketches, and Memoirs*, 2 vols (London: F. C. and J. Rivington, 1822), I, p. 14.

[3] D. H. Simpson, *The Twickenham of Laetitia Hawkins, 1760–1835* (Twickenham: Borough of Twickenham Local Historical Society, 1978), p. 25.

[4] Mary Poovey, *The Proper Lady and the Woman Writer: Ideology as Style in the Works of Mary Wollstonecraft, Mary Shelley, and Jane Austen* (Chicago: University of Chicago Press, 1984), p. 33.

[5] Hannah More, *Remarks on the Speech of M. Dupont: Made in the National Convention of France, on the Subjects of Religion and Education*, 2nd edn (London: T. Cadell, 1793), p. 64.

The Natural Daughter (1799), Helen Craik's *Adelaide de Narbonne* (1800) and John Moore's *Mordaunt* (1800) – go even further, giving 'walk-on parts to the likes of Robespierre and Marat, purely so that they might demonstrate their depravity, both political and personal'.[6] To fight the French 'contamination', both More and Hawkins focus on the domestic education of young women, especially their reading practices, as key to maintaining British national virtue. Both novels are primarily didactic in purpose, both hold to conservative moral, religious and political positions, both allow characters to speak with what Claudia Johnson has acutely called the 'egregious affectivity' of the age,[7] both betray anxiety about the role of women writers such as themselves engaging in the public fray, and both authors stress the crucial role of reading in moral and spiritual development, particularly for women. Reading provides the mechanism for developing virtue and then stands as virtue's test. More's hero, 'Coelebs', searching for a bride, contrasts those young women who read rubbishy Gothic and sentimental fiction with the heroine, Lucilla, whose favourite book is *Paradise Lost* and whose reading has been rigorously controlled for its Christian efficacy by her father. In contrast, Hawkins has a father control his daughter's reading to ensure that she never learn about religion at all; to his credit, the heroine has also never read a novel. The two novels' didactic aims are almost indistinguishable from each other, but their narrative strategies diverge considerably. While both More and Hawkins use a process of systematic staging to structure their narratives, More takes an almost fully static approach, either revealing moral lessons through the retrospective of conversation or setting 'lessons to be learned' in instructive tableaus. For her part, Hawkins chooses a more successful narrative strategy, taking her heroine from scenes of childhood to those of adulthood, dramatising how moral development occurs dynamically.

More's choice of a relatively static narrative was noted (and disparaged) by the multitude of reviews *Coelebs* occasioned. After all, More was a renowned polemicist and this was her first (and, as it came to pass, only) novel, though published anonymously. Almost all of the reviewers knew the secret of her authorship and named her directly (though they themselves were also writing anonymously); the reviewer at the *Scots Magazine* went further, conducting an extensive

---

[6] M. O. Grenby, 'The Anti-Jacobin Novel: British Fiction, British Conservatism, and the Revolution in France', *History*, 83.271 (July 1998), 445–71 (p. 459).

[7] Claudia Johnson, *Equivocal Beings: Politics, Gender, and Sentimentality in the 1790s* (Chicago: University of Chicago Press, 1995), p. 1.

stylistic analysis to prove that More wrote the novel, while his fellow at the *Monthly Review* added a wry rebuke of More's repressive piety: 'Report assigns this production to Mrs. Hannah More, and in some instances has associated with her name that of Miss Bowdler!' More's fame and the fact that the novel went through eleven editions within nine months probably accounts for the number of reviews; this author has located fifteen, but there were probably more. A few reviews were wholly commendatory, such as (unsurprisingly) that from the *Evangelical Magazine*, which contrasted the work with 'infidel and licentious novels' ('here [. . .] the reader will find the wisest maxims of life and conduct, and even the holy principles of religion'), while the *Literary Panorama* praised the static narrative by noting its 'models of excellence presented for emulation'. Most reviews begin by praising More's worthy didactic purpose, as in the *Monthly Review* ('it is the commendable object of the writer [. . .] to counteract the poison of novels by something which assumes the form of a novel'). Most, however, object to her execution, as in the *Monthly Magazine*: 'there is something incongruous in making a novel a medium for conveying to the world disquisitions on controversial divinity'. Reviewers could hardly fail to note the deficiencies of plot, as noted by the reviewer at the *European Magazine*: 'its construction is comprised in the title'. The anonymous reviewer at the *Edinburgh Review*, now known to be the great clerical wit Sydney Smith, was less kind: 'The machinery upon which the discourse is suspended, is of the slightest and most inartificial texture.' This 'mere work of shreds and patches', as it was termed by the *Universal Magazine*, ensures that the presentation of character will be inert, 'sketches which do not rise above the ordinary produce of circulating libraries'.[8]

The general verdict of these reviews seems to be that More had erred in trying to write a novel without any appreciation of what makes a novel successful. For while it is true that the publication of *Coelebs* played a crucial role in making novel-reading a more

---

[8] Anonymous reviews in order of citation: *Scots Magazine*, 71 (1809), pp. 435–41, 516–24; *Monthly Review*, 58 (1809), pp. 128–38 (p. 136); *Evangelical Magazine*, 17 (1809), p. 289; *Literary Panorama*, 6 (1809), pp. 259–68 (p. 268); *Monthly Review*, p. 128; *Monthly Magazine*, 27 (1809), pp. 663–7 (p. 664); *European Magazine*, 56 (1809), pp. 196–201, 282–7, 373–8 (p. 199); *Edinburgh Review*, 14 (1809), pp. 145–51 (p. 146); *Universal Magazine*, 11 (1809), pp. 327–36, 515–24 (p. 328); and *Monthly Mirror*, 5 (1809), pp. 223–36 (p. 228). Other anonymous reviews included those in the *British Critic*, 33 (1809), pp. 481–94; *The Satirist, or the Monthly Meteor*, 4 (1809), pp. 384–7; and *Scots Magazine*, 71 (1809), pp. 435–41, 516–24.

respectable pursuit, as Sam J. Pickering has argued, it is hard to escape the sense that More's intervention to reshape the novel as a
genre into her own design failed, exactly because novels must include
elements of the romance to succeed.[9] Even Thomas Love Peacock's
Menippean satires of the period, such as *Headlong Hall* (1815) and
Nightmare Abbey (1818), which are composed almost entirely of
conversation, have more plot than *Coelebs*. More's Lady Belfield
prophesies of the novel's action that it will have 'no cruel stepdame,
no tyrant father, no capricious mistress, no moated castle, no in-
triguing confidante, no treacherous spy, no formidable rival, not so
much as a duel, or even a challenge to give variety to the monotonous scene'; these are of course the staples of most novels of her
day.[10] And indeed, beyond Coelebs choosing Lucilla at the narrative's
end, a foregone conclusion from the outset, nothing much *does* give
'variety to the monotonous scene'. While moated castles as a novelistic fixture admittedly fell out of favour by the 1830s, novels since
have defied More and continued to enjoy all the privileges of romantic conventions. Jane Nardin makes a similar point in her comparison between *Coelebs* and Austen's *Mansfield Park*, following the
critical commonplace that Austen's novel reshapes the endogamous
plot of *Coelebs*. As Nardin argues, More constricts herself by putting
ideology, her 'single purpose to bring her readers to God', over art,
while Austen, with true 'artistic liberty', creates moral purpose in
a narrative well worth reading and with genuine suspense as to the
happy ending being achieved.[11]

There were far fewer reviews of *Rosanne*, largely because its first
edition in 1814 was also its last. These generally commended the
novel, but one reviewer objected to Hawkins' erudite footnotes,
many more than in More's novel, as 'little else than the disjointed
transcript of a common place-book'. The same criticism had been
made of her 1811 novel, *The Countess and Gertrude*, in the *Anti-
Jacobin Review*: 'That the writer possesses a great variety of knowledge will not be denied by her readers; but the major part, whom her

[9] This argument is elaborated in his 'Hannah More's "Coelebs in Search of a Wife"
and the Respectability of the Novel in the Nineteenth Century', *Neuphilologische
Mitteilungen*, 78.1 (1977), 78–85 (p. 78).

[10] Hannah More, *Coelebs in Search of a Wife: Comprehending Observations on
Domestic Habits and Manners*, 2 vols (New York: J. and J. Swords, 1810), I,
p. 186; further references are given parenthetically in the text.

[11] Jane Nardin, 'Jane Austen, Hannah More, and the Novel of Education',
Persuasions, 20 (1998), 15–20.

remote and scientific allusions will very frequently puzzle, will have reason to wish it less ambitiously, and less resolutely displayed.'[12] It fell to T.Q., the author of one letter to the editor of the *New Monthly Magazine*, to condemn Hawkins' footnote in which she suggests that children who have taken to deceit be treated to a hot match at the end of their tongue, in order to give them a taste of 'everlasting burning'.[13] The letter-writer properly fulminates: 'Such sentiments are shocking even from the bigoted monk of the darkest age – how highly reprehensible are they, then, from a female of the nineteenth century!'[14] While both Hawkins and More use footnotes to bolster their authority as authors (through quoting classical and other languages in their original Greek, Latin, German or French), Hawkins' notes are more voluminous and allow her a greater range of voluble comment, on female education, right conduct and anecdotes from the lives of the great (such as an early footnote to demonstrate the degeneracy of Voltaire, I, pp. 44–5).

Interestingly, we also have reviews of a sort of both novels from Jane Austen, found in her correspondence with her sister Cassandra. Of *Rosanne*, she writes: 'We have got "Rosanne" in our Society, and find it much as you describe it; very good and clever, but tedious. Mrs. Hawkins' great excellence is on serious subjects.'[15] Of *Coelebs*, Austen is dismissive; she may in fact never have read it at all, since she disliked aggressive didacticism in the service of religion within the pages of a novel.[16] We have, however, Austen's response to the title. She had evidently made a mistake about the spelling of 'Coelebs' in her last letter to Cassandra and had been chastised;

[12] Review of *Rosanne: or, A Father's Labour Lost*, by Laetitia Matilda Hawkins, *British Critic*, 4 (1815), pp. 670–1 (p. 671); review of *The Countess and Gertrude*, by Laetitia Matilda Hawkins, *Anti-Jacobin Review*, 45 (1813), pp. 263–72 (p. 264); this latter review is referenced in Lisa Wood's *Modes of Discipline: Women, Conservatism, and the Novel after the French Revolution* (Lewisburg, PA: Bucknell University Press, 2003), p. 81.

[13] Laetitia Matilda Hawkins, *Rosanne: or, A Father's Labour Lost*, 3 vols (London: F. C. and J. Rivington, 1814), I, p. 62; further references to this edition are given parenthetically in the text.

[14] T.Q., Letter to the editor, regarding *Rosanne: or, A Father's Labour Lost*, by Laetitia Matilda Hawkins, *New Monthly Magazine*, 3 (1815), p. 25; quoted in Wood, p. 81.

[15] James Edward Austen-Leigh, *A Memoir of Jane Austen*, 2nd edn (London: R. Bentley, 1870), p. 139.

[16] For more on Jane Austen's sense of how religious propriety should govern what enters a novel, see Laura White, *Jane Austen's Anglicanism* (Burlington, VT: Ashgate, 2011), pp. 65–6.

in response, she writes on 30 January 1809, with a return of playful fire:

> I am not at all ashamed about the name of the novel, having been guilty of no insult toward your handwriting; the diphthong I always saw, but knowing how fond you were of adding a vowel wherever you could, I attributed it to that alone, and the knowledge of the truth does the book no service; the only merit it could have was in the name of Caleb, which has an honest, unpretending sound, but in Coelebs there is pedantry and affectation. Is it written only to classical scholars?[17]

Austen's chastisement of novels like More's which display their learning too overtly raises the issue of the authority of women authors to enter the public sphere as political commentators, no matter how well disguised as novels these efforts might be. More's erudite footnotes, citing Lucan and Cicero among others, for instance, do nothing to disguise what Austen calls 'pedantry and affectation'; Austen evidently does not regard classical scholarship as a proper province for female writers *or* readers. And, as we will see, *Coelebs* works in exactly this seam of anxiety through its treatment of the proper education of women, including the question of how much classical learning is wise; underlying this question is inevitably another: is it proper for women to hold forth on moral, social and political issues, especially within the ideologically suspect mode of the novel?[18]

Susan Sniader Lanser has memorably noted that '[p]robably the best-selling novel by a woman [of the period] was [. . .] Hannah More's *Coelebs in Search of a Wife*, in which, if I may put it crassly,

---

[17] Jane Austen, *Jane Austen's Letters*, ed. by Deirdre Le Faye (Oxford: Oxford University Press, 2011), p. 172.

[18] Important scholarly considerations of *Coelebs* can be found in Mitzi Myers' recuperative appraisal in 'Reform or Ruin: "A Revolution in Female Manners"', *Studies in Eighteenth-Century Culture*, 11 (1982), 199–216; Kathryn Sutherland's 'Hannah More's Counter-Revolutionary Feminism', in *Revolution in Writing: British Literary Responses to the French*, ed. by Kelvin Everest (Philadelphia: Open University Press, 1991), pp. 27–64 (which further extends Myers' argument into the political province); Dorice Elliot's '"The Care of the Poor is Her Profession": Hannah More and Women's Philanthropic Work', *Nineteenth-Century Contexts*, 19 (1995), 179–204 (which hails More as a pioneer in the transformation of female philanthropy into a respectable profession for the Victorian age); and Anne Mellor, whose *Mothers of the Nation: Women's Political Writing in England, 1780–1830* (Bloomington: Indiana University Press, 2000), pp. 13–38, summarises the rehabilitation of More's literary and cultural reputation in the two decades previous.

a male narrator tells women how to please men'.[19] However, the homodiegetic narrative in More's *Coelebs* deliberately obscures the source of narrative authority. That is, while the narrative is dominated by the male voices of Coelebs, the narrator, and his mentor and ultimate father-in-law, Mr Stanley, both of whom offer copious wise commentary, there is no getting past the female engineer of that authority, More herself, bolstered by her plentiful commentary. As Lisa Wood has noted, More's other didactic narratives, including the highly successful *Cheap Repository Tracts* for the poor, use a heterodiegetic narrator whose voice is nonetheless markedly maternal. Wood goes on to say that in *Coelebs*, More usurped or at least displaced her own female voice, most likely because she was aware that the stakes were higher for a novel; writing a novel and thus participating in a morally ambiguous form, More feels the need to show the range of her historical, literary and theological expertise. Wood argues that the masculine voice here 'allows [More] to access male social and literary authority [. . .] and display her learning without transgressing the boundaries of female modesty'.[20] The female author and the two male figures of authority do speak as one ideologically, agreeing about theology, right conduct, right reading and even social niceties, but which predominates? An early reviewer professed not to be fooled by this ventriloquism: 'Coelebs [. . .] may attempt to disguise himself in the garb of a young man of twenty-four; but his eagerness to grasp the quill of religious controversy betrays the illusion, and sends him forth to the Holy Wars in the shape of an old lady of seventy!'[21] In Mr Stanley and Coelebs, More has created mouthpieces for her own views; there is no point in the novel in which More sets herself apart from either character, except to excuse Coelebs' romantic ardour for the heroine in volume 3.

More's novel is chiefly concerned to expose how a putatively Christian society such as Britain's lacks true piety and how fully reading practices determine a nation's character, for good or ill. There are stray criticisms of the French, certainly; young women who read French novels are in a parlous state regarding their souls, and Mr Stanley has gone so far as to purge his home of French decorative luxuries, arguing that the market for such goods damages

---

[19] Susan Sniader Lanser, *Fictions of Authority: Women Writers and Narrative Voice* (Ithaca, NY: Cornell University Press, 1992), p. 71.

[20] Wood, pp. 88–9.

[21] Review of *Coelebs in Search of a Wife: Comprehending Observations on Domestic Habits and Manners*, by Hannah More, *Monthly Mirror*, 5 (1809), pp. 223–6.

honest English labour and that the French in general have stained the current age with 'a spirit of independence, a revolutionary spirit, a separation from the parent state' (*I, p.* 127). However, this static narrative is mostly comprised of conversations, many led by the sage Mr Stanley; what and how to read predominates in these conversations as the concern of interest. There is an entire chapter, for instance, devoted to assaying the ethical merit of the flamboyant eighteenth-century poet Mark Akenside, chapters on when to shift a child from 'little story books' to 'such books as men and women read' (I, p. 190), chapters on the dangers of fictional romance (Cervantes is a model corrective), and, of course, chapters on how to interpret Scripture. Faulty reading is always at issue. One male character laments that ladies do not always properly attend as listeners: 'I have known a lady take up the candlestick to search for her netting-pin, in the midst of Cato's soliloquy; or stoop to pick up her scissors while Hamlet says to the ghost, "I'll go no further"' (I, p. 164).

The novel's epigraph could well be Coelebs' outburst: 'How many ways there are of being wrong!' (I, pp. 62–3). Our hero, orphaned at the novel's start, sets out to find the right wife; London provides numerous examples of the wrong sort. There are the two Ranby sisters who giggle mindlessly at the mention of Virgil but are proud of reading such things as D'Arnaud's *The Tears of Sensibility* (1773), Mrs Inchbald's melodrama *Emily Herbert: or, Perfidy Punished* (1787) or Mrs Haywood's witty *The History of Jemmy and Jenny Jessamy* (1753).[22] The daughter of Lady Bab Lawless, 'a Machiavellian mother' (I, p. 62), equally falls short of Coelebs' ideal, as does Miss Denham, the granddaughter of the 'formalist' Lady Denham, trained to 'walk precisely in [Lady Denham's] steps' (I, p. 63). Lady Denham is strict about not dining out during Holy Week but obsessively plays card games at home; moreover, she has no money to spare for a former servant whose house has burned down but still buys tickets to support

---

[22] This rather weepy set of novels, translated from French by John Murdoch in 1773, included *The Cruel Father, Rosetta: or, The Fair Penitent Rewarded, The Rival Friends* and *Sidney and Silli*. The Ranby girls also boast of having read Charlotte Dacre's *Zofloya: The Moor, a Romance of the Fifteenth Century* (1806); the rapturous prose of Wieland's *The Sympathy of Souls*, first translated into English in 1793; John Dent's *Too Civil by Half: a Farce in Two Acts* (1783); *The Resolute Lady: or, Fortunate Footman*, a selection of comic and sentimental songs, published in 1805, and yet another melodramatic novel, Elizabeth Gunning's *The Orphans of Snowdon* (1797).

an Italian singer. Coelebs notes her ladyship's reading, *The Week's Preparations*, a devotional work; it is ('awfully', in Coelebs' view) turned to a page which reads: 'Charge them that are rich in this world that they be ready to give' (I, p. 66). Though Lady Denham would be happy for Coelebs to marry her granddaughter, Coelebs exclaims, 'No! If Miss Denham were sole heiress to Croesus, and joined the beauty of Cleopatra to the wit of Sappho, I would never connect myself with a disciple of that school!' (I, p. 69). Leaving London, Coelebs muses to himself about the deficiencies of London society: 'Yet not one of these characters was considered as disreputable. There was not one that was profane or profligate. Not one who would not in conversation have defended Christianity if its truth had been attacked. [. . .] Yet how little had any one of them adorned the profession she adopted' (I, pp. 87–8). We will see roughly the same point made in Hawkins' *Rosanne*, where our heroine, come at last from France to England at the start of the third volume and expecting to join a richly observant Christian society, is appalled to find that most Christians practise their faith nominally.

So what kind of woman does Coelebs want? In the first chapter, he boldly proclaims that no less than an avatar of Milton's Eve, re-born in English society, will suit his expectations. Coelebs limns his bride-to-be, dismissing consummate beauty, saintliness and classical scholarship as criteria: 'I do not want a Helen, a Saint Cecilia, or a Madame Dacier' (I, p. 20). Nonetheless, his expectations, driven by his reading of Eve, require that

> she must be elegant, or I should not love her; sensible, or I should not respect her; prudent, or I could not confide in her; well-informed, or she could not educate my children; well-bred, or she could not entertain my friends; [. . .] pious, or I should not be happy with her, because [. . .] she will be a companion for eternity. (I, p. 20)

Not surprisingly, readers have often failed to warm to Coelebs and his exacting standards; More's biographer, Charles Brown Ford, notes he is an 'increasingly tedious robot' and a 'totally uninteresting prig'.[23] Nonetheless, his ideals are answered, for another Eve awaits: Lucilla, the daughter of Coelebs' best friend, Mr Stanley, whom he meets at Stanley Grove.

[23] Charles Howard Ford, *Hannah More: A Critical Biography* (New York: Lang, 1996), p. 237.

Lucilla is a paragon of all the virtues, marked most by her charitable garden work.[24] A model Methodist and genuinely humble, Lucilla is described by her mother as 'half a nun', and Lucilla confesses that she is convicted of her own 'inward corruption' (II, pp. 51, 53). Interestingly, though Lucilla is also highly intelligent and has read 'the most unexceptionable parts of a few of the best Roman classics' (II, p. 112) with her father every morning since she was a child, More does not endorse a classical education for all young women. Mr Stanley restricts Lucilla's exposure to Latin lest she become a pedant; he purposely keeps his second daughter, Phoebe, from the classics altogether, instead training her over-imaginative temperament through a corrective curriculum of mathematics. But Mr Stanley has since stopped Phoebe's mathematical studies: 'I never meant to make a mathematical lady' (II, p. 113).[25] More here and elsewhere insists that a daughter's reading must be carefully controlled and balanced, and, most importantly, feature Scripture and religious reading as its

[24] Several critics have discussed More's reshaping of Milton to suit her own feminist and evangelical purposes, especially her urging the domestic management of charitable gardens as the best use of time for female members of the gentry. The most thorough treatment is in Edith Snook's 'Eve and More: The Citation of *Paradise Lost* in Hannah More's *Coelebs in Search of a Wife*', *English Studies in Canada*, 26.2 (2000), 127–54; see also Wood, ch. 6; Elizabeth Kowaleski-Wallace's *Their Fathers' Daughters: Hannah More, Maria Edgeworth, and Patriarchal Complicity* (Oxford: Oxford University Press, 1991); Eileen Cleere's 'Homeland Security: Political and Domestic Economy in Hannah More's *Coelebs in Search of a Wife*', *ELH: English Literary History*, 74.1 (2007), 1–25; and Judith W. Page's 'Reforming Honeysuckles: Hannah More's *Coelebs in Search of a Wife* and the Politics of Women's Gardens', *The Keats-Shelley Journal*, 55 (2006), 111–36; Page notes: 'By linking [gardens] to women's charitable projects such as growing plants and produce for the poor, More assigns a public function to what might have been regarded as a private leisure activity and assigns value to the work in which women engage' (p. 112), while Cleere assesses the political dimension of Lucilla's model gardening: 'Lucilla's conversion of waste into food for a group of her father's hungry labourers seems less like an idealized domestic performance than a specific program for economic revival at a time of trade embargoes, French wars, and peasant uprisings. Hints of working-class agitation seem to compel many of Lucilla's domestic undertakings; indeed, Lucilla's daily home visits to poor families to assess their needs and administer comfort are deliberately undertaken in order to forestall the hungry cottagers from collectively descending upon the rich landowner and demanding assistance' (p. 10; I, p. 63 in More).
[25] The novel features several young ladies who have gone 'too far' in their education, such as a scientific lady described by Sir John Belfield, 'who talked of the fulcrum and the lever, and the statera, which she took care to tell us was the Roman steel yard, with all the sangfroid of philosophical conceit' (II, p. 72).

mainstay. Lucilla is a perfect reader, as we discover from Mr Barlow, the parish priest: 'Miss Stanley [. . .] is governed by a simple practical end, in all her religious pursuits. She reads her bible, not from habit, that she may acquit herself of a customary form; nor to exercise her ingenuity by allegorizing literal passages, [. . .] but that she may improve in knowledge and grow in grace' (II, p. 22).

A tableau of reading marks the novel's thematic and narrative climax. Coelebs is drawn to the door of a labourer's embowered cottage, where he comes upon Lucilla:

> kneeling by the side of a little clean bed, a large old Bible spread [. . .] before her, out of which she was reading one of the penitential Psalms to a pale, emaciated female figure, who lifted up her failing eyes, and clasped her feeble hands in solemn attention. (II, pp. 131–2)

This pathos-inducing scene, 'a subject not unworthy of Raphael' (II, p. 132), is followed by Lucilla's and Coelebs' conversation in which we learn that, beyond Scripture, *Paradise Lost* is her favourite book and that she has (improbably) learned all her gardening precepts from it; Eve is her favourite character (II, p. 136). The only mark of More's authorial embarrassment about manufacturing this colossal coincidence comes in Coelebs' reflection, 'It struck me as the Virgilian lots formerly struck the superstitious' (II, p. 135). Coelebs immediately proposes and is provisionally accepted; in the final chapter we learn that both fathers schemed since their offspring were in their cradles to raise them to marry, with *Paradise Lost* as their mutual pedagogical touchstone, and thus an Eve is ready-supplied when Coelebs comes to the end of his not particularly arduous search.

Hawkins' novel, a systematic exposure of modern French-inspired folly, is also replete with exempla of bad and good reading and provides a travesty of More's insistence that parents control their children's reading – Hawkins' loving parent, Bellarmine, does exactly that, but with the aim of excluding all religion! The novel begins with Bellarmine, the English son of a freethinker who insisted on atheistic, 'rational' principles for his son's education. Steeped in selfishness, the young man is seduced by the young wife of a wealthy man; when this man divorces her, she marries Bellarmine and bears him a daughter, the titular Rosanne. Pursuing amusement, the pair moves to Paris, where the wife runs away with yet another man, is abandoned by him and dies. After mixing in revolutionary circles, Bellarmine, now a cynical hypochondriac, takes advantage of the Revolution's chaos to buy a chateau on the Loire, where he retires with Rosanne and a

Mme Cossart, her freethinking governess. Bellarmine and the governess proceed to educate Rosanne in everything but religion – what both adults term 'superstition'.

Bellarmine's purchase of the Chateau-Vicq provides a moment for Hawkins to insert an anti-Jacobin reflection, for we learn that 'the exigencies of a noble family compelled them to sell it, and sorrow and desperation gave them fortitude to relinquish it' (I, p. 170); Bellarmine, on the other hand, having got the chateau at one-fourth its value, merely congratulates himself on a good purchase. Hawkins is happy here and elsewhere to make stray attacks on what the Revolution has wrought, but her prime targets are, as with More, habits of mind and behaviour rather than politics. She is, in fact, still carrying on her dispute with the Jacobin-leaning Helen Maria Williams, begun twenty years earlier with Hawkins' 1793 *Letters on the Female Mind*, ostensibly a conduct book but primarily an extended attack against Williams' *Letters Written in France* (1790) and *Letters from France* (1792), both of which detail Williams' exhilaration at the spectacles of the Revolution. As Elinor Shaffer notes, both Bellarmine's wife (briefly seen towards the beginning of the novel) and Mme Cossart are meant as caricatures of Williams, whom Hawkins accused of enjoying an illiberal delight in revolution. Of Mrs Bellarmine, for instance, we learn that when '[v]arious horrible events came in to vary the scene of minor excitations [. . .] Mrs. Bellarmine enjoyed them as she would have done the "spectacle of an opera"' (I, p. 105). Thus, the charge against Williams – and against Hawkins' two revolutionary-minded female characters – is that she creates a fanciful fiction of the Revolution that she mistakes for reality.[26]

This relegation of politics to a secondary concern occurs despite the fact that the action of much of the first volume and all of the second takes place in France. But Bellarmine's and Mme Cossart's experiences in Revolutionary Paris are described merely in the vaguest outline, and neither character has an important role to play on the revolutionary stage. Admittedly Mme Cossart during this period

[26] Julie Shaffer, 'From Indignation to Ambiguity: The Revolution in Laetitia-Matilda Hawkins's Letters and Novels', *English Studies*, 101.5 (2020), 550–69 (p. 562); Stephen Blakemore in 'Revolution and the French Disease: Laetitia Matilda Hawkins's Letters to Helen Maria Williams', *SEL: Studies in English Literature*, 36.3 (1996), 673–91, argues that Hawkins believes that 'Williams goes badly astray by 'presumptuously disdain[ing] all limit in entering the masculine political realm', p. 679.

attends Parisian salons, where 'the irascible as well as the grosser affections were features of intrigue – and [. . .] gave employment to all
the passions that were not engaged by illicit connexions' (I, p. 124).
However, we do not learn anything further about these salons or
what role Mme Cossart plays there; her attendance simply aids her
characterisation as a faddish thinker and allows Hawkins to criticise
French salons in general. The fact that *women* engage in these salons
draws as much venom from Hawkins as do the putatively poisonous
ideas they circulate; she argues that salons, the stage for the discussion of 'public business and the weightiest affairs, extensive learning,
and deep science', are degraded by 'the paltry interference of unprincipled females' (I, p. 124).[27] Here we see another manifestation of
Hawkins' opposition to female participation in public affairs, despite
the fact that her own writings, like More's, engage in issues of politics, religion and morality.

Neither Bellarmine nor Mme Cossart stays in Paris long, but Mme
Cossart is more damaged by French revolutionary ideas. She neglects
Rosanne to write her *magnum opus*, 'The Perfectibility of Human
Nature', the logic of which Hawkins describes as a compendium of

> things considered as they bore on other things, and those other things
> considered again as they bore on other other things, and then both to-
> gether considered as they regarded to another set of other things, all
> tending to show that the *ares* are better than the *have beens*; and that the
> *will be's* must be better than both, in the progress of this world's infinite
> eternity. (I, p. 246)

This is idealistic political philosophy reduced to rigamarole.[28]
Moreover, Mme Cossart secretly still indulges in partisan salons at
the Chateau-Vicq. Because Bellarmine's hypochondria has led him to

[27] Where Hawkins suggests Paris salons are ruined by women, More attacks *London*
salons as being ruined by *children*. She is concerned that revolutionary ideas about
child-raising have infected English households, creating homes in which children
rule. In London, Coelebs goes to a dinner party where he expects to meet an ar-
ray of men 'of sense, taste, and learning' (I, p. 38), but his hopes of high-minded
talk are ruined, for just as he has become fascinated by the conversation's turn
to excavations at Memphis, in flood a crowd of 'pretty barbarians', half a dozen
children who make conversation impossible (I, p. 42). As Mrs Stanley mourns
later in the novel, refashioning the family to adhere to new Romantic notions has
transformed the sphere of social practices into 'a children's world' (I, p. 127).

[28] Regarding *Rosanne*, Austen adds in that same letter to Cassandra noted above
that 'Madelle. Cossart is rather my passion' (Austen-Leigh, p. 131); her character
is certainly a broad caricature of vapid revolutionary enthusiasms.

retire to his own chambers much of the time, Mme Cossart is free to bring in like-minded thinkers from a nearby town. At age twelve, Rosanne is admitted to these gatherings, where she hears 'rejoicing over bloodshed, and hints of schemes that led to it: massacres and assassinations were the news, [. . .] and their conversations expressed approbation of rapine and treachery' (I, p. 213). This coterie is broken up by the new government, which lays hold on Mme Cossart's friends: 'some had paid the forfeit of their lives for their endeavours to promote the cause of general utility, and the rest [. . .] were dispersed' (I, p. 214) (presumably, this provincial nest of revolutionaries meets its fate sometime between Robespierre's arrest in July of 1794 and the establishment of the Directory in November of 1795).

This brisk scattering of would-be revolutionaries completed, Hawkins turns her focus to Rosanne and her father's venture of raising his child without religion. Such is the goal, but Hawkins so arranges her plot as to show instead how a child using reason and empirical observation will ultimately embrace Christianity. Thus, where in More's novel we simply learn from Mr Stanley's extensive conversation about the history of Lucilla's education, Hawkins' narrative *shows* Rosanne growing from the age of seven to young adulthood, with every major developmental shift in her understanding linked to moments in the action. The reader thus experiences Rosanne's education much more directly than Lucilla's, seeing the stages of her developing moral and spiritual views; the pleasure (at least for a Christian reader allied with Hawkins' cause, as would have been the case with almost all of Hawkins' initial readership) comes not only from Rosanne's two-volume transition into a devout Christian but also from the transition's naïve stages. For instance, when Rosanne first learns what 'revenant' ('ghost') means, she finds the idea ridiculous and amuses herself wondering about the 'revenants' 'in the ponds, [. . .] a "revenant" carp, or the restless spirit of an eel' (I, p. 261). An early reviewer from the *British Critic* also pointed to the heroine's naïveté as a factor in the novel's success, noting, for instance, that '[t]he first attempt of Rosanne to utter a prayer to that great Being, with whose existence she was but just made even acquainted, is a very finely drawn scene'.[29] We thus see Rosanne moving through the stages of primitive metaphysics and ethics; with More's Lucilla we only see the finished product, with

---

[29] Review of *Rosanne: or, A Father's Labour Lost*, by Laetitia Matilda Hawkins, *British Critic*, 4 (1815), pp. 670–1 (p. 671).

little to suggest that the creation of such a paragon of Christian belief and virtue was particularly difficult. The reader's active and sympathetic engagement with Rosanne's dynamic challenges in coming to a Christian worldview is much more likely to be didactically effective than the task of the reader in *Coelebs*, which is simply to accept Lucilla's full, complete and perfect Christian education as presented.

Hawkins' systematic staging of her heroine's education dominates the first two volumes (the third concerns the *father*'s Christian conversion and Rosanne's marriage plot). We begin by learning how thoroughly she is deprived of any knowledge of religion; because she has little contact with anyone but her governess and father, her reading is readily controlled. Admittedly, Bellarmine does allow her to learn about some of the more implausible pagan myths, such as Cadmus sowing dragon's teeth to grow warriors, but his aim is only to increase his daughter's religious scepticism. Otherwise, he suppresses religious information, as when he explains away the chateau's paintings of the Virgin Mary and Christ, respectively, as depictions of the Roman heroes Lucretia and Regulus. Rosanne dutifully pursues the rigorous scientific and rational education that her father sets for her, but she cannot help but be curious about death and other transcendental questions raised by her own perception of nature and her restricted contact with the Catholic servants. She is led to wonder if, as she has been taught, everything is the work of Nature and Necessity: 'who is this Nature? And what is this Necessity? – [. . .] How do I choose? – What makes me think? – Why does not the dog speak?' (I, p. 231). These are, of course, good questions; Hawkins expects that the Christian reader will have answers to them all (God made Nature, with its own laws, both physical and spiritual, and allows human beings, in distinction from the rest of the Creation, to employ their own agency, will and consciousness for good or ill; moreover, humanity has been given the gift of speech and language not vouchsafed to animals). The reader's pleasure is thus occasioned by a respect for Rosanne's having come on her own to such important questions. Since the novel is structured to show Rosanne's education, the reader can expect Rosanne ultimately to learn these things for herself. Jane West's 1802 *Infidel Father* provides an instructive counterpoint. This is another anti-Jacobin novel whose heroine, like Rosanne, is also brought up without any knowledge of Christian morality or theology. However, West's Sophia, another 'infidel'-raised heroine, ends disastrously as a suicide because she never grows to control her desires by reason or self-restraint; by contrast, Rosanne, even at a young age, perhaps improbably, puts her experiences to mental review and thus reasons her way to moral, ultimately to religious, understanding.

Because Hawkins is less committed to the Calvinist idea of natural depravity which so dominates More's theology, and to the Lockean idea that moral understanding is fundamentally experiential in origin, the narrative of Rosanne's moral education is structured by how Rosanne processes the limited moments of her young life. She is not exactly an example of John Locke's *tabula rasa*, however, for Hawkins often speaks of her character's temperament (loving and curious – she is 'curious in the eggshell' (I, p. 90)) as separate from her learning and as evidenced by Rosanne's earliest moments as a toddler. Her temperament protects her in that her curiosity aids her intellectual development and her amiability aids her burgeoning sense of the moral claims of others. The first test to develop Rosanne's moral compass is provided by a small parrot, a 'lory'. A village boy owns this colourful bird, and Rosanne covets it; using her position as the daughter of the estate, she takes it. Hearing of the boy's sorrow, she returns it, but soon learns that all that shifting about and change of diet has killed the bird. Her empathy for both the lory and the boy gives her the first sense of the 'sacredness of property' (I, p. 201). Here, Hawkins is following Locke's theories of moral sentiment in that Rosanne's moral reasoning is in line with natural law (theft brings bad results); her experience of the consequences of theft demonstrates to her the reality of good and evil. This parrot-based discovery also helps Rosanne come to a precocious anti-Jacobin objection, realising what she dislikes about that radical talk at Mme Cossart's salon: '"If", said she, "I was wrong in taking the lory, [. . .] why does Mme. Cossart seem so pleased about the effects of war, which, as far as I can understand, has no other purpose, but to kill people, or take away what belongs to them?"' (I, p. 214).

Having come to a sense of moral law, Rosanne is exposed to religion itself when she falls ill with a fever and is attended only by one faithful servant, the Catholic Nannette. Falling in and out of consciousness, Rosanne is aware of Nannette's ardent prayers and of the crucifix held over her body in supplication. Rosanne recovers and bends all her purposes to finding out more about what this strange behaviour might mean; she is impelled all the more by learning from Nannette's son that while Nannette caught the fever and died, she did so in full confidence of 'heaven' – for Rosanne, another baffling new idea. She overhears a labourer defending the Sabbath to the estate manager; this too is a new idea contrary to the utilitarian ethics of her father. She also begins to reason her way to the idea of a Creator

God by observing nature. Watching a fledgling bird, she asks, 'can it be supposed this bird created itself?' (I, p. 305). The lambs who instinctively know their own mothers similarly instruct her: 'I can see no difference between one lamb and ewe [. . .] but these creatures, I dare say, are never at a loss. [. . .] Who taught them this sagacity? It is Nature, I grant; but who made Nature?' (I, p. 306).

Rosanne's self-taught discovery of a Creator God, however, is inadequate to instruct her in Christianity; to understand such things as the crucifix, prayers, heaven and Sundays, Rosanne needs to read Scripture, and her quest to find, read and understand Christian texts structures all of volume 2. Rosanne finds a way to visit an English Christian neighbour, M. D'Orsette, and sees her first Bible: 'O! that is the Bible, is it? Can you tell me who wrote it? – May I see the title? Has it got the author's name?' (II, p. 10). Revelation follows revelation: '"What!" said Rosanne, striking her hands on her bosom, "did HE, after all, make the world and write this book, too? O! My head goes round! – I must read it, for this is just what I wanted to know"' (II, p. 15). Opening to *Proverbs*, Rosanne perceives 'sentences of advice': 'Do they resemble the Maxims of Rochefoucault? I have seen a few of *them*' (II, p. 11). Rosanne's naïveté rather confounds her hostess, whose knowledge of the Bible is itself spotty: '[M. D'Orsette] knew that Genesis came before Exodus, and that it was near mackerel-season when the story of Balak and Balaam was read at chapel' (II, p. 12). It falls to M. D'Orsette's four-year-old daughter Lisette to teach Rosanne about prayer — grace at meals, prayers before bed, and the Lord's Prayer. Hawkins endorses this mode of instruction from a little child: 'as Christianity is the same "out of the mouths of babes and sucklings", as from the pulpit, Rosanne could not be mis-led' (II, p. 61). Rosanne then finds her mother's Bible and Book of Common Prayer, long locked away in a chest, and proceeds to instruct herself in Christianity, though she hungers for someone to answer her many questions. By the end of the second volume, a visiting English cleric, Dr Grant, provides what is missing in Rosanne's religious conceptions and she becomes a fully instructed and faithful Christian.

None of this illicit reading and religious education happens without repressive treatment by her father: once her visits to M. D'Orsette are revealed, her cache of religious texts is discovered, and Mme Cossart is dismissed. Bellarmine demands Rosanne's Bible; she refuses. He locks her in; she continues her reading. All his scoffing and rationalism can no longer affect her, and she uses his life-long teaching about freethinking to oppose him: 'You did not mean, surely, my dear father [. . .] when you told me to use liberty of opinion, that liberty should end in having no opinion' (II, p. 115). In fact, despite himself, Bellarmine has strengthened Rosanne's religiosity because she gradually learns that her father is a hypocrite. Bellarmine has long contended that Nature and Reason give us no reason to fear dissolution; he instead wants his 'carcass' to be 'put in the first horse-cloth at hand – the gardener should dig a hole – any two of the men could take him neck and heels, ha! Ha! Ha!' (I, p. 339). But he locks himself up to avoid Rosanne's fever, and when there are those reports of a 'revenant' in the chateau, he again hides away in fear. It falls to Rosanne, curious and ignorant about ghosts, to discover that the 'revenant' is just a former servant in monk-like garb out for revenge. Similarly, when father, daughter and governess are caught in a storm while on a sailing excursion, Bellarmine and Mme Cossart are plainly terrified by the prospect of drowning, with Mme Cossart falling to her knees at the little boat's bottom. Rosanne learns by their behaviour what Bellarmine and her governess really believe: 'she could not forget that her father and Mademoiselle Cossart had been thoroughly frightened' (I, p. 265). As both Bellarmine and Mme Cossart have earlier postured against death as anything but a natural process, and nothing to be feared, their behaviour when threatened shows their hypocrisy.

Volume 3 fulfils the ironies of the novel's subtitle, *A Father's Labour Lost*. Rosanne at this point needs no further education – she has become, like Lucilla, perfectly good and Christian. Moreover, Bellarmine has brought her to England; she has escaped infidel France.[30] What justifies the final volume is threefold: Bellarmine's conversion, satire against the English social scene, and Rosanne's marriage to a man as good as herself, Sir Tancred Ormsted (Sir Tancred has also just inherited a fortune). The romance plot is weak and formulaic; indeed, Rosanne hardly seems to have any romantic feelings, there are no love scenes, and she does not even know whom she is marrying until the last chapter when she is given the news (there is also no proposal scene). Hawkins' satire against English manners and religious laxity is where the 'caricatures' that she defended in her advertisement emerge, figures such as Mrs Ductile, Miss Pathos, Mrs Firmly and Lady Lucrezia Sinister. Expecting the

[30] Since Rosanne and her father are smuggled into England on a fishing vessel, we can date their departure for England as occurring before the Treaty of Amiens in 1802, which amounted to a year-long truce in the war, reopened by Britain in May 1803.

English to be models of Christian virtue, Rosanne is surprised when society in Southampton is peopled by hypochondriacs, gossips and back-stabbers.

However, the third volume's greatest narrative interest lies in Bellarmine's conversion. The reader may initially be rather puzzled as to why the third volume is necessary. After all, at the start Bellarmine seems willing to put himself under Dr Grant's Christian tutelage, and by bringing Rosanne to England he is fulfilling a promise he made long ago to her grandmother, that she be brought up as a Protestant. Moreover, Rosanne is a confirmed 'angel' all through the third volume (she is so called by her father, Dr Grant and Sir Tancred, among others). Yet, though Bellarmine has been surreptitiously reading a book of religious instruction from Rosanne's personal library, Jacob Vernet's *Instruction chrétienne*, he seems marked by dread and guilt, and when he and Rosanne attend their first church service, the sermon – on confessing personal sin – only accentuates his desolation.[31] In fact, the first thing he does in England is to try to commit suicide (he is stopped by Dr Grant). Here Hawkins performs a narrative cheat. The reader has been led to believe that the worst of Bellarmine has already been related (that he had committed adultery with the wife of a friend, married her upon her divorce, and that he is a determined freethinker); moreover, Rosanne and Dr Grant have long forgiven him these faults. But these transgressions do not pose a sufficient impediment to a conversion which will take an entire volume, nor for that matter do they offer much narrative gravel. Thus, in one clumsy development after another, we learn of two past sins that Hawkins has not revealed before: Bellarmine not only has an illegitimate son with a woman now dead, but he once cheated a friend of his fortune. Both these happenstances now interfere with Rosanne's marital future through a variety of complexities not to our purpose (all is ultimately forgiven and comes right).

Hawkins is particularly lenient with her erring parental figure. The novel has featured, from beginning to end, formal litanies of Bellarmine's crimes, several times from the narrator, twice from Bellarmine himself, and once each from Rosanne, Dr Grant and Sir Tancred. The first of these recitals is harsh, but there is a marked amelioration in moral condemnation in the ensuing iterations. What an

---

[31] Published in five volumes in 1754, Vernet's *Instruction chrétienne* is a primer on Christian theology and practice. Vernet (1698–1789) was perhaps the representative Genevan theologian of his day, contending with such figures as Rousseau, d'Alembert and Voltaire about orthodoxy.

early reviewer noted of the faulty father in Hawkins' *The Countess and Gertrude* (1811) applies here with equal force:

> [He must be] distantly connected with the author. We can no otherwise account of her speaking of him always as a very worthy, kind-hearted, and respectable man, while she hardly ever makes him say or do anything, which does not [. . .] prove his conduct harsh, and almost constantly unfeeling, toward the amiable [heroine].[32]

These narrative contortions and illogicities are required so that Bellarmine's conversion, brought forth by the example of his daughter's piety, will be able to provide the central inversion of the narrative and explain the novel's subtitle, *A Father's Labour Lost*.

Ultimately, Hawkins' *Rosanne* is memorable for its implicit argument that Christianity can reveal itself to a questing mind, even in a secluded French chateau run on rigidly materialist principles, especially if that mind can in time avail itself of Scripture and religious reading. Bad reading cedes to good; Mme Cossart's 'The Perfectibility of Human Nature' remains unfinished, while Bellarmine turns instead to Rosanne's newly-instituted services of family prayer, conducted with the aid of the *Book of Common Prayer*. More's ideal education, as we see with Lucilla, has left far less to chance than that crafted by Hawkins for Rosanne. Instead of showing how a good child can reason itself into moral and religious principles through empirical observation and self-examination, More shows the results of carefully monitored education, especially in terms of what a good daughter should read. Raised to honour *Paradise Lost* and to emulate Eve through her orchards and groves, Lucilla was never in much danger of not being a consummate Christian. As with the novel as a whole, the battle was won before it begun. The contrast between these two novels reveals the much greater didactic strength of *Rosanne*'s dynamic representation. Nonetheless, both novels further the religious and conservative ends of British anti-Jacobins by providing ideal models, the already achieved perfections of Lucilla and the arduously won perfections of Rosanne, each due largely to right reading.

[32] Review of *The Countess and Gertrude*, by Laetitia Matilda Hawkins, *Anti-Jacobin Review*, 45 (1813), pp. 263–72 (p. 265).

Works Cited

Primary

[Anon.], Review of *Coelebs in Search of a Wife: Comprehending Observations on Domestic Habits and Manners*, by Hannah More, *British Critic*, 33 (1809), pp. 481–94

[Anon.], Review of *Coelebs in Search of a Wife: Comprehending Observations on Domestic Habits and Manners*, by Hannah More, *European Magazine*, 56 (1809), pp. 196–201, 282–7, 373–8

[Anon.], Review of *Coelebs in Search of a Wife: Comprehending Observations on Domestic Habits and Manners*, by Hannah More, *Evangelical Magazine*, 17 (1809), p. 289

[Anon.], Review of *Coelebs in Search of a Wife: Comprehending Observations on Domestic Habits and Manners*, by Hannah More, *Literary Panorama*, 6 (1809), pp. 259–68

[Anon.], Review of *Coelebs in Search of a Wife: Comprehending Observations on Domestic Habits and Manners*, by Hannah More, *Monthly Magazine*, 27 (1809), pp. 663–7

[Anon.], Review of *Coelebs in Search of a Wife: Comprehending Observations on Domestic Habits and Manners*, by Hannah More, *Monthly Mirror*, 5 (1809), pp. 223–36

[Anon.], Review of *Coelebs in Search of a Wife: Comprehending Observations on Domestic Habits and Manners*, by Hannah More, *The Satirist, or the Monthly Meteor*, 4 (1809), pp. 384–7

[Anon.], Review of *Coelebs in Search of a Wife: Comprehending Observations on Domestic Habits and Manners*, by Hannah More, *Scots Magazine*, 71 (1809), pp. 435–41, 516–24

[Anon.], Review of *Coelebs in Search of a Wife: Comprehending Observations on Domestic Habits and Manners*, by Hannah More, *Universal Magazine*, 11 (1809), pp. 327–36, 515–24

[Anon.], Review of *The Countess and Gertrude*, by Laetitia Matilda Hawkins, *Anti-Jacobin Review*, 45 (1813), pp. 263–72

[Anon.], Review of *Rosanne: or, a Father's Labour Lost*, by Laetitia Matilda Hawkins, *British Critic*, 4 (1815), pp. 670–1

Austen, Jane, *Jane Austen's Letters*, ed. by Deirdre Le Faye (Oxford: Oxford University Press, 2011)

Austen-Leigh, James Edward, *A Memoir of Jane Austen*, 2nd edn (London: R. Bentley, 1870)

Hawkins, Laetitia Matilda, *Anecdotes, Biographical Sketches, and Memoirs*, 2 vols (London: F. C. and J. Rivington, 1822)

——. *Letters on the Female Mind, Its Powers and Pursuits: Addressed to Miss H. M. Williams, with Particular Reference to Her Letters from France*, 2 vols (London: Hookham and Carpenter, 1793)

258   Laura White

——. *Rosanne: or, A Father's Labour Lost*, 3 vols (London: F. C. and
J. Rivington, 1814)

More, Hannah, *Coelebs in Search of a Wife: Comprehending Observations on Domestic Habits and Manners*, 2 vols (New York: J. and J. Swords, 1810)

——. *Remarks on the Speech of M. Dupont: Made in the National Convention of France, on the Subjects of Religion and Education*, 2nd edn (London: T. Cadell, 1793)

[Smith, Sydney], Review of *Coelebs in Search of a Wife: Comprehending Observations on Domestic Habits and Manners*, by Hannah More, *Edinburgh Review*, 14 (1809), pp. 145–51

T.Q., Letter to the editor (regarding *Rosanne; or, a Father's Labour Lost*, by Laetitia Matilda Hawkins), *New Monthly Magazine*, 3 (1815), p. 25

Secondary

Blakemore, Steven, 'Revolution and the French Disease: Laetitia Matilda Hawkins's Letters to Helen Maria Williams', *SEL: Studies in English Literature*, 36.3 (1996), 673–91

Brown, Ford K., *Fathers of the Victorians: The Age of Wilberforce* (Cambridge: Cambridge University Press, 1961)

Cleere, Eileen, 'Homeland Security: Political and Domestic Economy in Hannah More's *Coelebs in Search of a Wife*', *ELH: English Literary History*, 74.1 (2007), 1–25

Elliot, Dorice, '"The Care of the Poor is Her Profession": Hannah More and Women's Philanthropic Work', *Nineteenth-Century Contexts*, 19 (1995), 179–204

Ford, Charles Howard, *Hannah More: A Critical Biography* (New York: Lang, 1996)

Grenby, M. O., 'The Anti-Jacobin Novel: British Fiction, British Conservatism, and the Revolution in France', *History*, 83.271 (July 1998), 445–71

Johnson, Claudia, *Equivocal Beings: Politics, Gender, and Sentimentality in the 1790s* (Chicago: University of Chicago Press, 1995)

Kowaleski-Wallace, Elizabeth, *Their Fathers' Daughters: Hannah More, Maria Edgeworth, and Patriarchal Complicity* (Oxford: Oxford University Press, 1991)

Lanser, Susan Sniader, *Fictions of Authority: Women Writers and Narrative Voice* (Ithaca, NY: Cornell University Press, 1992)

Mellor, Anne K., *Mothers of the Nation: Women's Political Writing in England, 1780–1830* (Bloomington: Indiana University Press, 2000)

Myers, Mitzi, 'Reform or Ruin: "A Revolution in Female Manners"', *Studies in Eighteenth-Century Culture*, 11 (1982), 199–216

Nardin, Jane, 'Jane Austen, Hannah More, and the Novel of Education', *Persuasions*, 20 (1998), 15–20

Page, Judith W., 'Reforming Honeysuckles: Hannah More's *Coelebs in Search of a Wife* and the Politics of Women's Gardens', *The Keats-Shelley Journal*, 55 (2006), 111–36

Poovey, Mary, *The Proper Lady and the Woman Writer: Ideology as Style in the Works of Mary Wollstonecraft, Mary Shelley, and Jane Austen* (Chicago: University of Chicago Press, 1984)

Shaffer, Julie, 'From Indignation to Ambiguity: The Revolution in Laetitia-Matilda Hawkins's Letters and Novels', *English Studies*, 101.5 (2020), 550–69

Simpson, D. H., *The Twickenham of Laetitia Hawkins, 1760–1835* (Twickenham: Borough of Twickenham Local Historical Society, 1978)

Snook, Edith, 'Eve and More: The Citation of *Paradise Lost* in Hannah More's *Coelebs in Search of a Wife*', *English Studies in Canada*, 26.2 (2000), 127–54

Sutherland, Kathryn, 'Hannah More's Counter-Revolutionary Feminism', in *Revolution in Writing: British Literary Responses to the French Revolution*, ed. by Kelvin Everest (Philadelphia: Open University Press, 1991), pp. 27–64

White, Laura, *Jane Austen's Anglicanism* (Burlington, VT: Ashgate, 2011)

Wood, Lisa, *Modes of Discipline: Women, Conservatism, and the Novel after the French Revolution* (Lewisburg, PA: Bucknell University Press, 2003)

Part IV

Shaping the Future

Chapter 11

Pedagogy as (Cosmo)Politics: Cultivating Benevolence in Mary Wollstonecraft's Educational Works

Laura Kirkley

Before she became a professional writer, Mary Wollstonecraft was an educator: mistress of a school in Newington Green in the mid-1780s and later governess to the children of Irish Ascendancy aristocrats. Her first published works were explicitly pedagogical, but in almost every text in her extensive corpus, she reflects on how best to form self-governing moral subjects capable of committed (world) citizenship.[1] This emphasis on moral autonomy finds political expression through her republican resistance to arbitrary rule, which informs both *A Vindication of the Rights of Men* (1790) and *A Vindication of the Rights of Woman* (1792).[2] In the year between the publication of these famous political tracts, she produced illustrated second editions of two educational works, *Original Stories from Real Life* (1788) and *Elements of Morality, for the Use of Children* (1790). *Elements* is a translation from the German of Christian Gotthilf Salzmann's *Moralisches Elementarbuch* (1782–3; new edition 1785), but, as I have argued elsewhere, Wollstonecraft's interventionist translational strategy gives her version the status of a creative work in its own right.[3] In her preface, she invites the

---

[1] This essay reworks material from my book, *Mary Wollstonecraft: Cosmopolitan* (Edinburgh: Edinburgh University Press, 2022) with the permission of Edinburgh University Press.

[2] See Lena Halldenius, *Mary Wollstonecraft and Feminist Republicanism: Independence, Rights and the Experience of Unfreedom* (London: Pickering and Chatto, 2015).

[3] See Laura Kirkley, '"Original Spirit": Literary Translations and Translational Literature in the Works of Mary Wollstonecraft', in *Literature and the Development of Feminist Theory*, ed. by R. T. Goodman (Cambridge: Cambridge University Press, 2015), pp. 13–26.

reader to make intertextual connections between *Original Stories* and *Elements*, both of which feature pedagogical figures who give children the freedom to learn from experience instead of submitting blindly to authority. For Wollstonecraft, the resulting independence lays the groundwork for the fulfilment of our moral potential. She goes further than Salzmann, however, in modelling virtue as benevolence impervious to race, culture or creed – a cosmopolitan philanthropy, in the predominant eighteenth-century sense of 'love of humankind'. This philosophy shapes both her pedagogy and her politics. In her first published work, *Thoughts on the Education of Daughters* (1787), she enjoins her young readers to practise charity because 'goodwill to all the human race should dwell in our bosoms'.[4] In *Rights of Men*, she declares that 'all feelings are false and spurious, that do not rest on justice as their foundation and are not concentred by universal love'.[5] In *Rights of Woman*, she describes her feminism as the outgrowth of 'affection for the whole human race', and in *An Historical and Moral View of the Origin and Progress of the French Revolution* (1794), she argues for 'a more enlightened moral love of mankind'.[6] This essay examines how Wollstonecraft's cosmopolitan philosophy informs her theory of education, identifying crucial points of contact between the pedagogical content of *Original Stories*, *Elements* and *Rights of Woman*. Wollstonecraft reflects in all of these works on how best to suppress self-interest by cultivating reason, imagination and compassion. These are complementary assets in the progress to moral self-actualisation and have the potential to transform those in a state of unfreedom into the self-governing agents of a public culture of benevolence, the practical instantiation of love of humankind. Through my analysis of Wollstonecraft's representation of a Christian boy encountering a Jew, however, I suggest that tensions in her pedagogical discourse sometimes perform psychological impediments to the realisation of impartial philanthropy, revealing atavistic prejudices that bespeak the cultural conditioning of the educator.

---

[4] Mary Wollstonecraft, *The Works of Mary Wollstonecraft*, ed. by Marilyn Butler and Janet Todd, 7 vols (London: Pickering and Chatto, 1989), IV, p. 44.

[5] Ibid., V, p. 34. For a more detailed analysis of this passage, see Eileen Hunt Botting, *Family Feuds: Wollstonecraft, Burke, and Rousseau on the Transformation of the Family* (Albany: State University of New York Press, 2006), pp. 168–9.

[6] Wollstonecraft, *Works*, V, p. 65; Ibid., VI, p. 21.

Wollstonecraft's Cosmopolitan Pedagogy

The term 'cosmopolitan' has been deployed in support of many philosophical positions and competing political agendas, and evokes diverse models of travelling, nomadism and displacement, from the debonair jetsetter at home in the world to the rootless exile at home nowhere. In most cases, living a cosmopolitan life implies extending one's experiences and imagined community beyond the nation. A host of related terms – 'international', 'transnational', 'global' – also evoke the interdependency of races, nations and cultures, but cosmopolitan thought usually incorporates a distinctive ethical dimension, a recognition 'that there are moral obligations owed to all human beings based solely on our humanity alone'.[7] As a translator and a regular reviewer of European literature for the *Analytical Review*, Wollstonecraft engaged with Continental literary and philosophical systems. In developing her ethical framework, she also addressed the moral questions raised by our collective belonging to the human family. The foundations of this framework rest on two related beliefs in universal justice and universal benevolence, philanthropy undeterred by the boundaries of race, nation and social class. As Sylvana Tomaselli puts it, these guiding principles derived from Wollstonecraft's fundamental conviction that 'whatever the observable differences between human beings across time or diverse parts of the world, all shared the same God-given nature'.[8] From her earliest works to the end of her life, Wollstonecraft was preoccupied with a pedagogical dilemma tied to her cosmopolitan convictions, namely, how our instinctive affections might be developed into philanthropy embracing a borderless imagined community.

Never a stony rationalist, Wollstonecraft considered passions 'the auxiliaries of reason', motive forces for the philanthropic actions that could bring about practical change.[9] Well read in the Scottish sentimentalists, she also recognised human feeling as a vital component of sympathy, the capacity to walk imaginatively in the footsteps of another. Adam Smith's *Theory of Moral Sentiments* (1759) distinguishes sympathy from compassion, but suggests that, in the right

---

[7] Garrett Wallace Brown and David Held, 'Editors' Introduction', in *The Cosmopolitanism Reader*, ed. by Garrett Wallace Brown and David Held (Cambridge: Polity Press, 2010), pp. 1–14 (p. 1).

[8] Sylvana Tomaselli, *Wollstonecraft: Philosophy, Passion, and Politics* (Princeton: Princeton University Press, 2021), p. 65.

[9] Wollstonecraft, *Works*, V, p. 16.

conditions, sympathising individuals confronted with the spectacle of suffering may be motivated to benevolent actions. Influenced by her mentor, the rationalist theologian Richard Price, Wollstonecraft believed that benevolence should be 'universal': not simply an impulse to alleviate suffering in a particular context, but a rational principle of action predicated on the equality of all human subjects. Summed up in Price's *Discourse on the Love of Our Country* (1789), this cosmopolitan principle of 'Universal Benevolence' underpins a democratic political agenda, whereby 'love of country' entails extending human rights to all subjects within the nation and beyond it, regardless of the divisions wrought by narrower allegiances.[10] Hence Wollstonecraft instructs her readers that 'universal benevolence is the first duty and we should be careful not to let any passion so engross our thoughts, as to prevent our practising it'.[11] Whereas Price puts a premium on reason as the means to establish 'universal benevolence', Wollstonecraft gives more houseroom to sentiment and non-rational cognition.[12] At the same time, manifest in her many sketches of naughty children, naval-gazing lovers and negligent mothers are anxieties about the effects of 'selfish passions', the egotistical or clannish instinct to privilege the self or its perceived adjuncts over other less familiar candidates for our benevolence.[13] This is a natural human reflex, but it knits inequalities into the social fabric. Wollstonecraft therefore recommends educational reforms that mitigate self-interest by refining and redirecting feeling towards benevolent ends.

This imperative to form citizens capable of prioritising the welfare of distant and unknown others still preoccupies modern theorists of cosmopolitanism. How can we forge an imagined international

---

[10] See Richard Price, *A Discourse on the Love of Our Country*, in *Richard Price: Political Writings*, ed. by D. O. Thomas (Cambridge: Cambridge University Press, 1991), p. 180.

[11] Wollstonecraft, *Works*, IV, p. 30.

[12] See Barbara Taylor, *Mary Wollstonecraft and the Feminist Imagination* (Cambridge: Cambridge University Press, 2003); Susan Khin Zaw, 'The Reasonable Heart: Mary Wollstonecraft's View of the Relation between Reason and Feeling in Morality, Moral Psychology, and Moral Development', *Hypatia*, 13.1 (Winter 1998), 78–117 (pp. 104–5); Virginia Sapiro, *A Vindication of Political Virtue: The Political Theory of Mary Wollstonecraft* (Chicago: University of Chicago Press, 1992), ch. 2; Karen Green, 'The Passions and the Imagination in Wollstonecraft's Theory of Moral Judgement', *Utilitas*, 9.3 (1997), 271–82; Martina Reuter, 'The Role of the Passions in Mary Wollstonecraft's Notion of Virtue', in *The Social and Political Philosophy of Mary Wollstonecraft*, ed. by Sandrine Bergès and Alan Coffee (Oxford: Oxford University Press, 2016), pp. 50–66.

[13] See Wollstonecraft, *Works*, V, p. 193.

community that motivates self-sacrifice for the general good? For Martha C. Nussbaum, such a 'public culture of compassion' begins with intimate experiences of love.[14] In *Political Emotions: Why Love Matters for Justice* (2013), she focuses on the imagined community of the nation but addresses the same fundamental question of how to expand the average citizen's circle of concern beyond nearest and dearest, local and particular. To this end, she envisages pedagogical practices and collective cultural experiences that give citizens the means and opportunity to expand from localised acts of compassion to broader altruistic principles. The goal is 'to construct a *bridge* from the vividly imagined single case to the impartial principle by challenging the imagination, reminding people that the predicament to which they respond in a single vividly described case is actually far broader'.[15] In the pedagogical content of Wollstonecraft's works, one can trace a similar intellectual endeavour. Like Price, she is convinced that we can be led to adopt the principle of universal benevolence by our God-given faculty of reason. Yet she also sets great store by the imagination, which she regards as 'a sacred faculty, linking the fantasising mind to its Maker'.[16] The means to partial contact with the divine, the imagination can also forge connections between individuals, enabling the subject to picture themselves in the place of another. Once we see the world from the perspective of one who suffers, we may feel compassion for their plight, not simply because it violates our sense of justice, but also because we identify with their vulnerability in a way that affects our sense of wellbeing. This experience can move us to act benevolently on their behalf. Simply put, reason establishes the principle of universal benevolence, but compassion gives us an emotional grasp of its importance. This is what Wollstonecraft's textual persona Mrs Mason means when she declares that 'man is allowed to ennoble his nature by cultivating his mind and enlarging his heart', so that he can better experience 'disinterested love', another synonym for the philanthropic moral sentiment crucial to altruism.[17] In Wollstonecraft's eyes, the ques-

---

[14] Martha C. Nussbaum, *Political Emotions: Why Love Matters for Justice*, paperback edn (Cambridge, MA and London: The Belknap Press of Harvard University Press, 2015), p. 157.

[15] Ibid.

[16] Taylor, p. 21. See also Martina Reuter, 'Jean-Jacques Rousseau and Mary Wollstonecraft on the Imagination', *British Journal for the History of Philosophy*, 25.6 (2017), 1138–60.

[17] Wollstonecraft, *Works*, IV, p. 370.

tion is not whether human subjects have the potential to act from disinterested love, but whether it is possible to establish the social and cultural conditions that will unlock that potential.

Wollstonecraft identifies the patriarchal family as one of the principal barriers to human sympathies, but as Eileen Hunt Botting has demonstrated, she also envisages political and pedagogical change transforming the family into an egalitarian cradle of benevolence.[18] In *Rights of Woman*, she depicts the relationships between parents and children, brothers and sisters, as potential wellsprings of affection – if only legal and cultural changes could level the gendered hierarchies stoking familial conflict. 'Few, I believe, have had much affection for mankind', she observes, 'who did not first love their parents, their brothers, sisters, and even the domestic brutes, whom they first played with'.[19] In the right conditions, these formative relationships nurture the child's innate instinct for compassion, which then develops in tandem with their reason and imagination into a broader love of humankind. As Hunt Botting explains, the 'sympathy first shared between parent and child' acts as an 'emotional springboard for the habitual practice of compassion towards neighbours and strangers, fellow citizens, and foreigners'.[20] Mrs Mason invokes a similar idea when she describes the affective and ethical components of cosmopolitan fellow feeling: 'One being is made dependent on another, that love and forbearance may soften the human heart, and that linked together by necessity, and the exercise of the social affections, the whole family on earth might have a fellow feeling for each other.'[21]

What this beatific vision elides, however, is the tension between our instinctive loyalties and our moral obligations to the human family. In both the eighteenth century and the modern world, sceptics of the cosmopolitan worldview have pointed out that, while our first bonds of affection can lay the foundations for love of humankind, they are also liable to undercut it.[22] Wollstonecraft claims in

---

[18] See Hunt Botting, *Family Feuds*, p. 9.

[19] Wollstonecraft, *Works*, V, p. 234.

[20] Hunt Botting, *Family Feuds*, p. 147.

[21] Wollstonecraft, Works, IV, p. 412.

[22] Wollstonecraft's antagonist, Edmund Burke, was a well-known eighteenth-century sceptic of the cosmopolitan worldview expressed in Price's *Discourse*. See Edmund Burke, *Reflections on the Revolution in France* (1790), ed. by Conor Cruise O'Brien (London: Penguin, 1982), pp. 89–90, 160. For examples of present-day sceptics of cosmopolitanism, see Richard Rorty, 'Justice as a Larger Loyalty', in *Cosmopolitics: Thinking and Feeling beyond the Nation*, ed. by Pheng Cheah and Bruce Robbins (Minneapolis: University of Minnesota Press,

Rights of Woman that it is the 'recollection' of our 'youthful sympathies' that 'gives life to those that are afterwards more under the
direction of reason'.[23] In other words, the emotional groundwork
laid in childhood informs the adult practice of benevolence. What
this also means, however, is that the adult subject is still contending
with affects rooted in an earlier, less rational age. Reason accords
every human subject equal status, but the moral duty to exercise
benevolence impartially often clashes with human psychological
imperatives, ingrained attachments and antipathies. According to
Hunt Botting, Wollstonecraft seeks to avert this clash by conceiving
of personal fulfilment in a way that is reminiscent of the Aristotelian
concept of *eudaimonia*, which Nussbaum defines as 'human flourishing, a complete life'.[24] In this model, flourishing entails '[n]ot only
virtuous action but also mutual relations of civic or personal love
and friendship, in which the object is loved and benefited for his or
her own sake'.[25] Eudaimonistic emotions stem from the subject's
pursuit of personal fulfilment, but they can also drive benevolent
actions where these are perceived as constitutive elements of a life
well lived.[26] Likewise, Wollstonecraft recognises that subjectivity is
ineliminable. Education must therefore foster emotional as well as
rational investment in philanthropy so that children can fulfil their
virtuous potential which, in Wollstonecraft's ethical system, means
'cultivat[ing] an independent yet caring moral character'.[27] While
Aristotle regards reason as the defining human attribute and virtuous self-realisation as dependent on its cultivation, Wollstonecraft
insists that reason must work in tandem with compassion and a
sympathetic imagination to achieve a meaningful commitment to
universal benevolence. The question then remains as to how to foster these latent attributes in a child who has yet to experience the
pleasures of their fulfilment.

1998), pp. 45–58; Benedict Anderson, 'Nationalism, Identity, and the World-in-
   Motion: On the Logics of Seriality', in Cheah and Robbins (eds), pp. 117–34.
[23] Wollstonecraft, *Works*, V, p. 234.
[24] See Eileen Hunt Botting, *Wollstonecraft, Mill and Women's Human Rights* (New
   Haven and London: Yale University Press, 2016), p. 117; Martha C. Nussbaum,
   Upheavals of Thought: The Intelligence of Emotions (Cambridge: Cambridge
   University Press, 2001), p. 32.
[25] Nussbaum, *Upheavals of Thought*, p. 32.
[26] See ibid., p. 49.
[27] Hunt Botting, *Wollstonecraft, Mill and Women's Human Rights*, p. 117.

Confronting the same issue, Nussbaum turns to the concept of *eudaimonia* to model the psychology of a citizen capable of impartial altruism. She concludes that

> if distant people and abstract principles are to get a grip on our emotions, these emotions must somehow position them within our circle of concern, creating a sense of 'our' life in which these people and events matter as part of our 'us', our own flourishing.[28]

Those who adhere joyfully to the principle of universal benevolence do so because it fits with their conception of the good life. To experience altruistic fulfilment in the first place, however, the subject must take the leap of investing emotionally in the lives of unknown others. As Nussbaum points out, 'respect grounded in the idea of human dignity will prove impotent to include all citizens on terms of equality unless it is nourished by imaginative engagement with the lives of others and by an inner grasp of their full and equal humanity'.[29] Crucially, empathy (or 'sympathy', in Wollstonecraft's parlance) cannot do this work on its own. The ability to identify with the plight of suffering others is important, but acting on the principle of universal benevolence also demands compassion. Like Wollstonecraft, Nussbaum sees this kind of emotional investment germinating from the same soil as our intimate relationships: 'the type of imaginative engagement society needs', she argues, 'is nourished by love'.[30] 'Love', understood as passionate attachment to an autonomous subject, can give human shape to the ideal of a borderless human community. Once we identify the principle of universal benevolence with a loved one, we are more likely to invest emotional energy in the distant beneficiaries of our altruism, even though our connection to them is purely imaginary.

In *Original Stories*, Mrs Mason embodies universal benevolence. She is also the loved object inspiring her charges to adopt the same principle of action. Taking over the education of two girls, Mary and Caroline, after the death of their inattentive mother, she sets out to correct the flaws stemming from a faulty education. By recounting moral tales and staging learning experiences, she teaches them to draw rational conclusions from experience and rouses their latent compassion. Her peculiar mix of kindness and austerity quickly

---

[28] Nussbaum, *Political Emotions*, p. 11.
[29] Ibid., p. 380.
[30] Ibid.

dominates her charges' psyches: 'She was never in a passion, but her quiet steady displeasure made them feel so little in their own eyes, they wished her to smile that they might be something; for all their consequence seemed to arise from her approbation.'[31] Mrs Mason is both an authority figure directing her wayward charges and an object of love who inspires emulation. Despite profound grief at the death of her husband and child, she turns her thoughts towards others. Amongst the beneficiaries of her good deeds are an impoverished family from another county whom she shelters whilst they seek employment and a Welsh harper and his relatives whom she rescues from destitution. As she explains to Mary and Caroline, the purpose of human life is to unfold our innate capacity for 'disinterested love', which provides its own reward in eudaimonistic fulfilment: 'every part of creation affords an exercise for virtue, and virtue is ever the truest source of pleasure'.[32] Hence Wollstonecraft depicts Mrs Mason 'ever ready to smile on those whom she obliged', for the simple reason that 'she loved all her fellow creatures, and love lightens obligations'.[33] Instilling in her charges the importance of charity, she presents the girls with 'spectacle[s] of undeserved suffering' to exercise their compassion.[34] For instance, when an unkind boy steals a bird's nest, the children hear the mother bird's 'intelligible tones of anguish' and feel for the first time 'the emotions of humanity'.[35] By inviting the girls to imagine themselves in the place of the frantic mother bird, Mrs Mason also invites them to find a rational and benevolent means to alleviate her pain. The episode ends with Caroline buying the nest and returning it.

Crucially, Wollstonecraft presents impartial benevolence as impossible without moral independence. As Lena Halldenius explains in her fascinating study of Wollstonecraft's republicanism:

> [a] person whose mind has been habituated to dependence [. . .] will have no capacity to see beyond personal emotional ties or self-interested gratification. She will act benevolently only when it serves her own interests or pleases the narrow circle in which she moves.[36]

---

[31] Wollstonecraft, *Works*, IV, p. 388.
[32] Ibid., p. 370.
[33] Ibid., p. 393.
[34] Khin Zaw, p. 106.
[35] Wollstonecraft, *Works*, IV, p. 369.
[36] Halldenius, p. 31.

According to Halldenius, Wollstonecraft gives the faculty of reason the credit for instigating 'the move from being swayed by self-interest and partial commitments, toward being an agent acting on principle', but as we have seen, she also places considerable emphasis on a sympathetic imagination.[37] As her charges grow in moral independence, Mrs Mason slackens her hold over them. In a moment of metatextual allusion, she arms Mary and Caroline with the text of *Original Stories* and lets them embark on life in the temptation-ridden capital, not as her pupils, but as 'candidates for [her] friendship', a mode of relating predicated on equality.[38]

Mrs Mason never exerts arbitrary authority, but she watches Mary and Caroline constantly. By the time that Wollstonecraft wrote *Rights of Woman*, however, she recognised that this kind of unbroken surveillance would inhibit a child's emotional development and, in consequence, their capacity for altruism:

> Let a child have ever such an affection for his parent, he will always languish to play and prattle with children; and the very respect he feels, for filial esteem always has a dash of fear mixed with it, will, if it do not teach him cunning, at least prevent him from pouring out the little secrets, which first open the heart to friendship and confidence, gradually leading to more expansive benevolence.[39]

As hierarchy inheres in the parent–child relationship, Wollstonecraft's ideal system of national education is set up to give children the opportunity to develop 'social affections' as well as filial respect.[40] 'Of these equality is the basis', she writes, presenting affection between peers as an affective stimulus to the egalitarian principles that she vindicates.[41] The first sparks of benevolence are ignited within the family, but they burn brighter when the child establishes a broader circle of friendship. Accordingly, Wollstonecraft calls for state-funded co-educational day schools, a system calculated to develop 'the domestic affections, that first open the heart to the various modifications of humanity', as well as the 'social affections' fostered when children 'spend great part of their time, on terms of equality, with other children'.[42]

[37] Ibid.
[38] Wollstonecraft, *Works*, IV, p. 449.
[39] Ibid., V, pp. 229–30.
[40] Ibid., V, p. 229.
[41] Ibid.
[42] Ibid., V, pp. 230, 229, 230.

Describing a pupil dividing his days between home and school, Wollstonecraft portrays the different kinds of emotional sustenance he thereby receives, rooting the lessons taught by his parents and teachers in the habits and pleasures of childhood:

> I still recollect, with pleasure, the country day school; where a boy trudged in the morning, wet or dry, carrying his books, and his dinner, if it were at a considerable distance; a servant did not then lead master by the hand, for, when he had once put on coat and breeches, he was allowed to shift for himself, and return alone in the evening to recount the feats of the day close at the parental knee. His father's house was his home, and was ever after fondly remembered; nay, I appeal to many superiour men, who were educated in this manner, whether the recollection of some shady lane where they conned their lesson: or, of some stile, where they sat making a kite, or mending a bat, has not endeared their country to them?[43]

This pupil's upbringing favours the growth of moral independence as well as 'expansive benevolence'. He is allowed to exercise his reason independently but is not left completely adrift. Without the hierarchy instituted by the master–servant dynamic, he 'shifts[s] for himself' during the school day, but can still seek guidance 'at the parental knee'. That his 'father's house' is 'fondly remembered' implies a place of affection. The child is 'endeared' to his country because his childhood memories of it evoke feelings of safety, liberty and love. In the democratic republic at the heart of Wollstonecraft's political vision, children educated thus would connect egalitarian principles with their affections for the parents and educators who instilled them. These emotions would be eudaimonistic by virtue of being indissociable from the principles requisite to fulfil their virtuous potential. So far, this kind of education has produced only 'superiour men', but Wollstonecraft argues for pedagogical reforms designed to convert both sexes to the practice of universal benevolence fundamental to her political vision. The following section examines how Wollstonecraft's translational choices bring *Elements* into an intertextual conversation with *Original Stories*, reinforcing the eudaimonistic aspect of her pedagogy as well as her egalitarian and cosmopolitan convictions.

---

[43] Ibid., V, pp. 230–1.

Cosmopolitan Pedagogy: *Original Stories* and *Elements of Morality*

Wollstonecraft chose to translate Salzmann's *Elementarbuch* because their pedagogical systems had much in common.[44] Notably for our purposes, Wollstonecraft's emphasis on philanthropy resonates with Salzmann's iteration of Philanthropinism, a 'cosmopolitan, non-confessional, and pragmatic system of education' which conceived of the educator as an 'agent that fitted the natural human to the needs of civic life'.[45] Like *Original Stories*, the *Elementarbuch* depicts children learning through practical and emotional experiences, the latter of which Salzmann aims to replicate in his young readers. Like Wollstonecraft, he privileges children's moral development over book-learning, placing marked emphasis on compassion, benevolence and care for others beyond one's immediate circle. This overlap between their educational philosophies led to a correspondence and significant translational exchange between the German pedagogue and the Revolutionary feminist.[46] Their intellectual parity makes Wollstonecraft's alterations to her source text all the more conspicuous, highlighting trademark pedagogical features which she evidently considered essential in any text bearing her name.

One of these features is Wollstonecraft's preoccupation with cultivating moral independence. In chapter 15 of the *Elementarbuch*, Ludwig's mother warns him not to lean out of the window of their coach in case an accident befalls him. He sits down reluctantly, protesting that he does not see why it is dangerous, only to receive an immediate answer when the coach jolts against a large stone and the door is flung open. This incident furnishes an opportunity for Herrmann, Ludwig's father, to explain the importance of obedience:

Du mußt, sagte Herrmann, allemal gehorchen, wenn ich oder deine Mutter dir etwas befehlen, wenn du auch nicht weißt, warum wir es thun. Denn wir sind alter als du, und müssen also besser wissen, was dir gut oder schädlich sey, als du es selbst wissen kannst. Lieb haben wir

---

44 See ibid., II, p. 6.
45 Robert Sumser, '"Erziehung", the Family, and the Regulation of Sexuality in the Late German Enlightenment', *German Studies Review*, 15.3 (1992), 455–74 (pp. 457, 460).
46 See Laura Kirkley, 'Mary Wollstonecraft's Translational Afterlife: French and German Rewritings of *A Vindication of the Rights of Woman* in the Revolutionary Era', *European Romantic Review*, 33.1 (2022), 1–24.

dich auch. Wie kannst du also glauben, daß wir dir etwas sagen würden, das dir nicht gut wäre?

You must, said Herrmann, always obey when I or your mother command you to do something, even if you do not know why we are doing it. Because we are older than you, and must therefore know better than you can know yourself what will be good or harmful to you. We also love you. So how can you believe that we would tell you to do something, that was not for your own good?[47]

Herrmann emphasises that obeying parental commands will secure the child's wellbeing, not only because the parents have accrued greater wisdom through experience, but also because their actions are driven by love for their children. In *Elements*, Herrmann's English counterpart, Mr Jones, makes the same point about superior parental wisdom, but does not ask his son to trust that sound judgement derives from affection. Instead, he explains that, as the boy's reason develops, his parents will cease to give commands:

You must, said Mr Jones, always obey, when I or your mother desire you to do any thing, if you cannot guess why we bid you to do it; for we are older than you, and must know better what will be useful or hurtful to you. As you grow up and acquire more sense, by attending to our instruction, and observing what men do, you will know the nature of things yourself; and instead of commanding, I shall reason with you.[48]

In Wollstonecraft's version, the parent assumes that the child will one day attain moral independence. She thus represents the Jones children's affection for their parents as the inspiration for personal growth rather than blind obedience.

Throughout the text, the children's developing reason combines with compassion to prompt benevolent actions. In the *Elementarbuch*, Salzmann situates this moral progress within a class-bound society where people from different walks of life offer valuable moral insights or case studies in virtue. Nowhere is this clearer than in Ludwig's encounter with Ephraim, a Jew who cures both his toothache and his antisemitism. Ludwig is at first suspicious of the treatment, partly because he has been culturally conditioned to

---

[47] Christian Gotthilf Salzmann, *Moralisches Elementarbuch, nebst einer Anleitung zum nützlichen Gebrauch desselben*, new edn (Leipzig: Crusius, 1785), pp. 136–7. My translation.
[48] Wollstonecraft, *Works*, II, p. 79.

regard Jews as untrustworthy. In the Holy Roman Empire of the German Nation, as in other European nations, Jews had long suffered discrimination, persecution and violence at the hands of their professedly Christian compatriots. Salzmann's story contributes to growing literary representations of the *edler Jude* (noble Jew) begun by writers such as Christian Gellert and Gotthold Ephraim Lessing, whose work reflects and promotes the gradual – if disputed – shift towards religious toleration during the *Aufklärung*. In the later decades of the eighteenth century, arguments for religious toleration began to give way to a secular conception of virtue that would enable adherents of any or no faith to claim equal moral status and citizenship. Even so, Jewish emancipation did not occur in Germany until the nineteenth century.[49] Michael Scrivener observes that, in this period, the 'cosmopolitan dimension of Jews and Judaism becomes obvious in relation to nationalism', as in Britain, France and the German Nation, 'emancipation and cultural acceptance' depended on renouncing one's Jewish identity and 'assimilat[ing] entirely into the Christian public culture'.[50] In the German Nation, those who refused to convert struggled to find places to settle, which contributed to the antisemitic image of 'wandering Jews' as foreigners in their homelands. In this context, Salzmann's benevolent exchange between Ludwig and Ephraim not only refutes the antisemitic canard of Jewish predation on Christian children, it can also be read as a synecdochical model for the rising Christian generation embracing Jews as their compatriots.

When Ludwig's toothache subsides following Ephraim's treatment, he revises his opinion of Jewish people. Aligning antisemitism with ignorance, Salzmann presumes that education can dispel it, making Jewish integration a test case for the perfectibilist ambitions of enlightened pedagogues. He puts the moral message of the episode in Ephraim's mouth: '*Es giebt bey alle Religione gute Leute!*' (There are good people in every religion.[51] At the same time, Salzmann places this egalitarian principle in the context of the legal disenfranchisement and cultural prejudices that inhibit its

---

[49] See David Sorkin, 'The Jewish Question in Eighteenth-Century Germany', in *Discourses of Tolerance and Intolerance in the European Enlightenment*, ed. by Hans Erich Bödeker, Clorinda Donato and Peter Hans Reill (Toronto: University of Toronto Press, 2009), pp. 144–52 (p. 148).

[50] Michael Scrivener, *The Cosmopolitan Ideal in the Age of Revolution and Reaction, 1776–1832* (London: Pickering and Chatto, 2007), p. 147.

[51] Salzmann, p. 289 (emphasis original).

application. Ephraim complains about the *Leibzoll*, the mortifying
toll levied at Jewish travellers in the German Nation and otherwise
applicable only to livestock. In doing so, he compels the Christian
child to recognise the role played by antisemitic laws and attitudes
in driving Jews to commit the crimes cited as justification for their
oppression. 'Ich will zwar nicht widerstreite, daß es nicht auch viele
böse Leut unter unsere Nation giebt. Aber das ist ja kein Wunder,
da uns die Christe so stark drükke' (But I will not deny that there
are many wicked people amongst our Nation. But that is not to be
wondered at, because the Christians oppress us so severely).[52] When
Ludwig objects that many Jews are 'Betrüger' (swindlers), however,
Salzmann has Ephraim clarify his position:

> *Kann wohl seyn, antwortete Ephraim. Giebt unter unsere Nation und
> unter Christe Betrüger. Wenn aber unsere Nation betrüget, so sind die
> Christe selbst daran Ursach. Sie schneide uns ja alle Gelegenheit ab, uns
> zu nähre. Wenn der Christ etliche Söhne hat, so läßt er den eine ein
> Schuster, den andern ein Schneider, den dritte ein Priester werde, da fin-
> den alle ihr Brod. Uns arme Leut ist das aber nicht erlaubt. Wir müssen
> alle vom Schacher lebe. Wenn nun ein armer Jud fünf bis sechs Kinder
> zu ernähre hat, und mit seinem Schacher kaum etliche Pfennige verdiene
> kan des Tags – was soll er denn thun? soll er die Kinder denn verhungere
> lase? ist er nicht gezwunge zu betrüge oder gar zu stehle?*

That might well be, answered Ephraim. There are swindlers amongst
our nation and amongst Christians. But if our nation cheats, then the
Christians are themselves the cause of it. They cut off every opportunity
we have to earn our living. If a Christian has a few sons, then one can become a shoemaker, another a tailor, the third a priest, so all of them can
earn their bread. But that is not permitted to us poor people. We must
earn all our living from trade. Now if a poor Jew has five or six children
to feed, and if his trade can barely earn him a few pfennigs a day – what,
then, should he do? should he let the children go hungry? is he not then
driven to cheat or even to steal?[53]

In Salzmann's portrait of an antisemitic society, injustice causes Jewish
citizens to turn on their neighbours in a bid for survival. Having
first insisted that Christians and Jews are equally capable of evil, he
goes on to lay the blame for crimes committed by Jews squarely at
the feet of Christians. In the final lines, he invites compassion for

[52] Ibid.
[53] Ibid., pp. 289–90.

Jewish lawbreakers, who are banned from so many professions under German law that they are often unable to feed their children without resorting to theft and deceit. Yet this message about the relative virtue of Jews also reflects the antisemitism of the period, as Ephraim appears to accept the slur of widespread Jewish corruption, a common assumption in pro-emancipation works positing the ameliorative potential of an egalitarian society.[54] Impoverished Jews were indeed driven to desperate measures by antisemitic laws and prejudices, but there is no evidence that their criminality outweighed that of other marginalised groups; what is certain is that cultural perceptions of Jewish people were reflected and shaped by the caricatures of crooks and Shylocks permeating European discourse.

In comparison to their Continental counterparts, British Jews were relatively integrated into their society, but the ferocious opposition to the Naturalisation Bill of 1753 made it clear that this integration was contingent on denying them full citizenship and limiting them to poorly paying trades. As Scrivener puts it, '[t]hat Britain was the least unfriendly European country suggests the extent of the prejudice against Jews and how remote European culture was from realizing the cosmopolitan ideal'.[55] Part of the problem was that integration introduced 'a multicultural rationality' that contradicted the mounting nationalism of Britain and other European countries in the late eighteenth and nineteenth centuries.[56] Scrivener identifies ambivalence towards Jews and Judaism even in the progressive and explicitly cosmopolitan *Analytical Review*, which 'supported Jewish emancipation unequivocally at a time when few in either the Jewish or Christian communities gave it much thought', but which also published articles with antisemitic content and did not number Jewish intellectuals amongst its reviewers.[57] In *Elements*, Wollstonecraft's translation of Ludwig's encounter with Ephraim reflects these tensions, at times reinforcing Salzmann's repudiation of antisemitic prejudices and at times reinscribing them into her text.

---

[54] One important work was Christian Wilhelm Dohm's *Ueber die bürgerliche Verbesserung der Juden* (*On the Civic Amelioration of the Jews*), published in 1781 shortly before Salzmann wrote his *Elementarbuch*. For more on this aspect of the emancipation debate, see Michael Scrivener, *Jewish Representation in British Literature 1780–1840: After Shylock* (Basingstoke: Palgrave Macmillan, 2011), pp. 83–4.

[55] Scrivener, *Cosmopolitan Ideal*, p. 147.

[56] Ibid., p. 148.

[57] Ibid, p. 161.

Wollstonecraft changes Ludwig's name to Charles and cuts the allusion to the *Leibzoll*, almost certainly because of her avowed strategy of 'naturalizing' Salzmann's text for her British readership; but in omitting to insert a British equivalent, such as the discrimination meted out to non-Anglicans by the Test Acts, she also removes the opportunity for British child readers to learn about the oppression of their Jewish compatriots.[58] By removing cultural specificity from the encounter with Ephraim, however, Wollstonecraft gives herself scope to universalise the moral. She is quicker than Salzmann to stress that Jews do not have a monopoly on vice but, in Ephraim's dialogue, she places the emphasis on advocating love of humankind. Invoking biblical discourse to incorporate a call for fellow-feeling across religious divides, she claims the equality of all God's children:

> I do not deny but there are many wicked people among our nation, and how many Christians lie and steal! – but we are all men – descended from the same father, and serve the same God, and he who despises his fellow-creatures on account of their being called Jews, flies in the face of his Maker. We are commanded to love all men – we are all brothers, and should only despise those who steal, and commit crimes, which render them useless, if not a pest, to society.[59]

Wollstonecraft's rhetoric echoes her additions to an earlier chapter, which promotes compassion for the poor. In the *Elementarbuch*, when Herrmann's daughter, Luise, recoils from a poor woman and her unkempt children, Herr Friedlieb explains that the whole family has been struggling for subsistence since the woman's husband lost three fingers fighting with the Hussars. In *Elements*, the woman is the sole breadwinner because her husband was slowly poisoned working in a white lead manufactory. Having contracted 'lead palsy' or 'wrist drop' – now known as peripheral nerve disorder – which paralysed his fingers, hands and wrists, he can find few ways to earn money and his wife has 'sold one thing after another' to pay for hospital treatment.[60] This tale of rapid impoverishment stemming from the negligence of social superiors recalls the fate of Crazy Robin in *Original Stories*, who gradually loses his sanity as he watches his wife and children starve, sicken and die in poverty. While Salzmann never questions the social order, Wollstonecraft draws attention to

[58] See Wollstonecraft, *Works*, II, p. 5.
[59] Ibid., II, p. 149.
[60] Ibid., II, p. 135.

the suffering attributable to exploitative elites. Deploying biblical rhetoric, she depicts class distinctions as meaningless in the sight of God, again emphasising human commonality: 'we all descended from the same parents – all look up to the same God'.[61] In both cases, Wollstonecraft invites her young readers to join the fictional children in compassion for the victims of injustice. She thus seeks to stimulate a benevolent desire to palliate suffering, as well as a rational critique of the social order that causes it.

Despite imbuing *Elements* with subtle political commentary, however, Wollstonecraft stops short of mitigating crimes attributable to want; in her version of Ephraim's dialogue, a criminal is at best 'useless', at worst a despicable 'pest'. Nor does she translate Salzmann's suggestion that we might excuse Jews for dishonesty traceable to legal or social injustice:

> [B]ut if our nation cheat, the Christians themselves are the cause of it. They despise us, and do not allow us to gain our livelihood in an honest way; so many ignorant Jews are become cheats, because they think that they live among enemies; but there are many good Jews who tell truth, and give money to the poor; and such men deserve our love, whether they are Jews or Christians.[62]

In this bewildering passage, Wollstonecraft acknowledges antisemitic persecution in the same breath as she attributes it to the paranoia of 'ignorant Jews'. If her translational choices reflect her universalising project, then, her rhetoric betrays hostility to the very figures of difference that Ephraim's words ostensibly defend. As most modern theorists have recognised, universalist cosmopolitanism grants equal moral status to all human subjects, but it can also occlude otherness by painting their diverse experiences in broad brushstrokes liable to imitate the dominant culture.[63] By making Ephraim an exemplary educator, Salzmann and Wollstonecraft ostensibly bring

---

[61] Ibid., II, p. 138.

[62] Ibid., p. 150.

[63] See Timothy Brennan, *At Home in the World: Cosmopolitanism Now* (Cambridge, MA: Harvard University Press, 1997); Kwame Anthony Appiah, 'Cosmopolitan Patriots' [1997], in Cheah and Robbins (eds), pp. 91–114; *Cosmopolitanism*, ed. by Carol A. Breckenridge, Sheldon Pollock, Homi K. Bhabha and Dipesh Chakrabarty (Durham, NC: Duke University Press, 2002); David A. Hollinger, 'Not Universalists, Not Pluralists: The New Cosmopolitans Find Their Own Way', in *Conceiving Cosmopolitanism: Theory, Context, and Practice*, ed. by Steven Vertovec and Robin Cohen (Oxford: Oxford University Press, 2002), pp. 227–39.

the Jewish people he represents into a universalist moral fold; but Wollstonecraft's dialogue also makes him complicit in their marginalisation, echoing the emancipation debate about whether Jewish 'cheats' were social constructs whom education could reform.[64] In short, Wollstonecraft's pedagogical discourse reiterates the biases it purports to eschew. She devotes the closing lines, however, to praising Jews who practise virtue which, as in every part of her corpus, consists in sincerity and charitable giving. As beneficence depends on disposable income, her description confines Jewish virtue to the prosperous classes; however, by emphasising that 'there are many good Jews who tell truth, and give money to the poor', she goes some way to debunking the persistent stereotype of Jews as 'penny-pinching, double-dealing' miscreants.[65]

While recognising the troubling ambiguities in Wollstonecraft's treatment of antisemitism, it is essential to read her emphasis on common humanity in the context of her cosmopolitan pedagogical agenda. Foreshadowing her later critique of imperialism, her advertisement to *Elements* draws attention to one significant change in chapter 3, which teaches children to master fear and which Wollstonecraft adapts 'to lead children to consider the Indians as their brothers'.[66] In Salzmann's *Elementarbuch*, a terrified soldier runs straight into enemy hands. In *Elements*, the soldier falls from his horse as he rides full pelt to escape Native American pursuers conjured by his paranoid imagination. Incapacitated by a broken leg, he is rescued by 'one of those men whom we Europeans with white complexions call savages', who cares for him until he can return him to his camp.[67] Born of racist misconception, the soldier's dread of Native Americans is as unjustified as Ludwig/Charles' distrust of Jews. Significantly, although the soldier is 'the enemy of his country', the Native American recognises not his national identity, but their shared humanity, exemplifying benevolence that transcends racial divides and geopolitical conflict.[68] Likewise, in *Original Stories* Wollstonecraft discourages xenophobia with the tale of honest Jack, a sailor shipwrecked, lamed and captured by the French, who fought

[64] See Scrivener, *Jewish Representation in British Literature 1780–1840*, p. 83.
[65] Isaac Land, 'Jewishness and Britishness in the Eighteenth Century', *History Compass*, 3 (2005), 1–12 (p. 4).
[66] Wollstonecraft, *Works*, II, p. 6.
[67] Ibid., II, p. 28.
[68] Ibid., II, p. 29.

on the side of the Americans during the War of Independence. Jack owes his survival to the altruism of the local Frenchwomen, who brought food to his prison cell and nursed him back to health. He therefore rejects the Francophobia rife in eighteenth-century England: 'I for certain ought to speak well of the French; but for their kindness I should have been in another port by this time.'[69] In almost all of these tales, the subject of prejudice is stricken by illness or injury, and then healed by an Other whose foreignness makes them an object of fear or disdain. Such episodes emphasise that the members of every race, culture and creed contend with the vulnerabilities of the human body, and this ubiquitous condition succeeds in drawing together very different people in bonds of compassion. Moreover, the gratitude of the patient makes the healer an object of affection who embodies the benevolence that Wollstonecraft strives to impart to her readership.

Wollstonecraft's alterations to the *Elementarbuch* align the pedagogical theory of *Elements* with that of her *Original Stories*. She also brings a multiracial dimension to the theme of universal benevolence, subtly politicises the circumstances for charitable giving and emphasises the children's progress to moral independence, a prerequisite in her eyes for the 'expansive benevolence' fundamental to her cosmopolitan ethical framework. Like Nussbaum, Wollstonecraft understands that 'imaginative engagement with the lives of others is nourished by love', and in all of her pedagogical works, she strives to give universal benevolence a human face, either in the form of a textual alter ego like Mrs Mason or through the creation of racial and cultural others such as Ephraim and the Native American rescuer, whose salutary actions represent and promote altruism in the face of difference. Drawing attention to the misconceptions that divide citizens from each other, her tales mount a subtle challenge to racism, xenophobia, antisemitism and social inequity. This challenge is imperfect, however, because her pedagogical discourse at times betrays the prejudices she purports to reject. Nevertheless, having acknowledged the human potential for self-interest and factionalism, she strives to harness the human passions to a project of eudaimonistic fulfilment whereby the child learns to equate love of humankind with a life well lived. She thus positions her pedagogy as a means not simply to guide children towards rational self-government but

[69] Ibid., IV, p. 398.

also to construct the (world) citizens of a public culture founded on egalitarian principles and held together by compassion.

Works Cited

Primary

Burke, Edmund, *Reflections on the Revolution in France* [1790], ed. by Conor Cruise O'Brien (London: Penguin, 1982)

Price, Richard, *A Discourse on the Love of Our Country*, in *Richard Price: Political Writings*, ed. by D. O. Thomas (Cambridge: Cambridge University Press, 1991)

Salzmann, Christian Gotthilf, *Moralisches Elementarbuch, nebst einer Anleitung zum nützlichen Gebrauch desselben*, new edn (Leipzig: Crusius, 1785)

Wollstonecraft, Mary, *The Works of Mary Wollstonecraft*, ed. by Marilyn Butler and Janet Todd, 7 vols (London: Pickering and Chatto, 1989)

Secondary

Anderson, Benedict, 'Nationalism, Identity, and the World-in-Motion: On the Logics of Seriality', in *Cosmopolitics: Thinking and Feeling beyond the Nation*, ed. by Pheng Cheah and Bruce Robbins (Minneapolis: University of Minnesota Press, 1998), pp. 117–34

Appiah, Kwame Anthony, 'Cosmopolitan Patriots' [1997], in *Cosmopolitics: Thinking and Feeling beyond the Nation*, ed. by Pheng Cheah and Bruce Robbins (Minneapolis: University of Minnesota Press, 1998), pp. 91–114

Breckenridge, Carol A., Sheldon Pollock, Homi K. Bhabha and Dipesh Chakrabarty, eds, *Cosmopolitanism* (Durham, NC: Duke University Press, 2002)

Brennan, Timothy, *At Home in the World: Cosmopolitanism Now* (Cambridge, MA: Harvard University Press, 1997)

Brown, Garrett Wallace and David Held, 'Editors' Introduction', in *The Cosmopolitanism Reader*, ed. by Garrett Wallace Brown and David Held (Cambridge: Polity Press, 2010), pp. 1–14

Green, Karen, 'The Passions and the Imagination in Wollstonecraft's Theory of Moral Judgement', *Utilitas*, 9.3 (1997), 271–82

Halldenius, Lena, *Mary Wollstonecraft and Feminist Republicanism: Independence, Rights and the Experience of Unfreedom* (London: Pickering and Chatto, 2015)

Hollinger, David A., 'Not Universalists, Not Pluralists: The New Cosmopolitans Find Their Own Way', in *Conceiving Cosmopolitanism:*

Theory, Context, and Practice, ed. by Steven Vertovec and Robin Cohen (Oxford: Oxford University Press, 2002), pp. 227–39

Hunt Botting, Eileen, *Family Feuds: Wollstonecraft, Burke, and Rousseau on the Transformation of the Family* (Albany: State University of New York Press, 2006)

——. *Wollstonecraft, Mill and Women's Human Rights* (New Haven and London: Yale University Press, 2016)

Khin Zaw, Susan, 'The Reasonable Heart: Mary Wollstonecraft's View of the Relation between Reason and Feeling in Morality, Moral Psychology, and Moral Development', *Hypatia*, 13.1 (Winter 1998), 78–117

Kirkley, Laura, *Mary Wollstonecraft: Cosmopolitan* (Edinburgh: Edinburgh University Press, 2022)

——. '"Original Spirit": Literary Translations and Translational Literature in the Works of Mary Wollstonecraft', in *Literature and the Development of Feminist Theory*, ed. by R. T. Goodman (Cambridge: Cambridge University Press, 2015), pp. 13–26

——. 'Mary Wollstonecraft's Translational Afterlife: French and German Rewritings of *A Vindication of the Rights of Woman* in the Revolutionary Era', *European Romantic Review*, 33.1 (2022), 1–24

Land, Isaac, 'Jewishness and Britishness in the Eighteenth Century', *History Compass*, 3 (2005), 1–12

Nussbaum, Martha C., *Political Emotions: Why Love Matters for Justice* (2013), paperback edn (Cambridge, MA and London: The Belknap Press of Harvard University Press, 2015)

——. *Upheavals of Thought: The Intelligence of Emotions* (Cambridge: Cambridge University Press, 2001)

Reuter, Martina, 'Jean-Jacques Rousseau and Mary Wollstonecraft on the Imagination', *British Journal for the History of Philosophy*, 25.6 (2017), 1138–60

——. 'The Role of the Passions in Mary Wollstonecraft's Notion of Virtue', in *The Social and Political Philosophy of Mary Wollstonecraft*, ed. by Sandrine Bergès and Alan Coffee (Oxford: Oxford University Press, 2016), pp. 50–66

Rorty, Richard, 'Justice as a Larger Loyalty', in *Cosmopolitics: Thinking and Feeling beyond the Nation*, ed. by Pheng Cheah and Bruce Robbins (Minneapolis: University of Minnesota Press, 1998), pp. 45–58

Sapiro, Virginia, *A Vindication of Political Virtue: The Political Theory of Mary Wollstonecraft* (Chicago: University of Chicago Press, 1992)

Scrivener, Michael, *The Cosmopolitan Ideal in the Age of Revolution and Reaction, 1776–1832* (London: Pickering and Chatto, 2007)

——. *Jewish Representation in British Literature 1780–1840: After Shylock* (Basingstoke: Palgrave Macmillan, 2011)

Sorkin, David, 'The Jewish Question in Eighteenth-Century Germany', in *Discourses of Tolerance and Intolerance in the European Enlightenment*, ed. by Hans Erich Bödeker, Clorinda Donato and Peter Hans Reill (Toronto: University of Toronto Press, 2009), pp. 144–52

Sumser, Robert, '"Erziehung", the Family, and the Regulation of Sexuality in the Late German Enlightenment', *German Studies Review*, 15.3 (1992), 455–74

Taylor, Barbara, *Mary Wollstonecraft and the Feminist Imagination* (Cambridge: Cambridge University Press, 2003)

Tomaselli, Sylvana, *Wollstonecraft: Philosophy, Passion, and Politics* (Princeton: Princeton University Press, 2021)

Chapter 12

'The enemy of imagination'? Re-imagining Sarah Trimmer and Her *Fabulous Histories*

Jonathan Padley

For scholars of women's literary education, few names are better known than that of Sarah Trimmer (1741–1810). A prolific author and critic of children's literature, and a significant pedagogue, Trimmer dedicated her life to advancing education and conservative Anglicanism, with no little success. Commentators report that, in 1800, Elizabeth Newbery's catalogue of her uncle-in-law's renowned London bookstore shows that the shop 'stocked more titles by Mrs. Trimmer than any other author';[1] and, in its time, Trimmer's seminal periodical, *The Guardian of Education* (1802–6), 'dominated the field of children's literature reviewing'.[2] Her writing for children was unusually prominent in contemporary circulating libraries,[3] and her most celebrated children's book, *Fabulous Histories* (1786),[4] 'was a nursery staple for over a century'.[5] *Prima facie*, it is easy to agree with Frederick Joseph Harvey Darton's tautological statement that '[t]he importance of Sarah Trimmer is that she *was* important. [. . .] S]he made herself, in respect of her writings for

---

[1] Samuel F. Pickering, *John Locke and Children's Books in Eighteenth-Century England* (Knoxville: University of Tennessee Press, 1981), p. 61.

[2] M. O. Grenby, 'Introduction', in *The Guardian of Education: A Periodical Work, by Sarah Trimmer*, vol. 1 (Bristol and Tokyo: Thoemmes Press and Edition Synapse, 2002), pp. v–xli (p. xv).

[3] M. O. Grenby, 'Adults Only? Children and Children's Books in British Circulating Libraries, 1748–1848', *Book History*, 5 (2002), 19–38 (p. 22).

[4] References here are to a 1786 (I believe first) edition, from which later editions variously diverge (see notes 49, 60, 61 and 111).

[5] Mitzi Myers, 'Impeccable Governesses, Rational Dames, and Moral Mothers: Mary Wollstonecraft and the Female Tradition in Georgian Children's Books', *Children's Literature*, 14 (1986), 31–59 (p. 46).

and about children, completely typical of the [. . .] English upper middle-class'.[6]

Given that Trimmer's name is so well known and that her importance may be taken as read, it is noteworthy that Matthew Grenby – who has lately published most about her life and work – should refer to 'the vast gap [. . .] between [her] consequence to her contemporaries and her position on the margins of literary history today'.[7] This disparity can largely be attributed to what has become a received wisdom characterisation of her as 'the enemy of imagination':[8] a significant description in context because, as James Engell has put it, imagination was the conceptual 'quintessence of Romanticism'.[9] In imagination, Romanticism determined 'an idea whose power both to assimilate and to foster other ideas seemed virtually limitless'.[10] Jonathan Wordsworth reports that, for John Keats, 'that which is imagined will be found to be real' whilst simultaneously human imagination 'is in the same relation to its celestial "reflection", as human existence is to heaven'.[11] William Wordsworth discovered in imagination 'something mysterious, beyond human experience',[12] William Blake identified in it the opposite to self-negating rationalism,[13] and Samuel Taylor Coleridge thought of it as a faculty with layers ranging from tertiary 'fancy' to the primary means (at the very least) by which humans perceive everything.[14] Against this all-encompassing backdrop, to be imagination's enemy at the turn of the eighteenth century was essentially to be against Romanticism – to support the supposed reductive sterility of previous generations. In this way has Trimmer been denounced and the view of her been normalised as, in Grenby's words, 'the representative of all that was retrograde in the

[6] Frederick Joseph Harvey Darton, *Children's Books in England: Five Centuries of Social Life* (Cambridge: Cambridge University Press, 2011), p. 160.
[7] M. O. Grenby, '"A Conservative Woman Doing Radical Things": Sarah Trimmer and *The Guardian of Education*', in *Culturing the Child, 1690–1914: Essays in Memory of Mitzi Myers*, ed. by Donelle Ruwe (Lanham, MD: Scarecrow Press, 2005), pp. 137–61 (p. 137).
[8] Grenby, 'Introduction', p. xxii.
[9] James Engell, *The Creative Imagination: Enlightenment to Romanticism* (Cambridge: Harvard University Press, 1981), p. 4.
[10] Ibid., p. 3.
[11] Jonathan Wordsworth, 'The Romantic Imagination', in *A Companion to Romanticism*, ed. by Duncan Wu (Oxford: Blackwell), pp. 525–33 (p. 526).
[12] Ibid.
[13] Ibid., p. 527.
[14] Ibid., p. 530.

late eighteenth and early nineteenth centuries, whether in the political, religious or literary sphere'.[15]

Some excellent work has already been done to dispute this position,[16] and Trimmer has recently been the subject of a range of analyses.[17] As a contribution to this ongoing 'rehabilitation',[18] this chapter presents a case study of Trimmer's most famous title, *Fabulous Histories*, which turns precisely on its engagement of imagination, albeit under careful regulation. '[B]y the force of imagination',[19] *Fabulous Histories* connects its frame story of the Redbreasts – a family of subtly individualised talking robins, who converse in English, have complex interrelations and exhibit human-like morality – with its account of the human Benson family. This imaginatively enabled connection allows the book's primary purpose – the recommendation of Christian benevolence – to shine. By thus reimagining *Fabulous Histories*, I contend that Trimmer cannot be dismissed out of hand as imagination's enemy, and so thinking about her which is predicated on this presupposition must be revisited. This chapter reviews how Trimmer has become labelled as anti-imagination and considers why this is unsatisfactory, before offering a close reading of *Fabulous Histories* to demonstrate how imagination is imperative to its function.

To begin, let us unpack Harvey Darton's characterisation of Trimmer as 'important'.[20] Trimmer's life has been effectively summarised by Barbara Brandon Schnorrenberg[21] and Heather Weir,[22]

[15] Grenby, 'Introduction', p. xxii.
[16] For example, Nicholas Tucker, 'Fairy Tales and Their Early Opponents: In Defence of Mrs Trimmer', in *Opening the Nursery Door: Reading, Writing and Childhood 1600–1900*, ed. by Mary Hilton, Morag Styles and Victor Watson (London: Routledge, 1997), pp. 104–16.
[17] Robert M. Andrews, 'Women of the Seventeenth and Eighteenth-Century High Church Tradition: A Biographical and Historiographical Exploration of a Forgotten Phenomenon in Anglican History', *Anglican and Episcopal History*, 84.1 (2015), 49–64 (p. 60).
[18] Grenby, 'Conservative', p. 137.
[19] Sarah Trimmer, *Fabulous Histories: Designed for the Instruction of Children, Respecting Their Treatment of Animals* (London: T. Longman, G. G. J. and J. Robinson, and J. Johnson, 1786), p. x.
[20] Harvey Darton, p. 160.
[21] Barbara Brandon Schnorrenberg, 'Trimmer [née Kirby], Sarah (1741–1810)', in *Oxford Dictionary of National Biography* (2004), online edition <https://doi.org/10.1093/ref:odnb/27740> [accessed 1 March 2022].
[22] Heather Weir, 'Trimmer, Sarah (1741–1810)', in *Handbook of Women Biblical Interpreters: A Historical and Biographical Guide*, ed. by Marion Ann Taylor and Agnes Choi (Grand Rapids: Baker Academic, 2012), pp. 505–9.

though a 'full biography [. . .] has yet to be published'.²³ Nevertheless, from these and earlier accounts, it is plain that Trimmer was formidable, in the best sense: a driven mother, who learned about education to educate her twelve children; a practical leader, who went from volunteering at a Sunday school in Brentford to advising Queen Charlotte about setting up a Sunday school at Windsor; a scholarly literate, who as a child debated the niceties of *Paradise Lost* with Samuel Johnson, and went on to become a substantial critical commentator; a committed Anglican, whose diverse knowledge of Church, liturgy, biblical exegesis, history, literature and education was variously poured into her corpus. Though the exact size of that corpus remains a matter of some debate,²⁴ there is no doubt that Trimmer was both prolific and popular in her time.

Allowing for this historic consequence, then, wherefrom Trimmer's modern neglect? Again, the answer apparently lies in the fact that she has become defined as the enemy of imagination. Whilst there is no clear originator of this position, we may find an important early contributor in Charles Lamb's oft-quoted invective from a letter he wrote in 1802 to Samuel Taylor Coleridge, in which Trimmer is mentioned *en passant*:

> Mrs. Barbauld's stuff has banished all the old classics of the nursery; and the shopman at Newbery's hardly deigned to reach them off an old exploded corner of a shelf [. . .]. Mrs. B.'s and Mrs. Trimmer's nonsense lay in piles about. Knowledge insignificant and vapid as Mrs. B.'s books convey, it seems, must come to a child in the *shape* of *knowledge* [. . .] instead of that beautiful Interest in wild tales which made the child a man, while all the time he suspected himself to be no bigger than a child [. . .]
>   Damn them! – I mean the cursed Barbauld Crew, those Blights and Blasts of all that is Human in man and child.²⁵

²³ Pauline Heath, *The Works of Mrs. Trimmer (1741–1810)* (Saarbrücken: LAP LAMBERT Academic Publishing, 2010), p. 7.

²⁴ Pauline Heath identifies some forty-four works '[b]etween the appearance of her first book in 1780 and her death in 1810' (Pauline Heath, 'Mrs Trimmer's Plan of Appropriate Instruction: A Revisionist View of Her Textbooks', *History of Education*, 32.4 (2003), 385–400 (p. 385)). Elsewhere, Heath cites counts ranging from nineteen to thirty-one items (Heath, *Works*, pp. 2–3), and chronologically lists thirty-eight publications from 1780 to 1814 (ibid., pp. 290–2).

²⁵ Charles Lamb, 'Letter 101: Charles Lamb to S. T. Coleridge', in *The Letters of Charles and Mary Lamb 1796–1820*, ed. by E. V. Lucas (London: Methuen, 1912), pp. 259–62 (pp. 260–1).

At a stroke, Lamb helps initiate a tendency to dismiss Trimmer through rhetorical flourish as one of 'the cursed Barbauld Crew'. This group's children's material he finds insipid – restrictive, pragmatic and simple – in contrast with the 'wild tales' he favours and the 'beautiful Interest' they elicit, descriptors redolent of our earlier discussion of Romantic imagination. Thus, he summarily excoriates Barbauld and Trimmer as reductive didacts, lumping them together indiscriminately amongst derogatory readings of other period female authors. Grenby lists examples of similar practice,[26] and it is readily possible to find more, both general and specific. Paula R. Backscheider writes persuasively of the wider eighteenth-century propensity to circumscribe and lambast female authors and their writing.[27] More particularly, Harvey Darton asserts that Trimmer and Mary Martha Sherwood exhibit 'very plain and even truculent dogmatic leanings'.[28] Humphrey Carpenter describes Trimmer as 'the indomitable lady', whose chief characteristic, like many other women educationalists of her time, was '[s]evere piety'.[29] Alan Richardson typifies Trimmer as 'the arch-conservative' and states that 'the more aridly didactic children's books of the period 1780–1800 [are] exemplified by Trimmer's works'.[30]

The fuel upon which this collective fire feeds especially in Trimmer's case is her purportedly adverse attitude to fairy tales. As Tucker puts it, it is unsurprising that 'an eighteenth-century fairy tale opponent like Mrs Trimmer has been treated with scant respect', given that '[t]he whole notion of condemning fairy tales for children [. . .] came to seem wilfully wrong-headed, apparently attempting to deprive the young of imaginative material'.[31] What is surprising, however, is that such disrespect persists when it is not clear either that Trimmer was uncomplicatedly a fairy tale opponent or that she condemned fairy tales principally for their engagement of children's imaginations. Indeed, quite early in *The Guardian of Education*, Trimmer's five-volume

---

[26] Grenby, 'Introduction', pp. xxii–xxiii; Grenby, 'Conservative', pp. 142–3.
[27] Paula R. Backscheider, 'Women Writers and the Chains of Identification', *Studies in the Novel*, 19.3 (1987), 245–62.
[28] Harvey Darton, p. 158.
[29] Humphrey Carpenter, *Secret Gardens: A Study of the Golden Age of Children's Literature* (Boston: Houghton Mifflin, 1985), p. 7.
[30] Alan Richardson, *Literature, Education, and Romanticism: Reading as Social Practice, 1780–1832* (Cambridge: Cambridge University Press, 1994), p. 111.
[31] Tucker, p. 104.

magnum opus periodical for parents and pedagogues,[32] she receives certain collections of fairy tales somewhat favourably, naming them amongst a list of writing for children that evolved from John Locke's (for her, positive) 'idea of uniting amusement with instruction'.[33] She recalls fondly that '[s]ome of the books written in what may be called *the first period of Infantine and Juvenile Literature* in this country, we well remember, as the delight of our childish days, viz. *Mother Goose's Fairy Tales*; *Esop and Gay's Fables*; *The Governess*, or *Little Female Academy*, by Mrs. Fielding, &c. &c.'[34] Given this affectionate tone, it is then all the more noticeable when she afterwards reflects – rather than reminisces – that these and some other texts 'were mostly calculated to entertain the imagination, rather than to improve the heart, or cultivate the understanding'.[35] The key word here is 'mostly'. For Trimmer, uniting amusement with instruction is one thing. Favouring the former at the expense of the latter, however, is quite another. Her concern is not about imagination *per se* but rather about texts which charm imagination to the apparent detriment of '*the* PRINCIPLES OF CHRISTIANITY',[36] the advancement of which is one of the journal's key intentions. If we then consider some of her specific textual analyses with this in mind, we may find that *Mother Bunch's Fairy Tales* are 'only fit to fill the heads of children with confused notions of wonderful and supernatural events, brought about by the agency of imaginary beings',[37] and that *Little Red Riding Hood* and *Blue Beard* are problematic because 'the terrific images, which tales of this nature present to the imagination, usually make deep impressions, and injure the tender minds of children'.[38] In these cases, Trimmer's difficulty is neither that the stories are fairy tales nor that they engage imagination. Instead, it is more

---

[32] It is an important comment on Trimmer's character and self-belief that she decided to publish a serious periodical entitled the *Guardian of Education* at the start of the nineteenth century. This signals that she felt a work of such remarkable remit – which helped define children's literature as a type of writing (Grenby, 'Introduction', pp. xv–xvi) – was right for its time and that she was the right person to produce it.

[33] Sarah Trimmer, *The Guardian of Education, A Periodical Work [. . .]*, vol. 1 (London: J. Hatchard, 1802), p. 62.

[34] Ibid.

[35] Ibid., I, p. 63.

[36] Ibid., I, p. 2.

[37] Sarah Trimmer, *The Guardian of Education, A Periodical Work [. . .]*, vol. 2 (London: J. Hatchard, 1803), p. 185.

[38] Ibid., II, p. 186.

simply her view that their representations of supernatural (in places terrifying and horrific) events could, without moderation, mislead and injure young minds. Putting it another way, her problem is not with imagination but rather with what is presented to it.

Thus, the recurring insinuation, that Trimmer's moral didacticism necessarily led to her blighting and blasting imagination, extrapolated from her supposedly uncomplicatedly negative view of fairy tales, is ill-founded. Fortunately, scholars have started to challenge this attitude and its origins at root, both with respect to the wider period and its connection with the evolution of children's literature. John Brewer reports that attempts to complicate the morality vs imagination binary were already being made by the end of the eighteenth century,[39] and Jeanette Sky suggests that blithely reasserting their opposition obscures important 'cultural-historical facts'.[40] On writing for the young, Mitzi Myers decries the 'Whiggish view of children's literary history as a progress toward pure amusement and imaginative fantasy' and attacks the thinking that supports it: '[h]opelessly defaced by injunctions to improvement, commentators on children's literature imply, the moral tale excites a merely antiquarian interest, is necessarily devoid of imaginative force'.[41]

Amidst this increasingly nuanced milieu, there is a good case for considering Trimmer as something other than the enemy of imagination and for finding instead in her writing a balance between instruction and amusement; between delivering appropriate (for her, Christian) content and allowing it to engage imagination suitably. Schemas and material which unbalanced or disregarded one or the other side of this equilibrium, she condemned as inadequate. As an example, we know from *Reflections upon the Education of Children in Charity Schools* (1792) that she regarded the didactic staple of catechetical rote as an unsuitable framework to scaffold the goodness towards which she believed children were disposed by infant baptism. She writes that children's want of spiritual understanding can 'in a great measure [. . .] be ascribed to the prevailing method of [. . .] learning by rote lessons greatly above their capacities, and suffaring

---

[39] John Brewer, *The Pleasures of the Imagination: English Culture in the Eighteenth Century* (Chicago: University of Chicago Press, 1997), pp. 105–6.

[40] Jeanette Sky, 'Myths of Innocence and Imagination: The Case of the Fairy Tale', *Literature and Theology*, 16.4 (2002), 363–76. Sky's point concerns the agency in adulthood that (usually female) eighteenth-century moral educationalists wanted to foster in the period's children.

[41] Myers, p. 31.

[*sic*] them to read without reflection'.[42] Preferably, children should be given instruction that they can comprehend and assimilate, and thus 'render their minds capable of receiving lasting impressions concerning things of the utmost importance to their present and future happiness'.[43] On this front, Trimmer felt that Anna Laetitia Barbauld was correct in introducing 'a species of writing, in the style of *familiar conversation*, which is certainly much better suited to the capacities of young children than any that preceded it'.[44] Conversation, as opposed to rote, better suited the capacity of child learners, and let adult educators provide clarification where necessary to facilitate understanding. Thus, Trimmer's pedagogic position with respect to Christianity evolves, as it does with respect to fairy tales: good material and teaching for children must judiciously combine the right Christian content with the right approach to imparting it. Again, imagination is not rejected. Rather, it must be given access to the right stuff.

* * *

Having laid this foundation, we can now turn our attention to *Fabulous Histories*, Trimmer's best-known book for children. *Fabulous Histories* tells the story of two families: the robin Redbreasts (two parents, four children) and the human Bensons (two parents, two children). The Redbreasts live in a wall in the Bensons' orchard, and the third-person narrative turns upon the relationship between the two families. The conversations of both are reported in English, though neither is comprehensible to the other, and each family occupies half the text, pretty much to the page. Across twenty-four chapters, the book accounts for the period between the Redbreasts building their nest and their children leaving it. The narrative is episodic, weaving back and forth between vignettes of each family before moving to more developed sections, like the Bensons visiting the Wilsons (local farmers) and the young Redbreasts spending more time with their parents away from their nest. The final, twenty-fifth chapter adds a 'sequel of the history',[45] which summarises the main characters' endings.

---

[42] Sarah Trimmer, *Reflections upon the Education of Children in Charity Schools [. . .]* (London: T. Longman and J. and F. Rivington, 1792), p. 34.
[43] Ibid.
[44] *Guardian*, I, pp. 63–4.
[45] *Fabulous*, p. 220.

From both *Fabulous Histories'* original 1786 subtitle – *Designed for the Instruction of Children, Respecting Their Treatment of Animals*[46] – and its internal Advertisement, the text declares its intention to establish sound behaviour in children towards animals:

> It certainly comes within the compass of *Christian Benevolence*, to shew compassion to the *Animal Creation*; and a good mind naturally inclines to do so. But as, through an erroneous education, or bad example, many children contract habits of *tormenting* inferior creatures, before they are conscious of giving them pain; or fall into the contrary fault of *immoderate tenderness* to them; it is hoped that an attempt to point out the line of conduct, which ought to regulate the actions of *human* beings, towards those over whom the SUPREME GOVERNOR hath given them dominion, will not be thought a useless undertaking.[47]

Herein lies a variation upon a theme of Trimmer's baptismal sacramentology.[48] Compassion for animals is a regular part of Christianity, and a good mind orientates itself accordingly. Nevertheless, good minds can go awry if they are not appropriately supported, potentially in this instance to become either cruel or mawkish. For Trimmer, the good Anglican, the solution to this challenge is a properly taught and well-exampled *via media*: 'the line of conduct' – implicitly a moderated midpoint – between two problematic extremes, which needs to be protected from 'erroneous education' and 'bad example'.

In this core modality – the use of animal paradigms to help define the place and behaviour of children within the adult world – Christine Kenyon-Jones finds a primary example of Trimmer's innovative creativity:[49] '[a]long with Kilner, Trimmer was [. . .] the first to use this winning formula for children's fiction'.[50] However, whilst Trimmer's subtitle and Advertisement help clarify her purpose for *Fabulous Histories*, they tell less of how she proposes to deliver it, towards

---

[46] Ibid., p. i.

[47] Ibid., pp. vii–viii.

[48] 'And so far from allowing that children are naturally disposed to wickedness, we are fully persuaded, that by the gift of the Holy Ghost bestowed upon them in Baptism, they are disposed to goodness; but the animal nature in children [. . .] gains strength whilst their reason is weak and imperfect, and if left to themselves, passion and appetite will certainly increase' (*Guardian*, II, p. 468).

[49] Kenyon-Jones' citations are not to *Fabulous Histories* but are instead to an undated illustrated edition of *The History of the Robins* (see notes 60 and 61), published in London by Griffith and Faran (Christine Kenyon-Jones, *Kindred Brutes: Animals in Romantic-Period Writing* (Aldershot: Ashgate, 2001), pp. 54, 213.

[50] Kenyon-Jones, p. 56.

Jonathan Padley

which Kenyon-Jones also gestures when she writes that *Fabulous Histories* 'alternates between twin animal themes: one, concerned with how children should be brought up to treat animals [. . .] and the other using a story of animal [. . .] life as a fable to teach children how to behave correctly in life in society at large'.[51] The second of these themes particularly is not obvious in Trimmer's prefatory material. However, strikingly, her introduction does describe *Fabulous Histories* as 'a series of FABLES',[52] a format she regarded as 'particularly pleasing to children', into the meaning of which they enter 'with surprising facility, when their teacher takes proper pains with them; and if they should not perceive the whole moral, they will at least be greatly amused with birds and beasts playing at *make believe*'.[53] From this last, especially, we may infer an important fact about the aim for *Fabulous Histories* which Trimmer describes in her Advertisement. By defining her *Fabulous Histories* as fables (which of course she also does implicitly in the first word of the book's title), Trimmer consciously pushes them into the realm of make-believe. She reports that the meaning and amusement which are simultaneously present in *Fabulous Histories* cannot be accessed without an appeal to imagination.

    A fuller reading of Trimmer's introduction confirms that this is the case, as *Fabulous Histories* is described as a book

> in which the sentiments and affections of a good Father and Mother, and a family of children, are *supposed* to be possessed by a *Nest of Redbreasts*; and others of the feathered race are, by the force of imagination, endued with the same faculties: but, before [children begin] to read these Histories, they [should be] taught to consider them, not as containing the real conversation of Birds, (for that it is impossible we should ever understand,) but as a series of FABLES, intended to convey moral instructions applicable to themselves, at the same time that they excite compassion and tenderness for those interesting and delightful creatures, on which such wanton cruelties are frequently inflicted, and recommend *universal Benevolence*.[54]

Here, the direct reference to imagination makes plain its import, with some caveats. Trimmer lays out that readers must willingly suspend

[51] Ibid.
[52] *Fabulous*, p. x.
[53] Sarah Trimmer, *An Essay on Christian Education* (London: F. C. and J. Rivington, and J. Hatchard, 1812), pp. 183–4.
[54] *Fabulous*, pp. x–xi.

their disbelief to accommodate her book's representation of the impossible: a family of robins, and other birds, having human sentience
and sharing human conversation. We already know that Trimmer
favoured Barbauld's novel use of 'familiar conversation'[55] as a pedagogic tool in writing for children, so her emphasis upon discourse is
readily explicable. More notable, however, is that it occurs between
robins and that its appreciation requires what the Coleridgean imagination would describe as a 'willing suspension of disbelief',[56] highlighting again that Trimmer's thinking and Romantic proponents of
imagination were not persistently at odds. True, this demand is made
acceptable because the stories are identified as fables, so will likely be
regulated to children by teachers or parents, and from which 'there
is very little danger of [children] taking up improper ideas'.[57] The
controlled hesitation between imagination and reality[58] is intended
both to stimulate the compassion for animals that is highlighted in
the Advertisement (by drawing animals nearer and making them
less other) and convey the wider social lessons that are hinted at
by Kenyon-Jones (which might otherwise be less engaging). Between
these two – compassion and social lessons – lies the goal of *Fabulous
Histories*: the inculcation of universal (Christian) benevolence.

Far from being imagination's enemy, Trimmer actively calls for
imaginative engagement in readings of *Fabulous Histories*. True, she
calls for this engagement to occur in a regulated way which emphasises that elements of her text are fable-pretend, but she nonetheless regards it as strategically essential. Since this is the case, one
might be forgiven for assuming that talking birds would be *Fabulous
Histories*' central characters. Throughout the story, the Redbreasts
provide an avian analogue to the Bensons, and demonstrate a
range of Trimmer-endorsed maxims like the importance of family, obedience to parents and contentment with one's lot. Mr and
Mrs Redbreast are even described at the end as 'the Hero and Heroine
of my tale'.[59] However, despite this and the introduction's momentous declaration that *Fabulous Histories*' speaking creatures require

---

[55] *Guardian*, I, pp. 63–4.
[56] Samuel Taylor Coleridge, *Biographia Literaria*, in *Samuel Taylor Coleridge*, ed.
by H. J. Jackson (Oxford: Oxford University Press, 1985), pp. 155–482 (p. 314).
[57] *Essay*, p. 183.
[58] *Fabulous Histories* often uses the ends of chapters to transition between the imaginative story (in which birds can speak) and the realistic story (in which they
cannot) to maintain the boundary between the two.
[59] *Fabulous*, p. 220.

imagination to be rightly understood, the history of the robins is by and large unremarkable.[60]

Before speaking to why this history's ordinariness is important, it is worth taking a moment to document it, in and of itself. At the start of *Fabulous Histories*, Mr and Mrs Redbreast establish their nest in the security of the Bensons' orchard. They hatch four children – Robin, Dicky, Flapsy and Pecksy[61] – and the development of these little ones thereafter dominates the movement of the family's narrative. The narrator is at pains to point out that the names given to the young-lings are merely 'for the sake of distinction',[62] since robins, of course, do not really have names(!). Of the four, Pecksy alone grows up to be the robin equivalent of a model citizen: '[a]ll the little Redbreasts, excepting Pecksy, in turn committed some fault or other [. . .] but she was of so amiable a disposition, that it was her constant study to act with propriety, and avoid giving offence'.[63] She achieves this ideal state by being a 'happy medium betwixt self-conceit and timidity'.[64] She is willing to apply herself as she learns to sing and fly,[65] but she is equally willing to cede to the wisdom and guidance of her parents. Her character is an exemplary *via media* and she is thus rewarded at the story's conclusion by living near to her parents and enjoying their friendship.[66] Dicky and Flapsy, by comparison, are more vacuous

---

[60] In the early nineteenth century, *The History of the Robins* was incorporated as a subtitle to *Fabulous Histories* and became an alternative title to abridged editions. Donelle Ruwe remarks that Trimmer refused to endorse this, 'for she wished to be clear that she was not writing history but rather was writing an imaginative fabrication' (Donelle Ruwe, 'Guarding the British Bible from Rousseau: Sarah Trimmer, William Godwin, and the Pedagogical Periodical', *Children's Literature*, 29 (2001), 1–17 (p. 8)). In addition, as has been hinted and as we shall see, the Redbreasts' story is not the narrative's focus, making *The History of the Robins* a misnomer.

[61] Some commentators excise Robin from this list and/or list Dicky with an alternative spelling: 'Dicky, Flapsy, and Pecksy, the three young robins' (David Perkins, *Romanticism and Animal Rights* (Cambridge: Cambridge University Press, 2003), p. 30), and 'Trimmer's young robins (Dicksy [*sic*], Pecksy, and Flapsy)' (Kenyon-Jones, p. 56). I have not seen the editions of *Fabulous Histories* – or *The History of the Robins*, in Kenyon-Jones' case (see note 49) – which are cited in these instances so cannot confirm whether these references are errata or authentic variants.

[62] *Fabulous*, p. 4.

[63] Ibid., p. 25.

[64] Ibid., p. 95.

[65] Ibid., pp. 14, 82.

[66] Ibid., p. 226.

and are devalued in *Fabulous Histories* because they are vain and timid – too unbalanced. Their giddiness and minor greed eventually lead to their being captured and incarcerated in an aviary, where they learn in time the estimable lesson of becoming 'reconciled [. . .] to their lot'.[67] Robin, finally, thinks too much of himself for being the nest's firstborn. He is also by turns a disdainful lying tell-tale[68] and quick to anger,[69] for which faults he pays often by being ostracised from his family. On the most telling of these occasions, Robin fails to accept his father's advice on flying and suffers a fall, injuring a wing.[70] He is subsequently subjected to a period of isolation (typical, by this point in the narrative) and becomes genuinely contrite about his pride and stubbornness. However, the damage to his wing proves permanent and, whilst he eventually settles to a measure of contentment, he ultimately becomes reliant upon the Bensons' charity.[71]

Again then, this is a humdrum story, which begs the question of why Trimmer laid such stress in her introduction on the need to engage imagination as the means to hear the Redbreasts' conversations and appreciate their family life. To answer, we must concentrate on what the Redbreasts' presence brings to *Fabulous Histories*' wider narrative and where else Trimmer cites imagination in her text. In terms of what the Redbreasts bring to *Fabulous Histories*, we may combine the words of two commentators to identify that the robins' key quality is to be 'particularly anthropomorphic'[72] participants in a 'frame story in the fable tradition'.[73] That which their story frames is the tale of Mr and Mrs Benson and their children, Harriet (eleven) and Frederick (six), in which Mr Benson figures but little. As to other references to the imagination in Trimmer's text, there is only one other usage after the introduction, when Mrs Benson and the children visit the home of Farmer Wilson.[74] Wilson is described as

---

[67] Ibid.
[68] Ibid., pp. 19ff.
[69] Ibid., p. 86.
[70] Ibid., pp. 90ff.
[71] Ibid., pp. 225–6.
[72] Heather Klemann, 'How to Think with Animals in Mary Wollstonecraft's *Original Stories* and *The Writings of Woman; or, Maria*', *The Lion and the Unicorn*, 39.1 (2015), 1–22 (p. 7).
[73] Moira Ferguson, *Animal Advocacy and Englishwomen, 1780–1900* (Ann Arbor: University of Michigan Press, 1998), p. 8.
[74] Beyond these two references to imagination, *Fabulous Histories* contains two further uses of imagination cognates. The first is in a commentary from Mrs Wilson on the harmlessness and gentleness of her animals, which she attributes to the

'a very worthy man, possessed of a great share of natural good sense and benevolence of heart'.[75] The fact that he is benevolent is a strong signal that he is an admirable character, borne out by the solicitude that he and his family show towards the animals with which they work. During this visit, imagination is referenced in a discussion between Mrs Wilson and Mrs Benson about cleanliness, in which both women agree that they would not unnecessarily destroy the webs of garden spiders or the nests of ants: 'I am of the opinion, said Mrs. Benson, that it would be a good way to accustom one's self, before one kills any thing, to change situations with it in imagination'.[76]

In a book which takes such trouble to institute what it regards as good practice with respect to imagination, Mrs Benson's usage of 'imagination' here is critical because it sets up a very particular relationship between the anthropomorphic robins in the text's frame story and the human protagonists whose story the robins' frames. Within such a setting, it is impossible to view animals as dull beasts over which humanity has exploitive dominion. Rather – as a result of the Redbreasts' clear, simple and crucially proximal analogy to a nuclear human family – animals are contextualised as potentially advanced creatures over which humanity has the momentous responsibility of careful stewardship. The frame story of the anthropomorphic Redbreasts, predicated as it is upon regulated (not overactive) imagination, leads to a degree of what we might now describe as empathy

---

kind treatment they receive. In this, she declares that 'it is difficult to persuade some people that there is no danger, for they are apt to imagine, that every loose horse they see will gallop over them, and that every creature with horns will gore and toss them' (*Fabulous*, p. 173). The second is in Mrs Redbreast's analysis of an overheard conversation between two partridges who are incarcerated in the aviary. The partridges' discourse reveals that they are determined to be content with their lot, particularly because they realise that their prison makes them and their potential family safe from the perils of the outside world. About them, Mrs Redbreast observes that 'would every one, like these Partridges, try to make the best of their condition, we should hear but few complaints; for there are much fewer *real* than *imaginary* misfortunes' (*Fabulous*, pp. 206–7). These usages, of the verb 'to imagine' and the adjective 'imaginary', both have negative connotations: the first, against persons who have no meaningful knowledge of animals so are overly sensible of danger from them where it does not necessarily exist; the second, against people who feel oppressed by misfortunes which are arguably insubstantial. These are clearly distinct from imagination itself and are rather examples, as we shall see, of what happens when imagination is misguided and/or overactive.

[75] Ibid., p. 145.
[76] Ibid., p. 159.

from humans to animals. Where such empathy exists, the ground-less and antipathetic killing of creatures with whom humanity shares God's world (and elements of personality, intangibly made manifest by imagination) is unconscionable. How can one kill a creature with whom one is explicitly asked to change places in imagination; with whom one is asked to empathise?

This underlying hypothetical touches a range of germane contemporary thinking. There is more than a whiff of Locke's insight into 'unnatural cruelty': that the habit 'of tormenting and killing [. . .] beasts [. . .] harden[s children's] minds even towards men'.[77] There is also consonance with Thomas McFarland's description of Coleridge's approach to imagination 'as a means of connecting poetic, philosophical, and theological interests[; . . . connecting] the inner world of "I am" with the outer world of "it is"'.[78] Perhaps most tellingly is the alignment with the opening of Adam Smith's *The Theory of Moral Sentiments*:

> As we have no immediate experience of what other men feel, we can form no idea of the manner in which they are affected, but by conceiving what we ourselves should feel in the like situation. Though our brother is upon the rack, as long as we ourselves are at our ease, our senses will never inform us of what he suffers [. . . I]t is by the imagination only that we can form any conception of what are his sensations [. . .] By the imagination we place ourselves in his situation.[79]

As Robert Sugden phrases it, 'this is empathy in the modern sense': '[t]hrough this act of imagination, the spectator is cognitively able to attribute particular feelings of pain to the other person'.[80] Of course, none of this is to imply that Trimmer would have been an out-and-out advocate of Locke, Coleridge or Smith. However, it does evidence coincidence between her thinking and elements of live cognate philosophies.

---

[77] John Locke, *Some Thoughts Concerning Education and Of the Conduct of the Understanding*, ed. by Ruth W. Grant and Nathan Tarcov (Indianapolis: Hackett Publishing Company, 1996), pp. 90–1.

[78] Thomas McFarland, *Originality and Imagination* (Baltimore: John Hopkins University Press, 1985), p. 95.

[79] Adam Smith, *The Theory of Moral Sentiments*, ed. by Knud Haakonssen (Cambridge: Cambridge University Press, 2002), pp. 11–12.

[80] Robert Sugden, 'Beyond Sympathy and Empathy: Adam Smith's Concept of Fellow-Feeling', *Economics and Philosophy*, 18 (2002), 63–87 (p. 71).

After this, we may agree that at the core of *Fabulous Histories'* representation of Christian benevolence is a controlled, unsentimental, modern-day empathy. Furthermore, it is upon the realisation of this empathy that the text's institution of a right relationship with imagination turns. An examination of *Fabulous Histories'* early interactions in the Benson household finds that such empathy is writ large on numerous occasions, often in relation to food (since hunger is a readily empathetic experience). It also reveals that, where Harriet is the proverbial Pecksy (caring, intelligent, rarely in need of correction, and attentive to her parents' wills), Frederick is still very much on the learning curve of young childhood. In the narrative's first encounter with the Bensons, Frederick wants a large slice of bread to feed the birds outside the parlour window.[81] Mrs Benson cuts a roll for him but cautions him not to give good loaf to the birds since there are poor children who want food, and questions if he would favour feeding birds over a hungry boy. Frederick subsequently resolves to ask the Bensons' staff to gather scraps from the bread-pan and tablecloths so that the birds may still be fed without giving them food which is fitter for humans. On another day, Frederick, having overslept, hastens to feed his supplicant birds, barges into the parlour and attempts to open the window without acknowledging Mrs Benson.[82] Mrs Benson chastises him, both for neglecting his filial duty to greet her (his parent, upon whom he depends) and for neglecting his benevolent duty towards the birds (his pensioners, who depend upon him). Later still, Frederick desires to catch the Redbreasts in order that he might feed them incessantly.[83] Mrs Benson rhetorically asks whether he does not 'recollect one of [his] acquaintance who, if an apple-pie, or any thing else that he calls nice, is set before him, will eat till he makes himself sick? Frederick looked ashamed, being conscious that he was too much inclined to indulge in his love of delicacies'.[84] All these food-based examples see Mrs Benson nurturing Frederick's empathy: teaching him neither to indulge animals (or himself) nor to prioritise animals over humans, but still to treat animals with kindness and consider his dependents, especially since he is himself a dependent. À la Smith, Mrs Benson's strategy is to encourage Frederick to change situations in imagination with the (potentially) wronged

---

[81] *Fabulous*, p. 5.
[82] Ibid., p. 16.
[83] Ibid., p. 30.
[84] Ibid.

party, after the manner of her forthcoming conversation with Mrs Wilson.

Further lessons with food as a common denominator concern the practice of caging animals. At one point, Frederick does not listen to Mrs Benson (a bad sign, to ignore his parent) and pays attention instead to a butterfly that he wants to catch.[85] Again, his mother calls him to empathy: '[s]hould you like, Frederick, said she, [. . .] to have any body lay hold on you violently, scratch you all over, then offer you something to eat which is very disagreeable, and perhaps poisonous, and then shut you up in a little dark room?'[86] The question of confinement returns in similar terms as Mrs Benson queries Frederick's desire to cage the Redbreasts: '[a]nd would you really confine these sweet creatures in a cage, Frederick, merely to have the pleasure of looking at them? Should you like to be always shut in a little room, and think it sufficient if you were supplied with victuals and drink?'[87] As before, Mrs Benson engages Frederick's imagination. How would Frederick feel about being captured? Does he want to be shut up? If not, he should not seek to capture and shut up animals,[88] especially not in a book where animals are so thoroughly anthropomorphised in pages nearby.

Through Mrs Benson's instruction then, Frederick is taught neither to treat animals unkindly nor to set them on a pedestal above humans. Thinking back to *Fabulous Histories*' Advertisement, the balance between these two behaviours is set out as the *via media* to Christian benevolence: the middle way between the excesses of maliciousness and sentiment. Christian benevolence falls between a paucity and a surfeit of empathy, both of which extremes result from

[85] Ibid., pp. 8–9.
[86] Ibid., pp. 9–10.
[87] Ibid., p. 31.
[88] Mrs Benson cites keeping caged canaries as an exception to this rule, since canaries originate from countries with warmer climates and would die if not looked after (*Fabulous*, p. 32). This speaks to a wider theme in *Fabulous Histories* of collaborating with others and treating foreigners and people or creatures who look different with kindness and respect: the Redbreasts have good relations with other birds; Mrs Benson warns her children against unkindness to those whose dress and speech seems unusual to them; the Redbreast nestlings are told not to fear Joe the gardener just because his form is alien; and Mrs Redbreast speaks positively of the many foreign birds she has met (*Fabulous*, pp. 2–3, 33, 36ff., 83). Moira Ferguson interprets *Fabulous Histories* oppositely in this area, arguing that it 'upholds xenophobia and insular practices whilst subtly condoning colonial acts' (Ferguson, p. 26). This interpretative disparity could benefit from further study.

inappropriately engaged imagination. *Fabulous Histories* exemplifies these respectively in the persons of Edward Jenkins (the eldest child of a local family) and Mrs Addis (a widow with two children), with some careful preparation before either is introduced. It is therefore to consideration of these two characters that we will now turn.

Fabulous Histories introduces the problem of cruelty askance, partly through the butterfly episode but moreover after Mrs Benson's conversation with Frederick about his idea to cage the Redbreasts. As an alternative, Frederick (charitably) suggests that he might find the Redbreasts' nest and place it in a tree nearer the Bensons' home, to make it easier for him to feed the old robins and their hatchlings.[89] Mrs Benson commends his rationale but tells him that adult birds sometimes desert nests when they are moved. She continues that people who take birds' nests 'are quite insensible of the distresses they occasion',[90] though it is not clear whether she thinks such people are motivated by good or ill. Three chapters later, the narrative apparently abandons such obliqueness as Mr Redbreast recalls – in the narrative's only true history of the robins (note 60) – how his former nest of younglings was taken by three boys, causing his former mate to die of a broken heart.[91] Mr Redbreast's story imaginatively intensifies Mrs Benson's teaching because it makes the reader all too sensible of the distresses that may be occasioned by those who take birds' nests. Intriguingly, despite Mr Redbreast's perception that the boys who took his nest were 'barbarians' who cruelly exulted in their acquisition,[92] the narrative – like Mrs Benson earlier – does not clarify whether they intended harm, since they attempted to feed the young[93] and did not destroy the nest (in the narrative, at any rate). Whatever their motivation, however, they were incompetent to look after the nest, giving unsuitable food and failing to keep the nestlings warm.[94] There is a salutary warning here to children like Frederick to avoid callousness, and a subtle reinforcement of the more nuanced idea that successful benevolence requires more than mere intention. After these recollections, Mr Redbreast stoically encourages his new family: '[e]very bird does not meet with [. . .] cruel children'.[95] He also,

[89] *Fabulous*, pp. 33–4.
[90] Ibid., p. 34.
[91] Ibid., pp. 50ff.
[92] Ibid., p. 51.
[93] Ibid.
[94] Ibid., pp. 51–2.
[95] Ibid., p. 54.

perhaps to reinforce the lesson that one should not act on incomplete information, takes some responsibility for his aborted family, admitting that his youthful inexperience led him to build his stolen nest in an 'exposed situation'.[96] Finally, he (not unkindly) lays a portion of blame at the door of his parents, 'who were young and inexperienced themselves, and did not give [him] good advice'.[97]

This episode's imaginative engagement and resultant empathy are subtle. Irrespective of the boys' indeterminate intentions, their cruelty is reprehensible. However, so too is inadequate parenting and its corollaries: the boys are at least ill-informed, and Mr Redbreast did not have access to the sort of high-quality advice and experience that might have helped prevent the boys from stealing his nest. Enter Edward Jenkins and his sister Lucy, the children of a local family. Edward is a 'robust rude boy, turned of eleven',[98] Harriet's age, so old enough to know better than the narrative's subsequent account of his behaviour. The use of 'robust' is pointed too; it earlier described Robin,[99] insinuating that Edward shares Robin's wilful defects.[100] Trimmer leaves little doubt about his character. He takes nests 'to toss the young birds about'.[101] He blows out eggs, of which he has over a hundred, and threads the shells for Lucy to keep.[102] He is willing to tie a cat and a dog together for sport.[103] He throws cats off a roof, encourages the killing of a dog, flings a cockerel around until it dies, sets two other cocks to fighting, plucks feathers from a live chicken, drowns a litter of puppies in the sight of their mother and pulls the legs off flies.[104] His interactions with animals are a litany of cruelty. He is a character without imaginative empathy.

To make matters worse, Edward's father explicitly endorses his behaviour. When Mrs Benson attempts to remonstrate with Mr Jenkins about his son's conduct, Mr Jenkins 'applauded him as a lad of life and spirit'.[105] The irony of crediting a boy who blows

---

[96] Ibid., p. 50.

[97] Ibid., p. 54.

[98] Ibid., p. 55.

[99] Ibid., p. 28.

[100] Similarly, the adjective 'thoughtless' describes both Frederick and Edward (*Fabulous*, pp. 41, 66), hinting that Frederick should be careful that his thoughtlessness does not lead him to behaviour like Edward's.

[101] Ibid., p. 56.

[102] Ibid., pp. 56–7.

[103] Ibid., p. 61.

[104] Ibid., pp. 61–3, 65.

[105] Ibid., p. 65.

eggs and kills animals as 'a lad of life' is far from lost on Trimmer's narrative, as Mr Jenkins validates the Advertisement's assertion that children's misconduct stems from 'an erroneous education, or bad example'.[106] Both father and son totally lack the empathy which defines Trimmer's favoured characters: they are unable or unwilling to change places with animals in imagination, even in a story which is framed by anthropomorphic animals and has just recorded the history of Mr Redbreast's earlier nest as a witness to the impact of human cruelty. Lucy, comparatively, is less far gone. Whilst her conduct is – like Edward's – born from ignorance, she is less actively destructive and more laissez-faire: 'is there any harm in taking birds eggs? said Miss Jenkins; I never before heard there was'.[107] Unlike Edward, Lucy is transformed into a sympathetic figure when the narrative notes that 'she had no kind mamma to give her instruction', and Mrs Benson corrects Lucy's unempathetic misconception of birds 'as playthings, without sense or feeling'.[108] Lucy is permitted a degree of restoration as she gives the Bensons some nests that Edward recently brought her,[109] and she ends *Fabulous Histories* as a new benefactor to the Redbreasts.[110] Not so Edward, whose torturing progresses from animals to younger children at school, and who ultimately dies – with poetic justice – after he is thrown from a horse that he has mistreated.[111]

Edward and Lucy's behaviour results from their lack of imagination. With equal clarity, Trimmer attributes this to their poor parenting, though Edward in his death assumes full responsibility for the sins of his father, whereas Lucy is afforded the correction

[106] Ibid., p. vii.

[107] Ibid., p. 57.

[108] Ibid., p. 59.

[109] Ibid., pp. 74ff. Nevertheless, most of the nestlings perish: one is overfed and chokes to death (ibid., p. 119), and another falls out of a window and is mauled by a dog (ibid., p. 133). These are cautionary reminders that it is hard to look after animals away from their natural habitats, even when one genuinely wishes to do so.

[110] Ibid., p. 225.

[111] Ibid., pp. 221–2. David Perkins cites Edward as an example of a cruel child in children's literature whose viciousness towards animals progresses to viciousness towards people and leads to him being universally despised, in implied contrast with William Hogarth's Tom Nero in *The Four Stages of Cruelty* (1751), whose comparable progress leads him to the gallows (Perkins, p. 22). Perkins' contrast is strange because Edward ends *Fabulous Histories* just as dead as Tom, unless he (Perkins) was working from an alternative version of *Fabulous Histories* in which Edward reached a different conclusion (see note 61).

of Mrs Benson. At the other end of the spectrum from the Jenkins' cruelty is over-imagination, personified in Mrs Addis. As with the Jenkins family, Mrs Addis' introduction is prepared partly by the Advertisement and partly by a narrative preamble, a conversation between Mrs Benson, Mrs Franks and an unnamed gentleman in the Bensons' drawing room.[112] This discourse roams widely over the essence of animal nature, discussing mechanics, intellect and theology. Mrs Benson – sagacity itself – argues that God has placed animals within human stewardship but beneath human rank, so they should be treated neither brutally nor with excessive elevation (again, recalling the Advertisement). This last, she concludes, is 'really sinful',[113] and in so doing sets up the visit which she and Harriet make four chapters hence to Mrs Addis' home.

Mrs Addis' sinfulness is established from the very first sentence about her home, in which Harriet notices a 'very disagreeable smell' and is surprised to see several caged birds.[114] Mrs Addis is a widow who, like the Bensons and Jenkins, has two children: Charles (twelve) and Augusta (seven). However, the narrative focuses on Mrs Addis' feted animals, not her offspring. Charles is not even present at the family home, and Mrs Addis summarily writes him off without even mentioning his name: 'I am obliged to keep the boy almost continually at school, for he is so cruel to my *dear little precious creatures*'.[115] Mrs Addis' juxtaposition of an impersonal reference to her son with a fawning description of her animals is stark, as is her reference to Charles' cruelty: an unusual trait to find in the child of a woman who is ostensibly an animal-lover. Augusta appears soon afterwards but in a bedraggled condition: she is variously rendered as 'a little simpleton', 'sickly, dirty, and ragged' and 'a very vulgar figure'.[116] She too is quickly dismissed 'without so much as one tender kiss or kind expression',[117] but not before Mrs Addis nearly beats her for manhandling a kitten. Like the Jenkins siblings, the Addis children are vindictive to animals, and like the Jenkins, they are so because of their parenting. However, their conditioning is the result of parental neglect that has arisen from their mother's over-imaginative

---

[112] *Fabulous*, pp. 66ff.

[113] Ibid., p. 70.

[114] Ibid., p. 101. In comparison with Mrs Benson's caged canaries (see note 88), it is implied that Mrs Addis' caged animals are kept for her benefit rather than theirs.

[115] Ibid., p. 102.

[116] Ibid., pp. 103–4.

[117] Ibid., p. 105.

relationship with animals, rather than their father's lack of any such relationship, as in the case of the Jenkins.

In comparison with her children, Mrs Addis' animals are utterly indulged, particularly her monkey, who, upon breaking his restraining chain, is greeted thus by his owner:

> O my dear sweet pug, [. . .] are you come to see us? Pray shew how like a gentleman you can behave; just as she had said this, he leaped upon the tea-table, and took cup after cup, and threw them on the ground, till he broke half the set [. . .] till Mrs. Addis, though vastly diverted with his wit, was obliged to have him caught and confined.[118]

Mrs Addis' impropriety is writ large: her unchecked amiability with animals is as grotesque as Edward's physical cruelty is diabolic. Moreover, in the context of a book about anthropomorphic birds which privileges humanity's stewardship of animals, her behaviour is shown to be disadvantageous not only to her children but also her creatures. As Mrs Benson says to Harriet:

> Mrs. Addis [. . .] has absolutely transferred the affection she ought to feel for her child, to creatures who would really be much happier without it. As for puss who lies in the cradle in all her splendor [. . .] she would pass her time pleasanter in a basket of clean straw, placed in a situation where she could occasionally amuse herself with catching mice. The lap-dop [*sic*] is, I am sure, a miserable object, full of diseases, the consequences of a luxurious living. How enviable is the lot of a spaniel that is at liberty, to be the companion of his master's walks [. . .]![119]

And so Mrs Benson reimagines Mrs Addis' animals into more fitting circumstances. By doing so, she gathers weight to the sense of dissoluteness that results from Mrs Addis' transference of her affection away from her children. Mrs Benson's analysis is underscored when Mrs Addis forgets to treat her guests with the appointed social niceties when her parrot falls ill,[120] and even more when it becomes apparent that she has abandoned poor people who live nearby in favour of maintaining her animals in luxury.[121] Mrs Addis' over-imaginative outlook unbalances her and her children with respect to the created order – Charles grows up to be an animal-hater and Augusta an

---

[118] Ibid.
[119] Ibid., pp. 107–8.
[120] Ibid., pp. 108–10.
[121] Ibid., pp. 110ff.

animal-fearer[122] – and it makes her forego her most basic duty of charity. Like Mr Jenkins, she is demonstrably a botched parent and no route to Christian benevolence, and it is telling that she ends 'her days with sorrow and regret',[123] no longer amused by animals, aware of her errors, and estranged from her children. Her lonely demise is put down to her own inadequate childhood, in which her natural tenderness was improperly regulated.

*   *   *

As we can see then, *Fabulous Histories* testifies that Sarah Trimmer was no enemy of imagination. Certainly, she thought that imagination and access to materials that engage it must be regulated: as she writes in *The Guardian*, of content for children in general, '[t]he utmost circumspection is [. . .] requisite in making a proper selection'.[124] Nonetheless, to facilitate *Fabulous Histories'* articulation of Christian benevolence and the corollary that animals should receive stewardship not exploitation, imaginative engagement is specifically invoked and functionally essential. In chapter XVIII, Mrs Wilson says to Mrs Benson that she 'often wished that poor dumb creatures had somebody to speak for them'.[125] In *Fabulous Histories* they do. Mrs Benson speaks for them. The narrator speaks for them. They even speak for themselves through the anthropomorphic Redbreasts, assuming that imagination is engaged to allow their voices – and the text's thereby amplified teaching – to be heard. By speaking and being spoken for, the animals of *Fabulous Histories* illuminate through imagination the *via media* to Trimmer's desired Christian benevolence, negotiating a midpoint between the extremities of cruelty and sentiment that Trimmer felt did disservice to both humans and animals alike. They give voices to the voiceless, demanding that readers change places in imagination with those who might otherwise be ignored: the poor; the lowly; even, as in the case of animals, those who are quite literally unable to speak.

In the *Oxford Dictionary of National Biography*, Schnorrenberg's entry on Trimmer concludes that Trimmer's 'most important contribution was in showing how educational material could be made appealing to children'. The evidence is that in *Fabulous Histories*,

---

[122] Ibid., pp. 223–4.
[123] Ibid., p. 223.
[124] *Guardian*, II, p. 407.
[125] *Fabulous*, p. 160.

this appeal was made precisely through a regulated engagement with imagination. Thus, *Fabulous Histories* supports the arguments of Brewer, Sky, Myers et al., that it is spurious both to regard morality and imagination as necessarily odds with each another, and to assert that moral tales are inevitably devoid of imaginative force. Via *Fabulous Histories*, I find in Trimmer a writer who was actively and creatively engaged with her literary and philosophical peers, and for whom there remains a case to close the gap between her historic and modern consequence, that she may hereafter be more than just a well-known name. Certainly, the persistence of derogatory received-wisdom accounts of her person and work within conversations about women's literary education will not do. This case study of *Fabulous Histories* moves on the discussion and hopefully may become part of a wider process of reimagining Sarah Trimmer.

Works Cited

Primary

Coleridge, Samuel Taylor, *Biographia Literaria*, in *Samuel Taylor Coleridge*, ed. by H. J. Jackson (Oxford: Oxford University Press, 1985), pp. 155–482

Lamb, Charles, 'Letter 101: Charles Lamb to S. T. Coleridge', in *The Letters of Charles and Mary Lamb 1796–1820*, ed. by E. V. Lucas (London: Methuen, 1912), pp. 259–62

Locke, John, *Some Thoughts Concerning Education and Of the Conduct of the Understanding*, ed. by Ruth W. Grant and Nathan Tarcov (Indianapolis: Hackett Publishing Company, 1996)

Smith, Adam, *The Theory of Moral Sentiments*, ed. by Knud Haakonssen (Cambridge: Cambridge University Press, 2002)

Trimmer, Sarah, *An Essay on Christian Education* (London: F. C. and J. Rivington, and J. Hatchard, 1812)

——. *Fabulous Histories: Designed for the Instruction of Children, Respecting Their Treatment of Animals* (London: T. Longman, G. G. J. and J. Robinson, and J. Johnson, 1786)

——. *The Guardian of Education, A Periodical Work [. . .]*, vol. 1 (London: J. Hatchard, 1802)

——. *The Guardian of Education, A Periodical Work [. . .]*, vol. 2 (London: J. Hatchard, 1803)

——. *The Guardian of Education, A Periodical Work [. . .]*, vol. 3 (London: F. C. and J. Rivington, and J. Hatchard, 1804)

——. *The Guardian of Education, A Periodical Work [. . .]*, vol. 4 (London: F. C. and J. Rivington, and J. Hatchard, 1805)

——. *Reflections upon the Education of Children in Charity Schools [. . .]* (London: T. Longman and J. and F. Rivington, 1792)

Secondary

Andrews, Robert M., 'Women of the Seventeenth and Eighteenth-Century High Church Tradition: A Biographical and Historiographical Exploration of a Forgotten Phenomenon in Anglican History', *Anglican and Episcopal History*, 84.1 (2015), 49–64

Backscheider, Paula R., 'Women Writers and the Chains of Identification', *Studies in the Novel*, 19.3 (1987), 245–62

Brewer, John, *The Pleasures of the Imagination: English Culture in the Eighteenth Century* (Chicago: University of Chicago Press, 1997)

Carpenter, Humphrey, *Secret Gardens: A Study of the Golden Age of Children's Literature* (Boston: Houghton Mifflin, 1985)

Engell, James, *The Creative Imagination: Enlightenment to Romanticism* (Cambridge: Harvard University Press, 1981)

Ferguson, Moira, *Animal Advocacy and Englishwomen, 1780–1900* (Ann Arbor: University of Michigan Press, 1998)

Grenby, M. O., 'Adults Only? Children and Children's Books in British Circulating Libraries, 1748–1848', *Book History*, 5 (2002), 19–38

——. '"A Conservative Woman Doing Radical Things": Sarah Trimmer and *The Guardian of Education*', in *Culturing the Child, 1690–1914: Essays in Memory of Mitzi Myers*, ed. by Donelle Ruwe (Lanham, MD: Scarecrow Press, 2005), pp. 137–61

——. 'Introduction', in *The Guardian of Education: A Periodical Work, by Sarah Trimmer*, vol. 1 (Bristol and Tokyo: Thoemmes Press and Edition Synapse, 2002), pp. v–xli

Harvey Darton, Frederick Joseph, *Children's Books in England: Five Centuries of Social Life* (Cambridge: Cambridge University Press, 2011)

Heath, Pauline, 'Mrs Trimmer's Plan of Appropriate Instruction: A Revisionist View of Her Textbooks', *History of Education*, 32.4 (2003), 385–400

——. *The Works of Mrs. Trimmer (1741–1810)* (Saarbrücken: LAP LAMBERT Academic Publishing, 2010)

Kenyon-Jones, Christine, *Kindred Brutes: Animals in Romantic-Period Writing* (Aldershot: Ashgate, 2001)

Klemann, Heather, 'How to Think with Animals in Mary Wollstonecraft's *Original Stories* and *The Writings of Woman; or, Maria*', *The Lion and the Unicorn*, 39.1 (2015), 1–22

McFarland, Thomas, *Originality and Imagination* (Baltimore: John Hopkins University Press, 1985)

Myers, Mitzi, 'Impeccable Governesses, Rational Dames, and Moral Mothers: Mary Wollstonecraft and the Female Tradition in Georgian Children's Books', *Children's Literature*, 14 (1986), 31–59

Perkins, David, *Romanticism and Animal Rights* (Cambridge: Cambridge University Press, 2003)

Pickering, Samuel F., *John Locke and Children's Books in Eighteenth-Century England* (Knoxville: University of Tennessee Press, 1981)

Richardson, Alan, *Literature, Education, and Romanticism: Reading as Social Practice, 1780–1832* (Cambridge: Cambridge University Press, 1994)

Ruwe, Donelle, 'Guarding the British Bible from Rousseau: Sarah Trimmer, William Godwin, and the Pedagogical Periodical', *Children's Literature*, 29 (2001), 1–17

Schnorrenberg, Barbara Brandon, 'Trimmer [née Kirby], Sarah (1741–1810)', in *Oxford Dictionary of National Biography* (2004), online edition <https://doi.org/10.1093/ref:odnb/27740> [accessed 1 March 2022]

Sky, Jeanette, 'Myths of Innocence and Imagination: The Case of the Fairy Tale', *Literature and Theology*, 16.4 (2002), 363–76

Sugden, Robert, 'Beyond Sympathy and Empathy: Adam Smith's Concept of Fellow-Feeling', *Economics and Philosophy*, 18 (2002), 63–87

Tucker, Nicholas, 'Fairy Tales and Their Early Opponents: In Defence of Mrs Trimmer', in *Opening the Nursery Door: Reading, Writing and Childhood 1600–1900*, ed. by Mary Hilton, Morag Styles and Victor Watson (London: Routledge, 1997), pp. 104–16

Weir, Heather, 'Trimmer, Sarah (1741–1810)', in *Handbook of Women Biblical Interpreters: A Historical and Biographical Guide*, ed. by Marion Ann Taylor and Agnes Choi (Grand Rapids: Baker Academic, 2012), pp. 505–9

Wordsworth, Jonathan, 'The Romantic Imagination', in *A Companion to Romanticism*, ed. by Duncan Wu (Oxford: Blackwell), pp. 525–33

A Literary Life: A Transatlantic Tale of Vivacity, Rousing Curiosity and Engaging Affection

Lissa Paul

A literary life is a happy life, as Eliza Fenwick (1766–1840) makes clear in the title of her 1805 novel for children, *Visits to the Juvenile Library: Knowledge Proved to be the Source of Happiness*.[1] There on the shelves of the actual early nineteenth-century children's bookshop to which she alludes in the title – Tabart's Juvenile Library on New Bond Street in London – both the knowledge and the happiness temptingly featured in the story are available for purchase. But it is not quite that easy: to be literate, it is first necessary to become literate. And therein lies the plot.

Fenwick's novel centres on enticing five recently orphaned reluctant child readers into the rewards of a literary life. As they had been raised in Jamaica, the spoiled (White) children of plantation-owners, they had been accustomed to having an enslaved person attending to every whim. Because their early schooling had been at the hands of a sadistic 'master', they had learned to equate education in general and reading in particular with punishments typically inflicted on the enslaved. That is why, when they arrive in London, with their (enslaved) nanny, Nora, to the guardianship of 'the good Mrs. Clifford', as she is always called in the story, they want nothing to do with literate life. They are suffering, as the title of the first chapter clearly states, from 'The Mistakes of Ignorance', their misery stemming from the fact that they had never learned to be 'excited to activity of mind or body' (p. 7). In diagnosing their ills, the good Mrs Clifford notes that it is equally difficult 'to rouse the curiosity of these children or to engage their affections' (p. 5). Her challenge is to disabuse them of the

[1] Eliza Fenwick, *Visits to the Juvenile Library: or, Knowledge Proved to be the Source of Happiness* (London: Tabart, 1805), hereafter cited parenthetically in the text.

idea that education is a form of punishment defined by 'the terrors of rods, canes, dark closets and stocks' (to use Nora's terms), and to coax them into recognising being literate as a good thing (p. 15). In the novel, all ends happily as the children, and their enslaved nanny Nora, discover that becoming literate is physically, intellectually and emotionally rewarding.

Teaching people to become literate has of course long been at the heart of the educational project, though the word 'literacy' itself did not come into being until 1883 (*OED*). It would have been alien to Eliza Fenwick and her late-Enlightenment contemporaries. The reason for beginning this essay with *Visits to the Juvenile Library* is that it is both an account of the maternal pedagogical practices and the works of literature that supported those practices; it is defined, as Mary Wollstonecraft eloquently says, by 'a cultivated understanding, and an affectionate heart', which as she says, 'will never want starched rules of decorum'.[2]

For Fenwick, pedagogical and philosophical faith in the liberating qualities of a literate life informed her as writer, mother and teacher. She makes the case in her polemical 1795 novel *Secresy* (unmarked as being for children, though it is at least partly about the dangers of restricting access to education), and in the children's books she wrote and edited in the early 1800s for the publishing houses of Benjamin Tabart (1767–1833), his mentor, Richard Phillips (1767–1840), and later for William Godwin (1756–1836) and his second wife, Mary Jane Clairmont Godwin (1768–1841). What makes Fenwick's perspective of value in this volume of essays on women's literary education is that her views changed as she changed from British author early in her career to colonial educator in Barbados and North America. Fenwick transported the late-Enlightenment principles of the literary education that had shaped her early writing life in Britain to her teaching life, adjusting and redefining those principles as she moved across the Atlantic.

Fenwick's articulations of mothering and educating had been deeply informed by Wollstonecraft. In the mid-1790s, both were published authors, as well as young mothers and friends. The characteristics of the mother/teacher they embodied and promoted in their work are defined by Mitzi Myers in her inspiriting 1986

---

[2] Mary Wollstonecraft, *A Vindication of the Rights of Woman, with Strictures on Political and Moral Subjects* [1792], in *The Works of Mary Wollstonecraft*, ed. by Janet Todd and Marilyn Butler, vol. 5 (London: Pickering, 1989), p. 167 (ch. 5, section iii).

essay on Georgian children's books and the literary women who authored them. With reference to the character of Mrs Mason from Wollstonecraft's *Original Stories from Real Life* (1791), Myers demonstrates how 'qualities associated with women – nurturing, empathy, the habit of thinking in terms of human relationships' – define a maternal pedagogical style of the age.[3] 'Human relationships', as she says, are the key. The point that Myers makes in the essay is that unlike the authoritarian (patriarchal) approaches to pedagogy – emphasising what is being taught (curriculum) and how (direct instruction) – maternal teachers build their instructional practices on the cultivation of 'affection' and its cognates, including sensibility, curiosity and vivacity.

For twenty-first-century readers, the difference between feminine and masculine approaches to literary instruction might be best framed as the contrast between what is now called a 'child-centred' approach (emphasising the relationship between student and teacher) and a curriculum-driven approach (emphasising subjects being taught). For Fenwick, as demonstrated in *Visits to the Juvenile Library*, it was the difference between the authoritarian (essentially masculine) punishment model of education that had first turned the children into reluctant readers, and the 'nurturing' qualities that informed the good Mrs Clifford's programme of gradually enticing the children into the rewards of reading. At the heart of the difference between a curriculum-driven masculine authoritarian (you-must-do-this) approach and a maternal approach is the recognition that the child who wants to do something is more likely to do it than the child threatened with punishment. The key figure in the successful transactional relationship between the learner and the material to be learned is the maternal teacher whose instructional impulses are informed by affection.

'Affect', as Louise Joy explains, is 'the body thinking', and it is 'relational': it 'is not individual but transindividual; it is fundamentally social, shaped as much by what it interacts with as by the subject itself'.[4] Both ideas (affection and human relationships) permeate *Visits to the Juvenile Library* as they do more broadly the works and

---

[3] Mitzi Myers, 'Impeccable Governesses, Rational Dames and Moral Mothers: Mary Wollstonecraft and the Female Tradition in Georgian Children's Books', *Children's Literature*, 14 (1986), 31–59 (p. 43).

[4] Louise Joy, 'Affect', in *Keywords for Children's Literature*, ed. by Philip Nel, Lissa Paul and Nina Christensen, 2nd edn (New York: New York University Press, 2021), p. 7.

lives of the literary women of the period. Most famously, the relational quality of the educational project is captured by Ellenor Fenn in *Cobwebs to Catch Flies* (1783). It is in her introductory address to the child readers of her stories (it follows the address to their mothers) that she sets out her agenda:

> My Dears,
>   Do not imagine that, like a great spider, I will give you a hard gripe, and infuse venom to blow you up. No; I mean to catch you gently, whisper in your ear,
> *Be good, and you will be beloved;*
> *Be good, and you will be happy.*[5]

Like Wollstonecraft in *A Vindication* in 1792 or Fenwick in *Visits to the Juvenile Library* in 1805, Fenn speaks to the mantra of the maternal teachers of the age: to entice, or to use a term made famous by John Locke (1632–1704), 'cozen' children into their letters.[6] What is distinctive is that for Enlightenment mothers, the instructional project was already 'interactive', as Jill Shefrin and Mary Hilton note in their introduction to *Educating the Child in Enlightenment Britain*.[7] The contrast is with the top-down authoritarian approaches, the patronising, patriarchal methods of, for example, Jean-Jacques Rousseau in *Émile* (1762) or Thomas Day (1748–89) in *Sanford and Merton* (1783–9).

The philosophical heart of the entwined ideas of affect and human relationships in education likely began to quicken through David

---

[5] Mrs Lovechild [Ellenor Fenn], *Cobwebs to Catch Flies: or, Dialogues in Short Sentences, Adapted to Children from the Age of Three to Eight Years. In two volumes* [1783] (London: John Marshall, 1800), p. xi.

[6] John Locke, *Some Thoughts Concerning Education* [1693], in *Some Thoughts Concerning Education and Of the Conduct of the Understanding*, ed. by Ruth W. Grant and Nathan Tarcov (Indianapolis: Hackett, 1996), p. 114 (section 149). Although Locke gets credit for 'cozening' children into reading, he was likely reporting well-established maternal teaching practices. See Julia Briggs, '"Delightful Task!": Women, Children and Reading in the Mid-Eighteenth Century', in *Culturing the Child 1690–1914*, ed. by Donelle Ruwe (Lanham, MD: Scarecrow, 2005), pp. 67–82 (p. 72).

[7] The discussion on 'interactive education' is in response to an argument in *The Archaeology of Childhood: Children, Gender and Material Culture* (Walnut Creek, CA: AltaMira Press, 2005), p. 24, by Jane Eva Baxter on a change in emphasis from a (masculine) authoritarian instructive focus to an implicitly feminine model that is interactive and dialogic, *Educating the Child in Enlightenment Britain: Beliefs, Cultures, Practices*, ed. by Mary Hilton and Jill Shefrin (Farnham: Ashgate, 2009), pp. 6–7.

Hume (1711–76), in both his *Treatise of Human Nature* (1739–40) and *An Enquiry Concerning the Principles of Morals* (1748), as he links discussions of vivacity with imagination and the public good, all aimed at promoting a peaceful, just and good society. The 'Of Benevolence' chapter of the *Enquiry* begins when he asks rhetorically if it is 'a superfluous Task to prove, that the benevolent or softer Affections are VIRTUOUS'. He then lists the attributes that are essentially the ones 'the good Mrs. Clifford' attempts to cultivate in the lethargic and unhappy children in her care, including 'Esteem, Approbation, and Good-will of Mankind'. Hume ends by naming 'the Epithets' associated with those who achieve those qualities: '*sociable, grateful, friendly, generous,* [and] *beneficent*'.[8]

In *Visits to the Juvenile Library*, the lethargy and reluctance of the children to be interested in anything is attributable to their lack of affection, curiosity and 'vivacity' (a term Hume uses frequently). Their gradual acquisition of those attributes is calibrated by their degrees of literary acquisition. As the children – and ultimately their enslaved nanny, Nora – are gradually won over by the delights of the books at Tabart's Juvenile Library, they are liberated by literacy. As they improve, they are described in terms that distinctly echo Hume: 'the daily improvement of their manners, their tempers and understandings, not only won the entire affection of Mrs. Clifford, but the esteem and approbation of all her friends' (*Visits*, p. 92).

Although she does not say so in the story, at least four of the books that brought about such miraculous transformations in the children are by Fenwick herself – *Songs for the Nursery* (1805), *Presents for Good Girls* (1804), *The Life of Carlo* (1804) and *Mary and Her Cat* (1804), and there is a strong possibility that Fenwick is the anonymous author of a few more.[9] Besides her own work,

---

[8] David Hume, *An Enquiry Concerning the Principles of Morals* (London: A. Millar, 1751), pp. 22–3.

[9] Given that all four of the books as well as *Visits to the Juvenile Library* were published over a two-year period (1804 and 1805), Fenwick was obviously writing and publishing at breakneck speed. Although she can clearly be identified as the author of both *Presents for Good Girls* and *Mary and Her Cat*, the confirmation of the fact that she collected and edited the verses for *Songs for the Nursery* comes in a roundabout way; Charles Lamb links Fenwick to a unique contribution by Dorothy Wordsworth. See Lissa Paul, *Eliza Fenwick: Early Modern Feminist* (Newark: University of Delaware Press, 2019), pp. 111–12; also Iona Opie and Peter Opie, *The Oxford Dictionary of Nursery Rhymes* (Oxford: Oxford University Press, 1997), pp. 64–5. In a manuscript letter dated 7 April 1806, Fenwick wrote that she was going to see a theatrical production of 'The Forty

other books Fenwick promotes from Tabart's lists are by the literary women of her acquaintance, including Elizabeth Kilner's *A Visit to a Farm House* (1804), *A Visit to London* (1805) and a *Puzzle for a Curious Girl* (1801–2). Kilner, incidentally returned the promotional favour by endorsing Fenwick's *Visits to the Juvenile Library* in her *A Visit to London*.

The means by which the transformative miracle from reluctant to enthusiastic reader is achieved in *Visits to the Juvenile Library* stands as a textbook-perfect case study of the benefits of maternal pedagogy. It is exactly of the kind promoted by Eliza Fenwick and the late-Enlightenment literary women who were her part of her intellectual community, including Anna Barbauld (1743–1825), Maria Edgeworth (1767–1849), Ellenor Fenn (1743–1813), Mary Lamb (1765–1847), Jane Porter (1776–1850), Charlotte Smith (1749–1806) and, of course, Mary Wollstonecraft (1759–97). In their world, a literary life was at the heart of what it meant to be knowledgeable, to be educated and to be free. For the literary women of the age who were teachers too, encouraging children to embrace literary lives was also a potential source of income. Jane Porter, though not mentioned by Fenwick in *Visits to the Juvenile Library*, published her children's novel *Two Princes of Persia* on Tabart's first list in 1801. There is, as it happens, an extant letter from Eliza Fenwick to Jane Porter written not much later, dated 3 June 1802, enthusiastically confirming a meeting.[10] Although there is no way of knowing if publishing with Tabart was something the two women discussed at that meeting, the first three books for children (*The Life of Carlo*, *Mary and Her Cat* and *Presents for Good Girls*) clearly authored by Fenwick appear on Tabart's list not long after, in 1804.

Given that Fenwick published about a dozen books for children between 1804 and 1813, she must have been working relentlessly to make a financially sustainable literary life. Yet, despite her productivity and her innovative – still compelling – work, only one book turned out to be a bestseller. *The Class Book: or, Three-Hundred and Sixty-Five Reading Lessons* (1806) hit all the pedagogical aims she advocated, but as it was an anthology published under the pseudonym of

---

Thieves' to make a 'little pantomimic book' of it. By 1804, Tabart had already published several 'pantomimic' books.

[10] Eliza Fenwick to Jane Porter, 3 June 1802, Carl H. Pforzheimer Collection of Shelley and His Circle, New York Public Library. New York Public Library Digital Collections <https://digitalcollections.nypl.org/items/ad91ca10-c876-0139-1bfe-0242ac110004> [accessed 5 April 2022].

Rev. David Blair, she never received public credit for it at the time, nor any of the royalties, as she sold the copyright to her publisher, Sir Richard Phillips, for some ready cash.[11]

The Class Book completely conforms to the late-Enlightenment approaches to becoming literate: emphasis is on proper diction as well as introductions to works of literature and ideas necessary to being considered as a literate person. Fenwick kills two pedagogical birds with one stone: the readings provide texts on which diction could be practised as well as content designed to stimulate curiosity and affection. Each selection is about a page long, with subjects drawn from a wide range of topics, genres and periods – a 'miscellany' of useful knowledge. There are snippets of Shakespeare, fables, Greek and Roman history, advice, notes on writing, extensive (now racist) translated selections on natural history from George Leclerc, Comte de Buffon (1707–88), on science, philosophy, morality and geography and, for Sundays, Fenwick supplies suitably religious texts. There were also excerpts from contemporary authors: Anna Barbauld's 'Fourth Evening' from *Evenings at Home* is programmed for reading on 9 May, and it is followed on 10 May with 'Of an Early Taste for Reading', 'Essay V' from William Godwin's *The Enquirer: Reflections on Education, Manners and Literature.*

The preface – which I assume was written by Fenwick, though it is unclear, as Richard Phillips also wrote as 'Blair' – explains how her book differs from those by competitors who also claim to be offering selections on which children can practise speaking:

> Thus, in the teaching the art of reading it is an obvious waste of the precious period devoted to education, to confine the exercises in that art to the mere combination of words; or to compositions, the sole object of which was to prove the wit and genius of the writer; – to compositions which do not teach any thing, which are often unintelligible to young persons, and which, after a volume of them has been perused and re-perused for years, leave the mind in a state of listless curiosity and total ignorance.[12]

11. In a fragment from a letter dated 10 June 1832, from Niagara to the Moffat family, friends in New York, Fenwick explains that the publisher, Sir Richard Phillips, had 'engaged [her] assistance in his many enterprises and translations form the French, & compilations chiefly of school books'. She also says that she was paid '150 guineas for compiling' the book she wrote as Blair (see Paul, p. 72).
12. Eliza Fenwick, *The Class Book: or, Three-Hundred and Sixty-Five Reading Lessons, Adapted to the Use of Schools; for Every Day of the Year* [1806], 12th edn (London: Longman, Hurst, Rees, Orme and Brown, 1814), p. iii.

The last line on the risks posed by pointless reading exercises leaving 'the mind in a state of listless curiosity and total ignorance' echoes similar lines from *Visits to the Juvenile Library*. And although Fenwick does not say so, she appears to be channelling Mary Wollstonecraft's lines from *A Vindication of the Rights of Woman*; her disapproval is palpable as she questions the use of teaching children 'to recite what they do not understand' and speak in 'parrot-like prattle, uttered in solemn cadences, with all the pomp of ignorance and folly'.[13]

Fictional children, as Jean-Jacques Rousseau knew when he created Émile, are a lot easier to teach than actual children. In Fenwick's books for children published in the first years of the nineteenth century, female pedagogues emblematise the perfect maternal teachers, the 'Mentorias' that Myers describes in her 1986 essay. The term – a feminine version, obviously, of the masculine 'mentor' – likely begins with Enlightenment author Ann Murray and her 1778 treatise, *Mentoria: or, Young Ladies Instructor, in Familiar Conversations on Moral and Entertaining Subjects* (even in the title, interactivity is conveyed in the reference to 'familiar conversations'). The 'Mentorias of make-believe', as Myers defines them, 'possess the rationality to choose the good and the self-command to follow it'. She expands the definition, setting up the qualities that characterise Mentorias, the women in charge of teaching children to become literate:

> Theirs is an energetic vocabulary full of moral exercise and shaping up; their womanly virtues, sturdier than the usual conduct book ascriptions, run to self-control, endurance, usefulness, and an unsentimental compassion with a decided social reference. They specialize in moral management, of the self and of others. They both embody and love to talk about the power of being good and doing good. Mentorias never speak of women's rights, but they make large strategic claims for female nature and capacities and for woman's ability to make a difference in her social world. (Myers, p. 54)

The 'make-believe' Mentorias of Fenwick's fictions are of the kind that Myers describes. Real children, however, as parents and teachers know, are not nearly as tractable as fictional ones, and real Mentorias are unlikely to sustain the relentless good grace of the prototypes.

For Fenwick, by about 1811 it was clear that the fictional people in her children's books were not going to provide her with enough income to support and educate her actual children, Eliza Ann

---

[13] Wollstonecraft, *Vindication*, in *Works*, V, ch. 12, p. 235.

(born 1789) and Orlando (born 1798). Because her charming husband, John, had been given to drink and debt, by about 1800 Fenwick resolved to separate from him and take sole responsibility for their family. She had briefly – unsuccessfully – tried shopkeeping (first with her brother-in-law, then in William and Mary Jane Godwin's Juvenile Library) but had really concentrated in the first decade of the nineteenth century on earning her living as a writer of books, including textbooks, for children. Only after it became painfully clear that writing would not allow her financial independence did she reluctantly decide that she would have to teach.

Her first gig was as governess to the five eldest children of Moses Mocatta (1768–1857), a member of a prestigious Jewish banking family in London. In her letters to her friend, the author Mary Hays, Fenwick is critical of the children and uses unflattering terms to describe them in ways that are eerily reminiscent of the first fictional descriptions of the Mortimer children in *Visits to the Juvenile Library*, whose 'curiosity' was difficult to arouse and 'their affections' difficult to engage. 'The little girl', writes Fenwick of one of her actual charges, likely Bracha Mocatta (1795–1819),

> is a dull drudge who learns from want of vivacity and forgets again from want of intellect to comprehend. Tractable yet void of energy and fancy, she sticks close to me as a burr, without engaging my affection or stimulating in any way my temper.[14]

Fenwick is equally unflattering about the other Mocatta children. She describes the eldest as 'Dullness & frivolity personified'. Fenwick was clearly not modelling herself on the 'good Mrs. Clifford', Mrs Mason of Wollstonecraft's *Original Stories* or the 'make-believe' Mentorias about whom Myers writes. In that first phase of Fenwick's transition from writer to teacher, she appears to have regarded her governess gig as temporary, something that would give her enough of a secure income to educate and launch her two children before returning to her writing life. But as it became clear that the demands of her teaching life were not leaving the time or space or energy for

---

[14] Eliza Fenwick to Mary Hays, c. 1811, Fenwick Family Papers, Correspondence 1798–1855, New-York Historical Society Library. All transcriptions are mine, though versions of the Fenwick/Hays correspondence can also be found in *The Fate of the Fenwicks. Letters to Mary Hays: 1798–1828*, ed. by A. F. Wedd (London: Methuen, 1927) and on the website by Timothy Whelan, *Mary Hays: Life, Writings, and Correspondence*: <https://www.maryhayslifewritingscorrespondence.com>.

writing, Fenwick also gradually revised her expectations of the children in her charge and of herself as their teacher.

By 1812, Fenwick had accepted a new position as a governess, this time to the children of Robert Honner, in Lee Mount near Cork, Ireland, and seems more resigned to the fact that actual children are not as tractable as fictional ones. On 8 February 1813, she wrote to Mary Hays (who was also doing some part-time teaching in the period), confessing that she 'once thought very differently of the task of education to what I now do, & such doubtless is the case with you'. Fenwick then gives a startlingly moving description of her revised vision of the practice of educating children. Instead of the typical growth metaphor – characterised by James Thomson (1700–48) in *A Hymn to the Seasons* (1730) – she imagines intellectual fireworks:

> To be able to fix a willing delighted attention to communicate energy, to perceive ideas shooting expanding and maturing under your guidance & culture and to receive an intelligent need of affection & gratitude in return for y[ou]r labours from your pupils is a vision of very agreeable promise I grant you [. . .] (Eliza Fenwick to Mary Hays, 1 February 1813)

Fenwick is, however, clear on the tensions between writing and teaching, and she brings her visionary, starry version of the daily grind of teaching actual children back to earth. In commiserating with Hays, Fenwick admits to their shared responses to the unglamorous work of teaching: 'our wearied spirits exhausted patience', she writes, 'and harassed tempers have none of these pleasures to record I believe'. She advises Hays to get out if she can:

> Go then, dear Mary, you have no ties to bind you to such a species of servitude, whom necessity does not compel to silence your reluctance & bend your will and wishes to your circumstances, go & taste of liberty & society befitting your tastes and talents. (Eliza Fenwick to Mary Hays, 8 February 1813)

In early 1813, as Fenwick was struggling in Lee Mount with her conflicted feelings about teacher–student relationships, her daughter, Eliza Ann, was thinking about setting up an elite school for girls in Bridgetown, Barbados. Eliza Ann, an actress, had been in Barbados for just over a year, having gone there to perform with the repertory company that was starting up in the newly rebuilt theatre. It was supposed to have been a temporary gig, a way of helping her mother fund the completion of the education of her younger brother, Orlando. Although Fenwick had trained her daughter to be self-supporting as an actress, Eliza Ann was, at best, reluctant, regarding acting simply as one of the limited options available to women trying to support themselves. Within a year of her arrival on the island, she had met and married another actor in the company, William Rutherford (1783–1829), and had started to formulate a plan to open a school for the rich daughters of the plantocracy. The advantages must have been clear. Instead of being a paid member of the repertory company, she could be an independent businesswoman. Best of all, by convincing her mother to join her in the enterprise, they would both be free of the precarious financial dependency that had characterised their lives in Britain. As Orlando was just completing his education, he would be able to begin his working life in a new country. Although it would be a fresh start for all of them, in Barbados they would necessarily be in a morally compromised position. Although the slave trade had been abolished in 1807, Barbados was a slave-dependent colony, economically reliant on sugar produced by enslaved labour. As Fenwick had been on the side of the abolitionists, political reformers and proto-feminists of the late Enlightenment, she was acutely aware of the moral concessions that would come with the move. But her daughter – by 1813, referring to herself as Mrs Rutherford – was convinced that the benefits would outweigh all other considerations. On 28 December of that year, Eliza Ann Rutherford advertised on the front page of the *Barbados Mercury, and Bridgetown Gazette* for the new school, the Seminary for Young Ladies, she would soon be opening with her mother.

From the first advertisement for the school, the lineaments of the kinds of interactive pedagogical practices used in the school, built on the affectionate relationship between teacher and students, were evident. Mrs Rutherford, echoing her mother's February letter to Mary Hays, says that her 'chief endeavor' will be 'to fix the attention of her Pupils by gaining their affections, and to cultivate the better feelings of the heart', while she attempts the 'development of the youthful understanding'. The echo of Mary Wollstonecraft's lines from the *Vindication*, on educating for 'a cultivated understanding, and an affectionate heart', is audible.[15] The curriculum – at least in the first

---

[15] Wollstonecraft, *Vindication*, p. 167.

advertisement – focuses on Grammar and Reading, that is, on learning to become literate:

> READING, – *it might appear unnecessary to mention particularly, as that, at first sight, seems to be an art easily taught, and to be acquired with facility & yet, daily experience proves, that, to read well, is the attainment of few. The utmost care, therefore, will be taken for the improvement of the pupils in this very necessary branch of their studies, and the most approved classic authors, in prose and verse, selected for their perusal, according to their progress, by which the style may be formed and the taste improved.*[16]

Here, too, Mrs Rutherford echoes what sound like her mother's sentiments as developed in *The Class Book*, under the David Blair pseudonym. And there is something else identifying the instructional methods as being distinctly maternal: the fact that the selections will be made 'according to their progress'. The book chosen for each child is determined by attention to the interests and capacities of that child. The point is that the readings to be assigned in the school, like those chosen for *The Class Book*, were not arbitrarily selected, not curriculum-driven (as would be typical in an authoritarian, masculine model), but driven instead by attention to the 'progress' of the student. That is also the strategy used by 'the good Mrs. Clifford'.

In *Visits to the Juvenile Library*, *The Book of Games*, for instance, is introduced in the novel as something that encourages play, reading and – in keeping with the narrative drive of the story – happiness. Fenwick, in fact, develops the connections between reading and happiness in the story: the selection of a book is designed to arouse the child's curiosity; the child responds by expressing a desire to read it, and then demonstrates the ways in which that book becomes, in the case of the *Book of Games*, a happy part of the lived experience, the fabric of the child's life. The way in which Fenwick narratively deploys the *Book of Games* in *Visits to the Juvenile Library* is itself something like a masterclass in enticing children into literate lives. The sequence begins with Mrs Clifford, in conversation with one of the older boys, Arthur, about another boy of her acquaintance who had gone to Tabart's bookshop and purchased, for a younger cousin, 'the new Book of Games, to teach the little boy how to play'. What Mrs Clifford is doing, of course, is not only arousing his curiosity,

---

[16] *Barbados Mercury, and Bridgetown Gazette*, 28 December 1813, p. 1. Italics in the original.

but also perhaps slight envy for a child who will be able to play games to which Arthur does not have access. Suspicious of the ploy, Arthur responds: 'I cannot understand, Madam, what you mean by a *Book of Games*, to teach a little boy how to play. I never saw any books that did not hinder boys from playing' (*Visits*, p. 23). Mrs Clifford counters, by giving Arthur a little more context, saying that the book 'contains a very amusing history of several boys, and at the same time describes a number of delightful plays to which you, and your brothers, and sisters are entire strangers' (p. 24). It is a good tactic as it ratchets up the opportunity for envy, the sense that other children have access to pleasures that Arthur and his siblings do not. Fenwick employs a narrative strategy that speaks to her literary ability to control the tensions in the plot. She has Mrs Clifford leave the room, called out by 'some person who had affairs of business to transact with her' (p. 24). Then Fenwick cleverly uses the interlude to set up the clues that will lead both to the happy ending of her novel (*Visits to the Juvenile Library* itself), while within the story, the children have time to reconsider their aversion to being educated. 'Arthur and Henry', the two eldest boys,

> particularly longed for the *Book of Games*, but were ashamed to say so to each other, or to ask it of Mrs. Clifford, to whom they had expressed in the morning such an aversion to books; and when they went to bed, each of them, except little Louisa, dreamt of being carried to *Tabart's Juvenile Library*. (p. 31)

Only later are they able to play one of the games described in the book – trap-ball, a precursor of cricket. The sequence presents a lovely example of Fenwick's technical skill as an author: both the children in the story and the implied readers of *Visits to the Juvenile Library* are required to delay their gratification.

The one child not yet dreaming of Tabart's in *Visits to the Juvenile Library* is 'little Louisa', the youngest of the orphaned children. The story of her induction into a literate life is another example of the pedagogical principle that Fenwick and her daughter would bring to their first school a decade later. In the first advertisement for the Barbados school are lines promising that in teaching reading, the works are '*selected for their perusal, according to their progress, by which the style may be formed and the taste improved*'. The lines, of course, are obviously in the same register as those in the preface to the 1806 *Class Book*. They are also true in *Visits to the Juvenile Library*, as Fenwick has Mrs Clifford – recognising that Louisa is at the very beginning of the road to a literate life – select works 'according to [her] progress' in order to entice her into reading: 'a box containing an ivory alphabet, to teach her her letters, and a book of *First Lessons*, wherein she might soon begin to read' (p. 65). As it does not appear that a book with *First Lessons* as the exact title was on Tabart's lists at the time, the reference is likely generic and in reference to a genre modelled on Anna Barbauld's original, influential *Lessons for Children from Two to Three Years Old* (1778). Fenwick formally published her own contribution to the genre, *Lessons for Children*, a little later, in 1811, not for Tabart but for the Juvenile Library of William and Mary Jane Godwin. In the introductory 'Note to the Publisher', in her volume of *Lessons*, Fenwick uses language that reappears in the advertisements (like the one above) for her schools. 'This work', she says at the beginning of the 'Note', 'will be found precisely adapted to [. . .] progress the understanding' and the 'subjects and incidents will be found admirably calculated to excite a useful curiosity, and to seize upon the affections of the child'.[17] Here again is the linked triad of attributes associated with becoming literate: affection, curiosity and – in the reference to being able to 'excite' – Hume's sense of vivacity. The text is the mediating term that both ignites the spark and continues to warm body and mind after the lesson is complete. In her introductory note to *Lessons for Children*, she even obliquely alludes to it as a 'prequel' to her 1806 *Class Book*: 'In this edition also', she writes, 'the work is rendered a proper Class Book for very young pupils, [. . .]; and it is presumed that its readers will not be inclined to lay it aside when the Lesson is finished'.

By tacking between Fenwick's published work and her work teaching actual children, it is possible to see that both are infused with the same pedagogical drive and then brought to life by affection, curiosity and the sparks of 'vivacity' that connect teacher, student and text. As Fenwick moved physically and professionally away from her British life as a writer, she more completely inhabited her identity as a teacher first in the Caribbean and later in the United States and Canada. With each move, the closer she came to inhabiting the character of the 'make-believe Mentoria', the farther removed she became from her life as a creative writer. By the time she arrived in Niagara in 1829, both of the children that she had worked so hard

---

17 Eliza Fenwick, *Lessons for Children: or, Rudiments of Good Manners, Morals, and Humanity* [1811] (London: M. J. Godwin, 1813), Note to the Publisher, n.p.

to support were dead. Orlando died of yellow fever in Barbados in 1816, just as he was getting established in a career, and her daughter, Eliza Ann Rutherford, died in 1828 in New York. Her husband, William Rutherford (like Fenwick's husband, also given to debt and drink), had abandoned the family in 1818, just after the birth of their fourth child. Fenwick and her daughter had left Barbados in 1822 and had attempted to establish schools first in New Haven, then New York, on the model they had developed in Barbados. Her daughter, however, appears to have suffered from some kind of congenital heart disease, and grew weaker with each move. That is how Fenwick, in her early sixties, found herself solely responsible for raising and educating her four young grandchildren. And that is when she made the move to Niagara-on-the-Lake in what was then still the colony of Upper Canada to begin her final Seminary for Young Ladies.

In reviewing both Fenwick's advertisements for her North American schools and her personal letters, it appears that Fenwick became increasingly at home in her role as an educator. The annoyance she expressed about the tedious job of educating the Mocatta children in 1811 disappears. Instead, she seems to grow more aware of the success of her approach and appreciative of the praise she receives. In an advertisement in the *Niagara Farmer's Journal* on 22 April 1829, for example, Fenwick and her new partner Mrs Breakenridge promise to 'inspire' their students 'with a zeal for excelling in their studies; and where timidity of disposition or slowness of capacity render a child incapable of excelling others, still by noticing with approbation every step towards improvement to delight her with the consciousness of excelling her former self'.[18] Here Fenwick appears to merge herself with her own 'make-believe' Mentoria, 'the good Mrs. Clifford', actively embracing 'affect' as 'transidividual', as something 'fundamentally social, shaped as much by what it interacts with as by the subject itself'.[19] She expresses a conscious awareness that she can make a difference in the lives of the children in her care and that they can grow and change under her tutelage.

Letters that date from the final stages of Fenwick's career as an educator in North America confirm her success. One mother, for instance, was so pleased by the 'improvements' in her daughter that she

[18] Advertisement for the Niagara Seminary for Young Ladies, *Niagara Farmer's Journal*, 22 April 1829.
[19] Joy, p. 7.

sent Fenwick a fifty-dollar bonus 'as testimony of her gratitude'.[20] But
Fenwick's success as an educator was not limited to her actual work
as a teacher. She impressed a wide range of people in her orbit. Even
in her late sixties, when she could no longer work as a teacher and
school-owner in Niagara, she took on a final position as the mistress
of the boys' boarding house of Upper Canada College, essentially
the 'feeder' school for King's College (precursor to the University of
Toronto). In that role, Fenwick continued to work with the boys on
both their writing and their in-house theatricals. They recognised
her impact. In an 1837 letter, she acknowledges just how telling it is
that a teenaged boy should appreciate her influence: one 'of the most
gifted youths' of the college, she writes, a boy of seventeen, had made
a 'parting request' that she should 'correspond with him'.[21]

Fenwick did eventually retire to the Rhode Island home of her
friends Sarah (1806–88) and Alexander (1805–89) Duncan. The
couple had met in 1823 in New Haven at the ball Fenwick had organised for her first American school. Her family attended their wed-
ding and their respective families remained friends. The (wealthy)
Duncans eventually helped Fenwick fund the educations of her two
youngest grandchildren (the two eldest had, sadly, drowned in Lake
Ontario in 1834). It was a little earlier – though still at the very end
of her teaching career – that Fenwick, through the Duncans, unexpectedly renewed contact with an author whom she had known at
the beginning of her writing career, Jane Porter. While working in
Niagara, Fenwick, often with her granddaughter, Bessie (Elizabeth)
Rutherford, would holiday with the Duncans at their home in
Canandaigua, Upper New York State. As it happens, William Wood,
a neighbour of the Duncans, had been acquainted with Jane Porter
and had hosted her during her visit to America. On 10 September
1832, Wood wrote to Porter on the extraordinary coincidence linking in America two authors from among those making up the 'gal-
axy of talent' (he also named Maria Edgeworth and Felicia Hemans)
shining in Britain at the beginning of the century. He marvelled at
the fact that both Fenwick and Porter should find themselves in the
same 'corner' of the New World at the same time, and he describes

[20] Eliza Fenwick to the Moffat family, 7 January 1830, Fenwick Family Papers,
Correspondence 1798–1885, New-York Historical Society Library. There are no
online or print editions of letters written by Fenwick between 1829 and her death
in 1840.
[21] Eliza Fenwick to Reuben Moffat, 18 September 1837, Fenwick Family Papers,
Correspondence 1798–1885, New-York Historical Society Library.

Fenwick as 'the almost perfect Mrs. Fenwick'.[22] A letter from Fenwick to Porter (dated 30 August 1832) survives. In it, Fenwick provides updates on her own life, including the deaths of her children. Porter had, in fact, known both Eliza Ann and Orlando when they had been children. With just a trace of regret, Fenwick also alludes to the fact that her own writing life had ended. 'You have long lost sight of me', she writes to Porter, 'but *you* have been ever before me, in your works, and in the universal estimation of your highly gifted mind'.[23] And although there is no record of a letter from Porter to Fenwick, there is a record of the fact that they must have stayed in touch, at least occasionally over the next few years. On 31 October 1836, in a letter to her friend Adeline Moffat, Fenwick's granddaughter, Bessie Rutherford, writes, charmingly:

> Grandmama received a letter the other day from the authoress of 'The Scottish Chiefs'. [. . .] She talks of coming to this country, and promises to visit Grandmama. It was a kind unaffected letter, not a bit better than Grandmama's, not so good I think.[24]

There is no extant evidence indicating whether or not Jane Porter and Eliza Fenwick did reunite in North America. Fenwick had left her literary friends behind. Strangely, however, just a few weeks after Bessie Rutherford's letter confirming that Fenwick and Porter had been in touch, back in Britain, Mary Hays had written to Mary Shelley (on 30 November 1836), asking if she had 'ever learned the fate' of Fenwick and her family, as correspondence had broken off in 1828 and 'all enquiries respecting her proved fruitless'.[25]

At the end of this essay, several questions remain. Did Fenwick regret – as she suggests in the letter to Porter – abandoning her literary life because she had been forced into life teaching other people to be literate? Or was she, perhaps, too embarrassed to admit to her British friends that even her teaching life had not been enough to sustain – at least in the short term – her family? Were Fenwick's letters,

---

[22] William Wood to Jane Porter, 10 September 1832, Carl H. Pforzheimer Collection of Shelley and His Circle, New York Public Library.

[23] Eliza Fenwick to Jane Porter, 30 August 1832, Carl H. Pforzheimer Collection of Shelley and His Circle, New York Public Library.

[24] Elizabeth (Bessie) Rutherford to Adeline Moffat, 31 October 1836, Fenwick Family Papers, Correspondence 1798–1885, New-York Historical Society Library.

[25] Mary Hays to Mary Shelley, 30 November 1836, Abinger Papers, Bodleian Special Collections, University of Oxford, MS. Abinger c.49, fols 52–3.

as her granddaughter hints, her literary legacy? Fenwick did leave traces saying that she had also continued to write short fictions, but if they survive, they have not been identified. Alternatively, Fenwick's enduring contribution to literary education was her transmission of the late-Enlightenment pedagogical principles of affection, curiosity, vivacity and interaction. As those are the qualities that survive in her extant published work, in evidence of her impact as an educator and in her letters, perhaps it is enough to end by acknowledging that her literary remains are, in fact, her legacy.

Works Cited

Primary

Manuscript

Abinger Papers, Bodleian Special Collections, University of Oxford

Carl H. Pforzheimer Collection of Shelley and His Circle, New York Public Library. New York Public Library Digital Collections <https://digital-collections.nypl.org> [accessed 5 April 2022]

Fenwick Family Papers, Correspondence 1798–1885, New-York Historical Society Library

Published Sources

Barbados Mercury, and Bridgetown Gazette. Digitised copies are available through the Digital Library of the Caribbean (dLlOC) <https://dloc.com/cndl/results/?t=barbados%20mercury%20gazette> and through the British Library <https://eap.bl.uk/collection/EAP1086-1/search>

Blair, Rev. David [Eliza Fenwick], *The Class Book: or, Three-Hundred and Sixty-Five Reading Lessons* [1806], 12th edn (London: Longman, Hurst, Rees, Orme and Brown, 1814)

Fenwick, Eliza, *Lessons for Children: or, Rudiments of Good Manners, Morals and Humanity* [1811] (London: M. J. Godwin, 1813)

——. *Visits to the Juvenile Library: or, Knowledge Proved to Be the Source of Happiness* (London: Tabart, 1805)

Hume, David, *An Enquiry Concerning the Principles of Morals* (London: A. Millar, 1751)

Lovechild, Mrs [Ellenor Fenn], *Cobwebs to Catch Flies: or, Dialogues in Short Sentences, Adapted to Children from the Age of Three to Eight Years. In two volumes* [1783] (London: John Marshall, 1800)

Locke, John, *Some Thoughts Concerning Education and Of the Conduct of the Understanding*, ed. by Ruth W. Grant and Nathan Tarcov (Indianapolis: Hackett, 1996)

Niagara Farmer's Journal, Welland Canal Intelligencer, St. Catharines

Wollstonecraft, Mary, *A Vindication of the Rights of Woman, with Strictures on Political and Moral Subjects* [1792], in *The Works of Mary Wollstonecraft*, ed. by Janet Todd and Marilyn Butler, vol. 5 (London: Pickering, 1989)

Secondary

Baxter, Jane Eva, *The Archaeology of Childhood: Children, Gender and Material Culture* (Walnut Creek, CA: AltaMira Press, 2005)

Briggs, Julia, '"Delightful Task!": Women, Children and Reading in the Mid-Eighteenth Century', in *Culturing the Child 1690–1914*, ed. by Donelle Ruwe (Lanham, MD: Scarecrow, 2005), pp. 67–82

Hilton, Mary and Jill Shefrin, eds, *Educating the Child in Enlightenment Britain: Beliefs, Cultures, Practices* (Farnham: Ashgate, 2009)

Joy, Louise, 'Affect', in *Keywords for Children's Literature*, ed. by Philip Nel, Lissa Paul and Nina Christensen (New York: New York University Press, 2021), pp. 7–10

Myers, Mitzi, 'Impeccable Governesses, Rational Dames and Moral Mothers: Mary Wollstonecraft and the Female Tradition in Georgian Children's Books', *Children's Literature*, 14 (1986), 31–59

Opie, Iona, and Peter Opie, *The Oxford Dictionary of Nursery Rhymes* (Oxford: Oxford University Press, 1997)

Paul, Lissa, *Eliza Fenwick: Early Modern Feminist* (Newark: University of Delaware Press, 2019)

Index